KYOTO-CSEAS SERIES ON ASIAN STUDIES 24
Center for Southeast Asian Studies, Kyoto University

WAYWARD DISTRACTIONS

KYOTO-CSEAS SERIES ON ASIAN STUDIES 24
Center for Southeast Asian Studies, Kyoto University

WAYWARD DISTRACTIONS

Ornament, Emotion, Zombies and the Study of Buddhism in Thailand

Justin Thomas McDaniel

NUS PRESS
Singapore
in association with
KYOTO UNIVERSITY PRESS
Japan

The publication of this book is funded by International Program of Collaborative Research at the Center for Southeast Asian Studies (IPCR-CSEAS), Kyoto University and Asian Studies Fund at Kyoto University.

NUS Press
National University of Singapore
AS3-01-02, 3 Arts Link
Singapore 117569
Website: http://nuspress.nus.edu.sg

ISBN 978-981-325-150-2 (Paper)

Kyoto University Press
Yoshida-South Campus, Kyoto University
69 Yoshida-Konoe-Cho, Sakyo-ku
Kyoto 606-8315
Japan
www.kyoto-up.or.jp

ISBN 978-4-8140-0367-9 (Paper)

National Library Board, Singapore Cataloguing in Publication Data

Name(s): McDaniel, Justin.
Title: Wayward distractions : ornament, emotion, zombies and the study of Buddhism in Thailand/Justin Thomas McDaniel.
Other Title(s): Kyoto CSEAS series on Asian studies ; 24.
Description: Singapore : NUS Press; Kyoto, Japan : Kyoto University Press, [2021] | Includes bibliographical references and index.
Identifier(s): ISBN 978-981-325-150-2 (paperback)
Subject(s): LCSH: Buddhism--Thailand. | Buddhism and culture--Thailand. | Buddhism and art--Thailand.
Classification: DDC 294.309593--dc23

Cover image: Image taken from a liturgical illuminated manuscript from the late eighteenth century composed in Central Siam. Fogg Collection (London). Thai.Ms.#13. Photo by author.

Typeset by: Ogma Solutions Pvt Ltd
Printed by: Mainland Press Pte Ltd

Contents

List of Images

1

Introduction: Cajoleries, Non-Human Ontology and the Importance of Thin Description in the Study of Thai Buddhist Stuff

"Buildings must be shaped by internal laws without lies and games; all that is unnecessary, that veils the absolute design, must be shed."

– **Walter Gropius** (Internationale Architektur, 1925)

"Less is a Bore."

– **Robert Venturi** (Complexity and Contradiction in Architecture,1966)

The first idea to assemble a selection of my articles into a single volume came through a conversation with Yoko Hayami over a plate of *takoyaki* (octopus fritters) in Kyoto in the summer of 2014. One of her students had a hard time finding several of my articles in Japan. This difficulty in finding Southeast Asian research articles written in English, especially in research libraries in Asia, was a common complaint of students and local scholars, just as scholars working outside of Asia often lament the inability to access the work of scholars in Thai, Burmese, Korean, and other languages easily. We thought

Not Thai decorative art, but an American artist working in London inspired by Japanese art in the middle of the nineteenth century. This is James Whistler's Peacock Room, and it provides an instructive example of the benefits of "thin description", part of the author's materialist approach to Buddhism in Thailand. Courtesy of the Smithsonian Institution, which put this image in the public domain.

it might be easier for people to access this work if it was in a single volume, published in Asia. However, when I started to assemble past work, I struggled. I did not want to re-publish material that was already available in some form in my previous books on Thai ghosts and magic, Lao, Pali, Sanskrit, Shan, and Thai manuscript cultures, monastic education, or modern Buddhist architecture. That work is largely excluded in this volume. I also wanted to keep the focus on Thailand and so did not include my publications in Indian, Lao, and Japanese Studies for the sake of space. However, when looking through research I had conducted over the past 20 years, it was hard to find a cohesive theme. On the surface there is no consistent approach, scholarly discipline, theoretical agenda, nor subject matter. The work ranges from ethnographic and modern to pre-modern and historical, from textual to art historical, from material cultural to pedagogical.

While my work, outside of book-length studies, is characterized by diversity of subject, time-period, and method. In assembling these pieces, I noticed that I developed a pattern of sorts over time. I research and write a book over two to three years and then while editing the book in question, often driven by restlessness, I take on side-projects and explore a wide-range of subjects and questions. I find that these side-projects have inspired longer studies or bring new and interesting material to my teaching. I call these "Wayward Distractions" because they began as delightful distractions from my main research agenda but blossomed and became obsessions.[1] They took me in different directions. The subject matter is diverse and the writing is also quite different from piece to piece depending on the audience and journal in which it was originally published. The writing is caught somewhere between the designs of Gropius and Venturi. While I respect those scholars and artists who abide with the dictum that "less is more," and, like Gropius, don't believe that ornament should interfere with the function and the internal laws of an argument, like Venturi, I just don't operate that way.[2] I find it too boring. There is a beauty in laying out a scholarly argument clearly, using just enough evidence to prove a point, and avoiding dangling clauses, tangential asides, lengthy footnotes, and arbitrary adjectives. I certainly pound these writing guidelines into my students and some articles are short and to the point. But, more often, my writing reflects my approach to the subject matter.

My students and my colleagues have been a great gift to me and I have continually thanked them in the extensive acknowledgement sections of my books. There are far too many intelligent, caring, and creative people to list. They know who they are. I have had a truly blessed life because of them. I continually, often irritatingly, reach out to so many of them and lean on their expertise and generosity. I have presented work in these articles in this volume at venues in Asia, Australia, Europe, and North America and have received helpful comments from many audiences and editors. What has been most satisfying is witnessing my own students correct and challenge me. I am repeatedly and simultaneously enlivened and humbled by them like an aging sailboat hopelessly tacking back and forth looking for any sign of a breeze. They are the welcome winds of inspiration sweeping through the doldrums of my horse latitudes.

What I have given back to them has been a mess, because what has long attracted me to the study of the Buddhism are the surprising moments, the conflicted persons, the complex narratives, the vernacular architecture, the sumptuous art, and the generally non-canonical. It is probably what also attracts me to eating fatty food, spending too much money on albums, paintings, and amulets. It is why I pull my children out of school to do fun and pointless things that I justify by calling them "learning experiences." I have never had any interest or enough intelligence to exist in logic or philosophy courses, but spend my time researching decorative art, participating in rituals, reading illuminated manuscripts, and listening to music. My thinking and writing about Thai Buddhism over the past three decades has reflected these bad habits and frustrated the few readers that have tried to find my arguments amid the examples, asides, and suggestions. Malcolm Lowry's self-composed epitaph should be the first line in a critical review of anything I write: his "prose was flowery, and often glowery. He lived nightly, and drank daily, and died playing the ukulele." I am simply much more comfortable in the world of narrative, beauty, design, shared experience, music, and art.

Here, though, starts the road to recovery. In the introduction, reflecting on these articles and seeing trends and themes across them, in this first volume, I lay out three general approaches to the study of Thai Buddhist stuff and Thai Buddhist communities that I have found useful in the field and which have informed these wayward distractions. In the second volume (forthcoming, 2022), I will focus on textual and historical studies in Thai Buddhism. This might sound bold and self-indulgent. It is. However, I am not arguing that these are the approaches others should follow or that these are the only approaches. Indeed, I have learned a great deal from my colleagues, teachers, and students. Moreover, I often found that none of my approaches developed in the field fully captured the experiences I had. I am not interested in all-encompassing methods. I don't think that there is one way to study Thai Buddhism or any other subject. I find such efforts silly in general. This is a purely subjective collection and while it is shaped by "internal laws" that I hope to clarify below, let's hope, for both of our sakes, it is not too much of a bore.

An Introduction to Volume One

My children and I have a routine whenever we visit Washington DC. We pick a new museum or historical place to visit, we try a new place to eat, and then head over to the Freer Museum to sit in the Peacock Room. Anyone familiar with late nineteenth-century art is most likely familiar with this iconic dining room turned reflective gallery. A classic of the Japonisme or Anglo-Japanese design that was all the rage in Europe after the Meiji Restoration caused a flood of Japanese art and fashion to enter Europeans' department stores, galleries, and imaginations. The room was designed and executed by James McNeil Whistler, an American painter who spent most of his life in London, in 1876. Originally, this room, before being purchased in its entirety by Charles Lang Freer in 1904 and brought to the US, was in the stately row house of Frederick Richards Leyland in Kensington (London). Thomas Jeckyll was the person hired to design the dining room of the home, but because of an illness, he asked a young artist, Whistler, who was working in another room of the house, to finish executing his design. Whistler, whose non-narrative painting of a Caucasian woman dressed in Japanese robes and holding a fan called "The Princess from the Land of Porcelain" Jeckyll has already chosen for the dining room, did not follow Jeckyll's lead and completely changed his design, color-scheme, and overall impression of the room without informing the original designer. He worked in private and didn't allow anyone to enter the room. He kept handing Leyland's wife (with whom he was most likely having an affair) exorbitant bills for the supplies to redesign the room. Leyland grew suspicious and finally demanded to see the room. He was furious and only agreed to pay Whistler for less than half of the cost of the room's design. Their letters on the matter which survive are layered with resentment and invective. Whistler was incensed that someone he saw as merely a rich simpleton could not appreciate his art and at one point even broke into Leyland's house at night and painted two peacocks fighting in gold, one with a silver streak in its head plumage (Whistler had a distinct gray streak in his own hair) and one grasping at gold coins. He called the painting "Art and Money: or, The Story of the Room." He soon gave up his fight though and declared bankruptcy. Leyland's marriage ended. Jeckyll finally recovered well enough to visit the room and upon seeing it, he went home, covered himself in gold leaf and was later found unconscious on the floor. He died not too long after that bout of "insanity."

When my children sit in this very angelic room, with shelves of Chinese porcelain, lamps that look as if they are dripping from the ceiling, and calming blues and subtle golds, they have no idea of the lives it ruined and the controversy it stirred in London's elite circles. They enjoy the quiet bench in the middle of the room and the hushed tones of the occasional visitor on a weekday afternoon. It is a place to rest and let the mind wander. I make it a point of never asking my children "what do you think of this painting or this design?" "What do you see in this?" or "What do you think the artist was trying to say?" I hated when teachers would ask us those questions on field trips to museums when I was young. Isn't it okay, I remember thinking, not to want to "understand" everything? Some things don't have to have meaning. I have to think everywhere, why can't I just go to a museum not to think.

In 2015, a modern artist named Darren Waterston, was inspired by Whistler's Peacock Room and created one of the most elaborate installation pieces I have ever seen—"Filthy Lucre: Peacock Room Remix." He completely recreated the entire room to scale in the Sackler Museum (connected to the Freer). He reproduced the Whistler-

Leyland letters and projected them against the wall, piped in aggressive rock music, and violently dripped paint everywhere. The room, which one can walk into, like the original, is dark. The walls are cracked, the shelves broken, and even the painting of the Princess in the Land of Porcelain has her head covered in black smudged paint. Through the shutters, a reddish glow emanates, and the ceiling looks as if it will cave in. He even made dozens of his own ceramic vases, similar to the ones in the original room, just to break many of them and littered the shards on the floor. It was a massive effort to "break" the room. He took the room that had become a peaceful sanctuary to my children and countless other visitors over the past century, and returned the family turmoil, the jealously, the deceit, the ruin, and the violence. For all of those people who had appreciated the graceful beauty of this example of Japanese-British harmony, he wanted to pull back the curtain and reintroduce them to the story behind the room. He wanted us to read the room to discover a meaning.

The dedication and skill it took to create this installation, which was also for a time at the Mass MoCA, cannot be denied. However, after I told him the story of the room (something I had never done before), my son (12) lamented, "dad, I get it, trust me, I get what he is trying to do, but really, I would rather just go back to the regular room. That's, you know, *our* room." My daughter, 8, agreed and added "why would anyone ever want to eat in this dining room. Let's go back." I was a little disappointed that they were not the sophisticated modern art patrons that I wanted to raise, but I also had to admit, despite the "truth" of the controversial origins of Whistler's room, now, and for the century it has been in the Freer, it was devoid of controversy. It was a hidden space in the corner of a busy city filled with political strife, crime, ambition, and greed. My children were teaching me the art of thin description and something important about how we encounter art without meaning.

What Waterston had done was return the Peacock Room to the time of its creation to highlight the tension between artists and patrons to its greatest degree. In that return though, he turned what had become to many a sumptuous dining room into a crime scene. He turned it from a place of opulent distraction to a place to search for evidence—a lair of well-kept secrets and neglected emotions became a courtroom where everyone who entered had to relive the whole affair in gruesome detail. He returned meaning and interpretation to a place of forgetful repose. The distant and the exotic had become part of the city again, part of the economy of arguments.

Strange Attractors, Interpretative Communities, and Inciters of Emotion

The Peacock Room and the fascinating historical characters that were brought together because of it, as well as the wide variety of people that visit it today, encapsulate many of the reasons I engage in the type of research I do. Indeed, the Peacock Room is housed in the Freer Gallery of Art and Arthur M. Sackler Gallery, which comprise the

Smithsonian's National Museum of Asian Art. These two galleries are connected by an underground passageway but by entering one, you have unfettered access to the other. Therefore, visitors and researchers primarily interested in Asian Art will encounter the Peacock Room even though its connections to Asia, as we saw, are tentative at best. However, some of the most interesting questions that arise in research are the result of unexpected mixtures, juxtapositions, and moments of frisson. Abandoning perceived notions of identity and what Lorand Matory calls "trait geographies" has heavily influenced my projects.[3] I aim, but not always successfully, and my thoughts on this matter have changed significantly overtime, to question mega-categories and organizing rubrics like "religion," "art," "ethnicity," "nationality," and even "Buddhism." Even though it was prominent in my dissertation and first book, I also have attempted to abandon the false dichotomy I find often made between the "local" and "translocal" religious thoughts and practices in Thailand. I have not found that Thai Buddhists see their diverse practices as somehow "local" in comparison to some vague notion of a broader or more true Buddhist "tradition" unless a white person, like me, presents their practice as somehow non-traditional, apocryphal, popular, local, and some other modifier drawn from a position of privilege.

Many of these approaches and my intellectual struggles with them were first formulated early in my studies when I was inspired by the work, ironically, of the late Stanley Tambiah, who was often associated with structuralism and relatively hard categories. His three books and several articles that focused on Thai Buddhism, royalty, and society in the 1970s and 80s were comprehensive, provocative, and forward-thinking. In graduate school Tambi (as he was often called) was more of a comfort than advisor and seemed to use our conversations, to talk about Thai ritual, ghosts, and amulets. I was in the Sanskrit and Indian Studies Department and was not training to be an anthropologist, but Tambi, because of my experiences in Thailand and my occasional help with Thai texts, spent time with me and despite my irritating begging, never filled my alms bowl with career or publishing advice. He was a luminary in the field and I snuck over to William James Hall to steal some secrets of how to make it in the academic game and hear stories about his many research trips to Thailand. He wouldn't play my game. He seemed to disdain these aspects of university life at Harvard. It was an attitude that I find myself admiring more and more over time. Since my family had no real experience with academic life and I didn't complete any higher education, I was initially enthralled by the pomp and general self-congratulatory blow hardiness that often defines university days. Tambi, who had spent his entire career wading knee-deep in it, was slowly trying to emerge and dry himself off. Although we often disagreed, I miss the way he shook up the field of Southeast Asian religion. He had a long career of publishing many books, writing dozens of articles, and earning awards, presidencies, and fellowships. However, what I was impressed by and still try to impart to my students, is that Tambi respected and even celebrated the complexity and messiness of field work. Even though he has been labeled a structuralist in numerous reviews and studies, he often built structures simply to dismantle them. He was a vocal critic of other structuralists, especially Melford Spiro, and tried to complicate any model he dreamed up with ugly political and economic realities, historical anomalies, and cognitive contradictions. His field notes and highly-skilled observational acumen betrayed his most elaborate schema. He delighted in that fact and encouraged us to do that in his lectures.[4]

Tambiah inspired me to allow the messiness of history and society be laid bare, not to stuff the things into a closet when guests come over. The reader should see the process of research, the evidence that doesn't quite fit a well-conceived argument, and the misgivings and apprehensions of the author. The occasional hiatus, the distraction, from the main argument thus occasioned should remain. Therefore, my side-projects often involved looking at communities that didn't quite fit into the well-worn narrative of Thai ethnicity and Thai Buddhism being one in the same. It is often assumed and certainly promoted by many scholars and politicians in Thailand that to be Thai is to be Buddhist. Thailand is often said to be the most Buddhist country in Asia, with some 93–96 per cent of all citizens being Buddhist. However, the fact that the vast majority of Thais are Buddhists, does not make it a homogeneous place. There are many ethnicities in Thailand and many ways of being Buddhist. I wanted to reveal the neglected evidence of the diversity inherent to Thai Buddhist society.

In "This Hindu Holy Man is a Thai Buddhist," *Southeast Asia Research* 21, 2 (2013) I argue that there really is no such thing as a translocal "Hinduism" in Thailand. By looking closely at the figures of the Brahmin and hermits in Thai Buddhism, I argue that despite the prevalence of these figures in modern and pre-modern Thai art, literature, and ritual, it should not be assumed that the presence of statues of Brahmins, hermits, or deities like Indra, Śiva, Lakṣmī, Gaṇeśa, Brahma represents the presence of a definable Hinduism in Thailand. If I had a chance to rewrite this article, I would also start to argue that there is no such thing as Thai Buddhism either as established vis-à-vis Hinduism or some translocal imaginary of Buddhism. This article led to many productive conversations with younger scholars like Nathan McGovern, Arthid Sheravanichkul, Aditya Bhattacharjee, Trent Walker, and Susanne Ryuyin Kerekes. When we separate Hindu figures from the study of Thai Buddhist practice we do not see them as part of Thai Buddhism. In turn, no study of Thai Buddhism is complete if we relegate supposedly Hindu figures, stories, and rituals to a "foreign" accretion or influence.

Case in point, in reading through manuscripts for two edited volumes I published (*Illuminated Archives: Siamese Manuscript Collectors, Collections, and Connections,* Special Issue of the Journal – *Manuscript Studies*, 2017, and *From Mulberry Leaves to Silk Scrolls*, edited with Lynn Ransom, 2016) and a forthcoming book, *Cosmologies and Biologies: Illuminated Siamese Manuscripts on Death, Time, and the Body* (London: Holberton Books, 2022), I was struck by how many supposedly Hindu stories derived from Sanskrit literature I was finding in Thai Buddhist manuscript collections. In "Encountering Corpses: Notes on Zombies and the Living Dead in Buddhist Southeast Asia,"*Kyoto Review of Southeast Asia* (2012), I looked at the narratives of ghosts, animals, and the undead that have been popular in Thailand for the past several centuries and that are part of Buddhist story-telling culture. I concentrate on the *Vetāla–prakaraṇam* (*Collection of Stories of Zombies*) which is part of a whole genre of *prakaraṇam* texts that have circulated in Southeast Asia since, according to manuscript evidence, the fifteenth century. I emphasize that scholars of Buddhist history and practice in Southeast Asia need to pay more attention to both Sanskrit literary sources for supposedly the Pali-based Theravada Buddhist history instead of labeling those non-Theravada/non-Pali elements of Buddhist culture in the region simply "local" or indigenous or even animist. Like the supposedly Hindu communities of Thailand, I am trying to show that these forgotten and/or marginalized communities are actually what I call "strange attractors." This is a term I borrowed from theoretical mathematics which designates an influence that is seemingly everywhere but can't be isolated, identified, and analyzed. Strange attractors are part of chaos theory. Mathematicians and physicists use the term to explain the way when non-linear dissipated (i.e., chaotic) systems reveal patterned cohesion at the most fundamental mathematical and physical level. Because these forces are as yet not fully understood, they are called strange attractors. Any casual observer of Thai Buddhism will see, smell, and hear deep aesthetic, ritual, and linguistic similarities as they move from monastery to monastery, mural to mural, festival to festival. However, this apparent homogeneity, an essential Thainess (*khwam ben thai*), is something the Thai tourist board and Thai educational system consistently promotes. However, I argue that what we see as purely Thai is actually a shimmering result of diverse cultural, political, and religious, often foreign, forces. These forces are sometimes benign and the result of contact over time. Other times, they are the result of repetitive stress injury, so to speak, of strategic and manipulative forces seeking to maintain social control and erase diversity. The point, I attempt to make is that the heart of Thai Buddhism is often beat by non-Thai muscles.

No more so is this seen than in the research by Edward Van Roy. I was inspired by his research on the Chinese, Indian, Khmer, Malay, Mon, Tamil, Vietnamese, and other ethnic communities in the history of Bangkok. Pushing back on Tambiah and Van Roy here, I published an article, "Ethnicity and the Galactic Polity: Ideas and Actualities in the History of Bangkok" (*Journal of Southeast Asian Studies*, 2018) that looks closely at his valuable work, but questions the very idea of the well-known "mandala" model of Bangkok and expands on his history of Muslim (especially Malay and Persian) and South India (especially Chettiar) communities in the economic, royal, and religious life of the city. These communities, which were at the heart of power, especially under the third and fourth reigns of Bangkok history (1820s–70s) provide an alternative to the Buddhist and ethnic Thai-dominated histories of the city and central Siam/Thailand.

Another forgotten community in Thai Buddhism are nuns (*maechi*). Thai Buddhist monasticism is often presented as institutionally and ritually androcentric, if not downright misogynist. Many scholars have lamented the powerlessness of nuns and the lack of a "fully-ordained" Bhikkhuni order of nuns in Thai history.[5] However, Steven Collins and I in "Buddhist 'nuns' (*mae chi*) and the Teaching of Pali in Contemporary Thailand," *Modern Asian Studies* 44 (2010) argue that scholars have often been collaborators in that marginalization and in efforts to promote the launch of an Bhikkhuni order they have ignored the success of *maechi* in national Pali exams, their role in teaching monks at monastic universities, and the respect they are given as scholars of Buddhist literature and history. Their activity at the center of Buddhist educational life, although not ritual or ceremonial life, questions the very claim that Thai Buddhism is a male-dominated institution. This article has led to productive conversations with scholars like Monica Falk, Ayako Itoh, Claire Elliot, Martin Seeger, Kelly Meister, Joanna Cook, Suwanna Satha-Anand, and many others.

Not only are religious and ethnic communities in Thailand diverse, but the characters within Thai Buddhist literature are as well. Many literary works are like the Peacock Room that bring together many different people and conflicting ideas and interpretations. Particular communities at particular times have taken local stories, an idiosyncratic collection of "ancient" texts (which themselves are evolving repositories of a whole range of other local and translocal texts), and memories of their teachers' words. These sources have created curricula which both attempts to preserve this memory and these texts according to contemporary needs. Instead of describing "Buddhism" in the region, I have long been interested in how knowledge locally referred to as "Buddhist" has been formed and transmitted. How has this living episteme been transmitted from teacher to student?

To explore the curriculum of a particular religious community at a particular time and place is to look at its pedagogical methods, textual resources, physical practices, and educational structures, as well as at the relationship between the ideal religious authorities of the past and the constantly evolving lives of exegetes, pedagogues and novice consumers. By tracking changes over time the socio-historical forces which affect the way religious groups educate themselves and their society are apparent. In Buddhist Southeast Asia I believe that this approach highlights the texts and ideas that interpretative communities, both diachronically and synchronically, were and are aspiring to preserve and teach in particular ways.

I have been pleasantly surprised to find that this approach to studying texts in modern Theravada contexts has led to productive conversations with colleagues and practitioners in Burma, Sri Lanka, Nepal, and Cambodia as well. This approach to studying the ways texts are used in pedagogical settings and the formation of interpretative communities was seen in my book, *Gathering Leaves and Lifting Words* (2008). However, that book focused primarily on monastic communities in Laos and northern Thailand. In other articles that looked at interpretative communities I went outside of the monastery and looked at diverse range of ways to approach texts and the way they were taught, translated, catalogued, and repackaged by lay communities. Many of those articles will be re-published in the second volume in this series—*Further Wayward Distractions: Cacophonies, Erasures, and Transformations in the Study of Buddhism in Thailand* (2022). In this volume I include three articles that focus primarily on affect, longing and emotions. I include the first major article I ever published while I was a young graduate student. It is an article that was published in the *Journal of the Siam Society*, "Creative Engagement: The Sujavanna Wua Luang and its Contribution to Buddhist Literature" (2000), on a little known Tai Khoen Buddhist narrative that is popular for story-telling among Buddhist communities in northern Thailand and among the Lao, Shan, and Tai Leu and Tai Khoen in southern China. I focus on the values of love, attachment, and loyalty in this story and what it says about the interpretative communities that popularized it. This focus on the emotional content of Thai Buddhist art and texts would prove to be a subject that consistently distracted me for the next two decades.

I have often found in Thai Buddhist material love and attachment are featured as positive values. Indeed, the expression of extreme emotional attachment is common in Thai Buddhist stories. This might seem strange in a religion that is usually associated with emphasizing the dangers of desire and the suffering that often results from attachment to family and romantic partners. I question the negative association of love and especially marriage in "Beautifully Buddhist and Betrothed: Marriage and Buddhism as Described in the Jātakas," published in a volume edited by the late Steven Collins called *Reading the Vessantara Jātaka* (2016). Love and marriage are presented in many cases as admirable pursuits and, above all, beautiful. Through researching this side-project on marriage, I became increasingly interested in the role of beauty and pleasure in Thai Buddhism which leads me to another set of approaches to my studies of religion and culture in Thailand.

Cajoleries, Thin Description, and Non-Human Ontology

As my daughter said that day in the Peacock Room—"let's go back." Art historians are first trained to see, simply to see what is in front of them without interpretation, without reference, without articulating meaning. As my colleague, the great art historian, Gwendolyn Shaw, emphasizes—art historians have to learn how simply to describe first.[6] I took her advice in the study of Thai Buddhist art with a focus on "thin description." As Kant argued, we cannot experience reality "as such," since the only tool (our mind and senses) to experience reality is the very thing that makes all our observations subjective. But subjective does not necessarily mean non-empirical. Here is where I find Heather Love's work on "Thin Description" and "Surface Reading" (as opposed to Geertz's "Thick Description") important for the study of Buddhist art and material culture. Love criticizes the field of Literary Studies' "deep" reading of texts and the psycho-analytical analysis of characters. Her insights are important for scholars of Material Religious Studies as well. She states that

> by focusing exclusively on meaning, intention, language, and culture, critics have not attended fully to the behavioral components of experience and representation ... consider forms of analysis that describe patterns of behavior and visible activity but that do not traffic in speculation about interiority, meaning, or depth. Through its exhaustive, fine-grained attention to phenomena, thin description offers a model for close reading.... Thin description means, in effect, taking up the position of the device; by turning oneself into a camera, one could—at least ideally—pay equal attention to every aspect of a scene that is available to the senses and record it faithfully.... While it abjures the metaphorical depths of texts—hidden meanings, symbolic content, and repressed historical or psychic content—surface reading remains attentive (or even hyperattentive) to the text itself. Surface reading makes reading central, but it focuses on aspects of texts often seen as too obvious to be of interest.[7]

Later she shows that this is similar to the ways in which Erving Goffman practiced micro-sociological examination of stories. Love describes Goffman's approach as:

> it is descriptive: it defers virtuosic interpretation in order to attempt to formulate an accurate account of what the text is like. It also attends to what, in the text, is descriptive—it highlights its capacity to index and make visible forms of material and social reality. Goffman's empiricism can perhaps best be accounted for by emphasizing his affinities with the techniques of microanalysis. He analyzes social reality by focusing on observable elements of behavior: gesture, spacing, timing, dress, posture, eye contact, and so on. The key formulation of his method can be found in the introduction to *Frame Analysis*, where he identifies the key question to be answered in sociological inquiry: "What is it that's going on here?" ... Because he stops at the threshold of the person, refusing to speculate about affect, motivation, and character, the products of Goffman's method are perspectives, not persons; situations, not traits; behavior that belongs to no one.[8]

I care not if a particular set of ritual actions, a particular arrangement of statues on an altar, a particular type of gift, etc. are "Buddhist" (i.e., adhering to a pre-approved regimen or protocol established by a vague authority or discourse of "tradition"). Instead, I stay at the level of "surface reading" and "thin description." Like Geertz, I am using a literary metaphor for "reading" human behavior, but instead of following his famous method of "thick description," I am turning towards Love, Goffman, and as we will see, Material Culture and Affect Theorists like Daniel Miller and Eve Sedgwick, to take a micro-sociological approach and "thin" or surface reading of the ways Thai Buddhists interact with excessive Buddhist material in monastic spaces and how the material interacts with itself.

In many of these articles I argue that scholars of Buddhism should see what is in front of them in a monastery in Thailand (and in many other parts of the Buddhist world). In any Thai monastery, a forest of objects, ornaments, designs, images, and colors presents itself. There are burning sticks of incense, the sounds of chanting, and often the play of children, the smells from kitchens, or the haggling of merchants outside the monastery gates. We don't need to judge the interior intentions of the humans who engage in this activity. Furthermore, we also have to acknowledge that the objects in the rooms we see often don't have humans noticing them. Much of the time, they sit in the dark alone. If a flower wilts or a clock ticks in an empty monastery room does it smell; does it make a sound? One could argue that it does not matter. Sure, there are non-human actors and they exist in a flat ontology and in flat relations often with human actors, but it is their actions and their effects that only have meaning. I disagree here. If we want to get to the "why" of Buddhist expression—why are Buddhists so obsessed with excessively visually (and stimulating the other senses, of course) representing the dharma and the teachers of the dharma? Why are so many art schools, so many artisans, so much money, so much time, and so many resources spent to decorate a monastic space? Why do so many stories excessively describe nature, beauty, and emotions? The gaudy, gold, cacophonous, bejeweled, dusty, variegated, jumbled, almost technicolor and frankly sometimes loud, cluttered, and "unmeditative" spaces of monasteries in Thailand (often even more so in Tibet, Korea, Hong Kong, etc.) are overwhelming to the senses. They are a sea of senseless cajoleries. The flowers, the sculpted birds, the scattered shoes are ubiquitous on many monasteries. My largely Western students and foreign visitors to monasteries I encounter and occasionally give tours to often ask—why not just meditate? Why not just read or listen to teachings and texts? Why not use the money spent on this excessive ornament to help the poor surround the monastery? Why not use the resources for textbooks for students or to build handicapped-accessible ramps or better bathrooms for meditators? These are good questions. These are legitimate and not only foreigners ask them, many local Buddhists reflect on these issues themselves, but they reveal a problematic idea that there is a pure and transcendent or "original" set of universal Buddhist ideals that somehow many Thai Buddhists are either forgetting, ignoring, or actively dismantling.

Excess, abundance, and what one of my former students, calls "all the much" perpetuates and multiplies in Thai monastic spaces as it does in Tibetan, Japanese, Chinese, Burmese monastic spaces (and Catholic cathedrals, Hindu temples, Taoist shrines). Religion is often a celebration, not an austere retreat. To help answer these questions, I have tried to follow over the years my children back to Whistler's room so to speak. Whistler used the colors of his painting of the "Japanese" princess to guide the colors on the design in his room. The room's design was a type of cajolery that non-directly attempted to create certain undefined moods of general celebration and unapologetic waste. In that room filled with overwhelming and excessive ornament and non-narrative, non-figurative design, the painting becomes part of the ornament versus being studied independently. This often happens in the interiors of Buddhist monasteries (and the verses of Buddhist narrative poetry and prose).

What I have wanted to do across many articles in this volume is push back on Geertz (although his work in general was one of the greatest inspirations for me as I started my graduate studies) and the "cognitivist assumption" in the humanities that rituals, art, objects, and even stories have to have a cognitive or symbolic meaning or that they have to be a vehicle for advancing some deeper ethical or philosophical truth claim.[9] More specifically there is a baseline that runs through many of these articles and certainly my books that I am overwhelmed by Thai Buddhist complexity and beauty. So not only do the tangible literary or artistic expressions of Thai Buddhist practice need to be studied in terms of cognitive meaning, but many aspects of Thai Buddhism are even designed to be or simply are overwhelming so that they trigger a particular experience which is implicitly transcendent of meaning.

My thoughts on this are best expressed on the last page of Ottessa Mosfegh's brilliant novel—*My Year of Rest and Relaxation*. The book ends with the nameless protagonist watching a recording of the news that featured her closest friend Reva leaping from the flaming towers in lower Manhattan on September 11th, 2001.

> I watched the videotape over and over to soothe myself that day. And I continue to watch it, usually on a lonely afternoon, or any other time I doubt that life is worth living, or when I need courage, or when I am bored. Each time I see the woman leap off the seventy-eighth floor of the North Tower—one high-heeled shoe slipping off and hovering up over her, the other stuck on her foot as though it were too small, her blouse untucked, hair flailing, limbs stiff as she plummets down, one arm raised, like a dive into a summer lake—I am overcome by awe, not because she looks like Reva, and I think it's her, almost exactly her, and not because Reva and I had been friends, or because I'll never see her again, but because she is beautiful. There she is, a human being, diving into the unknown, and she is wide awake.[10]

I didn't hesitate to reveal (or "spoil") this ending. It is not the humbling ending that makes this one of the most striking pieces of fiction I have ever read, but the process of getting there. Sometimes beauty simply is. We can give it meaning, we can interpret it, often correctly, as a product of exploitation, of class, of competition, and/or of much larger historical, economic, and political forces. September 11th has been and should be interpreted in all those ways. Mosfegh knows this. The profundity and despair of that moment is not lost on her, but there is also something else in smaller moments that is much harder to articulate.

The process of learning with and from Thai Buddhists for the last nearly 30 years has been continually overwhelming and I have tried, and often failed to make sense of it. However, I do not think surface reading and thin description are necessarily shirking our humanist's duty to find, interpret, translate, and convey meaning. What I once thought of myself as failing in an endeavor or not having a keen or insightful enough of a mind to translate the meaning of what I was seeing in field work, I now see as simply an alternative, but not necessarily better or worse, approach. Indeed, in my own field of Religious Studies, Abraham Joshua Heschel provides another model of witness and gratitude. He famously wrote: "Our goal should be to live life in radical amazement [to] get up in the morning and look at the world in a way that takes nothing for granted. Everything is phenomenal; everything is incredible; never treat life casually. To be spiritual is to be amazed."[11] I am hoping that these articles reveal this amazement in a much more humble way, my amazement with the innovation and expression of Thai Buddhist practitioners. I do not want to define the wide variety of practices against the categories of a transcendent tradition.

Along the way, I have learned much not only from listening and learning from Thai Buddhists, but also through the "material turn" and "affective turn" in the study of Buddhism. There are too many excellent studies that have come out to mention, especially in Chinese, Japanese, and Tibetan Buddhist Studies on monastic architecture, Buddha images, mural paintings, reliefs, and even contemporary Buddhist art. I have been inspired by work by Fowler, Glassman, Pileka, Wang, Cate, Sharf, Tanabe, Geary, Levine, and many others who have shown the beauty, agency, and material history of art and architecture in premodern and modern Buddhist cultures. Perhaps the most revolutionary aspect of these studies is that they show that Buddhists often treat Buddha and other images as "living." These objects and the rooms themselves act on the ritualist, meditator, and visitor in Buddhist spaces. The work of Latour, Appadurai, Bennet, Miller, Morgan, Meyer, and other material culture and affect studies have been instrumental to the ways in which Buddhist Studies has theorized ways of understanding objects and built spaces in the history of Buddhist expression.[12] I have contributed as well to this material turn as seen in the articles collected here. What I have found is missing in this material turn is a study of cajolery of non-meaning. For me, the Peacock Room said much without trying to communicate anything at all.

These cajoleries often escape study.[13] What does the story teach us? What is the Buddha symbolizing? These questions and others like them search for meaning and intention. To step back from Geertzian "Thick Description" that looks for meanings, motivations, and underlying messages and stay at the surface level of material interaction. For example, I have tried to tackle the oft-heard criticisms of Thai monasteries being gaudy or overly ornamented by foreigners. I argue that the valuing of Buddhist material is not seen as a contradiction to simultaneously valuing meditation, personal austerity by nuns and monks, and renouncing the lay life. Indeed, contradiction between the Buddhist concepts of non-attachment and selflessness and the excessive ornamentation and material abundance of Buddhist ritual spaces are only a problem if we study Buddhism as single, over-arching, coherent whole and Buddhists merely as parts of that whole. However, I choose to study Buddhists not as products or expressions of a defined religion, but as negotiators of daily reality similar, as characters, not narrators or authors, of a story whose plot they are in the middle. Most Thai Buddhists are not particularly bothered by the unabashed accumulation of stuff in Buddhist monasteries. Moreover, they are active participants in producing and giving stuff and artisans and patrons donate funds to decorate monastic spaces and lavish them with non-functional, non-narrative, and non-meaningful (i.e., they do not didactically teach particular Buddhist ethical or historical lessons or information) ornamental design. However, these ubiquitous features of Buddhist spaces in Thailand and in many other Buddhist regions are rarely studied. Why? Attempting to answer this question led to an eventual book called the *Architects of Buddhist Leisure* (University of Hawai'i Press, 2018), which was a comparative study of Nepali, Japanese, Vietnamese, Singaporean, Thai, and Korean Buddhist public and leisure spaces, but it also led to two articles (included in this volume) on Thai art, one that focused on pre-modern art—"The Bird in the Corner of the Painting," *Moussons: Recherchesen sciences sociales sur l'Asie de Sud-Est* 23 (2014) and one that focused on modern art—"Strolling through Temporary Temples," *Contemporary Buddhism* (2017). In the first of the two articles especially, I argue, that the architects, installation artists, and visionaries that designed the often elaborate monastic spaces of the Theravada civilization in South and Southeast Asia did not just create functional spaces for ritual, religious instruction, ecclesiastical meetings, or meditation, but highly-stylized atmospheres that are filled with seemingly unnecessary, but beautiful objects. They and their teams of artisans, especially could be referred to as *ensembliers* more than architects. These *ensembliers* or decorators were often masters of the superfluous and arbitrary so that their spaces sanction luxury and enjoyment.[14] Like Whistler's Peacock Room, the overwhelming number of assembled natural and constructed sensual objects work to inhibit systematic learning. This does not mean they are simply a decadent jumble though. As Daniel Miller notes, some objects are important for the simple fact that they are not isolated and seen individually. They are important because we "do not 'see' them. The less we are aware of them, the more powerfully they can determine our expectations by setting the scene and ensuring normative behavior, without being open to challenge. They determine what takes place to the extent that we are unconscious of their capacity to do so."[15] They help form a festive atmosphere where one can be anonymous and absorb sensory delight. There is no test of merit or knowledge, no time spent debating with nuns or monks, and no designated time to enter or leave. Similarly, Michael Taussig asserted that when an object becomes expected and ordinary, it creates a space for non-contemplative practical memory.[16] It becomes "distraction." Distraction is a type of "apperceptive mode." The object is no longer studied individually, it is only noticed when it is absent. Cajoleries are unnoticed, but also ubiquitous in these spaces. With so many statues, murals, flowers, and burning incense sticks in many Buddhist spaces, a visitor is not encouraged to focus on an objective but get lost among a maze of a menagerie of distractions and diversions. These distractions are an important, but neglected aspect, in the study of Buddhist architecture. This is an important aspect of the growing field of Affect Theory. As Gregory Seigworth and Melissa Gregg write that to study affect is to study "of accumulative *beside-ness.*" It is the study of accumulation of encounters—a "supple incrementalism." The senses accumulate images, feelings, scents, and sounds constantly. This accumulation is at once "intimate and impersonal." It is the slow accretion of knowledge in the form of non-discursive impressions. It is not the systematic learning of facts, dates, titles, terms, narrative sequences, ethical standards, and logical progressions, but the body's "capacity to affect and be affected."[17] Thai Buddhist ornament and art, like ritual and music, are repetitious affective encounters. I assert that these affective encounters, these distractions, are as fundamental, if not more fundamental, to the ways Buddhists learn to be Buddhists, because they are more accessible and common, than ethical arguments, philosophical treatises, and doctrinal formulations.

One of the most consistent distractions I have had in the last 28 years of being involved in Thai Studies is the collection, trading, and study of Thai Buddhist amulets. I rarely wrote about amulets as I wasn't sure that anyone outside of "fans" and traders like me would be interested. However, I thought it might be wise to at least write up a summary of the scholarly resources for the study of Thai amulets (nearly all of which are in the Thai language and so hard to access for non-Thai readers). Benjamin Fleming and Richard Mann invited me to include this article in their edited volume *Material Culture and Asian Religions: Text, Image, Object* (Routledge, 2014). Surprisingly to me, this is one of the most requested article by strangers who email me. I have been asked for dozens of copies over the last couple of years and have been invited to speak on this subject often. I guess I am not the only scholar or enthusiast with this distraction!

This leads to the last article I have included in this section. Here I turn to empty monasteries, Buddhist spaces without Buddhists. I look at one of the most notable, but unstudied, features of modern Buddhist art in Thailand—the installation. In "Strolling through Temporary Temples," I describe the exponential growth in the number of large gallery and museum spaces in Thailand, especially in Chiang Mai and Bangkok, that invite artists to construct large and provocative installation pieces. Two artists in particular have created entire secular, monastery-like spaces to display their installations. These lay artists have redefined the nature of Buddhist art and have taken it out of traditional monasteries and royal court ateliers. They have also used art to question the role of monks and religion in modern society and have provided an important social, aesthetic, and intellectual critique. They also force us to reflect on non-human ontology.

In many articles in this volume, I have discussed the importance of the study of Buddhist material culture in a largely functional and human-centric fashion. However, what about objects, rooms, monasteries, monastic neighborhoods, etc. when humans aren't considered? Like the Peacock Room, Thai Buddhist Monasteries create atmospheres. The problem is reducing these atmospheres to an analysis of the "meaning" (for and to human agents) of an individual statue, mural, bird relief, flower, rain spout, recorded chanting, even feather, aroma of incense, aroma of gasoline from the parking lot, mirror shard (common decorative item in Thai monasteries), or even paint chip color shade or even a leaf fallen on the ground or an old broom leaning against a wall. We must resist that formalism, but we also must resist the opposite—reducing individual objects, sounds, and aromas or the total atmosphere they create to their capacity to act on human observers. Can we stretch thin description so thin that it can't be seen with human eyes? We must guard against reducing Buddhism to its individual pieces (undermining) nor ignore their physicality or their physical expression to their "objectness" and make them servants to the observer and their "function" (overmining). Objects, whether they be sensual or actual, as Graham Harman argues in several works on Object-Oriented Ontology, exist without the need of humans, human stories, human creators, human visionaries, human observers, or simple humans present in a room not noticing individual pieces of ornament and simply laughing or relaxing in the total aesthetic fact of the atmosphere. As he argues "works of art and architecture are misunderstood if we reduce them downward to their physical components or upward to their socio-political effects ... there is something in these works which resists reduction in either direction."[18] He argues that objects, whether as part of a total architectural space or an individual work (or even molecular or atomic component of an individual work) have a capacity for "emergence."[19] An object acts and an object is regardless of the observer and, I would argue further, that the object when placed in different configurations with other objects in a various tableaux, it has the capacity to emerge in different ways. Just as a person, if seen from afar, acts differently alone than with her colleagues or his friends or among strangers in a crowd. A train abandoned in a field and covered with flowers and weeds (thank you André Breton) is different from one on city tracks and full of fuel. The train changes the tracks and the fuel. The train in the meadow changes the direction and possibilities of the enveloping tendrils and pervades a home for insects, birds, and animals. A solitary Buddha image is different in an open field than it is surrounded by hundreds of other images, surrounded by flowers, incense, murals, chanting, with a donation box in front of it. The Buddha image in the meadow and the Buddha image surrounded (or better as one part of) an ornamental tableau creates emergent atmospheres whether humans are present or not. Most of the time the ornamental tableaux or the solitary image (which is exceedingly rare in any Buddhist context and it could be argued that the meadow or empty room is part of ornament as well) exists sans humans—largely all night long and in long-stretches of the mid-morning and mid-afternoon when there are no events, no chanting, no meditators, and no visitors in monastic spaces. The Peacock Room exists when the doors are locked. The atmosphere is there and has emergent, sensual, and actual existence regardless of its functions and much greater than the sum of its components.

It is this atmosphere that is emerging in different ways depending on the light, ambient sound, relative humidity and barometric pressure constantly whether humans observe it or not that is neglected by scholars of Buddhist art, architecture, literature, ritual, and history. If we are really going to respect the teaching of non-self and non-attachment, then we have to allow that Buddhist stuff (statues, flowers, mirror-shards, flowers, LED flashing lights placed behind Buddha images—esp. in Burma and Cambodia—gold flakes, reflections, figural drawings, painted flames, dust, lingering aromas, etc.) don't need us after they are placed and created. They have stories, they have origins, they have materials, they have socio-economic contexts, they have patrons, they have monetary value for sure. However, once they are in an atmosphere, they still act on each other and create atmosphere. The aroma and smoke of incense continues long after a human lights the stick. Flowers unfold and then wilt long after they are placed and admired. Murals retain their colors and images have their eyes downcast long after they are painted or forged. They are as much present to each other in a humanless room as they are to a room full of people kneeling, chanting, or checking their cellphones. As Harman argues "objects interact among themselves even when humans aren't present ... [we need] to be aware of the relations between objects that have no direct involvement with people."[20]

So if we think about the history of the study of Art History as a discipline, we know that formalism came at a time where art historians wanted to show that their discipline was a "science" like any other and didn't need a study of humans, but a close study of the formal properties of a piece of art. This movement was subsumed by Art History turning to other sciences—Psychology and Anthropology—seeing how art, especially under the studies of Alfred Gell, Rudolph Arnheim, and Erwin Panofsky in very different ways, but all taking human-art work interaction as the main force of their work. Harman and others like Manuel DeLanda want to remove the necessity of humans from the understanding of an object's agency and see the effects objects have on each other.[21] In a sense it seems Art History could be returning to the non-human (although this is an emerging and certainly not widespread "turn" at the moment), but the return is to a vastly different space than Formalism provided.

If we remove the necessity of the human observer and see these spaces and the objects within them creating atmospheres and being there in an assembly for each other—in object to object, tableau to tableau relationships—whether humans are also objects in the room or not, then we can (1) breakdown the human-object dichotomy; (2) see artisans (most often nameless) as practicing, at least partially, selflessness; (3) acknowledge the egoless relations between objects; (4) respect the presence of Buddhas (in the form of images) in a room partaking in the atmosphere of beauty and sensory delight; (5) honor the Buddha without judging the seemingly selfish petitions and merit-seeking gifts and actions of Buddhists; (6) understand, as Robert Brown, did more than 20 years ago, that murals and other "art" in a monastic space are not there for humans, it is there for the Buddha image to delight in and by which to be honored; the Buddha it is true witness and appreciator of the ornament, not the human visitor;[22] (7) and better understand the seemingly uselessness or wastefulness of Buddhists gift givers, patrons, artisans, and anonymous people that drop coins in a donation box at a monastery and not the open hands of the beggars outside its gates. It is hard to understand this seeming waste, excess, and lack of compassion while maintaining the human-object divide, without understanding that the Buddha is the observer, not the Buddhist. It also respects the respect (and desire for him not to feel lonely, Thai: *wawei/nga*) Buddhists have for the Buddha in image form after the doors of the monastery are locked and the lights turned off.

The story of the Peacock Room, the betrayal, the affair, the money, the scandal, and the bequest and the movement of the room to the Smithsonian can teach us that every room, every work of art has a biography that includes the materials, the patrons, the artists, the delivery workers, the paint suppliers, the trees, and the carpenters. These are important factors to consider. However, equally important factors to consider are that my children and thousands of visitors to the Peacock Room or any Buddhist monastery can delight in the atmosphere and have their senses overwhelmed and their ration suspended in and by beauty without ever knowing one single fact about the artist, the controversies, the decisions, and the history of the room or any individual object in it. It is also important to acknowledge that the room exists and commands security guards and alarms and inspires writers and home decorators long after visiting hours are over and the doors are shut.

Conclusion

The approaches above are an attempt to provide shape and significance to the diversity of subjects and arguments this collection of articles offers. When I say "my approach," it is similar to the way I might say "my office." I didn't build it, I don't pay the utilities, I don't repair the roof, I don't pay the insurance, I rarely clean it. My office and the other material conditions that contribute to the ways I can easily lead my privileged life are supported by hundreds of people, most of whom, I rarely meet. The sidewalks I walk on, the police that protect me and my property, the people fighting to keep my air clean and those that fight to keep polluting it, don't know me and I don't know them. I can cite my parents, my deans, my friends, the staff and faculty I have had the chance to meet as supports that allow me to occupy the space I call my office, but those "known" people are just a few of the many. I make great efforts to site the countless teachers, students, friends, experts, books, articles, etc. that have in some small way contributed to "my approach," but I am sure I miss many. Who is to say which conversation, which moment, led to the first cognitive moment that lead to being open to a new approach?

Basically, I have long been interested in complex individuals with conflicting influences and seemingly contradictory views. I am interested in the ways in which places like the Peacock Room come into existence and how they are continually reimagined and reinterpreted. I emphasized that individual agents (texts, statues, teachers, magicians, etc.) are always in situated relationships with other people, art, texts, memories, and objects. This permits a study that takes into account an agent's capacity and authority to be complex and contradictory. The lives of texts, objects, and people are not their own, but told and retold by many others. The study of agents is actually the study of the ways many people construct agents. This way of thinking about agency has, I hope, the advantage of recognizing situatedness, what might be called dependent co-arising (Pali: *paṭiccasamuppāda*) in Buddhist terminology. When one writes, gives talks, and the like they become an unwitting voice "representing" the area of their research. Scholars are often thrust into the role of "expert" or "resource" especially when asked to give interviews to news outlets, large gatherings at museums or public venues, and the like. While I wanted to write about individual Thai Buddhists, objects, events, and texts in the past and present, I found myself speaking about Thai Buddhism in general. I am hoping that this collection will reveal, but certainly not resolve, that struggle.

Notes

1 This title is inspired by a British punk band named Joy Division.

2 Mies van der Rohe was the originator of the phrase "less is more" when describing his approach to design.

3 Lorand Matory, *Black Atlantic Religions* (Princeton: Princeton University Press, 2009): introduction.

4 Bernard Formoso and I wrote [in French] a dedication and review of Tambiah's work shortly after he passed on—"Stanley Jeyaraja Tambiah (1929–2014)," *Éditions de l'EHESS* | L'Homme no. 212 (2014): 63–70.

5 Louis Gabaude, in a talk at the Theravada Civilizations Conference at Arizona State University in May 2016, argued that the very term "ordination" or "ordained" is a Catholic term that makes little sense when used in a Thai Buddhist context.

6 Personal communication, September 2017.

7 Heather Love, "Close Reading and Thin Description," *Public Culture* (2013) 25 [3 (71)]: 401–34.

8 Ibid.: 426–7.

9 I thank Donovan Schaefer for his comments on this section and his help in clarifying this issue.

10 Ottessa Mosfegh, *My Year of Rest and Relaxation* (New York: Penguin, 2019), p. 289. I thank her for giving a talk and reading at the University of Pennsylvania in March 2020 and for further conversations with me about her work and the idea of beauty without meaning. I also thank Corey Loftus for introducing me to her work in 2018.

11 Abraham Joshua Heschel, *God in Search of Man: A Philosophy of Judaism* (Philadelphia: Jewish Publication Society, 1955), p. 33.

12 See especially, Bruno Latour, "Where are the Missing Masses," in *Shaping Technology-Building Society*, ed. Wiebe Bijker and John Law (Cambridge, Mass: MIT Press, 1992), pp. 225–59; Arjun Appadurai, *The*

Social Life of Things (Cambridge: Cambridge University Press, 1988); Jane Bennett, *Vibrant Matter: A Political Ecology of Things* (Durham: Duke University Press, 2010); many works by David Morgan, but see his most recent book *The Thing About Religion* (Chapel Hill: University of North Carolina Press, 2020); Birgit Meyer, "'Material Approaches to Religion' Meet 'New Materialism': Resonances and Dissonances," *Material Religion* 15, 4 (2019). Some of the work that has inspired my thinking on art and material culture in Buddhism includes: Stanley Abe, "Inside the Wonder House: Buddhist Art and the West," in *Curators of the Buddha: The Study of Buddhism under Colonialism*, ed. Donald S. Lopez Jr. (Chicago: University of Chicago Press, 1995); Richard Davis, "From the Lives of Indian Images," in *Religion, Art, and Visual Culture*, ed. S. Brent Plate (New York: Palgrave, 2002), pp. 176–81; Sherry Fowler, *Murōji: Rearranging Art and History at a Japanese Buddhist Temple* (Honolulu: University of Hawai'i Press, 2005); Gregory Levine, *Daitokuji: The Visual Cultures of a Zen Monastery* (Seattle: University of Washington Press, 2005); Forrest McGill, ed., *Emerald Cities: Arts of Siam and Burma, 1775–1950* (San Francisco: Asian Art Museum, 2009); Fabio Rambelli, *Buddhist Materiality: A Cultural History of Objects in Japanese Buddhism* (Palo Alto, CA: Stanford University Press, 2008); Robert Sharf, *Living Images: Japanese Buddhist Icons in Context* (Palo Alto, CA: Stanford University Press, 2002); Eugene Wang, *Shaping the Lotus Sutra: Buddhist Visual Culture in Medieval China* (Seattle: University of Washington Press, 2005); Sarah Fraser, *Performing the Visual: The Practice of Buddhist Wall Painting in China and Central Asia, 618–960* (Palo Alto, CA: Stanford University Press, 2003); Apinan Poshyananda, *Modern Art in Thailand: Nineteenth and Twentieth Centuries* (Oxford: Oxford University Press, 1992); Sandra Cate, *Making Merit, Making Art: A Thai Temple in Wimbledon* (Honolulu: University of Hawai'i Press, 2003); Jessica Falcone, "Waiting for Maitreya: Of Gifting Statues, Hopeful Presents, and the Future tense in FPMT's Transnational Tibetan Buddhism," PhD diss., Cornell University, 2010; David Geary, "Destination Enlightenment: Buddhism and the Global Bazaar in Bodh Gaya, Bihar," PhD diss, University of British Columbia, 2009; Hank Glassman, *The Face of Jizō: Image and Cult in Medieval Japanese Buddhism* (Honolulu: University of Hawai'i Press, 2012); Patricia Jane Graham, *Faith and Power in Japanese Buddhist Art, 1600–2005* (Honolulu: University of Hawai'i Press, 2007); Clare Harris, *The Museum on the Roof of the World: Art, Politics, and the Representation of Tibet* (Chicago: University of Chicago Press, 2012); Richard Jaffe, "Buddhist Material Culture, 'Indianism,' and the Construction of Pan-Asian Buddhism in Pre-War Japan," *Material Religion* 21, 3 (2006): 266–92; Klemens Karlsson, "Material Religion and Ethnic Identity: Buddhist Visual Culture and the Burmanization of the Eastern Shan State," in *The Spirit of Things: Materiality and Religious Diversity in Southeast Asia*, ed. Julius Bautista (Ithaca, NY: Cornell Southeast Asia Program Publications, 2012), pp. 61–78; Borteh Ly, "Of Trans(national), Subjects and Translation: The Art and the Body Language of Sopheap Pich," in *Modern and Contemporary Southeast Asian Art: An Anthology*, ed. Nora A. Taylor and Boreth Ly (Ithaca: Cornell University Press, 2012), pp. 117–30; Ian Reader and George J. Tanabe Jr., *Practically Religious: Worldly Benefits and the Common Religion of Japan* (Honolulu: University of Hawai'i Press, 1998); Andrew Watsky, *Chikubushima: Deploying the Sacred Arts in Momoyama Japan* (Seattle: University of Washington Press, 2004); Cynthea Bogel, *With a Single Glance: Buddhist Icon and Early Mikkyo Vision* (Seattle: University of Washington Press, 2009). I am also indebted to the study of ornament and design in Asian religions: Jonathan Hay, *Sensuous Surfaces: The Decorative Object in Early Modern China* (Honolulu: University of Hawai'i Press, 2010). One excellent collected volume that features three articles on Balinese, Japanese, and Indonesian ornamental art (although not Buddhist) are found in Morgan Pitleka and Jan Mrázek, eds., *What's the Use of Art?: Asian Visual and Material Culture in Context* (Honolulu: University of Hawai'i Press, 2008).

[13] I thank Trine Brox, Elizabeth Lane Williams-Oerberg, Hannah Gould, Jane Caple among others that included me in the workshop on Buddhism and Waste in Helsinor, Denmark in 2019. The discussion there inspired much of my recent work on Buddhism and excess and some of this material will go into their collected volume with Bloomsbury Press on the subject (forthcoming). Unfortunately, I could not

contribute to their volume, but owe them a debt of gratitude for their encouragement and feedback. Brox and Williams-Oerberg particularly helped me rethink my assumptions.

14 Witold Rybczynski notes that the notion of the *ensemblier* as separate from the architect began to emerge at the Exposition Internationale des Arts Décoratifs et Industriels Modernes in Paris in 1925. I thank him for his advice (personal communication, Fall 2012). See also his *Home: A Short History of an Idea* (New York: Penguin, 1986), p. 180. See also Edward Hollis's *The Memory Palace: A Book of Lost Interiors* (Berkeley: Counterpoint, 2014).

15 See also the introduction to Justin McDaniel, *Architects of Buddhist Leisure: Socially Disengaged Buddhism in Asia's Museums, Monuments, and Amusement Parks* (Honolulu: University of Hawai'i Press, 2016) where I first engaged with and provide a more expansive reflection on this idea. Daniel Miller, "Introduction," in *Materiality*, ed. Daniel Miller (Durham: Duke University Press, 2005), p. 5. For a powerful mix of autobiography and anthropological study on the capacity to affect and be affected by ordinary objects, see Kathleen Stewart's *Ordinary Affect* (Durham: Duke University Press, 2007) and Farshid Moussavi's work at the 2013 Venice Architecture Biennale takes a creative approach to "Architecture and Affects." See http://www.nytimes.com/2012/12/03/arts/design/defining-the-emotional-cause-of-affect.html?_r=1&

16 Michael Taussig, "Tactility and Distraction," *Cultural Anthropology* 6, 2 (1991): 147, 153.

17 Gregory Seigworth and Melissa Gregg, "An Inventory of Shimmers," in *The Affect Theory Reader*, ed. Gregory Seigworth and Melissa Gregg (Durham: Duke University Press, 2010), pp. 1–28.

18 Graham Harman, *Immaterialism: Objects and Social Theory* (New York: Polity, 2016), p. 12. See also his larger work on this subject in *Object-Oriented Ontology: A New Theory of Everything* (New York: Penguin, 2018) and *Art and Objects* (New York: Polity, 2019).

19 Ibid., p. 6.

20 Harman, *Immaterialism*, p. 6.

21 See Manuel DeLanda, *Assemblage Theory* (Edinburgh: Edinburgh University Press, 2016): introduction.

22 See Robert L. Brown, "Narrative as Icon: The Jātaka Stories in Ancient Indian and Southeast Asian Architecture," in *Sacred Biography in the Buddhist Traditions of South and Southeast Asia,* ed. Juliane Schober (Honolulu: University of Hawai'i Press, 1997), pp. 64–110.

2

Creative Engagement: The *Sujavaṇṇa Wua Luang* and Its Contribution to Buddhist Literature*

Introduction

The *Sujavaṇṇa Wua Luang* (SWL), an apocryphal Buddhist *Jātaka* story written in Khün, employs translocal literary practices to express local values, religious beliefs and practices. The Khün composer(s) of the SWL found the complex narrative structure, compelling chain of events and prestigious classical language of the canonical *Jātaka* to be an excellent vehicle to comment upon local historical events, political and social concerns, and cultural values and practices. Studying the SWL in this light will lay the basis for a new understanding of the relationship between canonical and vernacular literature in Southeast Asia.

The SWL is a non-classical or apocryphal Buddhist *Jātaka*. Traditionally these *Jātakas* tell the story of a Bodhisatta who was born as a prince and performed meritorious acts involving sacrifice of limbs, wealth, family or even his own life. These

---

* Originally appeared as "Creative Engagement: The *Sujavanna Wua Luang* and Its Contribution to Buddhist Literature," *Journal of the Siam Society* 88 (2000): 156–77.

Artisan in the Shan region of Burma near the Thai border. Photo by author.

miraculous and tragic tales are among the most popular stories in all of Buddhist literature. A total of 547 *Jātakas* are canonical. However, in Southeast Asia there are over a hundred apocryphal *Jātakas*, which in many instances have little in common with the canonical tales aside from plot structure and having a Bodhisatta as the main character. Often these non-classical *Jātakas* are grouped together in collections with classical *Jātakas*, the most common collection being the *Paññāsa-Jātaka* (50 *Jātakas*) found in manuscripts in Burma, Thailand, Laos and Cambodia.[1] The main events of both the canonical and non-canonical *Jātakas* are depicted in sculpture and painting throughout Southeast Asia and the values emphasized in them are a common theme of traditional Buddhist sermons. The questions I am concerned with are: why would writers in Southeast Asia write new *Jātakas* when there were 547 canonical ones attributed to the historical Buddha himself? What can the differences between the canonical and the non-canonical *Jātakas* tell us about religious values, textual practices and historical changes in Southeast Asia in the medieval period?

Summary of the *Sujavaṇṇa Wua Luang*[2]

A summary of the SWL is as follows: One day the Buddha overhears two monks recounting a story they heard of a woman who became pregnant after drinking the urine of a bull and gave birth to a child who would become a Buddhist monk. The Buddha then uses this occasion to relate the story of himself in a former life when he was the Bodhisatta Sujavaṇṇa. Sujavaṇṇa was the son of the good King Jambu Ekarāja and Queen Suvaṇṇabhūmā. Indra observed the queen practicing Buddhist precepts and decided to bless her with Sujavaṇṇa who was actually one of his sons in the 33rd heaven. The King of the Bulls, Usubharāja, wanted to pay homage to Sujavaṇṇa. Usubharāja was invisible to humans and only left large footprints on the ground when he walked. The people became frightened when they saw these huge footprints, but Jambu Ekarāja assured them that these footprints were left by an *Arahant* (an enlightened person). After visiting the humans, the King of the Bulls decided to bathe in the river. While he was bathing, a piece of the fruit he was eating fell into the river, and a young woman named Khemavatī who was bathing down river picked it up and ate it. The fruit, combined with her practice of Buddhist precepts, caused Indra to impregnate her with a daughter named Ummādantī, who was one of Indra's wives in the 33rd heaven. Ummādantī agreed as long as Indra would assure her that she would be able to marry a future Buddha. Ummādantī was born and one day she went to a great celebration at the palace. She was so beautiful that many princes wanted to become her husband, but the other women were jealous of her and ridiculed her for being an illegitimate child that was abandoned by her father. They called her a wild beast (not aware that she was in fact the daughter of a bull) and told her to go play with the animals (foreshadowing her travels to the land of the bulls). Ummādantī begged her mother to let her go to find her father who Khemavatī told her was Usubharāja.

Khemavatī allowed her and Ummādantī travelled through the forest guided by a golden deer, who, in reality, was another son of Indra.

She reached a large dirty cowshed which was the home of Usubharāja and she cleaned it before its owner returned home. Usubharāja saw this clean stable and knew that it must be the work of a great person. The gods caused Usubharāja to be sick and have to remain at home the next day where he saw the beautiful Ummādantī. She made the proper respectful salutations and offered Usubharāja puffed rice and after some miraculous events told him that she was his daughter. The other bulls brought her delicious fruit from the forest. They built a miraculous one-pillar palace for Ummādantī and this is the reason why today bulls' horns are in all different directions, because they had been twisted and turned by the work of building. Indra created a glorious park for her with fruit groves and crystal clear pond. The bulls were given an endless supply of sweet grass to eat, so they no longer had to go into the forest to search for fruit.

Then Indra magically inspired Sujavaṇṇa to go into the forest to hunt deer. Carrying the sword of victory the prince entered the forest and chased the golden deer who led him to the one-pillared palace. Ummādantī allowed Sujavaṇṇa to stay in the palace because he possessed a protective mantra. Sujavaṇṇa had no way of climbing the pillar and had to chant a mantra to give him the power to reach Ummādantī. The mantra requested that the gods give him power to fly because he had achieved many of the Buddhist perfections (*pāramī*) and acquired merit for the sake of reaching Nibbāna and escaping the cycle of rebirths (*vaṭṭa-saṃsāra*). After he had flown up to Ummādantī, she tested him further with riddles involving Buddhist doctrine, which he answered with skill. The king and queen were worried when their son did not return from his hunting excursion and consulted a *purohita* (a Brahman spiritual advisor and soothsayer), who was knowledgable in regards to the three Vedas and trained in the use of mystical diagrams (*yantra*) and *mantras*. He told the king through his interpretation of these *yantra* that the prince would return on the eighth day of the crescent moon of the seventh month (which turned out to be correct). Ummādantī and Sujavaṇṇa remained alone in the one-pillared palace for seven days (without marrying) and then flew on a magical horse first to her mother in the city of Rājagaha and then to the parents of Sujavaṇṇa in Jetuttara. They felt obligated to show respect to their parents. When the jealous women saw that Khemavatī was the mother of a glorious being, they repented for their earlier improprieties. The couple was married and had a boy and girl, who in turn married each other.

One day Sujavaṇṇa realized that everything was impermanent and decided to become a Buddhist renunciant and go into the state of homelessness (*pabbajā*). He decided to give up his flesh and his own life to anyone who requested it. He prayed to Indra, Brahma and even hell beings. Then Indra changed into the form of an old brahmin and asked for Sujavaṇṇa's limbs. The earth shook and trembled because of the great selfless act of Sujavaṇṇa. Then Indra returned the limbs to Sujavaṇṇa and

Sujavaṇṇa ascended a jeweled throne to preach the word of the Buddha. He gave a sermon about the first noble truth of suffering and instructed people to maintain the Buddhist precepts, listen to sermons and take refuge in the Buddha, the Dhamma and the Sangha so as to annihilate *taṅhā* (craving).

Then Indra changed his form into an ogre and requested the eyes of Sujavaṇṇa. Sujavaṇṇa willingly tore them from their sockets, but then Indra returned the eyes which could see even farther than before. Sujavaṇṇa made the resolution to become a Buddha during his 199,000th life during the time of the Buddha Dhammadassī. Then he was reborn at that time as a king and gave to the poor every day and practiced the ten behavior rules of a good Buddhist king. He also practiced meditation (*bhāvanā*) and the subjects of meditation (*kammaṭṭhāna*) and became aware of impermanence. He decided to give up anger, lying, committing adultery, destroying reliquaries, cutting the bodhi trees and causing dissension among the saṅgha. Ummādantī also became a renunciant. They practiced the spiritual exercises to achieve the perfection of asceticism (*nekkhammapāramī*) and *jhāna* meditation. They were reborn in the 33rd heaven and lived in a jeweled palace.

The Buddha appears in the narrative again and tells the monks that he told this story so that they would be able to realize *Nibbāna*. He states the *āṇisaṃsa*: that anyone who copies the SWL, reads it to an audience and offers the text to a temple and honors the text with flowers will obtain the three joys (living in wealth, living in heaven and realizing *Nibbāna*). The Buddha identified himself as Sujavaṇṇa, Jambu Ekarāja as Suddhodhana (the father of the Buddha), Suvaṇṇabhūma as the mother of the Buddha, Mahāmāyā, Usubharāja as Sāriputta, the golden deer as Ānanda, Khemavatī as Gotamī, Sugandha, the son of Sujavaṇṇa as Rahula (the son of the Buddha) and Indra as Anuruddha.

Linguistic Features

The SWL is written in a mixture of Pāli, traditionally associated with Theravada Buddhism, and the extremely local Khün language only spoken in and around the city of Chiang Tung (also known as Jengtung, Kengtung and Kyaington) in the Shan regions of upper, eastern Burma, about 300 kilometers from the present-day northern border of Thailand. Khün is a member of the Tai family of languages and its script is similar, although certainly not identical, to Yuan, Lü or Tham scripts which are used in Laos, eastern Burma and northern Thailand alongside the more common Fakkham and Lao scripts.[3] A northern Thai, Shan and/or Lao person would most likely be able to understand a Khün speaker at a basic level. However, Khün is largely incomprehensible to a central Thai speaker. Khün reveals a great deal of lexical borrowing from Chinese, Lao, Shan and Thai; however, there are numerous words not traceable to any other language (although a more serious study of the Ahom language of Assam might lead to better etymologies). The manuscript of the edition that I am using for this chapter was found at Wat Hnong Kham in Chiang Tung. It comprises seven *phūks* (bundles of palm leaves) and is a relatively standard length, although, due to the popularity of this *Jātaka*, there are numerous recensions, including manuscripts as long as 17 *phūks*.[4] Besides the manuscripts, the story is often depicted in art. In his edition, Anatole-R. Peltier, includes numerous stitched drawings in narrative sequence on a colored flag that depicts the story. The story is often retold at the Cullakaṭhina ceremony at temples in Chiang Tung at the end of the raining season. The numerous recensions, sculptures and stitched drawings all attest to the popularity of the story.[5]

Each *phūk* of the Wat Hnong Kham recension begins with a short Pāli summary of the *phūk*'s contents, consisting of approximately 7 to 60 words. These summaries get shorter as the narrative progresses. For instance, the Pāli summary at the beginning of the third *phūk* is of average length and reads: "*namo tassatthu tadā kiāe devatā ummdantī gacchāma silaṃ oruyanti* (then, at that time, the deities addressed Ummādantī, 'let us go to the mountain')." This is translated in Khün as "*nai kāla mūa devabut devatā flūng phān phaeo mā rap ao nāng no gaeo mūa yū plāi phāg mïi neramit yang dī yū*. . . (at that time, the son of the glorious and magnificent deity went to receive the Lady of the Gem who was living at the top of a mountain, then he built a residence...)."[6] Any reader of both languages will immediately see that the Khün is not an exact translation of the Pāli, in fact the Khün provides more detail and the Pāli is simply an outline, or what Levi-Strauss might call a mytheme, of the main action of the *phūk*. If one could only read or understand the Pāli, this narrative would be quite vacuous, telling the audience little more than who went where at what time. The Pāli may not have been intended to be translated and instead was meant to provide a frame to the main Khün narrative. In addition, Pāli in northern Thailand and the Shan territories often is non-standard and its consistency of errors could simply reveal the existence of a local dialect of Pāli and/or reflect the non-standardized nature of Pāli in Southeast Asia in general.[7] The Khün seems to be using the relatively simple Pāli statements as cues to the narrative sequence of the story, but the Khün writers had a free hand in creating details, expanding on the fortunes of characters and adding branch stories not contained in the Pāli. This should not suggest that there was a Pāli original on which the Khün text is based, especially due to the frequent errors in Pāli grammar and syntax, but that the Pāli framed the story and gave it a sense of religious authority, temporal authenticity and could have been used to comment on contemporary events. We will return to these issues below.

The Pāli is not limited to these initial summaries, however, on every page of the Wat Hnong Kham edition there are intertextual Pāli words or short phrases usually followed by Khün translations. For example, in the fourth *phūk* there are intertextual Pāli words and phrases like: "*sattaṃ yojanamaggaṃ* (a path measuring seven yojanas)" and others like "*so mahāsatto* (the great being)." These Pāli words and phrases are often, but certainly not always, followed by a direct Khün translation which reveals a good understanding of Pāli. The former phrase is followed by "*an wā hanād nag klāi yūo yoj nap wā dāi 7 yojanakanā* (this means the way was very far and long measuring seven *yojanas*)." The latter two words are followed by "*an wā mahāsat* (the great being)."[8] These intertextual Pāli words and phrases are extremely common. They are known as "*plae roi*" or "thread translations," because the Pāli is weaved through the vernacular text.[9] These Pāli words add no additional information to the narrative and seem completely arbitrary; however, like Latin, French or German words and phrases often used in English texts, like *sui generis*, *a priori*, or *wissenschaft*, they add both a sense of prestige and scholarliness to the text as well as providing foreign words that present complex ideas or descriptions in concise ways. For example, in the fifth *phūk* the Pāli term "sakuṇṇā (birds)" followed by the Khün "*an wā nok dang lāi noi yāi an yū dāo pā māi himaphān* (this means every type of bird, small and large, that lives in the Himaphan region)."[10] As you can see, the general Pāli term for birds is more concise than the Khün; however, since the text provides a lengthy translation of the term, I do not believe that the Pāli is employed for conciseness, like "*a priori*," but instead to maintain a sense that the Khün is merely a translation of the original Pāli. The composer of the text must have known Pāli well enough to translate basic words and phrases. Furthermore, the Pāli in general adds no additional detail or semantic feature to the narrative as a whole, it seems merely to provide a consistent transition between *phūks* and a consistent reminder that the Khün is a translation of a yet-to-be discovered Pāli original. However, since there has never been any indication in inscriptions, the canon, *Paññāsa-Jātaka* collections or anthologies that an original existed, we cannot and indeed should not assume that this text is a translation of an original Pāli text.

To conclude this section on the particular linguistic features of the SWL, it should be noted quickly that Khün, like Thai, Lao, Khmer, Sinhala and Burmese, contains numerous Pāli derivatives that are so common that the speakers may not be aware that they come from Pāli. Similarly, English speakers are not always aware that many of the words they use come from German, French, Latin, or Sanskrit. These derivatives are found throughout the Wat Hnong Kham recension of the SWL and reflect centuries of contact between the local language and the classical languages of Pāli and Sanskrit. These derivatives should not however be compared with the examples of thread translations seen above, because almost universally the Pāli terms used in thread translations are distinguished by being in the original Pāli versus a derivative form which has undergone local phonetic changes, like Khün "*dit* (direction)" for Pāli "*dis(a)* (direction)," (there are no sibilants in final position in Khün) as well as by being set apart from the other words in a given line by "*an wā* (this means)" after the Pāli word. All these examples of the use of two languages in one text demonstrate a textual example of the interplay between the classical, translocal world which Pāli and Buddhism represented and the local, vernacular world of the Khün. These linguistic features have narrative counterparts as we will see in the next section.

Cultural Values, Religious Beliefs and Religious Practices

In terms of religious beliefs, cultural values and spiritual practices the SWL has many features in common with canonical *Jātakas*. However, by closely examining the differences between canonical *Jātakas* we can be witness to the simultaneous processes of Buddhist acculturation and the construction of a regional cultural independence. The SWL is different from canonical *Jātakas*, especially the *Vessantara-Jātaka*, which is by far the most well-known in Southeast Asia. As we have seen, the SWL is very similar to the canonical type due to its main character being a Bodhisatta and because it involves self-sacrifice, renunciation and the lives of royalty and the gods, as well as some sort of journey. However, the Khün writers inserted many new features into this known form, including:

(1) an emphasis on monogamy;
(2) a greater attention to the value of romantic love;
(3) an acceptance of sibling marriage;
(4) a focus on achieving the three joys;
(5) frequent references to the practice of local and/or brahmanistic magic;
(6) meditative practices which included the *kammaṭṭhana* (specific objects of meditation);
(7) an explicit importance placed on copying, honoring and listening to the text;
(8) and a greater emphasis on the perfection of knowledge and renunciation.

Although there are many other important themes and values expressed in the SWL (like the emphasis placed on the connection between physical beauty, wealth and spiritual power, the importance of giving and the period of asceticism in the forest) these particular eight features are largely local innovations on the canonical *Jātaka* type. By focusing on them, Khün creative strategies for manipulating classical literature for their own purposes will emerge.

Local cultural values

The Khün have a great affection for romantic tales. One of the most famous love stories in Khün is the *Along Chao Sam Lo*. This story relates the story of two rich and beautiful young people who fall in love and conceive an illegitimate child, but they are not permitted to marry by the young man's mother. The young lady, U Piem, and her unborn baby, die from wounds inflicted by the mother. The young man, Sam Lo, commits suicide when he learns of her death.[11] In the *Chao Bun Hlong*, another non-classical Khün *Jātaka*, there are numerous scenes describing great feelings of passion and lust felt by young women towards one of the heroes, Bun Hlong. Besides this overflowing expression of passion, there are also passages describing undying love beween Bun Hlong and the young woman, Bimba.[12] In manuscripts Peltier copied at monasteries in and around Chiang Tung, there are seven stories that could be called romances, which laud the intense love of the main characters. For example, in the *Ratana Saeng Beu* (Peltier's transliteration: *Rttn Sēṅ Bbēe*), non-classical *Jātaka*, the hero gives up the ascetic life, because he longs for his wife and when he could not find her, he sends a parrot to fly all around the world to deliver love letters to her. When he finds her, her father refuses to give her away in marriage, so the hero attacks the father's kingdom with an army and wins the girl. Truly this is more of a romance than a Buddhist morality tale.[13]

The SWL does not completely abandon the promotion of Buddhist sexual morality or promote the attachment which love brings, but it also does not mark romantic love as a hindrance to spiritual advancement. In the SWL, Sujavaṇṇa and Ummādantī are depicted as a couple very much in love.[14] In the fifth *phūk*, Ummādantī is worried that because she is a daughter of a bull, Sujavaṇṇa will be attracted to the firm-breasted, fully human women and reject her because of her dubious ancestry when they return to the city together. She begs his faithfulness. Sujavaṇṇa assures her that he will only love her. He declares: "*thī rak khot sāi jai nang yā dai song sai lāi yūang jai fon fūang glā bai ... phī bao liao chāk nong sak an thāe lāe* (my love untie the knots of your heart, give up this intense doubt and that heart of yours which flitters and flutters to and fro ... your man (literally elder brother) will truly not stray away from you even for one instance)."[15] These heartfelt expressions continue for several lines and Sujavaṇṇa states that Ummādantī is more beautiful than all other women and that he loves her (*hū pen yai kwā nāng thang lāi ... rak nāng no thai nak nā* ... I see you as greater than all other women ... I love you deeply).[16] While the romantic theme and orations of love are subjects of literature in all languages and across all cultures, what is important for our purposes is that this explicit promise of monogamy as well as Ummādantī's request of faithfulness from Sujavaṇṇa is largely unknown in canonical Pāli *Jātakas*. Furthermore, the ardent love a Bodhisatta so eloquently expressed for a female is never expressed in a context where it is not designed to be a lesson against lust and attachment. For example, in the canonical *Paduma Jātaka* the Bodhisatta expresses feelings of love towards his wife by saving her from being eaten by his brothers but does not show any passion or proclaim his love verbally. Moreover, he is punished for his attachment to her because she has an affair with a criminal. The Bodhisatta is taught that attachment is suffering (J.11.321–3). Furthermore, in the *Suruci Jātaka* we find an example of a queen who asked her husband to be monogamous, but when she cannot bear a son for him, he marries 16,000 other women (J.IV.314–25). In the *Asankha Jātaka* it is said that women are a stain to the religious life (J.III.250). In fact, the Pāli word most commonly used for love, *sineha*, is found only in three canonical *Jātakas*. In the *Kaṇha*, love or affection is associated with delusion (*dose vā lobhe snehe va*) (J.IV.11). In the *Guṇa*, it is used in the sense of a lion showing affection to a she-jackal who had saved his life (*sineham karomi*: I show/make affection) (J.II.27). In the *Abhiṇha*, it is used to express the platonic friendship between an elephant and a dog

(J.I.190). The term, *raga*, commonly translated as "passion," is universally an unskillful (*akusala*) quality in a person and is supposed to hamper spiritual advancement. It is usually found in a triad with *dosa* and *moha* (delusion).[17] This is certainly not the case in the SWL. In this tale, Sujavaṇṇa gladly dedicates himself to his princess and promises his faithfulness. This faithfulness is maintained throughout the story. Even after Sujavaṇṇa has sacrificed his eyes and legs and has retreated to the ascetic life in the forest, he still feels attachment for his wife. He worries about her being left alone in the world and takes her with him into the forest to live as a renunciant.[18] They live there until both are freed from mental defilements (*kilesa*) and passed away together and are reborn as husband and wife in heaven. This is truly an undying love!

Even though the canonical *Jātakas* cannot be called romantic tales and they do not promote monogomous relationships, Jaini has pointed out the prevalence of these themes in the *Paññāsa-Jātaka* collections. For example, he lauds Madrune Terral, who published an edition of the Khmer/Thai version of the *Samuddaghosa-Jātaka* from the *Paññāsa-Jātaka*, because her "translation and grammatical notes introduced to scholarship a beautiful love story not found in the Theravāda canon or its commentaries." The *Paññāsa-Jātakas* themselves often relate tales of longing and separation of young lovers. For example, the *Sakhapattarāa-Jātaka* describes how the Buddha courted his wife Yasodharā in past lives and in one scene Yasodharā, born in the past as Ratanavatī, attempts suicide due to the loss of her lover.[19] The *Sudhanukumāra-Jātaka*, Jaini notes, is very similar to the well-known love story of Sudhana and Manoharā, which is performed in plays in Thailand and Burma. Jaini has related its story to a tale in the *Divyāvadāna* and the *Mahāvastu*.[20] The *Lokaneyyapakaraṇam* (LP), a non-canonical *Jātaka* also offers what Jaini calls "a startling defense of the superiority of monogamy over polygamy. LP is the only place in Pāli literature where a Bodhisatta refuses to accept the king's offer of a royal princess for a second wife." He was not familiar with the SWL, so we cannot fault him for not noticing the support of monogamy in Khün Buddhist literature. What is important is that monogamy was a value promoted by some Southeast *Jātakas* and two of these non-canonical *Jātakas* are truly love stories. These elements, since they are largely unknown in canonical *Jātakas*, reflect a local creative insertion.[21]

There is no good ethnographic material available about Khün marriage patterns.[22] In his travel journals, F.J. Harmand did not give any specific information about family and marriage rules among the Khün or surrounding tribes.[23] Francis Gamier did not note a particular value placed on monogamy among the Khün or their neighbors, but he did often comment on the number of Catholic converts in the area in the mid-nineteenth century, which could have had an influence on Khün marriage rules. The little ethnographic material available on Tai-speaking peoples in the region points to some practice of monogamy. For example, the San Chay people in northwestern Vietnam practice strict monogamy.[24] Among the central Lao, monogamy is the rule.[25] The Bo Y and the Tho also practice monogamy.[26] While these customs may be ancient, because of the difficulty in dating the SWL, which I will discuss below, it is impossible to say if the emphasis on monogamy seen in the SWL and in other Southeast Asian non-canonical *Jātakas* was influenced by local customs and morality, local or translocal religious and secular literature or was just a creative insertion by the author or authors of the text. However, it reflects a local innovation contained within a translocal literary structure.

Besides the romantic elements of the SWL and the unusual emphasis on the value of monogamy, another local value is expressed in this story. After our heroine and hero return to Jetuttara and rule as queen and king, they have two children—a girl and a boy. When these children are of age they are married to each other. This particular event is completely arbitrary. It plays no essential part in the plot or progression of the narrative. This is confirmed when the Buddha reveals that the people in the story who lived during one of his former lives would be reborn as well-known figures from the life of Gotama, like Sāriputta, Mahāmāyā and Ānanda. He even includes Sugandha, Ummādantī and Sujavaṇṇa's son as being Gotama's son Rahula in a past life. Sujavaṇṇa's daughter, Saṅkharī, is not mentioned. I believe that this element of the story was added to express a local value in sibling marriage, like that honored by Zoroastrians.[27] The only other suggestion of a non-platonic sibling relationship in the regional literature is from the *Sin Xay*, in which the king, Phaya Kutsalat, expresses his deep love for his sister and gives her half of his kingdom. When she is kidnapped by a giant snake, he pines after her, becomes depressed and abdicates the throne to become a monk, vowing to search for his sister for the rest of his life.[28] Sibling marriage or incest is unknown in canonical *Jātakas* and is twice criticized as sinful in other canonical texts. *Micchādhammamarāga* (wrong and unlawful or unrighteous passion) is used in reference to two family members marrying in the *Dīghanikāya* (D.iii.70).[29]

Religious beliefs

At the end of the SWL (*phūk* seven) the Buddha requests that the monks honor the SWL with gifts (*dai pūjā dūai vatthu gan tāng tāng*), copy (literally 'build') it and listen to it (*dai srāng lae dai fang*), preach it and write it (*dai thet lae dai kien*), study it and memorize it (*dai rien lae taem ān*), to encourage (people to know it) and call attention to it so that people can listen to its truth (*dai chak chern pok tuan thān heu dai fang dham*), etc. (188). If they perform these deeds, each one will go to Nibbāna as well as experience the three joys. These joys (*sukh ying*) are: (1) living as a very wealthy royal person (*mahāseṭṭhī lae gasatarā*) with much rice and other abundant things; (2) being reborn in heaven; and (3) realizing Nibbāna. These three joys are not seen as contradicting each other and the monks who perform the duties listed above with faith (*saddha*) will achieve them all. This *ānisaṃsa* (deed performed in the hope of receiving merit) statement at the end of their narrative with the particular emphasis on the three joys is not found in canonical *Jātakas* but is a common feature in Buddhist literature in Southeast Asia. *Ānisaṃsa* passages are found at the end of dedicatory inscriptions, on the bases of Buddha images, in the colophons of copies of both canonical and extra-canonical texts, and elsewhere. Their inclusion at the end of a *Jātaka* reveals its locative specificity in Southeast Asia, especially with the mention of the three joys which are found at the end of most non-canonical *Jātakas* in the *Paññāsa-Jātaka* collections of Southeast Asia. What is also interesting about this *ānisaṃsa* section of the text is that it is accompanied by an unusually large number of Pāli words and phrases that are translated into Khün. This is probably because requests for merit at the end of texts and on inscriptions were quite formulaic and common in northern Thailand, Laos and eastern Burma. However, a more important point to make for our purposes is that the SWL shows local innovation by conflating the possible worldly material and the soteriological goals of the monk who studies, honors, copies and reads the text into the three joys. At the end of the canonical *Jātaka* the Buddha simply informs the audience how the characters in the story relate to him and people during his present lifetime. Only in the *Paññāsa-Jātaka* collections in Southeast Asia and independent non-classical *Jātakas* like the SWL do we find this emphasis on the three joys and the specific instructions by the Buddha that those who honor the *Jātaka* will obtain the three joys.

Religious practices

There are a number of specific religious practices mentioned throughout the SWL which strike any reader familiar with canonical *Jātakas* as strange. The first practice is that of making *yan*. *Yan* (skt: *yantra*) are mystical diagrams used with *mantras* for casting spells of protection, causing misfortune to befall enemies, or to gain wealth, love or prestige. Their origin is sometimes traced back to the Harappan civilization of the Indus Valley (2400 BCE), but they did not become popular until their use in Tantric rituals in India and Tibet in 700–1200 CE. Today they are commonly used by Brahman priests. They are not mentioned as being employed in the Pāli canon, but they are extremely common in northern Thailand and Laos, where they are made by Buddhist monks and lay religious specialists alike and are found in most homes, businesses and temples or tatooed or worn on shirts by practitioners of this form of magic.[30] They are used in the SWL. In the fourth *phūk* Sujavaṇṇa composes and studies a *yan*, a *man* (skt: *mantra*) and then a specifically Vedic *man* in order to prove to Ummādantī that he is not afraid of her father or her ancestry (*kien man yan lae mantapet*). What is interesting is that Sujavaṇṇa is the future Buddha. In the canon there are innumerable places where the Buddha criticizes the employment of Vedic magic and *mantras*.[31] However, the canonical texts often present ideals that may not reflect the actual practices of Buddhists at any time or in any place. The practice of composing *yan* and *man* should not be seen as separate from "Buddhist" practice, namely, the maintenance of precepts and the striving to perfect *pāramī*. For example,

Sujavaṇṇa is well skilled in their usage. He is able to dispel fear and fly up to Ummādantī in the one-pillared palace owing to the power of his *man* as well as his *pāramī* and the collection of merits he has acquired aimed at true omniscience coupled with his desire to escape the round of rebirths (*vaṭṭasaṃsāra*) and realize *Nibbāna*.[32]

Other Brahmanistic practices that had been adapted and localized in the Khün region are explicitly mentioned in two other passages. Later in the fourth *phūk* King Jambū Ekarāja and Queen Suvaṇṇabhūmā are worried because their son did not return from his hunting excursion. They summoned their *purohit* (skt: *purohita*), a Brahman court priest/ritual specialist, and their *Brahm* (skt: *Brahman*) attendants, who were skilled in the three Vedas (*fūng chop tripet*) to tell them what had happened to their son. The *purohit* and the brahmins were successful in discovering where Sujavaṇṇa was and correctly predicted when he would return. In this section it is unclear how the purohita knew this, but in the first *phūk*, it states that the *purohit* practiced astrology (*hūrū*; Thai: *horāsāt*) to decipher a dream of Suvaṇṇabhūmā and to predict the birth of her son. This may have been the practice of the *purohit* in the fourth *phūk*. These practices localize the SWL, demonstrate the syncretic nature of Khün religion in general. They certainly were not only common among Buddhist and Brahmans, but local religions in the region. Finally, practices such as these are found in other works of Khün literature. For example, the *Kalasa Grüa Dok*, a romance written in Khün, but set in Benares, describes the hero getting tattoos in red ink from his waist to his feet to ward off knives and spears. In the *Chao Bun Hlong*, the mother of two banished sons ties golden threads around their wrists to prevent disease and avoid tiger, snake, scorpion and spirit attack. This is a common practice among the Khün people but is largely unknown in India.[33]

Other practices in the SWL have more in common with canonical *Jātakas* but take on a different role and a greater emphasis. The practice of perfecting *pāramī* is common throughout the Buddhist world, but takes on different forms in different places. In most canonical *Jātakas*, especially the *Vessantara-Jātaka*, the *pāramī* of giving (Pāli: *dāna*) is most important and most commonly practiced by bodhisattas. Furthermore, 27 out of the 50 *Jātakas* in the *Zimme Paññāsa* recension of the *Paññāsa-Jātaka* are primarily about the perfection of giving. The *pāramī* of giving plays a very significant role in the SWL. Sujavaṇṇa gives away his wealth, kingdom, legs and eyes. There is also a heavy emphasis on the *pāramī* of renunciation (Pāli: *nekkhammapāramī*).[34] The text states that Sujavaṇṇa and Ummādantī practice *nekkhammapāramī* in order to remove *kilesa* (defilements) and escape from the cycle of rebirths in *saṃsāra*. According to standard *Abhidhamma* descriptions, removing *kilesas* is the last step before realizing enlightenment. Therefore, the practice of the *nekkhammapāramī* would seem to be logically the last type of practice our heroes should perform. However, this practice is rarely the theme of *Jātakas* and the term *nekkhammapāramī* is never mentioned in the canonical *Jātakas*. The most common *pāramī* in the canonical *Jātakas* is the *dānapāramī* (perfection of giving).

Practices such as *bhāvanā* (meditation) and the development of *metta* (loving-kindness) are frequently mentioned in the SWL. This is not unusual in comparison to classical *Jātakas*; however, the specific emphasis on the practice of the *kammaṭṭhāna* (basis of action; a mode of meditation; analytical meditation) is relatively uncommon in *Jātaka* literature.[35] There are only about 14 out of 547 *Jātakas* which refer to a specific type of *kammaṭṭhāna* and less than half that number refer to *kammaṭṭhāna* in an uncompounded form. For example, in the *Kassapamandiya-Jātaka*, the term *kammaṭṭhāne* is used, but no specific practice is mentioned. Whatever it might be it leads to Arahant-ship (J.III.36). This same ambiguity is found in the *Apaṇṇaka-Jātaka*, *Tittha* and *Mudulakakhaṇa*. In the *Dubbalakaṭṭha* there is a reference to a specific *kammaṭṭhāna* which was, judging from its name, used to gain awareness of death—the *maraṇasatikammaṭṭhana* (J.I.414). These specific types of *kammaṭṭhānas* are enumerated and described by Buddhaghosa. He lists 40 different types of *kammaṭṭhānas* in the *Vissudhimagga* and they are frequently referred to the *Dhammapada*, both are popular texts in Southeast Asia and have numerous regional vernacular commentaries.[36] The composer(s) of the SWL may have been familiar with the *kammaṭṭhāna* concept from these works, but why the writer felt the need to emphasize them as specific practices of Sujavaṇṇa and Ummādantī on several occasions is unknown.[37] We may speculate that since the *kammaṭṭhānas* were supposed to be practiced only under the instruction of a trained meditation teacher, that depicting Sujavaṇṇa as practicing them without any formal instruction was designed to demonstrate his imminent Buddhahood (since the Buddha is distinguished from an *arahat* because he achieved enlightenment on his own without teaching from another). This particular practice emphasized in the SWL warrants a study of its own and cannot possibly be fully explained here; however, what is important to note is that they cast light on some regional religious practices that are often not present or not emphasized in Pāli *Jātakas*.

Creative Engagement: Old Forms in Service of New Concerns

Vernacularization and localization

As should now be evident, the SWL contains many features not commonly found in canonical *Jātakas*. The first reason for these novelties might be simply the creativity of Khün writers and storytellers. Jaini notes that Buddhist authors in Southeast Asia had a "penchant . . . to embellish old canonical tales with new elements drawn from the indigenous cultures of their own native regions."[38] These writers clearly took common themes from traditional Khün, northern Thai and Lao literature and incorporated them into the traditional form of the canonical Pāli *Jātaka*. They drew from local beliefs, practices and values.

Why did the writer(s) of the SWL choose the structure of a classical form of religious literature as a vehicle to carry their own literature? One explanation could be that the writer(s) wanted to give their new story a sense of temporal legitimacy. Canonical *Jātakas* were written in Pāli and explicitly claimed to be the word of the historical Buddha, Gotama (*Buddhavacana*), spoken over 2,400 years ago. Philologically, the SWL contains numerous Pāli passages which are translated into Khün or individual words or phrases which are either translated or must have been familiar enough to the reader to be left untranslated (thread translations). Since, there is no manuscript or any historical suggestion that there was ever an original Pāli version of the SWL, we cannot assume that the SWL is a translation of an Pāli *Jātaka* that has been lost, especially since there are numerous non-canonical *Jātakas* in Southeast Asia. Moreover, the few Pāli passages that are translated are mere *phūk* introductions or *mantras* that if strung together would not offer a clear understanding of the plot or any detail of the story. Even if there was an original Pāli version of the SWL, the numerous unique elements of the story demonstrates a plethora of local innovations. Still, by employing Pāli passages, words and phrases, throughout the text a sense of classical temporal authenticity is created and works to raise local innovations to the level of *Buddhavacana*.

This use of Pāli and Khün also reflects what Pollock called, "vernacularization;" namely, it took a cosmopolitan text-type, the Pāli *Jātaka*, and used the literary structure of that text-type for its own purposes. The SWL was composed in a vernacular language in such a way to emphasize its connection to some Pāli original. However, it "vernacularizes," or perhaps regionalizes the Pāli source text or at least the genre of texts. It mimics the genre of the Pāli *Jātaka* and therefore "domesticates" it. The composers of the SWL, as Pollock writes discussing South Indian vernacular poets, "define themselves in significant if variable ways on the basis of literature they share, and they create new literatures in service of new definitions."[39] Jaini also notes that the apocryphal *Jātakas* collections use the canonical form to comment on contemporary concerns. For example, the *Mahāumagga-Jātaka* of the *Lokeyyapakaraṇa Jātaka* collection

> provides a framework within which our author builds a tension between a Brahmin court-chaplain (*purohita*) who is identified as an adherent of the Śiva-sāsanā (Śaivism) and the Bodhisatta Dhanañjaya, the son of a merchant, who although very young, stands up for the Buddha-sāsanā. One major purpose of the LP [*Lokeyyapakaraṇa*] would thus appear to show the conflict between the eventual triumph of Buddhism over the Śaivism of the Śaivite court brahmans of Siam and Burma that took place during the fourteenth century [sic].[40]

Furthermore, there was a religious motivation for this localization. Jaini writes: "Buddhist monks took such canonical *Jātakas* as models for their repetitive literary endeavours, much in the same way that they reduplicated Buddha-images or stūpas *ad infinitum* as an expression of their deep faith."[41] These are ongoing concerns, whether polemic or spiritual, which the canonical texts confront.

The creation of a regional identity

By working within a canonical structure, the SWL is able to carve out a place for its local creative innovations and communicate them in a form that would be familiar to other Theravadin Buddhists in the region. The one institutional and intellectual entity that most of mainland Southeast Asia, excluding Vietnam, had in common was Theravada Buddhism, known in Pāli as the *sāsanā*. Looking at Sri Lankan historical chronicles, like the *Mahāvaṃsa* and the *Dipavaṃsa*, Gananath Obeyesekere shows that Sinhalese speakers largely identified with the "*sāsanā*." Obeyesekere writes that:

> It is *sāsanā* that takes place. In the doctrinal tradition *sāsanā* refers to the universal Buddhist community or church that transcends ethnic and other boundaries. This meaning coexists with another meaning that is found in post-canonical historical texts: *sāsanā* is the Buddhist 'church' that is particularized by the physical bonds of the land consecrated by the Buddha.[42]

The *sāsanā* is a conceived reality by which intellectuals across Southeast Asia understood themselves as being a part. If we understand this, we can examine regional Buddhist literature as forming a connection with the *sāsanā* that in turn defined themselves as distinct regional expressions of that *sāsanā* vis-à-vis other regional dynastic polities. The composer(s) of the SWL used the structure of classical *Jātakas* and wrote in passages, words and phrases of a cosmopolitan language which linked the Khün temporally and religiously to Sri Lanka and India (i.e., to the Buddha) and used the translocal prestige of the Theravada. This could have been designed to authenticate the Khün region politically and religiously vis-à-vis the other Buddhist peoples around it or simply could be a sign that Khün writers wanted to participate in a larger intellectual and religious world. The *sāsanā* was a conscious concept, continually reasserted in texts, that had regional cohesive force.[43] It was a pre-modern conceptual category, like the Catholic conception of "the church," with which local agents could and certainly did identify with. The composer(s) of the SWL, either consciously or unconsciously, used a form of literature with well-known themes and characters to connect themselves to the *sāsanā* and define itself as a legitimate Buddhist polity (or at least cultural polity). This effort to distinguish itself as an innovative contributor to the Buddha *sāsanā*, is also seen in Khün temple layout and architecture. Temples in Chiang Tung possess the same elements as Southeast Asian temples; namely, a *vihāra*, *uposatha* hall, a *cetiya*, a *sāla*, etc., but the style of the temple buildings are unique when compared to other regional polities in Southeast Asia as well as to Sri Lankan and Indian Buddhist temples.[44] We have already noted the regionality of the Khün script and vocabulary and when seen in its total historico-cultural context, efforts by Khün artisans and writers to both participate in the translocal Buddhist culture and establish their independent contribution become apparent.

The *Chiang Tung State Chronicle* also reflects an effort to create a regional identity. It provides a long history of its city, beginning with the rise of Buddhism in India to the advent of Buddhism in Chiang Tung and giving detailed information about the activities of its kings and temple abbots in service of the Buddha *sāsanā*. It is an attempt to establish a clear lineage from the Buddha to Chiang Tung Buddhist practice and institutions. This chronicle, like the *Jinakālamālī* and *Tamnān Mūlasāsanā* of Chiang Mai and many other regional chronicles, organizes the history of Chiang Tung into linear chronology that is methodical and detailed in order to convey, without a doubt, a clear, legitimate progression of Buddhism from its founding to its royal patronage in Lān Nā.[45] I believe that the SWL, like the *Chiang Tung State Chronicle*, is a further attempt to connect the Khün to the larger *sāsanā* and claim a place in its intellectual and literary history. The Chronicle also creates a sense of spatial authenticity for Chiang Tung as a place where the Buddha predicted his religion would flourish. The chronicler(s) relate a story of how the historical Buddha visited Chiang Tung and deposited eight of his hairs there. One passage reads:

> Lord Buddha, the Omniscient, with a retinue of forty-nine arahant disciples, came to the Subhāsudebba Hill during his preaching tours and left behind eight hairs of his head. He then came to Coṃḍoy and accepted honey from Gāng Āy-ān, washed the lid of his alms bowl at Tunga Lake ... and made the prophecy, saying, 'In the future this valley will be named Mönglang, the valley stream will be named namphii, and the place where I am sitting now will be named Coṃḍoy.' Having made the prophecy, the Lord came to the hill in the middle of the lake. Ananda Thera took the Lord's iron staff and planted it in the ground and took the alms bowl to wash it in the lake at the foot of the hill ... [and the Buddha declared] 'Six hundred and twenty-nine years after the Nibbāna of the Tathāgata king will bring the Sāsanā and establish it in this state without a doubt.'[46]

This short passage, which is similar to visits and predictions made by the Buddha to places in Southeast Asia reported in other regional chronicles of Chiang Mai, Lān Xāng and other places, demonstrates how important it was to the chronicler(s) to state that the Buddha not only was temporally but also spatially connected to Chiang Tung. The Buddha left both a relic of his body (i.e., eight hairs), *sarīrikacetiya* and relics of use (i.e., the bowl and staff), *paribhogikacetiya*. This gave the land itself a sort of high Buddhist property value.

What this chronicle does explicitly in terms of creating temporal and spatial authenticity for Buddhism in Chiang Tung, I believe the SWL does implicitly. Although this can only be a speculative endeavour at this point without more historical evidence, the SWL does demonstrate that the only aspect of culture, practice and belief that was common to all groups of characters in the story (bulls, the poor, merchants, women, men, people from Rājagaha, people from Jettuttara, royalty, brahmans, etc.) was their general recognition of the qualities of a bodhisatta in Sujavaṇṇa and the belief in power of his perfections. Moreover, the Buddha, by associating different characters like Sāriputta with the King of the Bulls, Ānanda with the golden deer, Mahāmāyā with Suvaṇṇabhūmā, etc. demonstrates their inherent connection under the power of his teaching and to the story of his life. The Buddhist values depicted in this story unify these individual groups.[47]

The oldest manuscript of the SWL dates from 1843. Some versions of the story are undoubtedly much older, perhaps dating from the heyday of Khün and northern Thai literature in the early sixteenth century before the Burmese invasion. Dating is notoriously difficult with these texts which may explain why scholars who have studied Khün literature have refrained from speculating on the original dates of any individual work.[48]

Almost all of the major works of Khün literature that are known to us have manuscripts which have been copied and re-copied several times in the last 30 years. This practice suggests, due to the climate and the shifting political fortunes of the Chiang Tung region, that the preservation of literature through copying is deemed as the essential practice of monks or at least as a proper gift for monks (since almost every manuscript has been found in a monastery) and could have been going on for centuries. A date as early as the sixteenth century, if not earlier, may also be probable in the light of the similarity of many Khün tales to older literature from Laos and Burma from that time. However, there is no way at the present time to confirm this.

This concern with dating the SWL is of secondary concern, though, to the purposes of this study. I mention it now to begin a discussion regarding the commentaries the SWL could have been making on local historical events. For example, the story, although similar to canonical *Jātakas* and to other works of Khün and Lao literature, has many elements that could suggest that its composer(s) had other aims besides presenting a didactic and moralizing tale in the tradition of Buddhist birth stories. The concern with bringing the world of the bulls together with the kingdom of Jambū Ekarāja might be a subtle reference to peace treaties and envoys being sent to kingdoms in neighboring Chiang Tung. The prince royal, Sujavaṇṇa, travels to major urban sites, Jettuttara and Rājagaha, to visit his parents and new in-laws and crowds come out to greet and approve of his new bride. The women from Sujavaṇṇa's birthplace repent their former ridicule of Ummādantī who was half-bull.

Could this royal procession and conciliation between two adversaries be based on an actual historical tribal alliance or perhaps be an attempt to encourage tribal peace in an area that has been traditionally occupied by many different ethnic groups and been fought over by competing dynastic polities?[49] This is a difficult period for historians to understand, due to conflicting historical sources. Barbara Andaya notes that Burmese chroniclers mentioned Chiang Tung, the city where the SWL was probably written, as a tributary state, while the *Pāḍaeng Chronicle* refers to Chiang Tung as an independent city which ruled over surrounding tribes and the ruler of Chiang Tung "was possessed of great glory and power without peer, and there was no one, either within or without the state, to rebel against his authority, nor did he submit to the ruler of Ava (Burma)."

This emphasis on Chiang Tung's power and the fact that there were "no rebellions," considering conflicting sources, may suggest that rebellions were indeed a problem. Historians do know that the area was fought over for more than 300 years. The *Chiang Tung State Chronicle* tells of wars that were continually fought between Laos (Lān Xāng), China, Chiang Mai, Burma and the Khün.[50] Not only were the kingdoms of Lān Xāng, Chiang Mai and Ava competing for power in this region, but there were many Shan groups, like the Mau Shan, Gwe Shans and other ethnic tribes like the Lü, Dai Doi and the Wa who consistently raised armies, demanded tribute from each other and disrupted trade routes.[51] The Burmese invaded the region ten times from 1613 to 1739. Furthermore, the Burmese often attempted to patronize local monasteries to encourage the monks to gather support for the Burmese among the populace.[52] Could the Burmese have been encouraging the writing of stories that emphasized peace between different groups of peoples?[53] The practice of marrying sons of one royal family to daughters of another royal family is a common way in Southeast Asia (not to mention of course medieval Europe, Africa and South Asia) for one family to acquire more land and power or to make alliances with other families. Chiang Tung is located on the edge of Burma, northern Thailand, northern Laos and southern China. This position is not only precarious in the present but has been an area continually conquered and re-conquered by competing forces. Its present geo-political location reflects its historic location between the competing empires of Burma, the Shan, Chiang Mai, Yunnan and Lān Xāng. This area has been historically unstable because of the practice of local rulers to make alliances with whichever neighboring kingdom was the most powerful at the time and playing one faction against the other. Moreover, this area is home to several different hill tribe peoples, like the Lü, Yao, Shui, Li, Mulao and many others. These tribes speak different dialects, have different styles of dress, religious customs and occupations. The SWL's focus on the unification of two different peoples could have been a commentary on the frequent interaction the Khün must have had with their neighbours. I am not suggesting that these motives were the only ones for the composition of the SWL or other Khün stories, but the pre-occupation with the unification of or relations with two or more kingdoms or peoples was undoubtedly influenced by socio-historic events that were taking place during the composers' lives.

Pierre Bourdieu, studying regional myth and ritual, sees these cultural expressions as a strategy for "transgressing and reshuffling cultural categories in order to meet the needs of real situations."[54] In his study of the manipulation of cultural symbols by ethnic peoples to generate authenticity for their existence as a regional political entity, Bourdieu notes that through political speeches, literature and ritual, certain politically marginalized peoples attempt to draw boundaries around themselves to emphasize their very existence as a unique and defineable people. "Regionalist discourse," he writes, "is a performative discourse which aims to impose as legitimate a new definition of the frontiers and to get people to know and recognize the region that is thus delimited in opposition to the dominant definition . . . the effectiveness of the performative discourse which claims to bring about what it asserts in the very act of asserting it...."[55] Could the use of cosmopolitan, classical and translocal genre of literature that has been localized, altered and re-configured work to help define the Khün as an independent people with their own contribution to Buddhist literature? Was this story an assertion of an autonomous culture? Were the canonical *Jātaka* or even other regional non-canonical *Jātakas* written by the Lao, Burmese, Vietnamese, Cambodian or Siamese considered the "dominant definition" against which the Khün are defining themselves? This claim to a distinct place within the Buddhist world of Southeast Asia could both work to connect the Khün culturally with its neighbors as well as separate themselves as unique. Is then, the writing of the SWL an act in service of creating the Khün culture, instead just merely a reflection of it? In the war-torn region of Chiang Tung, was the creation of local literature an act of claiming independence and a striving for cultural survival?

The practice of literature

The dynamic interplay between the local and translocal has been the subject of numerous anthropological studies in the past 30 years. Many anthropologists have examined how religious ritual and myth are used locally to deal with the anxiety produced when confronting the translocal. Insights into changes in ritual and myth may generate insight into how translocal literature, like canonical *Jātakas*, can be localized and re-told in reaction to local historical events. The practice theory was developed by Marshall Sahlins's *Culture and Practice Reason* in 1976 and Pierre Bourdieu's *Outline of a Theory of Practice* in 1977. Sahlins argues against structuralist understandings of ritual and myth because they tend to see their object of study as static. For example, Sahlins points out that Radcliffe-Brown saw structures in ritual and myth as stable and prescriptive, while they should be seen as relationships continually made and re-made out of practice.[56] Sahlins wanted to see how change over time and continuity worked together in ritual. He demonstrated in a much-debated study of Hawaiian myth and ritual that Hawaiians used traditional systems of symbols and of social organization to understand and deal with historical events like the arrival of Captain Cook on the Hawaiian Islands in 1778.[57] This major historical event or series of events changed the ritual involving the god Lono. Cook was incorporated into the ritual and sacrificially killed. This allowed the Hawaiians to assess and negotiate the new events through established patterns. Sahlins writes that the new "event becomes ... interpreted ... the event is a relation between a happening and a structure (or structures): an encompassment of the phenomenon-in-itself as a meaningful value, from which it follows its specific historical efficacy."[58] The Hawaiians used their own "frames of interpretation" to articulate their feelings within existing ideological forms and to make sense of new events and ideas. Sahlins sees this reaction as a form of resistence.

Jean Comaroff takes cues from Sahlins to understand how ritual incorporates new religious ideas and practices when two religious systems come into contact. Studying the Tshidi of South Africa, she contends that Zionist practices of the Tshidi show a creative re-conceptualizing of Christian and traditional Tshidi religious practices. This re-conceptualizing reflects an attempt to use traditional symbols to maintain control of traditional religious ideas in the face of new religious ideas being brought in by foreign colonists.

This use of practice theory by anthropologists studying Thai culture is becoming popular for those scholars working in Thailand. For example, the most recent issue of *Tai Culture* features two articles by Yoko Hayami and Kiyoshi Hasegawa that study the engagement of the Lü and the Karen people with the dominant cultures of China and Thailand respectively. Hayami argues that the Karen adopt the dominant religious practices of their rulers while holding onto their religious beliefs. She sees the Karen as localizing the dominant power's religious forms in ways that their traditional beliefs have a place within the new religious practices. Hasegawa studied the Lü, who have been Theravada Buddhists for centuries, but continue to practice spirit cults that were the main religious forms before the advent of Theravada Buddhism in the region. Theravada Buddhist practices have been modified so as not to conflict with local belief; furthermore, the Chinese culture of the ruling elite in the Lü territory in Yunnan province has also been subject to a process of negotiation, where Lü beliefs and practices are able to survive.[59]

All of these particular perspectives on the practice theory have one thing in common; namely, how traditional rituals and myths are used as tools, either explicitly or implicitly, to understand and culturally incorporate contemporary events. The insights gained from this theory on ritual help us see how the SWL shows the practice theory at work in literature. Still, we cannot simply transfer the practice theory as formulated by Comaroff and Sahlins onto the SWL, but the SWL instead shows us how the practice theory can be expanded to talk about literature. Moreover, I do not see the SWL as a form of resistance to a foreign culture. Indeed, by the time the SWL was composed, the Khün had centuries of familiarity and belief in Theravada Buddhism. Instead the SWL may be seen as an articulation of a particular understanding of the Theravada in an attempt to make sense of a world in which the religion of the Buddha constituted the overarching and dominant system of belief and practice. The Khün people used a foreign, translocal literary practice and plot structure to express their local practices, beliefs, values, social and historical concerns and vernacular language. This text is a negotiation in the form of a narrative. Whereas Captain Cook was incorporated into traditional Hawaiian ritual structure, the SWL incorporates local religious, cultural and linguistic elements into a non-native literary structure. The complex narrative structure, compelling chain of events and translocal ideological commerce proved to be an excellent vehicle to express local historical events, political and social concerns and religious values. Further research along these lines might lead us far in determining the different modes of interaction between classical, translocal literature and local, vernacular literature among the various peoples of Southeast Asia. Hopefully, with these theoretical tools, we can see the evolution of Pāli and vernacular local Buddhist literature as processual and dynamic reflecting strong ties to the past and engagement with the present.

Conclusion: Where Do We Go from Here?

This study of the *Sujavaṇṇa Wua Luang* has elucidated the ways in which classical Buddhist narratives found in the canon and local Buddhist-influenced literature in Southeast Asia interact with each other. What I have attempted to show is that Khün *Jātakas* cannot be seen as merely bad translations, evidence of lost classical *Jātakas* or word commentaries on classical Pāli canonical texts. The new elements in texts like the SWL reflect local innovations and creative engagement with canonical stories. Clearly, the structure, sequencing, themes and lessons of the SWL are very similar to the canonical *Jātaka* form. Still, numerous novel features brought out in this study reflect the Khün composer(s)' explicit efforts to incorporate local elements into the classical form in order to emphasize local practices, values and beliefs. These new elements might be: (1) an effort to communicate Buddhist lessons in a way that would be more conducive for a local audience to understand; (2) conscious attempts to raise themes and motifs of local literature to the level of canonical Buddhist literature; (3) subtle comments of socio-historic events that were shaping the lives of the composers and the audience; (4) efforts to create a sense of temporal authenticity for the text by linking it to classical literature and the words of the Buddha or; (5) attempts by the composers to emphasize their place and unique contribution to the Buddhist *sāsanā*, which was the one over-arching unifying agent of the multiple cultures of Southeast Asia. Certainly these motivations for employing a classical form of literature to express local ideas, make sense of local events or legitimize local literature are not mutually exclusive and could all have been factors in the creation of stories like the SWL. What is important to note is that the Khün writers actively appropriated a classical literary structure and used it as a vehicle to carry their own religious beliefs and cultural practices. Like a banner flying high above a citadel, the SWL used a familiar method of communication to assert its cultural independence and individuality.

I believe that this method of examining texts like the SWL could be used in looking at other non-canonical *Jātakas* in northern Thailand and Laos. Texts like the SWL are found in other scripts and in temple libraries in neighboring cities and towns, which attests to their literary popularity as well as their effectiveness as religious pedagogical tools. Therefore, before individual texts can be seen as reflecting a specific people's cultural practices or religious teachings, one must determine their origin (as much as that is possible). This will hopefully lead to an accurate determination of the language, socio-historical context and location in which they were originally composed. Then one can examine the text as a creative endeavor to promote local doctrinal and ethical teachings as well as cultural customs versus a passive use of literary genres written for the sake of prestige, profit or pulp entertainment. Furthermore, by examining versions of a text like the SWL written in languages like Yuan and Lao with an eye to their differences, the same process of appropriating well-known texts and genres for the purpose of asserting local creativity or remarking on local concerns may be observed.

Where do these speculations about and insights into the SWL lead us in future research? First, the SWL calls into question the notion of a closed Buddhist canon in Southeast Asia. As mentioned in the introduction, the SWL is one of perhaps hundreds of non-canonical *Jātakas* that are attested in various places and in various languages in Southeast Asia. Like the well-known *Paññāsa-Jātaka* collections of Burma, Laos, Thailand and Cambodia, which contain dozens of *Jātakas* not found in the Pāli canon, the SWL clearly adapts the structure of the canonical *Jātaka* but adds new elements. However, the prevalence of these non-classical texts and the fact that their manuscripts are often found bound with canonical *Jātakas* suggests that these non-classical *Jātakas* might have been considered canonical or at least reflect an effort to expand the number of texts usually thought of canonical. This might indicate that the notion of the closed canon commonly held today was only loosely interpreted at individual monasteries which copied, created and kept these collections of canonical and non-canonical *Jātakas*. We must expand our notion of the canon to understand the relation between local Pāli and vernacular Buddhist literature in Southeast Asia. This study of the SWL hopes to show the importance of comparing local Pāli and vernacular literature in the study of Buddhism in Southeast Asia even if we blur the lines between concepts of canonical and non-canonical.[60]

Second, this study suggests one more way to re-interpret the notion of the Indianization of Southeast Asia promoted by the pioneering scholars George Cœdès, Paul Mus, and D.G.E. Hall. They emphasized different ways in which Southeast Asian literature, art, religious belief and ritual could be traced back to Indian culture. While these individual studies taught later scholars much about the importance of seeing South Asian antecedents to Southeast Asian culture, studying Pāli and Sanskrit and locating points of contact between the two sets of peoples, they tended to depict Southeast Asian peoples as passive receptors of Indian cultures with very little creative innovation of their own.

The SWL shows us the richness and diversity of vernacular Buddhist literature in Southeast Asia and the importance of not only studying it diachronically in relation to its possible classical antecedents, but also synchronically in relation to other similar types of local literature among the various linguistically, ethnically and culturally related peoples of mainland Southeast Asia. A longer version of this paper compared the SWL, not only to classical *Jātakas*, but also to Lao, Khün, Burmese and Thai narratives. I hope to include these findings in a later publication. I believe that this comparison is essential in order to further understand the origins, evolution, motifs, linguistics and lessons of Southeast Asian Buddhist literature, because it allows us to see individual works in their total context both socially and historically. This diachronic and synchronic thick description of religious and secular literature in the different culturally, historically and linguistically distinct regions of Southeast Asia will allow us to see how doctrines, practices, literary styles, lexical items, cultural values and artistic expression have constantly changed and adapted over the centuries in these regions in response to foreign influences. The nature of the geography, historical position, languages, literatures and cultures of the peoples of Southeast Asia demands an understanding of the ways these cultures have creatively engaged with each other and with influences from the peoples of China, India and Europe. The SWL, as I hope to have shown, is an excellent example to justify this methodology. Furthermore, I hope that now the SWL can be seen as both a representative example of local Khün literature and a precious and unique contribution to worldwide Buddhist literature.

Notes

1 These collections of 50 *Jātakas* are different in three recensions (Cambodian, Thai and Lao) and only 15 *Jātakas* are common to all. There is also a collection of ten *Jātakas* found in Laos. See Sachchidanand Sahai, "The Rama *Jātaka* in Laos: A Study in the Phra Lak," *Phra Lam* I (1996): 9 (Delhi: B.R. Pub.). Probably the best overall study on the *Paññāsa-Jātaka* is in Thai and written by Niyada Lausunthorn. She gives a detailed history and analysis of the various recensions of the *Paññāsa-Jātaka* in Southeast Asia and attempts to connect them to canonical *Jātakas* and the *Jātaka-aṭṭhakathā* in Pali as well as Sanskrit birth stories. While she is rarely expansive in her discussion of these similarities and the obvious Indian antecedents to certain individual *Jātakas* in the collections of 50, she does provide the reader with a detailed philological and comparative evidence. In the second part of her book she demonstrates that Thai poetical literature has been inspired and influenced by the *Paññāsa-Jātaka* collections. This is an excellent source for anyone interested in the study of Thai literature. The weakness of Niyada's work is that she does not highlight (except for pp. 111–19) *Jātakas* that demonstrate Southeast Asian creativity. She mentions individual *Jātakas* that were drawn from local historical chronicles and folktales but does not speculate on the nature and reasons for the Southeast Asian creativity, nor does she consider in depth the effects local poetical literature may have had on the *Jātakas*. See Niyada Lausunthorn, *Paññāsa-Jātaka: Prawat lae kwām samkhan thī mī to wanakam roi krong khong thai* (Bangkok: Mae Kamphaeng Pub., 1997). For more information on the *Paññāsa-Jātaka* collections in general, see Padmanabh Jaini, "The Apocryphal Jātakas of Southeast Asian Buddhism," *Indian Journal of Buddhist Studies* 1, 1 (1989): 22–37. Jaini's research has uncovered that often times the titles of the various stories were common in the different collections, but the contents were quite different. See also Sap Phrakopsuk, *Vanakhadijathok* (Bangkok: Wat Porohit, 1984): introduction; and the study by Prince Savang Phouvong, et al., sous la direction d' Henri Deydier, *Un Fragment inconnu du Paññāsajātaka laotien*, ed. Jacqueline Filliozat and Anatole Peltier (Chiang Mai-Paris-Vientiane: École Française d'Extrême-orient, 1995–97), pp. 3–4. This source gives specific information on the Lao manuscripts of the *Paññāsa-Jātaka*, as well as a brief introduction to the different Indochinese collections in general. The researchers found over 2,000 manuscripts of these collections, demonstrating their popularity. The popularity of *Jātakas* is also proven by the thousands of representations of different *Jātaka* stories, especially the Vessantara-Jātaka, on temple murals, bas-reliefs and even in modern children's stories. For examples of these depictions of *Jātaka* stories, see McGill, Forest, "Painting the 'Great Life'," in *Sacred Biography: Buddhist Traditions of Southeast Asia* (Honolulu: University of Hawai'i Press, 1997), pp. 195–217; Arunsak Kingmanee, "Suvanna-Jātaka on the Bai Serna

of Wat Nonsila-atwararam," *Muang Boran* 22, 2 (1996): 138–61. There are also dozens of editions of individual *Jātakas* like the Vessantara, Mahosadha and Mahājanaka, which give abridged vernacular versions of the Pali original including pictures depicting dramatic scenes. There are also comic book versions of these *Jātakas*. For a good example of one of these popular, abridged editions see the Lao: *Prawetsanthonhom* (Vientiane: Sun gan kon kwa, 1993), pp. 1–67; English readers should see Elizabeth Wray, Clare Rosenfield, and Dorothy Baily's *Ten Lives of the Buddha: Siamese Temple Painting and Jātaka Tales* (New York: Weatherhill, 1972). This book shows how ten popular *Jātakas* are depicted on murals. Short summaries of the stories are given to accompany the murals.

2 Anatole-Roger Peltier (ed.), *Sujavaṇṇa Wua Luang* (Chiang Tung: Publié á l'occasion de l'offrande du Cullakaṭhina Monastere du Wat Tha Kradas, 1993), p. 174.

3 One of the most notable characteristics of epigraphy in Southeast Asia is the unusually large number of scripts employed to write both classical and vernacular languages [for a general introduction to epigraphy in Thailand and Laos, see George Cœdès, *Prachum Charuksayam: Phak Thi Nung, Charuk Sukhothai* (Bangkok: Bangkok Times Press, 1924), pp. 13–23. This edition also includes a French translation by Cœdès. French readers see pp. 1–5 of the French section. See also his "On Some Siamese Inscriptions," *Journal of the Asiatic Society of Bengal* 34 (1865): 27–38; Natwipha Chalitanon's *Prawatisat Niphon Thai* (Bangkok: Thammasat University Press, 1984), pp. 29–82; and Lefevre's "Etude," *BEFEO*, no. 50.2 (1962): 395–405]. Readers of Thai should consult the introduction to each chapter of Katannyu Chuchun's *Aksonboran Thi Chai Banthuk Wannakam Thai* [Bangkok: Khanakammkan Wichai Haeng Chat (National Research Council), 1987] for a good summary of the history of Thai scripts.

4 See Peltier, *Sujavaṇṇa Wua Luang*, p. 242. Note: all translations of both Pāli and Khün are by Justin McDaniel, unless otherwise noted.

5 Peltier also found a version of the story in Lao in Vientiane and at the Chiang Mai University Social Research Institute manuscript collection in Chiang Mai, northern Thailand. There are also incomplete Lü versions. Ibid.

6 Ibid., p. 66.

7 See K.R. Norman, "Pali Literature," *A History of Indian Literature*, vol. 7, pt. 2, ed. Jan Gonda (Wiesbaden: Otto Harrassowitz, 1983), pp. 140–4 for notes on the particularities of northern Thai Pāli; namely: "unhistorical gemination of consonants and the converse, unusual retroflexion of dentals, and unusual spellings" p. 144. Charles Hallisey, in a personal communication, notes the common confusion of number and gender in Southeast Asian Pāli. See also Padmanabh Jaini (ed.), *Paññāsa-Jātaka* or *Zimme Paññāsa*, Vol. II (London: Pali Text Society, 1983), p. xlii. Jaini provides a word list of particular anomalies in the spelling of many Pali words in the *Paññāsa-Jātaka*. Still, these common idiosyncrasies of Southeast Asian Pāli cannot account for all the anomalies of the Pāli in the SWL. Saddhatissa has a different opinion and calls the non-standardized Pāli of Laos, "poor Pali." He notes that in many non-classical texts in Laos there is the use of Pāli words and phrases which reflect a poor knowledge of grammar. See his "Pāli Literature from Laos," in *Studies in Pāli and Buddhism*, ed A.K. Narain and L. Zwilling (Delhi: B.R. Pub., 1979), pp. 330–2.

8 Peltier, *Sujavaṇṇa*, p. 99.

9 I thank Prapod Assavavirulkaharn for an explanation of the practice of thread translations.

10 Peltier, *Sujavaṇṇa*, p. 137.

11 See Anatole-Roger Peltier (ed.), *Along Chao Sam Lo* (Chiang Mai-Paris: École Française d'Extrême-Orient, 1988).

12 See Anatole-Roger Peltier (ed.), *Chao Bun Hlong* (Chiang Mai-Paris: École Française d'Extrême-Orient, 1992).

13 See Peltier, *La Litterature Tai Khoeun*, pp. 227–8.

14 See Peltier, *Kalasa Grua Dok*, introduction. He notes that romance is one of the most dominant subjects of all Khün literature.

[15] Peltier, *Sujavaṇṇa*, p. 126.

[16] Ibid., p. 128.

[17] See J.I.61 as an example.

[18] Peltier, *Sujavaṇṇa*, ch. 7.

[19] Jaini, *Paññāsa-Jātaka*, Vol. I, pp. 100–28.

[20] Ibid., Vol. II, p. xviii and Vol. I, pp. 129–59.

[21] Jaini also points out another story in the *Lokaneyyapakaraṇam* in which the author states that one of the main characters should not be faulted for being sexually promiscuous. See Jaini, "The Apocryphal Jatakas," pp. 32–3.

[22] We cannot say that monogamy was a value of the Khün people in general. In fact there are numerous narratives in Khün which mention men having two or more wives and they are not criticized for this practice. See manuscripts 16, 135, 188, and 202 of Peltier, *La Litterature Tai Khoeun*.

[23] See F.J. Harmand, *Laos and the Hilltribes of Indochina* (Bangkok: White Lotus, 1997).

[24] Dang Nghiem Van, Chu Thai Son, and Luu Hung, *Ethnic Minorities in Vietnam* (Hanoi: The Gioi Pub., 1993), p. 126.

[25] Ibid., p. 134.

[26] Ibid., pp. 111 and 140.

[27] There are other Khün stories that speak of family customs not found in most of South Asia. For example, in the *Kalasa Grüa Dok*, a Khün romance, there is mention made of divorce as if it was a common practice. Divorce is largely unknown in Indian literature. Furthermore, practices like smoking opium, eating magic tubers for super-human strength, performing the *yāt nām* ceremony, summoning soothsayers who can bring people back to life and shape-shifting magic through the power of silk-thread are present in Khün stories. See Anatole-Roger Peltier, trans., *Kalasa Grüa Dok* (Chiang Mai: Chiang Mai University Social Research Institute, 1989).

[28] See Thao Nhouy Abahy, *Sin Xai*, p. 361.

[29] This term, although used for incest, is also used for any unrighteous passion in the *Dhammasaṅgaṇi* (189, 201, 214).

[30] For an excellent study of the history of *Yan* and their use in modern northern Thailand, see Daniel Levy's "Yan in Northern Thailand," a thesis completed in partial requirement for a Bachelor of the Arts and Sciences, Harvard University, 2000. See also Madhu Khanna, *Yantra: The Tantric Symbol of Cosmic Unity* (London: Thames and Hudson, 1994) and Insom Chaichomphu, *Yan Lae Katha Khong Thi Muang Nua* (n.d., n.p.). This last source gives detailed information on the particular symbols and *mantras* used with particular *yantras*.

[31] See Levy, "Yan in Northern Thailand," pp. 75–8. Levy notes that there has been a continual tension throughout the history of Buddhism over whether magical practices involving *mantras* should be permitted or forbidden by Buddhists. There are several textual examples which confirm Levy's point. For example, a passage from the *Brahmajāla*, the first sutta of the *Dīghanikāya*, the Buddha mentions fire ritual (*aggi-homaṃ*) and offering oblations from a spoon (*dabbi-homaṃ*) within a list of "low arts" such as palmistry, divination, astrology, drawing blood from the right knee as a sacrifice to the gods (*lohita-homaṃ*), looking at the limbs and saying a *mantra* to predict whether a person will have a good birth (*aṅga-homaṃ*), poison *vijjas*, mouse *vijjas*, *mantras* to protect against arrows (*saraparittānaṃ*) etc. that ascetics and brahmans perform for those who provide them with alms. At the end of this list he states that these practices are for the "man of a low-class" (*puthujjano*) and Gotama remains aloof from them. This suggests that those ascetics and brahmans (*samaṇa-brāhmaṇa*) who receive alms and perform these deeds are fooling the faithful (*saddhā*). For other examples of the Buddhist criticism of Vedic magic see M.I.l.2.3.12 (82), Dh.VIII.107 and Th.2.143. However, the Buddhist texts occasionally acknowledge the efficaciousness of the magic coupled with the association of its practice with the world of attachment and desire as explicitly seen in the *Saṃyutta Nikāya*. The *Aggika* section contains a noteworthy passage

in which the Buddha refuses alms from the Brahman skilled in the three Vedas, because his fire rituals and mantras are producers of mental poisons and Buddhas do not chant verses from the Vedas. By refusing this rice offering from the brahman, the Buddha emphasizes that he is not one of those who sacrifices or attends to the fire. Furthermore, he is not a *vijjācaraṇasampanno* (one who is proficient in the ritual and knowledge of brahmans). The Buddha is one who is *khīṇasavam kukkuccavūpasantaṃ*. This section follows a chapter in which the Buddha warns against the dangers of attachment, because it is *na brāhmaṇo sujjhati koci loke* (S.VII.1.3.1) The two sections that follow the *Aggika* section tell about the attachment to the visible world that is associated with bearing children and accumulating wealth. Taking all of these polemical passages as a group we can see an explicit polemic against those members of society who participate in activities that foster a connection to the visible world of existence. However, by criticizing these activities, the Buddhist texts undermine the very basis of Vedic religion and epistemology. The criticism of Vedic magic did not just come from the Buddhists, there was also an occasional internal critique by Upaniṣadic writers. For example, two *Upaniṣads* that provide the most explicit attacks on Vedic magic and Vedic practice and learning in general are the *Maitri* (MaiU) and the *Muṇḍaka* (MuU) *Upaniṣads*. The dating of these two texts are far from confirmed and the authorship, of course, is unknown. Both of these texts are later Upanishads, meaning that they were probably composed sometime between the third and the first century BCE in comparison to the BĀU and the CU which were probably composed in the sixth and fifth centuries BCE. Their late date and their more direct critique of Vedic practices might suggest a Buddhist, Jaina or Ajivika influence. See especially MuU.1.2.7-13, and MaiU.4.3.

32 Peltier, *Sujavaṇṇa*, pp. 104–6.

33 Peltier, *Kalasa Grüa Dok*, p. 19.

34 Peltier, *Sujavaṇṇa*, pp. 173–4.

35 This was the primary focus of one of the most important scholastic Lao religious texts, the *Mūlakammaṭṭhāna*. This, Saddhatissa notes, was an important meditation manual for the Lao, giving detailed instruction of 40 *kammaṭṭhānas*. See Saddhatissa, "Pali Literature From Laos," p. 329.

36 See also J.1.116 for another example. These practices are well-known in Thailand. They were practices by one of the most famous forest monks in Thailand and Laos named, Achan Mun Bhuridatta Thera. See Achan Maha Boowa Nyanasampanno, ed., *The Venerable Phra Acharn Mun Bhuridatta Thera: Meditation Master* (Udon Thani, Thailand: Wat Pa Ban That, 1982), pp. 45 and 221. A modern monastery in Central Thailand has its monks sit staring at rotting corpses when meditating. See a description of these practices in *Suat Mon Lae Phakinnakadhammawinai* (author unknown) (Phichit, Thailand: Wat Pha Kao Noi, 1997).

37 Ibid., pp. 173–6. On a recent research trip to northern Thailand and Laos I was able to collect dozens of manuscripts of vernacular commentaries of the *Vissudhimagga*, *Dhammapada* and numerous other Pāli texts. These manuscripts have been continually composed, copied and recopied from the sixteenth century onwards and are some of the most common texts in various temple libraries throughout the region.

38 Jaini, "The Apocryphal Jatakas," p. 22.

39 Sheldon Pollock, "The Cosmopolitan Vernacular," *Journal of Asian Studies* 57, no. 1 (1998): 8, 27. See Pollock's critique of the prevailing "paradigm for understanding the social foundations of Sanskrit cosmopolitan culture, namely, legitimation theory and its logic of instrumental reason: Elites in command of new forms of social power deployed the mystifying symbols and codes of Sanskrit somehow to secure consent." Ibid., p. 13.

40 Jaini, "The Apocryphal Jatakas," p. 31.

41 Ibid., p. 35.

42 Gananath Obeyesekere, "Buddhism, Nationhood and Cultural Identity: The Pre-colonial Formations," rough draft of unpublished paper, p. 1.

43 For the contemporary debate on notions of regional and national consciousness reflected in literature

see Keith Taylor, "Surface Orientations in Vietnam: Beyond Histories of Nation and Region," *Journal of Southeast Asian History* 51, no. 4 (1998): 949, 970; Wheeler's "Challenges to Narrative History: Bifurcated History and Surface Orientations," unpublished paper, January 1999, pp. 1–23; Prasenjit Duara, *Rescuing History from the Nation: Questioning Narratives of Modern China* (Chicago: University of Chicago Press, 1995); John Breuilly, "Approaches to Nationalism," in *Mapping the Nation*, ed. Gopal Balakrishnan (New York: Verso, 1996), pp. 146–74; Ernst Gellner, *Nations and Nationalism* (Ithaca: Cornell University Press, 1983); Benedict Anderson, *Imagined Communities: Reflections on the Origins and Spread of Nationalism* (London: Verso, 1991) (revised from 1983); Eric Hobsbawm, *Nations and Nationalism since 1870* (Cambridge: Cambridge University Press, 1987); Partha Chatterjee, *Nationalist Thought and the Colonial World: A Derivative Discourse* (Minneapolis: University of Minnesota Press, 1993).

44 See Sao Sāimöng Mangrāi, *The Pāḍaeng Chronicle and the Jengtung State Chronicle* (Ann Arbor: University of Michigan, Center for South and Southeast Asian Studies, 1981), pp. 7–10. See also plates 1, 5, 6, 7, 11, 13, 14, 15, 17, 18 and 19 for examples of Khün temple architecture. Anyone familiar with South and Southeast Asian Buddhist temple architecture will notice the major differences in Chiang Tung temples immediately.

45 There are several other shorter extant *tamnāns* written in Thai Yuan including the *Tamnān Muang Ngon*, *Yang Chiang Saen*, the *Tamnān Muang Suwannakhomkham*, the *Tamnān Singhanawatikuman* and others which attempt to create temporal and spatial authenticity for their respective *muang* (city-states) through linking their *muang* with the lineage of the Buddha and justifying their temples as authentic "depositories of merit." Wyatt notes that they are "localized in their subject, they are at the same time universal in quality." Wyatt, however, dismisses their political motivation for authenticity when their local power was being threatened by Chiang Mai, Lān Xāng and later Ayutthaya (*Studies in Thai History*, pp. 5–11). These histories are designed to justify local rule associated with the local leaders' possession of Buddhist relics. This subject of relics is too vast to be discussed here and I encourage the reader of Thai to consult Sanguan Chothisukrat's *Prachum Tamnān Lān Nā Thai*, Vols. 1 & 2 (Krung Thep: Odeon, 2515 [1972]); and Prasert na Nagara, *Tamnānmunla-satsāsanā Chiang Mai Chiang Tung* (Krung Thep: Ekasanwichakan Samakhom Prawattisat, 1994). Camile Notton's *Annates du Siam, I-III: Chronique de Xiang Mai* (Paris, 1932) is also an excellent collection. For a brief history of later Sri Lankan and mainland Southeast Asian chronicles in Pali see K.R. Norman, "Pali Literature," in *A History of Indian Literature*, vol. 7, pt. 2, ed. Jan Gonda (Wiesbaden: Otto Harrassowitz, 1983), pp. 140–4. See also P. Schweisguth, *Étude sur Ia littérature Siamoise* (Paris: Imprimerie Nationale, 1951), pp. 43–4; O. Frankfurter, "Events in Ayudhya from Chulasaka-raj 686–966," *Journal of the Siam Society* 6, no. 3 (1909): 38–62; A.P. Buddhadatta, *Jinakālamālī* (London: Pali Text Society, 1962), pp. 125–6. See also Cœdès, "Documents sur l'histoire politique et religieuse du Laos occidental," *BEFEO* XXV, nos. 1–2 (1925); as well as the English translation entitled *The Sheaf of Garlands of the Epochs of the Conquerer*, trans. N.A. Jayawickrama (London: Pali Text Society, 1968), and Donald Swearer and Sommai Premchit, *The Legend of Queen Cama: Bodhiramsi's Camadevivamsa, a Translation and Commentary* (Albany: SUNY Press, 1998), pp. 63–6. Northern Thai inscriptions usually focus specifically on establishing temporal authenticity through detailed succession lists, but by the fact of their immobility they can be seen as suggesting a value to the place they occupy. For a good example of one of these lists concerning the royal line of King Mangrai inscriptions see Cham Tongkhamwan, "Kham An Silacharuk Wat Phra Yun Changwat Lamphun," *Sinlapakon* I (1957): 61–9; as well as James Pruess (ed.), "The That Phanom Chronicle: A Shrine History and its Interpretation," Cornell University Data Paper, no. 104. Donald Swearer and Sommai Premchit, "A Translation of Tamnān Mulasasana Wat Pa Daeng: The Chronicle of the founding of Buddhism of the Wat Pa Daeng Tradition," *Journal of the Siam Society* 65, part II (1977).

46 Sao Sāimöng Mangrāi, *The Pāḍaeng Chronicle and the Jengtung State Chronicle*, pp. 211–12.

47 In the *Chiang Tung State Chronicle* there is an example of inter-regional warfare and shifting alliances.

Sao Sāimöng Mangrāi's translation reads:

> [T]he Khüns mustered together five thousand men and came to fight in the direction of Jenglek, but were unsuccessful, and they went to seek help partly from the Lüs and partly from the Yeus [Shans, known to Thais and Tai-Yuans as Nio]. Fāghamraep [Khamhaepph of Hsenwi] brought a contingent to help. Hmün Benglong, Hmün Naen, and Fāghamraep brought forces to fight Saen Yī. The Lüs, Loes, and Yāngs took Jenggong in the rear. Saen Yī was defeated and fled. Hmün Benglong and Hmün Naen led in driving out the Yons up to Hinkongūa great number of Yons were killed and very many elephants and horses lost. The defeated Saen Yī retreated to Jengsaen. Brayā Kaeuyoḍjenggrāy ordered the execution of Saen Yī at Jengsaen and allowed Prince Jenggong to rule Mongbhyāk [a substate and sixty miles south of Kengtung City] (*The Pāḍaeng Chronicle and the Jengtung State Chronicle*, p. 243).

Swearer and Sommai's specific study of the reigns of Lān Nā monarchs in the fifteenth and sixteenth centuries unequivocally establishes this link. Donald Swearer and Sommai Premchit, "The Relationship between the Religious and Political Orders in Northern Thailand (14th to 16th centuries)," *Religion and Legitimation of Power in Thailand, Laos and Burma*, ed. Bardwell Smith (Chambersburg, PA: Anima Books, 1978), p. 31.

48 Although Anatole-Roger Peltier has cornered the market in studies of Khün literature, he has almost completely refrained from performing any research on or speculating on the dating of most of the Khün texts for which he has produced editions. The very few other scholars that have worked on Khün material have also been unable or unwilling to conduct any serious investigation into the dating of these texts. I imagine that the SWL could have composed as early as some of the non-classical *Jātakas* in the *Paññāsa-Jātaka* collection, making the text as much as 400 years old.

49 For good sources on the frequent periods of political instability of Southeast Asia in the medieval periods (1350–1820), see Stuart-Fox, *Lao Kingdom of Lāng Xāng*, chapters 3–4; D.G.E. Hall's *A History of Southeast Asia* (New York: St. Martin's Press, 1955), pp. 182–300; and Nicholas Tarling (ed.), *The Cambridge History of Southeast Asia*, vol. 1, parts 1 & 2 (Cambridge: Cambridge University Press, 1999), pp. 137–67 (part 1) and 75–89 (part 2).

50 Sao Sāimöng Mangrāi, *Jengtung State Chronicle*, pp. 231–65 (see esp. p. 243 for an example of inter-regional warfare).

51 Ibid., pp. 201–4.

52 Barbara Andaya, "Political Development between the Sixteenth and Eighteenth Centuries," *Cambridge History of Southeast Asia*, p. 85.

53 For example, in the *ānisaṃsa* section of the *Sankhapattarāja-Jātaka* (10) of the *Zimme Paññāsa-Jātaka* collection, there is a line that reads: "sīmaṃ janapadaṃ khemi, subhikkhaṃ bhavatu niccaṃ ... (let the boundaries of the kingdom be secure (and) prosperous forever)" (P.I.10,123). This is an explicit example of this non-canonical *Jātaka* inserting political concerns into the text, especially since various Burmese kingdoms over the last 900 years have been occupied with maintaining peace and security in the border areas of their kingdoms. Also remember that Chiang Tung has been on the borders of Burma since the sixteenth century.

54 Pierre Bourdieu, *Outline of a Theory of Practice*, trans. Richard Nice (Cambridge: Cambridge University Press, 1977), p. 133. See also his article "Structures, Habitus, Power: Basis for a Theory of Symbolic Power," in *Culture/Power/History: A Reader in Contemporary Social Theory*, ed. Nicholas Dirks, Geoff Eley, and Sherry Ortner (Princeton: Princeton University Press, 1994), pp. 155–99.

55 Pierre Bourdieu, *Language and Symbolic Power* (Oxford: Polity Press, 1991), p. 223.

56 Marshall Sahlins, *Islands of History* (Chicago: Chicago University Press, 1985), p. 26.

57 This study was attacked by G. Obeyesekere in *Apotheosis of Captain Cook: European Myth-making in the Pacific* (Princeton: Princeton University Press, 1992) and Sahlins offered a lengthy rejoinder with the

book *"How Natives Think" about Captain Cook for Example* (Chicago: University of Chicago Press, 1995).

58 Sahlins, *Islands*, p. xiv.

59 See Yoko Hayami, "Buddhist Missionary Project in the Hills of Northern Thailand," *Tai Culture* 4, 1 (1999): 53–76; and Kiyoshi Hasegawa, "Buddhism and Spirit Cults among the Tai Lü in Yunnan," *Tai Culture* 4, 1 (1999): 32–51.

60 K.R. Norman believes that a canon of religious texts can either be closed or open. By closed, he means that it consists of a fixed number of texts or utterances to which all additions would be considered the work of theologians, but not the work of the prophet or first promoter of the faith. Norman's study of the canonical tradition of Theravadan Buddhists shows that even though they claim to have a closed canon, many of the works contained therein are not and do not claim to be the words of the Buddha. Therefore, other parameters for canonicity, whether they be chronological, topical or other must be examined (*A Philological Approach*, p. 140). Even the canon was considered closed before the common era, there are texts like the *Milinda Panha*, *Petakopadesa* and the *Nettipakarana*. Origen used the term canon as an adjective with the phrase *scriptuae canonicae*, but the first nominative use was not until the fourth century [Brevard Childs, *Introduction to the Old Testament as Scripture* (Philadelphia: Fortress Press, 1979), p. 50]. In the Jewish tradition, the definition of canon was simply "sacred writings" that would not "defile the hands." However, examining the philological evidence, we see that the canon meant simply a collection of texts written in a fixed historical period. These texts were decided as sacred by consensus and usually were determined as canonical by their status of being taught as the divinely inspired words of God. Marvin Pope, in his translation and historical study of the *Song of Songs*, elucidates the difficulty in defining canonical and non-canonical works. He gives detailed comparative philological evidence (by connecting to Egyptian love poems or extracting its secular topics) to show that it could be considered non-canonical in the basis of date, literary integrity, authorship, language style and topic [Marvin Pope, trans. and commentary, *The Anchor Bible: Song of Songs* (Garden City, New York: Doubleday & Co., 1977), pp. 18, 29–33, 41–9, 66–7, 72 and 85]. In scriptural traditions throughout the world and across history, canonicity is often defined, not necessarily arbitrarily, but definitely eclectically based on multiple and over-determined factors. Childs writes:

> The term canon has both a historical and theological dimension. The formation of the canon of Hebrew Scriptures developed in a historical process, some lines of which can be accurately described by the historian. Semler was certainly right in contesting an exclusively theological definition of canon in which the element of development was subsumed under the category of divine Providence or Heilsgeschichte of some sort. Conversely, the formation of the canon involved a process of theological reflection within Israel arising from the impact which certain writings continued to exert upon the community through their religious use. To seek to explain the historical process leading towards the formation of the canon solely through sociological, political, or economic forces prejudices the investigation from the start (*Introduction*, p. 58).

This shows us that the canonical process is not on-going and limitless as maintained by James Saunders, but restrictive. However, the restrictions come under shifting rubrics of historical, literary, etc. Jonathan Z. Smith believes that the necessarily limiting function of the word canon that separates canon from commentary is a "radical and arbitrary reduction" [*Imagining Religion: From Babylon to Jonestown* (Chicago: University of Chicago Press, 1982), p. 43]. He states that the only formal element that truly defines a canon is "closure" (p. 48). The reduction "represented by the notion of canon and the ingenuity represented by the rule-governed exegetical enterprise of applying canon to every dimension of human life is that most characteristic, persistent, and obsessive religious activity" (ibid.). The making of the canon was a natural development of a religious people who seek to define their religion.

บ้านยาโกเบ

3

Ethnicity and the Galactic Polity: Ideas and Actualities in the History of Bangkok*

Siamese Melting Pot: Ethnic Minorities in the Making of Bangkok

Edward Van Roy's *Siamese Melting Pot: Ethnic Minorities in the Making of Bangkok* is a tour de force and one of the most important books on the history of Bangkok and late-modern Thai history ever to be published. It is clearly written and presented, it provides excellent maps, and brings to light little-known sources and surprising facts about the history of the most iconic neighborhoods in the city. It exposes the histories of various Muslim, Mon, Lao, Vietnamese, Chinese, European, Indian, and other communities in late Ayutthaya and Bangkok, as well as highlights various ways of seeing Bangkok as a feudal city, a vibrant port-city, or a galactic polity. Van Roy also reveals the complexities of defining ethnicity and class in Bangkok's changing neighborhoods. In this review article I will look closely at two issues Van Roy exposes that need some theoretical and critical interrogation: the "galactic polity/*mandala*" and "ethnicity." Then I will provide a short vignette about the Chettiar community in Bangkok and the idea of Hinduism in Bangkok history that both supports and

* Originally appeared as "Ethnicity and the Galactic Polity: Ideas and Actualities in the History of Bangkok," *Journal of Southeast Asian Studies* 49, 1 (2018): 129–48.

Courtyard behind the Immaculate Conception Catholic Church associated with the Vietnamese Community of Bangkok. Also known locally as "Bot Baan Yuan." Photo by author.

supplements Van Roy's excellent research. I write this not to discount or criticize Van Roy's monumental achievement, but because I believe a book this important to the field deserves serious attention and engagement.

Whither the Galactic Polity?

Unlike most scholarly studies of urban history, Van Roy leaves the theoretical reflections and critical questions about how to think about the history of ethnic diversity, city planning, and foreign influence on the history of late modern Bangkok largely until the very end of his book. In this way, they seem less like guiding principles and more like reflections and afterthoughts. Clearly, Van Roy feels more comfortable in the wonderful world of details and curiosities than he does in the realm of theory. We, the readers, benefit from this.

His book comes off less as a didactic prescription of how to understand the history of Bangkok and more of a delightful stroll through the network of shifting neighborhoods that make up one of the planet's great cities. I continually found myself thrilled to learn a fascinating tidbit about a street that I had walked down many times or a palace or monastery that I thought I knew well. While I have been researching the history of the Portuguese, Indian, Lao, Persian, Vietnamese, and Tamil histories of Bangkok for many years as a kind of hobby and thought I knew a lot, I was struck by the level of care Van Roy took in assembling his evidence. Even the most seasoned historian of Bangkok will learn many things from Van Roy's years of service to the field. The legendary Thai scholar Anake Nawigamune may be the only person I have read that knows the streets of old Bangkok better. The problem though with leaving theoretical reflections until the end of the book is that it is hard to determine where Van Roy stands. Should we see Bangkok as a *mandala*, as an ethnically diverse port-city, as the center of a feudal monarchy, or as a melting pot? It seems that Van Roy doesn't quite know himself or, perhaps, is telling us not to settle on one definition (if this is the case, I concur) and enjoy the process of speculating and reflecting.

Regardless of how Van Roy wants us to consider Bangkok, I want to argue for what it isn't. It is not a *mandala* in anything but a purely symbolic idea that was abandoned early in the Chakri Dynasty. The competing terms "*mueang*" (city-state), "*mandala*" (galactic polity), "theatre state," and others have been applied to cities in Asia for decades. In this chapter, I cannot review all of these terms, but they are models scholars have employed to understand the ways in which royal symbolism, architectural decisions, and ethnic and class divisions have factored into the design of certain cities' historical cores—Angkor, Ayutthaya, Beijing, Bagan, Madurai, Kathmandu, and Kyoto being perhaps the best examples. No matter how we define the ways in which the monarchs and planners of these cities laid out palaces, reliquaries, monasteries, parade grounds, and canals, it is evident that spatial and temporal authenticity and connecting the microcosm of the city to the macrocosm of the universe was essential in their decision-making.

Perhaps the most enduring cosmological cum topographical model in defining cities in Asia is the *mandala* (Sanskrit: *maṇḍaḷa*/Thai: *monthon*). Since Van Roy ends his book with a reflection on this term, I will offer some thoughts on it here. The best study on the appropriateness of the concept of the *mandala* in Thai historiography is Stanley J. Tambiah's *World Conqueror and World Renouncer*, where Tambiah defines the *mandala* as a "galactic polity."[1] When I was Tambiah's student we clashed about the usefulness of this term in Thailand, but it is still a very good term to think with. In short, a *mandala* is a kingdom defined by a strong urban center, ritually and symbolically reinforced as well as mythologically enhanced, and ruled by a god-king (*dharmaraja*; *cakravartin*). Before the eighteenth century there were only vague understandings of borders to these galactic polities in Asia, and power simply radiated out like heat from the center. Architecturally, topographically, and cosmologically these galactic polities—based on configurations of 5 (four spokes coming out of a central hub), 9, or 33—were concentric models as seen in Negeri Sembilan, Mataram, Ayutthaya, Hanthawaddy/Pegu, and Thaton, among others. Tambiah summed up his approach in a 1977 response to reviewers and critics of his studies on Buddhism in Thailand:

> For better or for worse, I consider my writings on Buddhism, society, and polity as situated at the confluence of anthropology, indology, and history ... the challenge ... has been to find my way towards a historical anthropology informed by indological learning ... let us all applaud the efforts of those linguists, philologists and grammarians who have dedicated their careers to composing meticulous translations of texts and painstaking glossaries and dictionaries ... for the benefit and enlightenment of scholars in other disciplines.[2]

From there he goes on to praise the *Sacred Books of the East* series of translations and the Pali Text Society. His turn towards Indic texts and indologists takes him away from local texts and local scholars. He extensively cites Pali canonical texts and the great indologists: André Bareau, Ananda Coomaraswamy, Louis de la Vallée-Poussin, among others. He looks past Thai history to Indian history, past Thai language sources to Pali and Sanskrit sources, and sees that Buddhist civilizational force was actually founded in Brahmanic cosmology and Vedic ideas of kingship. Tambiah's turn towards Indology revealed (largely non-Buddhist) structural aspects of Thai royal symbolism, cosmology, and social organization that influenced the work of Prapod Assavavirulhakarn, Yoko Hayashi, Richard O'Connor and many others.

Like Tambiah, Van Roy seems to force the model of the *mandala*/galactic polity to work too hard to accommodate a city like Bangkok that was never more than symbolically a *mandala* with the god Indra/the king and Mount Meru/city pillar (*lak mueang*) at its center. He seems to know this though and his own evidence argues against him. He writes that:

> Premodern Siam was replete with examples of cultural borrowing and adaptation from the Brahman tradition of South Asia. In Old Bangkok, the heir to that tradition examined in this book, application of the mandala as the template of symmetrical urban space was tacitly accepted ... the mandala provided the essential template for the city's original physical structure and social organization (p. 250).

Yet, throughout the book, he shows how quickly and painlessly that structure was abandoned repeatedly for what he calls "petty pragmatic reasons" (p. 250). Then he criticizes scholars like Sunait Chutintaranond, Chris Baker, Neil Englehart, and Maurizio Peleggi for their "blunt assertions" that the *mandala* model simply does not work for Bangkok (p. 251). His counter-evidence remains allusive, however. Van Roy seems to waver between seeing the symbolic center as part of a larger symbolic *mandala*, which included a central circle encompassing parts of both sides of the Chao Phraya River (p. 5), and detailing clear evidence to the contrary, such as the city wall which was determined by the river's flow, for example, when he writes: "supporting the specious claim that the entire Vietnamese community was situated within the city wall (contradicting the city's *mandala* principles)" (p. 207).

Indeed Van Roy demonstrates that the *mandala* was never much more than a symbolic ideal and that the city wall was a practical necessity of a city founded by war refugees and the remnants of the Ayutthaya ruling class. He shows that the city's symbolic center was moved from Thonburi to its present location only two weeks after the founding of the city for defensive purposes. Furthermore, after the move, he shows that the *mandala* model did not last long and had been fundamentally altered thrice during the first reign of the Chakri Dynasty. The city had to be expanded to accommodate waterways, swamp drainage, and worries of "imminent attack." He also states strangely that this *mandala* was overlooked by the "great celebratory monument (*phra prang*) of Wat Arun [Temple of the Dawn], erected in the Second Reign as a visionary rendering of Mount Meru" (p. 4). This is a very odd statement considering that the *mandala* model does not require overlooking monuments.[3] Furthermore, competing monuments symbolizing Mount Meru, like Phu Khao Thong (Golden Mountain), outside the center of the supposed *mandala* were built much later and for other practical reasons. Indeed, if the actual center (*axis mundi*/Mount Meru) was really that important symbolically for the Chakri kings, they could have easily enlarged the city pillar, which sits in an oft-forgotten, hard-to-visit traffic circle to the side of the Grand Palace. The palace could have been built around it. The city pillar could also figure more in the ritual, tourist, and historical literature of the city if the *mandala* concept was so important. Except for a minor annual ceremony, the supposed sacred center of the city has been long forgotten and is a minor monument compared to the

Temple of the Emerald Buddha ("stolen" from the Lao), Wat Arun, Wat Chetuphon/Pho, Wat Suthat, Wat Kalayanamit, Wat Benjamamophit, Wat Rakhang, and others.

Within the first four reigns (and certainly after), the royal family itself had lavished monastic and palatial building funds far outside the symbolic center that did not follow any strict observance of the *mandala* symbolism. Furthermore, Van Roy states that a "sizeable Chinese immigrant community was evicted from the delimited area [of the city pillar/symbolic center]" of the city, but then he shows that within the first 50 years of the kingdom, members of ethnic groups like the Malay, Mon, Vietnamese, Chinese, Lao, Indian communities were well-established (largely through the resettling of war captives/slaves) and the granting of land within the supposed sacred-center (see maps, p. 5). Many of these groups were not only war captives from Kings Rama I and Rama III's military campaigns in the Malay, Khmer, Cham, Vietnamese, Lanna, and Lao regions, but also ethnic groups (especially Muslims) that abandoned Ayutthaya when the Burmese invaded in 1767 and who were some of the city's earliest residents (for example, see pp. 137, 142, 152). Indeed, Van Roy's own evidence shows that Bangkok was ethnically diverse even before Rama I took the throne and established the city pillar. One could even argue that the early Chakri kings, with their Mon, Persian, and Chinese blood, were foreign invaders into an ethnically diverse set of villages that was turned into Bangkok/Thonburi and that the ethnic minorities of the early city were the Siamese (something Van Roy acknowledges himself) (p. 20). Within the first 100 years of Bangkok, ethnic communities were not only an essential part of the original *mandala* circle, but Malay, Mon, and Lao communities were within the original city fortress—whose walls were largely built by foreign workers (see pp. 111 and 119). The *mandala* as an idea was simply mapped over an already diverse urban core by an already ethnically diverse royal family.

It was not just that "foreign" ethnic communities were at the very heart of the *mandala*, but that their symbols and family members were part of the ruling Chakri Dynasty itself. The Emerald Buddha, the palladium of the kingdom, was, of course, a Lanna image that had been moved to Laos and then taken as war booty to Bangkok. There were also other Lao Buddha images in royal temples in Bangkok that Van Roy does not mention. Wat Srapthum (or more properly: Wat Pathum Wanaram Ratchawihan) is striking. It sits in the center of the busiest high-end commercial district in Bangkok—Siam Square. This is the equivalent of Rodeo Drive in Los Angeles, the Champs-Élysées in Paris, or Orchard Road in Singapore. There are no less than nine luxury department stores within two blocks of the monastery. The Royal Thai Police headquarters complex is directly across the street. The high-rises surrounding it cast shadows over the entire grounds. The main juncture for the BTS Skytrain is some 460 meters from its front entrance. Princess Sirindhorn's palace is behind the monastery. Despite its busy location, the monastery is actually a "forest" monastery of the Thammayut (Mon) lineage. It also was a place far outside the center of the original city in which King Mongkut (Rama IV) wanted to establish an important temple. In this way, the *mandala* was forced to shift and important royal connections were brought to the Lao community it seems, not vice versa. The monastery was originally built in a swampy area outside of the main city along the Saen Saep Canal in the 1840s. It was also an area that Lao refugees were forcibly settled after the wars with Laos between 1778 and 1827. It is ironic that this undesirable and overgrown malarial district in the suburbs of Bangkok would become over the next 150 years the country's financial center. It became symbolically and ritually important long before that. Indeed, the three main Buddha images (Luang Pho Soem, Luang Pho Saen, and Luang Pho Sai), along with dozens of smaller ones at the monastery, are proudly noted as Lao war booty stolen in 1827 and placed at the monastery in 1865.[4]

Across the river, another Lao image that was brought to Bangkok was placed at Wat Hong, a few hundred metres south of Wat Arun and next to the Ton Son Mosque (originally known as the Kudi Yai mosque/masjid). These foreign images were symbolically and ritually important and connected directly with patronage of the Chakri royal family. The Ton Son/Kudi Yai mosque was a former center of royal power and wealth. The original mosque Kudi Yai was founded in 1688 by the Cham and for a short time, an important Muslim official under Thaksin, Chao Phraya Sri Ongkaraksa (great grandfather of Queen Srisulalai, see below), resided there.[5] It is in the middle of Kudi Yai, an area with remnants of the Cham, Malay, and Persian Muslim communities. Very close by, of course, are the main Portuguese Catholic Church of Santa Rosa, a Chinese shrine to Kwan Yin and other deities, the resting place of General Taksin's ashes and monument (the founder of Bangkok after Ayutthaya) and the Royal Thai Navy Headquarters. It was also next to the former location of the Thonburi Grand Palace.[6] Ton Son mosque was rebuilt in 1827 in a style similar to the Dusit Grand Palace (the mosque prominently displays a drawing of this older building in its entranceway) during the reign of King Rama III, but in 1952 this building was replaced by the present building, which features a more classical Muslim minaret. This erased the physical memory of its royal sponsorship, but through interviews, I discovered that the local community is aware of this connection today. The entire area was essential for royal power in the first three reigns. Indeed, Kudi Jin, across the canal from the Ton Son Mosque, was named after a Chinese shrine and home for Mahayana priests, most likely on the grounds of present-day Wat Kalayanamit—a temple directly connected to the Chinese community on land given to King Rama III by a wealthy Chinese family. As Van Roy notes, it was not until the move of the royal shipyards about a kilometer away that the area declined (p. 138). However, in early Bangkok history, this area could be seen as much as a center of power in the early history of Bangkok as Ratanakosin Island and East Thonburi (the supposed center of the *mandala*) and arguably was the important center in the city for trade, military power, and wealth concentration. This is one of the many reasons it seems strange that he does not see the problems with the *mandala* as a useful concept for the study of Bangkok history.

Yet another example that questions the actual functioning power or guiding principles of the *mandala* is the fact that prominent Muslim families, mosques, and family members were part of the Chakri royal family. Even though Van Roy has an excellent section on Persian, Cham, Malay, and other Muslim communities (in one of the best researched chapters) and their history in Bangkok, he strikingly does not mention the fact that King Rama III, the greatest single sponsor of temples and palaces, as well as the greatest military leader in Bangkok's history, had a Muslim mother. He mentions Queen Srisulalai once but fails to mention that she was a descendant of Sultan Sulaiman. Sultan Sulaiman was a Persian Muslim who himself was the son of Dato Mogol, a Persian who founded the Kingdom of Singkora (not Patthalung and Songkhla) in southern Thailand in the early 1600s. Sultan Sulaiman ruled that kingdom from 1620 to 1668 and it was host to Dutch, Persian, Portuguese, Malay, Japanese, and other traders and resisted against Ayutthayan rule in several battles. Sultan Sulaiman's sons, Mustafa, Hasan, and Hussein, could not resist Ayutthayan rule, however, and were forced to take up prominent positions in the Ayutthayan court in exchange for their kingdom's independence. Chao Chom Mandariam (from the Arabic name: Maryam) was the daughter of Phra Chonnipheng who was descended from Hasan and the wife of Phra Chongajan, the leader of Nonthaburi (just north of Bangkok). Chao Chom Mandariam was one of the wives of King Rama II and her son was elevated above the first queen's son, Mongkut (eventually King Rama IV), for a number of reasons that are too complicated and controversial to describe here.[7]

King Rama III did not deny or hide his mother's religion or ethnicity. Indeed, he promoted it openly. His very first act as king, before any military or building plans, was to elevate his mother as Queen Srisulalai, making her the highest-ranking Muslim in Thai royal history. Second, he built a mosque in her honor, not far from Ton Son mosque. The queen's mosque, Masjid Bang Luang, which Van Roy mentions (p. 139) but does not connect to her, is known as Kudi Khao (White Religious Building) locally. Local officials and neighbors proudly talk about their royal connections. Their mosque is unique, because it is in the design of a Thai Buddhist monastery of the Rama III period with a few notable changes in color, placement of the altar—to face Mecca—and number of pillars. The Muslim *minbar* and *mirop* inside the mosque are of a mixed Chinese–Persian design and the flowers on the architrave are Chinese, similar to other Rama III period Buddhist monasteries like Wat Nang, Wat Ratchaorot, Wat Kalayanamit among many others. King Rama III had built it to replace a former Cham mosque dating back to 1767.[8] His mother's Muslim heritage was celebrated during her life and her family was well-supported. She received a full royal funeral in 1837 at the Dusit Throne Hall of the Grand Palace and her ashes were put in a Golden Urn (Phra Got) like those of her husband the king.[9] Even though she supposedly never "converted" to Buddhism, it seems she was given a Buddhist funeral and cremation. A major monastery, Wat Chaloemprakiat-worawihan, was subsequently built in Nonthaburi in honor of the Queen's parents (who were also Muslim) and the queen herself. Therefore, we have a Muslim queen who was treated as a Buddhist after her death but honored for her heritage by her son during her lifetime. The family remained prominent through the years; one of her descendants was the famous commander-in-chief of the Royal Thai Army and Prime Minister Chavalit Yongchaiyudh.

Van Roy should not be faulted for not describing Queen Srisulalai in his chapter on Muslims in Bangkok, because, it may have associated her with "indigenized Persians" (p. 142). This might also explain why there are so few references (pp. 121, 146) to the Persian Bunnag family, perhaps the second most powerful family in Bangkok's history, who had long converted to Buddhism and had their own sponsored temple, Wat Prayun (whose decorative iron fences were originally in the Grand Palace as a gift from the British), on the edge of the same Kudi Jin area where prominent Portuguese, Cham, Persian, and Chinese religious buildings are located. However, the fact that prominent Bunnags led the important Western Trade Department and controlled the highest positions in foreign ministry and military circles in the nineteenth century shows that their Persian Muslim connections were recognized. The Western Trade Department oversaw Siam's relations with India and Persia/Iran. Even today, the Bunnags are a well-respected family with prominent positions. Since Queen Srisulalai was posthumously "converted" to Buddhism and the Bunnags had converted in the Ayutthayan period, Van Roy does not see them as ethnically foreign (it is also strange that every other chapter of this book is organized by ethnic rubrics: Chinese, Lao, etc., but this chapter is organized by religion: Islam). This was probably a difficult choice for Van Roy and shows the complicated relationship between religion and ethnicity in Bangkok and in this book, as I will describe below.

For now, what is important is that the story of Queen Srisulalai shows the difficulty with using the *mandala* concept when discussing Bangkok's ethnic, religious, symbolic, and political history—the very center of the kingdom was physically and ethnically diverse from the very beginning. In this way, Van Roy's own very well-argued book falls victim to Tambiah's mistake—assuming that Brahmanic/Indological cosmology and symbolism (albeit filtered through Khmer, Javanese, and Tamil intermediaries and interpreters) actually mattered in practical terms to General Taksin and the Chakri kings. Indeed Van Roy's work is so refreshing because it shows the fascinating results of the "petty practical" decisions that leaders, monks, architects, business owners, and immigrants have to make because of the realities of water management, trading partners, conflicting landownership claims, intermarriage, and warfare.

As I argue in *Architects of Buddhist Leisure*, we need to look at history, especially in cities, as a history of the ways certain historical agents "get stuck at local optima."[10] They settle on a series of small "goods" and abandon the optimal "perfects" that they initially wanted to reach in the end. Along the way, many agents have to develop alternative plans or, in computational-speak—"low-level adaptive algorithms"—and give up ideal outcomes or overarching models.[11] Sometimes lives and material creations are simply the product of a series of local optima. Architects have to settle on a series of local optima as do buildings. Buildings are never places fixed in time that begin at the golden-shovel ceremony or end at the ribbon-cutting. They are ever-evolving. Van Roy's book shows this perfectly and the theoretical overtures to the *mandala* concept seem arbitrary and distracting even though this is one of the terms he claims his book was designed to "defend" (p. 235). In this way, he is similar to the great Tambiah. Tambiah respected and even celebrated the complexity and messiness of ethnographic and historical work. Even though he has been labelled a structuralist in numerous reviews and studies, he often built structures simply to dismantle them. He was a vocal critic of other structuralists, especially Melford Spiro, and tried to complicate any model he dreamed up with ugly political and economic realities, historical anomalies, and cognitive contradictions. His field notes and highly-skilled observational acumen betrayed his most elaborate schema. He acknowledges this himself (undoubtedly after some criticism of his book):

> In this analysis of the traditional kingdoms of Southeast Asia as pulsating galactic polities, I hope I have escaped being impaled on the horns of a dilemma by not resorting to any of the following frameworks, to the exclusion of others: (1) the "archaic" cosmological mentality which entails the acceptance of the galactic structure as a given cultural system that serves as its own explanation without resort to historical or sociological factors, i.e., an extreme form of priority attributed to the cultural order that verges on idealism; (2) a simple-minded determinism which believes it can directly and pragmatically generate the political and ideological superstructure of the galactic polity from a type of ecological and economic base; (3) a model of patrimonial domination that focuses on the imperatives of power and political control as the true arena for the emergence of the galactic structure; (4) a certain kind of laissez faire utilitarianism as portrayed by the so-called "central place" theory....[12]

Ethnicity and the Idea of Ethnicity

Van Roy's use of the *mandala* concept overshadows perhaps his sophisticated use of ethnicity as a lens through which to understand the history of late-modern Bangkok (i.e., "ethnohistory," see p. 234). He effectively and often brilliantly shows that one cannot begin to understand Bangkok without seeing it as essentially diverse and not a Siamese city that happens to have some other ethnicities because of historical circumstance and benign acceptance. He undertakes an "ethnology" of Bangkok in Geertzian terms to see how ethnicity undergirds the history of every neighborhood. Not since Leonard Andaya's masterful *Leaves of the Same Tree: Trade and Ethnicity in the Straits of Melaka* (2008) has a historical study of Southeast Asia taken ethnicity so seriously and as well as a conceptual category. Like Andaya, whose book he surprisingly does not cite, Van Roy sees ethnicity not as an "identity stamped on the soul ... [but as an] aspect of learned behavior ... a highly malleable social construct" (p. 235).

There are many things to praise here. I will only mention what I believe are the two real strengths of his book in regards to ethnohistory. First, Van Roy shows that non-Siamese ethnic groups were not simply historical curiosities, but central in the intellectual, economic, social, and cultural history of Bangkok. For example, arguably the most respected and influential scholar monk of nineteenth-century Bangkok history was actually half-Vietnamese. Somdet Phra Paramanuchit Jinorot (also known as Prince Wasukri, 1790–1853) was the supreme patriarch of Thai Buddhism (Phra Sangkharat) and the son of King Rama I and one of his royal concubines, Jui, a Vietnamese noblewoman and daughter of Ong Wang-tai (Thai title: Phraya Phakdinuchit), one of several high-ranking Vietnamese royals who escaped Vietnam after the Tay Son peasant rebellion of 1778. Prince Nguyen Anh also gave his sister to King Rama I as a concubine and he went on to return to Vietnam and rose to become the famed Emperor Gia Long who united Vietnam, while his sister built one of the first Vietnamese Buddhist monasteries in Bangkok (pp. 207–9).

Many members of the Lao royalty and commoners also held prominent positions in the early reigns of the Chakri Dynasty. Van Roy shows that after the defeat of Vientiane in 1779, many of the Lao elite were resettled in Bangkok and were "permitted to retain their positions as vassal rulers and ranking officials" (p. 107). Lao artisans were valued in the Royal Artisans' Department and served in the Siamese court as architects, goldsmiths, etc. Princess Khamwaen of Laos was elevated to the rank of First-Class Royal Consort and became a confidante of King Rama I (p. 113). She sponsored the building of two prominent Lao monasteries in Bangkok—Wat Daoadoeng and Wat Sangkhajai. These were two of several Lao monasteries in Bangkok's history. Prince Tissa of Laos was awarded the lucrative "Bangkok spirits monopoly (*akon sura*)" (p. 112).

Other prominent foreigners include the Portuguese envoy Carlos Manuel de Silviera, who was elevated to the noble title of Luang Aphai Wanit and was key in building the military of early Bangkok (p. 58), and Princess Roja (Siri Rochana) of the Lanna Kingdom (now northern Thailand), who was elevated to the rank of queen, as consort of the viceroy Bunma (p. 214). There were foreigners like the well-known Bishop Pallegoix of France who was a close adviser to King Rama IV, Dr. Dan Beach Bradley of the United States who was a royal physician and influential in the birth of printing in Thailand, and, of course Anna Leonowens, who wrote the famous book, *The English Governess at the Siamese Court*, which was published in 1870 through the help of New England abolitionists.[13] Her story was made famous by Rodgers and Hammerstein's musical (and later film adaptation), *The King and I*.[14] The list could go on and on to include prominent foreigners not mentioned by Van Roy like the royal photographer, Robert Lenz of Germany; Ekaterina Desnitskaya (Katya) of Russia who married Prince Chakrabongse Bhuvanath (40th child of King Rama V/ Chulalongkorn) and bore the first half-European/half-Siamese child into a Siamese royal family in 1905; Annibale Rigotti, the Italian architect of Siam's first bank, the reconstructed Portuguese Santa Cruz Church, and several other important royal buildings; and, of course, the great Florentine artist, Corrado Feroci, who moved to Thailand in 1923. This Italian national ended up becoming a Thai citizen in 1944, adopting a Thai name (Silpa Bhirasri), and having a state funeral in 1962. He is a national hero in Thailand. He founded and directed the first professional art school, which eventually became the first university dedicated to the arts in Thailand. He is considered the "father of Thai art." He designed many of the prominent statues of the royal family and a number of important Buddhist and national monuments. Of course, I am not including any foreign influence after 1940, considering that Van Roy's book largely is about ethnic diversity in Bangkok before the Second World War.

Second, although Van Roy does not explicitly state it, he shows well how religion and ethnicity do not necessarily go hand-in-hand in Bangkok's history. He has two well-researched sections on Vietnamese and Khmer Christians (he also has larger sections on Vietnamese Buddhists in Bangkok). He looks at the Vietnamese Catholic community descended from more than two hundred war captives in the 1830s resettled in the area formerly known as Ban Yuan (Vietnamese Area/Village), off Soi Mitrakam (near Samsen Road and the present National Library). While most Vietnamese Buddhists were settled in other areas in Kanchanaburi and other parts of Bangkok, this small Vietnamese Catholic community flourished here and still survives today, although most of its members no longer speak Vietnamese and the local Catholic School has largely ethnically Thai students.[15] Vietnamese ethnic pride is still present though, especially for church-goers at St Francis Xavier Church (built in 1863). Unlike most Vietnamese Buddhists, Van Roy notes that the Vietnamese Catholics largely intermarried with Thais in the area.

Van Roy also has a short section describing the Khmer Catholic community. Four or five hundred Catholics were brought from Cambodia to Bangkok in the first reign (1781) and many of these were ethnically Portuguese, but some were Khmer converts to Catholicism. The church was locally referred to as Bot Ban Khamen (Church of the Khmer Village). They were settled in Ban Portuket in the Samsen area of Bangkok. There was actually an earlier Portuguese Church (the Dominican Church of the Immaculate Conception) built in 1673 under the reign of King Narai of Ayutthaya (p. 62). I wish there was more about the existing church building in the book. Known as "Wat Noi" (Little Temple), it was built in 1834 and replaced by the new church in 1883, and was where Bishop Pallegoix once resided. Wat Noi has been transformed into a small private museum, only open by appointment and for special occasions.[16] The museum has a wealth of information about the Catholic community, including nearly every death record, Portuguese ivory images, silver and brass ritual objects for mass (several that look to be made in Goa), cremation volumes documenting the lives of individual Thai Catholics in the neighborhood, travel accounts of holy sites in Israel and Italy, and the like. These are primarily from the 1930s to the 1950s and are in Thai, with a few books in Latin like the *Missale Romanum*, as well as a few hymnals in English published by Westminster Press (Philadelphia). Some more detail on the impressive Catholic statuary would have also helped show the contributions of the community to religious art and material culture in the city.

What I found important about these sections, as well as his sections on the Lao and Cham, is that he shows well how religion, ethnicity, language, and customs remained separate in some neighborhoods and became thoroughly blended in others. It is very difficult based on Van Roy's detailed evidence to state unequivocally that there was a particular way that ethnic groups have been assimilated and controlled under the Chakri in Bangkok's first 150 years. This is why I found the choice of title "melting pot" unfortunate, as he clearly shows that Bangkok was not always a melting pot—it could be argued that it was a "salad," a "honeycomb," or a "mosaic," or, as I like to say, a "Jackson Pollock" in different neighborhoods at different times.

However, in his Mon section (which I found enlightening in general) he does not point out well enough that certain ethnicities have had a symbolic power far beyond their actual numbers or political/religious/social power in Bangkok's history. He has a long section (pp. 99–104) discussing the "fading of the Mon ethnicity," in terms of population due to a natural erosion of group identity and language through intermarriage and public schooling (I would add the fact that the Mon are a stateless people who are often in a precarious position in Burma). This is true, for example, it is very difficult to find Mon language teachers in Bangkok (I have tried!) and there were few Mon in positions of actual institutional power after the end of the nineteenth century. However, in many ways, I would argue, the Mon hold a place of great prestige in the minds of many Thais, especially devout Buddhists. On this point, Van Roy only makes three brief mentions, spread out in different chapters, about the founding of the Thammayut lineage/sect (Dhammayuttika Nikāya) by King Mongkut (Rama IV) in 1833 (before he rose to the throne, when he was a monk). King Mongkut himself said that he had to create a new lineage through the Mon, because most Siamese monks he witnessed did not follow what he saw as the proper monastic code (*paṭimokkha*). He was inspired by Phra Sumetthamuni—the abbot of a Mon monastery, Wat Bowon Mongkhon—and created this new lineage at Wat Samorai, a Mon monastery, near the residence, coincidentally (or perhaps not) of the above-mentioned Ban Portuket/ Ban Bot Khamen and the residence of Bishop Pallegoix (pp. 61, 82, 89–90).[17] It was a strange location, aside from the fact that it was a non-royal temple, for a future king to reside.

Mongkut was not merely inspired by the Mon—he worked to incorporate their Buddhist knowledge and language into the heart of Siamese Buddhism. For example, in approximately 1841 he invented the Ariyaka script. From my archival research and orthographic comparisons, Ariyaka is a radical adaptation of two scripts: Mon and Greek, which are two languages that the polyglot king studied as a monk and as a king, with foreign missionaries (Bishop Pallegoix being the most influential) and with Thai experts.[18] Intensely interested in other forms of Theravada Buddhism in Sri

Lanka, Burma (including the Mon), and Cambodia, King Mongkut was attempting to reform Siamese monastic discipline on the basis of what he believed were universal and "original" standards. He may have developed the script because the one factor that ties the Buddhist communities of South and Southeast Asia is the Pali language. He read Pali. He invited Sri Lankan, Khmer, Mon, and Burmese monks to study at Wat Bovorniwet (which notably still has a large number of international monks in residence).[19] The one factor inhibiting universal Theravada communication in Pali was the fact that each Theravada group used its own script for writing Pali (Sinhala, Tham, Mon, Burmese, Khmer, Yuan, Shan, Tai Khoen, etc.). I suspect that he devised the Ariyaka script to solve this problem. The monastery's own annals state that he wanted to spread the teachings of Buddhism and so he had "monastic codes of conduct" (*paṭimokkha*), "some chanting books" (*nangsue suat mon bang*), and "other texts" printed in the Ariyaka script (*akson ariyaka*) in order to replace manuscripts. Actually, only four texts were ever printed in this script: *Suat Mon, Bhikkhu Paṭimokkha, Bhikkhuṇī Paṭimokkha*, and the *Dhammapada*. Therefore, before he was King Mongkut, Vajirañāṇo Bhikkhu/Prince Mongkut invented an actual new script (and a typewriter) to replace Khom/Khmer and Siamese/Thai in writing Pali. This script was inspired, partly, by Mon. The order went on to become and remains the most prestigious lineage by virtue of its direct connections to the royal family, despite Thammayut monks being very much a minority in Bangkok, like the Mons. This is just one small example, but it shows that the idea of a people can have power far greater than their numbers. To be fair, Van Roy shows this very fact well in his discussions on the Khmer and the power of the symbolism of Angkor in Bangkok (pp. 200–6).

Vignette: The Chettiars and the Idea of Hinduism in Bangkok

Van Roy's book's significance for Thai Studies and Urban Studies of Southeast Asia cannot be undervalued. He brings a level of historical detail and exposes seriously understudied places and communities in Bangkok. Inspired by his work, I want to offer a short vignette—that supplements his book, as well as supports the two major questions, on ethnicity and the *mandala* schema I raise above.

Although, Van Roy describes numerous non-Siamese Muslim, Christian, and Buddhist communities in Bangkok's history, he curiously leaves out almost any mention of Hindus (not to mention the much smaller Sikh, Jewish or Armenian Orthodox communities, which had large trading communities in Penang, Yangon, Singapore, Chennai, Kolkata, Mumbai, Melaka, and other coastal cities in South and Southeast Asia, but not nearly as large in Bangkok) even though he employs the Brahmanic/Hindu concept of the *mandala*. Now, it is hard to criticize Van Roy for what he left out, when he wrote about so many subjects (I haven't even had time to discuss his excellent section on Chinese communities in Bangkok) and did so much research. No single book could ever fully cover a subject as big as the history of immigration and diversity in a city as large as Bangkok. However, I do find it odd that he left out one community considering he makes a slight reference to one of their members—Vaiti Padayatchi (p. 150)—and it supports some of the larger points I believe he is trying to make about the nature of ethnicity in Bangkok history. Van Roy notes that Vaiti was a partner with Mhd. Thamby Saibu Maraikayar, a Sunni Muslim livestock dealer—both had moved to Bangkok from Singapore on packet steamers (which brought many Singaporean/Malay/South Asian traders and goods to Bangkok in the nineteenth century). However, we learn nothing more about him or his religious/ethnic background. Indeed, Thamby and Vaiti were both Tamils from South India, one Hindu and one Muslim, and they worked together in cattle grazing and slaughtering (which is quite a strange livelihood for a Hindu for obvious reasons which are not explored in the book). The missed opportunity here was that this strange fact of history would actually support Van Roy's excellent point about religion and ethnicity not always going together. Vaiti and Thamby were partners and perhaps their shared Tamil language and heritage trumped their differences in religion. To say that Vaiti was a "Hindu" only tells us part of a much larger story. Vaiti was a Chettiar.

Chettiars, which (full disclosure) is a group about whom I am writing a book, were among the most well-known ultra-wealthy families of the late nineteenth and early twentieth centuries. They ran transnational networks, accumulated wealth, controlled entire industries, effectively owned or controlled banks, started arts and culture foundations, and built a string of architecturally unique mansions that have largely been lost to the history of economics, banking, charity, and architecture. Also known as the Nagarathar or the Nattukottai Chettiar Families or Chetty, in less than a century between the 1850s and 1940s, this community largely controlled banking/lending and cattle/sheep-herding, as well as trade in timber, salt, diamonds, arrack, and pearls. They financed most of the opium trade in Malaysia and Singapore in the late nineteenth century and dominated the ship-chandling industry in the region.[20] Some Chettiars went on to become major politicians, founders of universities, and founders of large multinational banks like the Indian Overseas Bank and the India Bank; and R.K. Shanmukham Chetty was the first finance minister of independent India. With this wealth the Chettiars were also responsible for building over 70,000 mansions (that looked like ornate fortresses called Nattukottai or "land-forts"), and a string of major Hindu temples in the region.

One of the largest of these temples is in Bangkok and is known in English/Tamil as the Sri Mariammam Temple and in Thai as Wat Umadewi or Wat Khaek. It is the most prominent Hindu temple in the city and was founded by Vaiti in 1879.[21] Chettiar families were not only some of the wealthiest in Tamil Nadu, but established homes, temples, and offices throughout Southeast Asia.[22] In Tamil Nadu, the families were nearly all associated with one of nine temples: Ilayathangudi, Mathur, Vairavanpatti, Iraniyur, Pillaiyarpatti, Nemam, Iluppakudi, Soorakudi, and Velangudi and the 96 villages that supported them.[23] These temple clans and sub-clans formed very close-kin trading/business/landed-gentry families that were able to work together, accumulate wealth, and support each other. Indeed, the name Chettiar comes from Sanskrit *'sresṭḥin* (Pali: *setṭḥi*) for wealth and is where Thais get the term for a very wealthy person/millionaire: *mahasetthi*. A form of *setthi/'sresṭḥin/chetti* is also a common term for wealthy person in Lao, Shan, Indonesian, Malay, and Burmese. Starting largely in the 1820s, but growing significantly in the 1880s, British colonialism was a convenient vehicle for moving these locally wealthy families from their agricultural and banking base in Tamil Nadu to colonial trading cities like Penang, Melaka, Bangkok, Singapore, Yangon, Kandy, Ipoh, and as far as Zanzibar, Durban, and various towns in the Caribbean. Dutch and French colonial officials also worked with the Chettiars to establish local financing firms and provide for both local and colonial entrepreneurs to raise capital to begin new trading routes and diversify commodity production, expand land cultivation, and further gem extraction. Chettiars were well-respected for keeping meticulous records, learning local languages, and being responsible, yet not excessively strict with payment schedules.[24] Indeed, they were successful not necessarily because of shrewd business practices or strong-armed techniques, but because of consistency, efficiency, and trust.[25] The families worked so well together and were so generous with payment plans and local charity (*mahimai*) that they became legendary throughout South and Southeast Asia.[26] They not only supported their own communities, but donated to Catholic churches, Buddhist monasteries, and other local institutions both in the Madras Presidency and abroad. They became so successful that in some areas they were controlling over 50 per cent of all lending services and their credit network enabled them to act as intermediaries for colonial powers in far flung places. For example, in certain towns in Burma, they were responsible for over 90 per cent of loans to farmers (helping the British expand the rice frontier deep into the country) and ran over 1,500 different companies in the country by the 1930s.[27]

Most Chettiar finance agents went on short trips away from their homeland (usually no more than three years when they were around 22 years old) and had strict rules about marriage and landownership in various villages in Tamil Nadu.[28] The main deity of many of their temples is the Tamil saint, Pattinathar, a descendant of Kubera (the God of Wealth). However, in Southeast Asia and East Africa, Sri Mariammam becomes the primary deity of the temples, most likely connected to protecting the visiting Tamil business people from diseases like cholera, smallpox, and malaria.[29] Some families, like the Padayatchi in Bangkok and the Pillai in Kuala Lumpur and Singapore established more permanent local ties.[30] While most families were making money abroad to bring back and build large mansions, shrines, and temples in towns like Karaikudi, Devakottai, Kulipirai, and Pillamangalam Alagapuri, some built large temples in coastal trading towns of Southeast Asia, Africa, and Latin America. These temples were not only places of worship, but also gathering places for Chettiar families and were surrounded by small shops selling food and gifts. *Hundial* shops popped up around the temples too which sold promissory notes for remittances transferred back to extended families in Tamil Nadu. *Nakarattar-vitutis* or *matams* (lodging houses for visiting Chettiars and business associates that also served as small shrines, libraries, study-rooms, and kitchens for families and priests) were often adjacent to these temples in Bangkok, Singapore, Calcutta, Medan, Colombo, and Penang. They served as a mixture of hotel, travel agency, bank, and monastery. The temples and *vitutis* were managed by *panchayats* (councils of elders) that settled disputes, arranged rituals, set the interest rates (on the sixteenth day of every month, to be precise), and the like.[31] Some even supported small *patasalais* (Vedic training schools for Brahmin boys), although rarely did these thrive outside of India.[32] These local families in Bangkok, Yangon, Saigon, and other places expanded from moneylending to owning or partnering in rice mills, rubber refineries, sawmills, and urban real estate.[33]

The Great Depression in the 1930s, the increase in competition from Multani, Gujarati, and Marwari moneylenders, the growth of markets outside of their expertise in Japan and China, local laws like the Moneylenders Bill of 1936 in Singapore, and the disruptions of the Second World War eventually led to the collapse of Chettiar dominance in South and Southeast Asian finance networks.[34] The Chettiars are disappearing from memory as producing some of the wealthiest families in the world for a century (although some descendants like the billionaire Ravi Pillai, now living in Dubai, and many others, continue to hold vast sums of wealth, but no longer invest in local Tamil village construction). However, in Southeast Asia, the Chettiar Hindu temples continue to operate and thrive, and the Chettiars still organize themselves through local *panchayats*. Many have integrated into local communities, marrying locally, and losing the ability to speak Tamil. In some cases, as in Saigon's Sri Mariammam Temple on 45 Truong Dinh Street, nearly all ties with the Chettiars have been lost. The temple is owned by the government and the *panchayat* has five members (two of Khmer ethnicity and three of Vietnamese), none of whom speak Tamil or have ever visited India. The chanting is in a Khmer–Sanskrit mixture that they claim is in the spirit of the Tamil original. However, they still celebrate some of the traditional Chettiar festivals, especially the annual sixth of October festival.

In Bangkok, there are still Tamil families connected to the Sri Mariammam Temple, but most visitors are Thai Buddhists and the main shop next to the temple is called "Three Jewels: Buddha, Dharma, Sangha;" although it sells Hindu posters, temple offerings, and Indian sweets, the owners are a Buddhist family who also sell Buddhist products. Although the networks of moneylenders, landowners, traders, and *hundial* shops have largely disappeared, the buildings and the largely non-Tamil and non-Hindu visitors are lasting and colorful landmarks in port cities on three continents. Van Roy's book is excellent for its exposure of the Tamil Muslim communities (compared to the more influential Persian, Malay, and Javanese Muslim communities of Bangkok) in Bang Rak, Khlong San, Kudi Jin, and other neighborhoods in Bangkok. I merely wanted to show that the Tamil Hindu community was also prominent and their temple is still hugely popular today among Buddhists, tourists, and the small, but influential Hindu community of Bangkok.

Besides supporting Van Roy's work on the flexibility and multiple ways of being "ethnic" in Bangkok, a study of Hinduism in Bangkok also further complicates the very idea of the Brahmanic cosmological basis of the *mandala* model.[35] There are only a few small Hindu temples actually staffed by Brahmin (usually Tamil) priests like Wat Umadewi (Sri Mariammam), a few small shrines near Si Yaek Ban Khaek, the Punjabi community's Wat Thepmontian, the small Visṇu temple serving Northern Indians on Soi Wat Prok, and the Thewasathan (discussed below). Furthermore, there are very few Hindu temples outside of Bangkok and only one in Thailand's second largest city of Chiang Mai.[36] However, like the very important influence of the Mon on Siamese/Thai culture and religion, the influence of Hinduism far outweighs the "Hindu" or Indian ethnic population. It is the idea of Hinduism and Brahmin ritual power that carries weight in the culture of Bangkok, but like the *mandala*, it largely exists in the mind and has cultural capital, not practical power. In Siam Square and Ratchaprasong (perhaps the two busiest intersections in Bangkok) tourists, shoppers, and explorers will undoubtedly pass many shrines on street corners, at bus stations, and on Buddhist monastic grounds to supposedly "non-Buddhist" deities.[37] There are shrines to "Hindu" deities like Gaṇeśa, Brahma, Śiva, Indra, and the Brahma-like "Jatukham Ramathep."[38] These are quite popular and visited by hundreds of Thai Buddhists everyday. This is not just a modern phenomena, Hindu goddesses and gods populate Thai Buddhist texts like the *Traiphum Phra Ruang*, many Pali and vernacular *jātakas*, *desanā*, *sutta* texts, as well as astrological (Thai: *horasat*), and ritual (*chalong/pithi*) texts. Van Roy notes this himself in the very beginning of the book in his references to the symbolic power of the god Indra in Bangkok. The long history of Hindu statuary in Thailand has been well-studied. There are statues, bas-reliefs, and mural paintings of Harihara, Śiva, Laksṃī (or Bhū-Devī), Gaṇeésa, Brahma, Indra and others found in the area we now call Thailand dating back 1,200 years as clear evidence. Indeed, art historians and historians working under the early rubric of "Hinduization" or early Hindu influence on Thailand like Georges Cœdès, Subhadradis Diskul, Stanley J. O'Connor, Alexander B. Griswold, and many others have unearthed or identified hundreds of statues of Hindu deities at Si Thep, Phimai, Lopburi, Suphanburi, Phanom Rung, among many other places. Museum collections at the National Museum of Thailand and numerous regional museums like the ones at Sukhothai, Ayutthaya, Kampaeng Phet, and collections like the Asian Art Museum (San Francisco), Guimet (Paris), British Museum (London), and Tokyo National Museum all contain numerous examples of imagery from Thailand that curators and historians refer to as "Hindu."

It is not just that the idea of "Hinduism" or Indian culture has importance in Bangkok history far beyond the numbers of ethnic Indians in the city, but their legacy also shows the problem with the *mandala* concept. While the idea of India is important, the actual role of Brahmins is not at the center of the *mandala* and they do not have much influence on the actual activities of the royal family. The royally-sponsored Brahmin temple is near the edge of the old city walls and not in the center of the supposed Bangkok *mandala*. Nor did court Brahmins have an office within the vast walls of the Grand Palace. They work out of the Thewasathan (Place of the Gods/Devas; also known as Bot Prahm). This is the royally-sponsored temple founded in 1784. There are less than 15 actual Brahmins (ordained Phra Prahm) in all of Thailand and few intact Brahmin families left.[39] There is no evidence that there were many more in early Bangkok history as well and they are almost never mentioned by name in royal chronicles of Bangkok. Certainly, they had and still have influence on royal and other ceremonies. This can be seen in murals, like the ones at Wat Ratchapradit Sathitmanasimaram near the Grand Palace and the Ministry of Defence and in King Rama V's writing on the 12 royal ceremonies. The most useful information I gained was from Phra Maharatchakhru Phithisriwisutthikhun, the chief royal Brahmin in Thailand and teacher to many of the present Brahmins.[40] In this very informative session I learned that there are no exceptions to the rule that in order to become a Brahmin in Thailand, one must come from one of the brahmanic bloodlines (*ben luk-lan khong Phra Prahm*) that he claimed stretched back over 1,200 years in Thailand and were invited to come from the Nakhon Sri Thammarat area in southern Thailand to serve the Siamese royal family. These lines were originally from the Tamil region of India, but only oral records exist. Many of these families have long intermarried with local Thai Buddhists and are at this point ethnically Thai. None of the Brahmins was born in India and none speak a modern Indian language well. Most had either never visited India or had gone there on a short tourist trip. He admitted that a recent two-week visit to India came after a gap of seven years. He also admitted that they use primarily Thai language books and some Thai–Sanskrit glosses in their study. He had in his possession some Sanskrit ritual manuscripts which were composed in what he called "*akson tamin boran*" (Old Tamil Script).[41] He emphasized that none of the Brahmins knew Sanskrit grammar, but were trained to chant Sanskrit mantras during rituals. There is no school at the Thewasathan and no formal curriculum. Instruction and ordination is done on a one-on-one basis and over his whole life (he is near retirement age) he has trained fewer than 25 people (he has been the primary trainer for the last couple of decades) and has the most students. Clearly, he is treated with great deference by all the other Brahmins and staff. Training does not take place in any serious way in Bangkok or anywhere else in the country. Several of the Brahmins in present-day Thailand are in fact from his own bloodline and I had a chance to meet one of his cousins, who also serves in the royal rituals. They do not produce books, hold regular classes, seek converts, promote the building of Hindu temples, have regular publicized visits from famous Brahmins from India, nor have a public lecture series. The point is that there are certainly Indic influences in almost every part of Thai cultural life, from architecture to astrology to dance to nomenclature to governance to ritual. The Indic cultural sphere includes much more than religious expressions, whether they be Mahāyānist, Theravadin, or Hindu (or another broad and relatively arbitrary category).[42] However, Hinduism is an umbrella term for a number of loosely related religious teaching lineages, philosophical systems, ritual programs, narrative tropes, and aesthetic tendencies largely centered on Vedic ritual, Deva puja, and ascetic, tantric, and yogic practices. Buddhism, Jainism, particular schools of Christianity, Sikhism, and certain forms of Zoroastrianism also were born in the Indic cultural sphere. We should not conflate "Hindu religious" influence and "Indian cultural" influence which is a problem with which Van Roy's book struggles, and it is in that struggle that we, the readers, benefit. However, Hinduism as a religion, like the *mandala* as a concept, is not actually a guiding force in Thai culture.

Edward Van Roy has produced through decades of observation, research, and walking through the city a book unlike any other and I believe it will launch many a research study, inspire historians, anthropologists, and even tourists in Bangkok. Despite my reservations about some of his approaches, I stand in awe at the way he carefully and meticulously collected information and presents it with clarity and purpose. I highly recommend *Ethnicity and the Galactic Polity: Ideas and Actualities in the History of Bangkok* for students at any stage in Thai, Southeast Asian, and even Urban Studies more broadly.

Notes

1 Stanley J. Tambiah, *World Conqueror and World Renouncer: A Study of Buddhism and Polity in Thailand Against a Historical Background* (Cambridge: Cambridge University Press, 1976), p. 102.

2 Stanley Tambiah, "The Galactic Polity: The Structure of Traditional Kingdoms in Southeast Asia," *Annals of the New York Academy of Sciences* 293, 1 (1977): 69–97.

3 Wat Arun was placed there for other more practical reasons and its *phra prang* was largely built under the third reign in place of two former temples; it is not Siamese, but Chinese, Persian, and Khmer in its architecture, symbolism, and design.

4 See descriptions of the movement of these Lao images in King Mongkut's chronicle, *Phra Ratchaphongsawadan Krungratanakosin Ratchakan thi 4* [Royal history of Bangkok under the reign of King Rama IV] (Bangkok: Cremation volume for Mormchao Chongkonni Watthanawong, 1965), pp. 98, 152, 319, and 384–91.

5 Relatives of Queen Srisulalai are buried in the cemetery of Ton Son mosque, and their graves can be visited today.

6 Thank you to Sri Chalaidecha (an administrator at the mosque) for pointing this out to me and showing me photos and letters from members of the Thai royal family on their visits. See also an edition of the magazine published by the mosque, featuring a visit of King Rama VIII (Ananda Mahidol) and his brother, King Rama IX (Bhumipol)—*Warasan thi ni Ton Son* [Ton Son Magazine] 10 (Aug. 2549 [2006]) that discusses the royal connection to the mosque.

7 See Phra Bhiksu Gaisri Kittisiri Chanthonpanya, *Ratchakan thi 3 haeng boromchakri mahakasatanuson* [King Rama III Memorial Book](Chiang Mai: Suthin, 2551 [2008]), esp. pp. 75–91.

8 I also thank Thongchai Likhitpornsawan and Anake Nawigamune for taking me there on a visit and introducing me to the imam and his family.

[9] Chao Phraya Thipakorawong, *Phra ratchaphongsawadan krungratanakosin ratchakan thi 3* [trans.], 7th ed. (Bangkok: Krom Silpakorn, 2547 [2004]), p. 75. Wat Nang Nong, a Buddhist monastery in Thonburi, was also dedicated to his Muslim mother.

[10] Justin T. McDaniel, *Architects of Buddhist Leisure: Socially Disengaged Buddhism in Asia's Museums, Monuments, and Amusement Parks* (Honolulu: University of Hawai'i Press, 2016), p. 81.

[11] Ibid., p. 82.

[12] Tambiah, "The Galatic Polity," p. 91.

[13] Leonowens was Anglo-Indian (Indian/Welsh), not a governess, and never lived in England.

[14] See, for example, Alfred Habegger, *Masked: The Life of Anna Leonowens, Schoolmistress at the Court of Siam* (Madison: University of Wisconsin Press, 2014). Susanne Kerekes and I recently studied the influence of Dr Dan Beach Bradly's wife on manuscript collecting in Bangkok. See Susanne Ryuyin Kerekes and Justin McDaniel, "Siamese manuscript collections in the United States," in *Collections and Collectors in the History of Siamese Manuscripts*, ed. Justin McDaniel, special issue, *Manuscript Studies* 2, 1 (2017): 202–38.

[15] I thank several teachers there for details about the school's history and student body.

[16] I have visited Wat Noi twice (thanks to Arthid Sheravanichkul for arranging the trip the first time) and document its contents extensively in a forthcoming publication.

[17] Surprisingly, Van Roy does not discuss the importance of Wat Paramai at Koh Kret, a largely Mon island in the Chao Phraya a few miles north of Bangkok with an impressive collection of Mon manuscripts.

[18] See two books produced by Prince Wachirayan (printed after his death) describing King Mongkut's Ariyaka script: Somdet Phra Mahasamanachao Krom Phraya Wachirayanwororot, *Akson Ariyaka* [Ariyaka Script] (Bangkok: Mahamakut Withayalai, 2501 [1958]); Somdet Phra Mahasamanachao Krom Phraya Wachirayanwororot, *Katha Chadok lae Baep Akson Ariyaka* [Buddhist Verses and the Ariyaka Script] (Bangkok: Wat Boworniwetwihan, 2514 [1971]). The Bhumipol Foundation also produced a study of the Ariyaka and other scripts: *Akson Khom lae Akson Boran Thong Thin* [The Ariyaka Script and Original Ancient Scripts] (Bangkok: Munitthi Bhumipol, 2519 [1976]). Phra Sugandha (Dr Anil Sakya) has edited and reprinted one of Mongkut's four texts produced in Ariyaka script in Suat Mon [Mantras] (Bangkok: Mahamakut University Press, 2004). I thank him for his helpful advice and for showing me some of the first editions of books produced on King Mongkut's Ariyaka script printing press. See also Justin T. McDaniel, *Lovelorn Ghost and the Magical Monk: Practicing Buddhism in Modern Thailand* (New York: Columbia University Press, 2011).

[19] King Rama III is said to have sent his half-brother, who outranked him and was passed over for the throne by Rama III, to be the abbot at Wat Boworniwet. This monastery was outside the city walls (symbolically significant, as Van Roy argues). King Rama III may have sent him there because he disapproved of the founding of the Mon-influenced Thammayut.

[20] David West Rudner, *Caste and capitalism in colonial India: The Nattukottai Chettiars* (Berkeley: University of California Press, 1994), p. 85.

[21] In Thailand, ethnic Indians and other South Asian peoples are commonly referred to as *khaek*, often glossed as "guest" and "foreigner" in dictionaries, but also a derogatory term for dark-skinned foreign laborers. *Si khaek* refers to a yellowish-brown mustard color—and is a term which Pakistanis, Indians, Sri Lankans, and other South Asians in Thailand avoid for themselves.

[22] See, for example, the history of the Vaithi Padayatchi family—landowners and wealthy sheep and cow herders in Tamil Nadu: http://pallavar-vanniyar.blogspot.com/2012/02/padayatchi.html.

[23] S. Muthiah, Meenakshi Meyappan, and Visalakshi Ramaswamy, *The Chettiar heritage* (Chennai: Lokavani-Hallmark, 2000), p. viii.

[24] Rudner, *Caste and capitalism*, pp. 67–73.

[25] David West Rudner, "Banker's trust and the culture of banking among the Nattukootai Chettiars of colonial South India," *Modern Asian Studies* 23, 3 (1989): 417–58. See also Heiko Schrader, "Chettiar finance in colonial Asia," *Zeitschrift für Ethnologie* 121, 1 (1996): 101–26. Schrader notes that the practice of sons of wealthy Chettiars apprenticing for other Chettiar families created bonds and decreased excessive nepotism (p. 105).

[26] Muthiah et al., *The Chettiar heritage*, pp. viii and 58. See also Sean Turnell and Alison Vicary, "Parching the land? The Chettiars in Burma," *Australian Economic History Review* 48, 1 (2008): 1–25.

[27] Rajeswary Brown, "Chettiar capital and Southeast Asian credit networks in the interwar period," in *Local suppliers of credit in the Third World, 1750–1960*, ed. Gareth Austin and Kaoru Sugihara (London: Macmillan, 1993), p. 262. See also S. Chandrasekhar, *The Nagarathars of South India* (Madras: Macmillan India, 1980), for an introduction to Chettiar history and a good bibliography of studies of the Chettiars in Southeast Asia.

[28] Schrader, "Chettiar finance": 105. See also Paul Kratoska, "Chettiar moneylenders and rural credit in British Malaya," *Journal of the Malaysian Branch of the Royal Asiatic Society* 86, 1 (2013): 61–78.

[29] I thank a priest at the Sri Mariammam Temple in Bangkok, who wanted to remain anonymous, for explaining the role of Sri Mariammam today.

[30] Vineeta Sinha, "Unravelling 'Singaporean Hinduism': Seeing the pluralism within," *International Journal of Hindu Studies* 14, 2–3 (2010): 253–79. The temple in Singapore is no longer connected to the original Pillai family, but has been since 2005 under the administration of the Sri Samayapuram Mariammam Pallaigal, which is a modern form of *panchayat*. Their main work is maintaining the temple, hosting annual festivals, and raising money for children's education. They also welcome Hindus (and even Taoists and Buddhists) from all backgrounds and are no longer a Tamil temple as has happened with many other Chettiar temples abroad. See Vineeta Sinha, "Mixing and matching: The shape of everyday Hindu religiosity in Singapore," *Asian Journal of Social Science* 37 (2009): 83–106.

[31] Rudner, *Caste and capitalism*, pp. 123–7; Schrader, "Chettiar finance": 107.

[32] Brown, "Chettiar capital," pp. 259–61.

[33] One exception was the *patasalai* in Yangon, which expanded into the Chettiar's Residential High School in 1928. Muthiah et al., *The Chettiar heritage*, p. 67.

[34] Schrader, "Chettiar finance": 118. Kratoska, "Chettiar moneylenders": 72. See also Medha Kudaisya, "Marwari and Chettiar merchants, c.1850s–1950s: Comparative trajectories," in *Chinese and Indian business: Historical antecedents*, ed. Malik Kudaisya (Boston: Brill, 2009), pp. 85–119.

[35] On Hinduism in Bangkok, see Justin McDaniel, "This Hindu holy man is a Thai Buddhist," *Southeast Asia Research* 21, 2 (2013): 191–210. See also the recent and excellent study by Nathan McGovern, "Balancing the foreign and the familiar in the articulation of kingship: The royal court Brahmans of Thailand," *Journal of Southeast Asian Studies* 48, 2 (2017): 283–303.

[36] Hindi is still taught at the Rongrian Bharat Withayalai (Indian High School); however, besides this subject (which is not taken by all students) and some Indian cultural events and instruction, this is a "*matrathan*" (standard) Thai high school with a government-approved curriculum. Indeed, most students are either Thai Buddhist or Muslim, and some Thai-born/ethnic Indian high school students. Instruction is in Thai. Funerals for the small ethnic Indian community take place near Wat Yannawa in Bangkok. Child blessings usually take place at the Thewasathan or are performed by Brahmins in private homes.

[37] On the shrines, see Justin McDaniel, "The gods of traffic: A brief look at the Hindu intersection in Buddhist Bangkok," *Journal of the International Association of Buddhist Universities* 2 (2009): 49–57. For background on the figure of Brahma, see Nathan McGovern, "Brahmā worship in Thailand: The Ērawan Shrine in its social and historical context" (Masters' thesis, University of California, Santa Barbara, 2006).

[38] See for example, Georges Cœdès, *Les états Hindouisés d'Indochine et d'Indonésie: Histoire du Monde Tome VIII* (Paris: E. de Boccard, 1948); Subhadradis Diskul, *Hindu gods at Sukhodaya* (Bangkok: White Lotus, 1995); Hiram Woodward, *The art and architecture of Thailand: From prehistoric times through the*

thirteenth century (Leiden: Brill, 2005); Stanley O'Connor, "Hindu gods of peninsular Siam," *Artibus Asiae* supplementum 28 (1982): 1–73; Theodore Bowie, A.B. Griswold, and M.C. Subhadradis Diskul, *The sculpture of Thailand* (Sydney: Visual Arts Board, 1977); Louis Frederic, *The temples and sculptures of Southeast Asia* (London: Thames & Hudson, 1965); Robert Brown, *The Dvaravati wheels of the law and the Indianization of South East Asia* (Leiden: Brill, 1996); Gauri Devi, *Hindu deities in Thai art* (Varanasi: Aditya Prakashan, 1998). See also the catalogues (many online) for the museums at Ayutthaya (http://www.thailandmuseum.com/thaimuseum_eng/bangkok/main.htm); Chiang Mai University Center for Art and Culture (http://art-culture.chiangmai.ac.th/index.php); and Kampaengphet (http://thaimuseum_eng/kamphaengphet/main.html), among others.

[39] They are (in order of rank): Phra Maharatchakhru Phithisriwisutthikhun (family name: Khawin Rangsiphrahmanakhun), Phra Ratchakhru Siwachan (Thawon Bhavangkhanan), Phra Khru Sathanathamuni (Arun Sayomaphop), Phra Khru Yananasayambhu (Khachon Nakhanawethin), Phra Khru Sitthikhayabadi (Khon Komonwethin), Phrahm Sombat Ratanaphrahm, Phrahm Sisonphan Rangsiphrahmanakhun, Phrahm Phisana Rangsiphrahmanakhun, Phrahm Bhatihari Sayomaphop, Phrahm Bharikhawut Nakhanawethin, Phrahm Khawankhat Ratanaphrahm, Phrahm Phathan Wuthiphrahm, Phrahm Kharan Buransiri, and Phrahm Thawutthi Komonwethin. From this list, you can see that these positions are often a father-brother-uncle-son affair.

[40] I thank Arthid Sheravanichkul for helping me arrange this interview and to the Buddhist monk Phra Sompong Santikaro for his help at the Thewasathan.

[41] Although I did not closely read or translate them, from their appearance they were central Thai-style *samut khoi* manuscripts from the mid-nineteenth century.

[42] Of course, there are problems with the terms Hinduization and Indianization which have been discussed in Southeast Asian Studies for three decades. The two main problems being they suggest that (1) the influence was only one-way and that Southeast Asian writers, thinkers, and artists had no influence on Indic culture; (2) there was no creative engagement with Indic art, literature, science, etc., and so Southeast Asian cultural producers accepted Indic culture wholesale and did not adapt it. Prapod Assavavirulhakarn's *The ascendancy of Theravāda Buddhism in Southeast Asia* (Chiang Mai: Silkworm, 2010) is a good example of how to examine Indic influences on Thailand in a sophisticated and balanced way. See also the seminal articles by Ian Mabbett: "The Indianization of Southeast Asia: Reflections on the pre-historic sources," *Journal of Southeast Asian Studies* 8, 1 (1977): 1–14; and "Indianization of Southeast Asia: Reflections on historical sources," *Journal of Southeast Asian Studies* 8, 2 (1977): 143–61. Many major textbooks on the region and the *Cambridge History of Southeast Asia* also discuss problems with the Indianization approach to understanding Southeast Asian culture. The concomitant problems with "Hinduization" or "Hinduism in Thailand" have not been extensively explored. Of course, in Japanese, French and even Victorian English, Hindou, Hindoo, and Hindouisme sometimes have a wider lexical import and can often be equivalent with "Indian culture" and do not always simply specify the "Hindu" religion as they do in contemporary English. John Holt's study *The Buddhist Vishnu* (New York: Columbia University Press, 2004) tackles the problem of separating Buddhist and Hindu deities in everyday practice in Sri Lanka and is highly recommended.

4

Beautifully Buddhist and Betrothed: Marriage and Buddhism as Described in the *Jātakas*

For my 22nd birthday, I visited my friend (now wife), Christine, who was a Peace Corps volunteer in Nepal. She had to conduct a children's health survey near the Tibetan border, close to the town of Simikot. She asked if I would like to tag along. I had saved up a little money as a teacher in Thailand, where I had been living since graduating from college, and decided to follow her as she could speak the language and I was interested in the region. After the short flight and a two day walk into the mountains along the border, we decided to knock at the door of a remote monastery and see if we could spend the night. We were greeted by a Tibetan nun and, to my surprise, her seven children. They were all dressed in monastic robes. Christine spoke to her in Nepali and she welcomed us and said that we could stay in her husband's room since he was away performing a funeral in another village. I was shocked, not by her hospitality, but by her robes, her children, and the casual mention of her husband—a monk! My shock was rooted in three basic misconceptions I held about religion, monastic life and Buddhism. First, in Thailand, where I had been learning as much as I could about Pali, Theravada Buddhism, and monastic life, monks are forbidden to marry. There are no exceptions. Second, growing up studying in exclusively Catholic schools in an Irish family, my ingrained belief was that priests, monks, and nuns do not and should not marry. Third, the Buddhist introductory textbooks, suttas, and monastic codes I

Tranquil pond and pavilion on the grounds of the Sathiradhammsathan Meditation and Education Center outside of Bangkok. New sites like these have become popular for wedding venues. Photo by author.

had been reading made no mention of Buddhist marriage or the ability of monks and nuns to marry.

Fast-forward 15 years later and I teach Buddhist Studies at an American university and my students still read a textbook that makes no mention of monastic nuptials. Scholars have largely avoided the study of Buddhism and marriage. However, even though there have not been many publications to date, over the past few years there has been a growing interest in Buddhist monastic marriage and family life among Buddhist Studies scholars, especially those who research Indian and Japanese Buddhism. Monastic marriage has a complicated and controversial history in Japan as noted by Covell, Jaffe, Reader, Tanabe, and others. However, strikingly it has not been a controversial issue in Thailand or Southeast Asia in general. Although there has been a push by some in the vocal elite to restart the *bhikkhunī* (nun) lineage in Theravada Buddhism, there has not been any serious suggestion that monks or nuns should be permitted to marry. This is strange since marriage and the married life is such a significant part of Buddhist narrative literature in Southeast Asia, especially Thailand.

Marriage and the love felt by married or monogamous couples are often seen as leading to the dangers of attachment and desire in Buddhist teachings. Nuns, monks, Buddhas, and Bodhisattas are seen as abandoning love and marriage, in most cases, to gain enlightenment. In fact, the Pali word most commonly used for love, *sineha*, is found only in three canonical *jātakas*. *Sineha* (literally an "oily substance" or discharge like semen) can also mean affection or even lust. In the *Guṇa Jātaka*, it is used in the sense of a lion showing affection to a she-jackal who had saved his life (*sineham karomi*: I show/make affection).[1] In the *Abhiṇha*, it is used to express the platonic friendship between an elephant and a dog.[2] In the *Kaṇha*, love or affection is associated with aversion and greed.[3] Abandoning the life of romantic love and family attachment is praised. For example, in the *Suruci Jātaka* we find an example of a queen who asked her husband to be monogamous, but when she cannot bear a son for him, he marries 16,000 other women.[4] In the *Āsaṅkha Jātaka* it is said that women are a stain to the religious life.[5] However, in other stories it is a woman that abandons the path of motherhood and wifehood and is praised for choosing the ascetic life, as in the story of the nun named Sukkā.[6] Both women and men ideally should refrain from love and marriage. Romantic, dedicated, or passionate types of love, it seems, are not soteriologically or ethically productive drives or emotions in Buddhism.

However, nothing is ever so straightforward in Buddhist literature. Looking broadly at Pali and vernacular literature, *sineha* is not necessarily a dominant emotion in marriage and loyalty, dedication, and attachment to one's spouse are not universally condemned. Husbands and wives are described as loyal and devoted, but not necessarily full of uncontrollable *sineha* that leads to delusion and attachment. Many stories seem to either suggest that you can live a married life without the suffering of attachment or that the suffering that marriage (and having children) often causes can be soteriologically productive and ethically pedagogical. Other stories in Buddhist literature circulated or composed in Thailand explicitly promote the virtues of falling in love, marriage, and monogamous dedication. Some stories speak of the virtue of marriage and married love even within narratives that are ultimately focused on teaching the dangers of attachment. In other words, the divisions between asceticism and the attachments of love often found in married life are not so clear cut.

Students of Buddhism are regularly told, quite correctly, that non-attachment is a virtue for both the laity and the monastic community. Non-surprisingly, therefore, the study of married or monogamous love has largely not been part of the field of Buddhist Studies. Love and marriage necessitate, it seems, attachment and dedication.[7] However, positive views of marriage and the married life are a significant part of Buddhist narrative literature in Southeast Asia, especially Thailand. Why is this the case? If non-attachment is lauded and if the ideal Buddhist life is that of a nun and monk, and nuns and monks cannot marry then one would assume that Buddhist teachings in Southeast Asia would either ignore the subject of married love or condemn it as a hindrance to leading an ideal ethical life.

In this article, I will approach the subject of marriage through the lens of the most popular story in the Thai Buddhist cultural tradition, the *Vessantara Jātaka*. Since the Vessantara, like many other Buddhist narratives circulated in Thailand, has married couples as the main protagonists, I will describe, as much as space allows, the ways in which the relationship is treated in a selection of Buddhist texts, sermons, and murals. I will show that even though the very idea of permitting marriage among Buddhist monastics in Thailand is unheard of, that the stories Thai Buddhists enjoy and the ones nuns and monks ritually perform and teach show the virtues of marriage and loyalty between wife and husband. Despite the ideal of "non-attachment," committed, supportive and romantic relationships are greatly valued in Thailand. Below I provide a selection of examples from a variety of narratives. My seemingly random choices of stories is based in my effort to show how pervasive these stories are and they are found throughout canonical, extra-canonical, Pali and vernacular texts in many regions and literary traditions of what we now call Thailand.

Marriage in Narrative Art and Literature in Thailand

The murals on the ordination hall of Wat Kongkaram (Ratchaburi Province, Central Thailand) are a good example of the complicated teachings on marriage. It was built in the eighteenth century and was originally a monastery used by the Mon ethnic community in the area. The murals on the interior walls are drawn from several sections of several different stories. There are scenes from the story of Prince Siddhattha's "Great Departure" into the ascetic life, the Thai *Three Worlds of King Ruang* (*Traibhūmikathā*) cosmology, and scenes from various *jātakas*, some included in the last ten, like the *Temiya*, *Suvannasama*, and the *Nimi*. Among these more common *jātakas* is a rendering of erotic and violent parts of the *Cullapaduma* (the

193rd story in the canonical collection). In this story, a king becomes nervous that his seven sons will try to kill him and take over the throne. Therefore, he exiles all of them with their wives. In the forest, desperate for food, the brothers devise a sinister plot to kill each of their wives over seven days. They plan to cut up the wives and roast the pieces of their flesh, muscles, organs to consume them and stave off hunger. The youngest brother, being compassionate and in love with his wife, goes along with the plot. However, every night, instead of eating his portion of his roasted sisters-in-law, he hides his portion. On the seventh night, instead of killing his own wife, he gives the brothers the portions of their spouses he had saved and escapes with his wife deeper into the woods. As they wander in the forest without food for many days, she starts to starve to death. Even though he is starving too, he puts her needs first (beautifully depicted in the mural)—he cuts open his knee and she feeds on the blood dripping from it. Nourished by his blood, they wander deeper into the forest. Finally, along a stream, reminiscent of the forest hermitage in the *Vessantara Jātaka*, he makes a humble home with his wife and they go about collecting fruit and water. One day, the prince, Cullapaduma, sees a man floating in a small boat in the stream. The man has no arms, no legs, and no nose. He has been tortured by the king (the prince's father) and thrown in a boat to float away and die a slow and agonizing death in the wilderness. Cullapaduma and his wife take pity on the man and bring him into their hut. Every day the wife takes care of the man's wounds while Cullapaduma searches for food and water. This is similar to the *Vessantara Jātaka* as well, but gender roles are reversed there, Maddī goes looking for food and water while Vessantara stays at home and meets with the physically hideous Jūjaka (see below). Over time, Cullapaduma's wife falls in love with the armless, legless, and noseless man and has a sexual affair with him while Cullapaduma is out looking for food. She wants to kill her husband so she can marry the tortured man. She plots to lead Cullapaduma to the edge of a cliff and push him down to his death. Her plan works, but instead of falling to his death, Cullapaduma gets caught in some tree branches growing out from the cliff face and is fed by a lizard who rescues him.

Now, this story, while certainly showing the dangers of marriage and depicting Cullapaduma's wife as unappreciative and maliciously cunning, spends a great deal of time describing the love between the couple. Cullapaduma is honoured for his dedication to his wife and in the end, when Cullpaduma returned to be king he does not have his former wife punished. He simply allows her to live the life of poverty she has chosen with her new husband. The story does not discount Cullapaduma's love for his wife. Indeed, it emphasizes that it is one of his virtues as a Buddhist hero. Perhaps this is why the muralist chose to depict the tender scenes of love between the couple on the monastery walls more than other scenes.[8] Murals depicting love scenes are not simply in small rural temples, but in central urban royal temples in Bangkok. For example, in Wat Suthat (a first-rank royal monastery), there are paintings from the Thai version of the Panji theme from Java, the *Inao*. It is of Princess Bussaba asking a Buddha statue to hear her plea and return her true love to her. Even though this scene is not in any known Javanese or Malay version of the story, here we see a creative muralist inserting a "Buddhist" scene into a foreign love story.[9]

The *Dhammapada-Atthakathā* (*Dhammapada Commentary*) is a collection well-known in Thailand which forms the content of multiple monastic examinations and from which many sermons are drawn. There are several stories that feature married couples in this collection. Unlike the wife in Cullapaduma, often in this collection, wives are depicted as loyal, loving, and often clever in teaching their husbands or avoiding the violent aggression of men. For example, in the *Bālavagga*, the fifth story in the collection, there is the long tale of Dinnā, the youngest wife of 100 kings, who is tricked into being sacrificed to a tree-spirit by the jealous King of Benares. Sakka (the god Indra) uses this event to teach the jealous king, the tree spirit, and the other assembled kings and queens the meaning of true merit making. Dinnā is said to be superior in her understanding of merit and intention to all others. She speaks highly of the value of marriage and states that wives should honor their husbands above all other kings, gods, and spirits. Although this might seem androcentric (as many Buddhist stories do), the importance of marriage as a loyal relationship is promoted. In other parts of this story, four kings are destined to spend 240,000 years boiling in a cauldron in the Avīci hell because of stealing wives away from other men. In another section, Queen Mallikā teaches her husband with the help of the Buddha the value of marriage and the dangers of pursuing other men's wives.

Although there are other stories from the *Dhammapada-Atthakathā*, most notably the heartbreaking stories of the two wives and mothers *Paṭācārā* and *Kisa Gotamī*, that offer soberly lessons about the sorrow that comes with attachment to husbands and children, there are other stories that recount the affection between wives and husbands. Indeed, even *Paṭācārā* and *Kisa Gotamī*, seem to speak highly of the love between husbands and wives, even though they ultimately teach the lesson of the suffering that comes when love is lost.[10] However, the story of *Kukkuṭamitta*, a hunter who marries a wealthy woman who falls in love with him despite his lowly profession, actually features a section where the Buddha chides other monks for thinking that all marriage is unsuitable. The Buddha states "If in his hand there be no wound, a man may carry poison in his hand. Poison cannot harm him who is free from wounds. No evil befalls him who does no evil." This means that if a wife and a husband have already gained enough merit to enter onto the path to enlightenment, they can perform actions that are outwardly signs of attachment and desire (like being married and having children or being a hunter and killing animals), but they are unscathed by these actions. They are married, but not attached.

This message is taught in a much more bizarre way in the famous story of Sorreya.[11] In this story, a man is rewarded for his attraction for the arahant, Mahākaccāyana (known for his handsomeness). The story goes that Sorreya, who was married and had two children, saw Mahākaccāyana on the road. He wished that the arahant should either become his wife or that his wife's skin should somehow look like the golden skin of the arahant. This wish led him to be magically transformed from a man to a woman. He was shocked by this spontaneous sex-change and ran away to hide in the forest. Later living as a woman with beautiful skin led her/him to being married (as a woman) to a treasurer's son, bearing two children with him, and living a comfortable life. When s/he meets Mahākaccāyana again years later, s/he transforms back into a man. He decides to become a monk, apparently to be closer to the true object of his attraction, Mahākaccāyana, a male arahant. The desire for a spouse with golden skin and the love s/he experienced in her/his previous two marriages is not criticized. Indeed, Mahākaccāyana seems to reward him for it and he gains arahantship because his previous merits allowed him to have two marriages and two sets of children (as a man and as a woman) in one lifetime and be detached from both situations.

In Southeast Asia, there are several extra-canonical Pāli *jātakas* from the so-called *Paññāsa (Fifty) Jātaka* collection(s) and *jātaka*-like vernacular stories circulated among the Shan, Khoen, Lue, Lao, Burmese, Khmer, Mon, and Thai language communities that speak highly of marriage. A few examples will suffice to make this point. In the *Akkharalikhita Jātaka* (*Birth Story of the One Who Writes Letters*) we find a long list of the benefits of writing and producing Buddhist texts. Included in this list are the benefits of being a good wife and a good husband. Verses 24, 28, and 29 read:

> those [husbands] who take care of their wives and children ... will be reborn in heaven ... a woman who diligently attends her husband, her parents-in-law, her friends, and other relations, attains to the highest happiness and the foremost position. A woman who is endowed with virtues and is respectful to her husband and others becomes beautiful and is always reborn in heaven.[12]

Later it states that the Buddha, when he was a Bodhisatta in a previous existence, "surpassed all other men of the entire Jampudīpa in beauty and form, and who resembled the Mahābrahmā of the Rūpa world, enjoyed marital happiness with both human females as well as celestial maidens ... having lived to the full extent of his life, after his death he was reborn in heaven."[13] In the *Brahmakumāra Jātaka*, the Buddha, in a previous life, was born as a prince in Benares. At 16 years old he was betrothed to a beautiful princess who "was endowed with every auspicious mark, and she was given to good conduct and good religious practice. She was extremely pleasing to the Bodhisatta."[14] Later, the story makes a point about the auspicious marriage and being born in a good family to emphasize to the reader the importance of associating with good people—a "man becomes worthy by learning the good law from good people."[15] As is seen in many other *jātaka* stories, in the end, it states that the Bodhisatta's wife went on to be reborn as Yasodharā and the Bodhisatta as Gotama. They were linked in the past and remained bound to each other through time.

There are many other examples of praise for marriage in Pāli stories in Southeast Asia. We find even more in stories lauding marriage in vernacular languages that often have the same format as *jātakas* but have no known Pāli equivalent. The Khoen (an ethnic group who largely follow Theravada Buddhism living along the Chinese, Burmese, Thai, and Lao borders) have a great affection for romantic tales. One of the most famous love stories in Khoen is the *Along Chao Sam Lo*. This story relates the story of two rich and beautiful young people who fall in love and conceive an illegitimate child, but they are not permitted to marry by the young man's mother. The young lady, U Piem, and her unborn baby, die from wounds inflicted by the mother. The young man, Sam Lo, commits suicide when he learns of her death.[16] In the *Chao Bun Hlong*, another non-canonical Khoen *jātaka,* there are numerous scenes describing great feelings of passion and lust felt by young women towards one of the heroes, Bun Hlong. Besides this overflowing expression of passion, there are also passages describing undying love between Bun Hlong and the young woman, Bimba.[17] In manuscripts Anatole Peltier copied at monasteries in and around Chieng Tung, there are seven stories that could be called romances, which praise the intense love of the main characters. For example, in the *Ratana Saeng Beu*, a non-canonical *jātaka*, the hero gives up the ascetic life, because he longs for his wife and when he could not find her, he sends a parrot to fly all around the world to deliver love letters to her. When he finds her, her father refuses to give her away in marriage, so the hero attacks the father's kingdom with an army and wins the girl.[18]

One of the best-known stories among the Khoen and other Tai ethnic groups in the region is the *Sujavaṇṇa Wua Luang,* a vernacular *jātaka* composed in Khoen.[19] A short summary of the *Sujavaṇṇa Wua Luang* is as follows: One day the Buddha overhears two monks recounting a story they heard of a woman who became pregnant after drinking the urine of a bull and gave birth to a child who would become a Buddhist monk. The Buddha then uses this occasion to relate the story of himself in a former life when he was the Bodhisatta Sujavaṇṇa. One of Indra's wives, Ummādantī agreed to be reborn in the human realm as long as Indra would assure her that she would be able to marry a future Buddha. Ummādantī was born and one day she went to a great celebration at the palace. She was so beautiful that many princes wanted to become her husband, but the other women were jealous of her and ridiculed her. Ummādantī was ashamed and went to live alone in the forest. There she ended up living with the king of the bulls. He rewarded her loyalty and service to him by building her a miraculous one-pillar palace. Then Indra magically inspired the Bodhisatta, Prince Sujavaṇṇa, to go into the forest to hunt deer. Carrying the sword of victory the prince entered the forest and chased the golden deer who led him to the one-pillared palace. Sujavaṇṇa had no way of climbing the pillar and had to chant a *mantra* to give him the power to reach Ummādantī. Ummādantī allowed Sujavaṇṇa to stay in the palace because he possessed a protective *mantra*. The *mantra* requested that the gods give him power to fly because he had achieved many of the perfections and acquired merit for the sake of reaching Nibbana and escaping the cycle of rebirths. After he had flown up to Ummādantī, she tested him further with riddles involving doctrine, which he answered with skill. The king and queen were worried when their son did not return from his hunting excursion and consulted a *purohita* (a Brahman spiritual advisor and soothsayer), who was knowledgeable in regards to the three Vedas and trained in the use of mystical diagrams (*yantra*) and *mantras*. He told the king through his interpretation of these *yantra* that the prince would return on the eighth day of the crescent moon of the seventh month (which turned out to be correct). Ummādantī and Sujavaṇṇa remained alone in the one-pillared palace for seven days (without marrying) and then flew on a magical horse first to her mother in the city of Rājagaha and then to the parents of Sujavaṇṇa in Jetuttara. They felt obligated to show respect to their parents. The couple was married and had a boy and girl, who in turn married each other. One day Sujavaṇṇa realized that everything was impermanent and decided to become a renunciant.[20] He decided to give up his flesh and his own life to anyone who requested it. He prayed to Indra, Brahma and even hell beings. Then Indra changed into the form of an old Brahmin and asked for Sujavaṇṇa's limbs, which he gave freely. Then Indra returned the limbs to Sujavaṇṇa and Sujavaṇṇa ascended a jeweled throne to preach the word of the Buddha. He gave a sermon about the first noble truth of suffering and instructed people to maintain the Buddhist precepts, listen to sermons and take refuge in the Buddha, the Dhamma, and the Saṅgha. Ummādantī also became a renunciant. They practiced the ascetic exercises together to achieve the perfection of asceticism (*nekkhammapāramī*) and *jhāna* meditation. They were reborn in the 33rd heaven and lived in a jeweled palace.

The writers of the *Sujavaṇṇa Wua Luang* do not mark romantic love as a hindrance to spiritual advancement. Sujavaṇṇa and Ummādantī are depicted as a couple very much in love.[21] Their children which have a sibling marriage also live happily together. In the fifth *phūk* (section) Ummādantī is worried that because she is a daughter of a bull, Sujavaṇṇa will be attracted to the firm-breasted, fully human women and reject her because of her dubious ancestry when they return to the city together. She begs his faithfulness. Sujavaṇṇa assures her that he will only love her. He declares: "*thī rak khot sāi jai nāng yā dai song sai lāi yūang jai fon fūang glā bai ... phī bao liao chāk nong sak an thāe lāe* (my love untie the knots of your heart, give up this intense doubt and that heart of yours which flitters and flutters to and fro ... your man (literally elder brother) will truly not stray away from you even for one instance)".[22] These heartfelt expressions continue for several lines and Sujavaṇṇa states that Ummādantī is more beautiful than all other women and that he loves her ("I see you as greater than all other women ... I love you deeply").[23] Sujavaṇṇa gladly dedicates himself to his princess and promises his faithfulness. This faithfulness is maintained throughout the story. Even after Sujavaṇṇa has sacrificed his eyes and legs and has retreated to the ascetic life in the forest, he still feels attachment for his wife. He worries about her being left alone in the world and takes her with him into the forest to live as a renunciant.[24] They live there until both are freed from mental defilements (*kilesa*) and passed away together and are reborn as husband and wife in heaven. This is truly an undying love!

Jaini has pointed out the prevalence of these themes in the *Paññāsa Jātaka* collections. For example, he acknowledges Madame Terral, who published an edition of the Khmer/Thai version of the *Samuddaghosa jātaka* from the *Paññāsa Jātaka*, because her "translation and grammatical notes introduced to scholarship a beautiful love-story not found in the Theravāda canon or its commentaries." The *Paññāsa Jātaka* stories themselves often relate tales of longing and separation of young lovers. For example, the *Sakhapattarāja Jātaka* describes how the Buddha courted his wife Yasodharā in past lives and in one scene Yasodharā, born in the past as Ratanavatī, attempts suicide due to the loss of her lover.[25] The *Sudhanukumāra Jātaka*, Jaini notes, is very similar to the well-known love story of Sudhana and Manoharā, which is performed in plays in Thailand and Burma.[26] The *Lokaneyyapakaraṇam,* a non-canonical *jātaka* also offers what Jaini calls "a startling defense of the superiority of monogamy over polygamy. [This] is the only place in Pali literature where a Bodhisatta refuses to accept the king's offer of a royal princess for a second wife."[27] He was not familiar with the Sujavaṇṇa story or vernacular Buddhist literature in Southeast Asia, so we cannot fault him for not noticing the support of monogamy in Southeast Asian vernacular Buddhist literature. What is important is that marriage and monogamy was a value promoted by some Southeast Buddhist narratives and some of these non-canonical *jātakas* can be read as stories of dedicated love.[28]

Maddī and Vessantara

I have had a great pleasure of watching many performances (which includes Pali chanting, vernacular Thai chanting, and a dramatic performance of the story) of the *Vessantara Jātaka* in Thailand, or as it is called there—*Mahachat kham luang* or *Mahawessandon Chadok* or by the name of the larger annual performance and chanting of the story—*Thet mahachat* that is part of the larger national celebration—often called the *Bun Phra Wet.* I want to note that if a person had never read the older Pali telling of this story (which most Thai people have not) they might assume from the dramatic performance that it is more about the love between Maddī and Vessantara than about the value of giving (*dāna*). Indeed, the most popular sections of the story are about Maddī and Vessantara living in the forest with their children and the suffering experienced by both when Vessantara gives their children away to Jūjaka. It is an ethical Buddhist narrative, but it is also an emotionally wrenching love story—love between a woman and a man and their dedication to their children.

The love between Maddī and Vessantara is complex and often infuriating. In both Pali and Thai tellings Vessantara is portrayed as being infatuated with Maddī's beauty. For example, in at least 40 verses Maddī's physical beauty is described and she is often introduced in various parts of the story as the Princess Maddī, "on whose every limb sat beauty..." [Pali: sabbaṅgasohanā].[29] Moreover, her family and even Vessantara's own mother considers her almost too good for Vessantara. There is a very long passage begging Maddī not to go with her children into the forest exile with Vessantara (CG 27). Vessantara agrees that the forest is no place for his wife and children and that they would miss the comforts of court life and be attacked by insects, wild beasts, and disease. However, Maddī will hear nothing of it. She emphatically tells his parents: "I would not wish for any joy that was without my Vessantara." Then she offers a speech about the duties of a wife:

> A woman obtains a husband by many kinds of behavior; by holding her figure with corsets and stays of cowbone [Pali: bahuhi vata cariyāhi kumāri vindate patiṃ udarassuparodhena gohanubbeṭhanena ca] by tending the sacred fires, by sweeping out water ... a river without water is bare ... and bare and defenceless is a woman who is a widow ... that woman is honoured who shares the poverty of her husband as well as his riches ... I will follow my husband always, wearing the yellow robes, for without Vessantara I would not want even the whole earth ... [W]hat sort of heart have they got, those callous women who can wish for their own comfort while their husbands are suffering? (CG 29-30)

While it could be argued that Maddī was more afraid of being a widow than loving her husband, she could have stayed in comfort in the palace without fault according to the king and queen. Moreover, as the story progresses her love for Vessantara is obviously not simply because of social pressure. Maddī shows her continued love and dedication by collecting their food and water taking care of the children. She never complains, even when her husband is callous and unfeeling. For example, one night Maddī has a dream in which her limbs are severed, her eyes dug out, and breast split open by a Brahmin (man wearing saffron robes and a red flower garland). She wakes up in panic and goes to see Vessantara. They do not sleep together because Vessantara has regulated the "proper" times for them to be alone and warned her against "improper desire." He says to her "Why have you broken our agreement?" (CG 54). To which she responds "[M]y lord, it is not improper desires which bring me here, but I have had a nightmare." She told him and although he knew what the dream meant, as he had earlier that day agreed to give his children away to the Jūjaka as servants (for Jūjaka's young wife Amittatāpanā), he pretended as if he did not know. He dismissed her dream and made her feel silly. The next morning he tricks her to staying away from the hut and the children while he happily gave their children away (CG 55). The children beg for him to wait for their mother to come home before he gives them away, but he ignores their tears. Later he does show an emotional attachment to his children and is described as "trembling like a rutting elephant seized by a maned lion, or like the moon caught in the jaws of Eclipse, his feelings unable to bear it, he went into the leaf-hut with eyes full of tears" (CG 62). Later, "tears that were drops of blood poured from his eyes. Realizing that such pain overcame him because of a flaw in him, his affection, and for no other reason, and certain that affection must be banished and equanimity developed, he plucked out that dart of grief" (CG 65). However, the feeling he shows over the loss of his children, is not shown to his wife. While Maddī was returning to the hut, a trip that was magically delayed by the interference of Indra [discussed below], she declares to wild beasts who have blocked her way "I am the wife of that glorious prince who was exiled, and I shall never desert him, just as the devoted Sītā never deserted Rāma" (CG 67). Vessantara is no Rāma it seems, subject to proclamations of love. Even though she implores him to tell her what happened to the children. He remains silent and allows her to believe that her children have been killed by animals. She cries out "This is worse pain. I feel a wound like the tearing of a dart, because today I do not see my children ... this is a second dart which shatters my heart: today I do not see my children, and you will not speak to me." Then, she threatens suicide: "O Prince, if tonight you do not explain to me, in the morning you will surely see me dead, all life gone" (CG 69). When he finally speaks, he does not tell her what happened to the children. Instead he suggests that it is her fault that they are missing. He states coldly:

> Indeed, Maddī, famous princess of lovely hips, you went out this morning to gather food. Why have you returned so late this evening?... You are beautiful and attractive, and in the Himālayan forests live a lot of people like ascetics and magicians. Who knows what you have been doing.... Married women do not behave like this, going off into the forest leaving young children. You did not so much as ask yourself what was happening to your children or what your husband would think (CG 70).

After this callous and unfounded accusation, Maddī finally stands up for herself. She explains the reason for the delay and the wild beasts that surrounded her.[30] Then she asserts "I look after my husband and children" and then tells Vessantara about the gifts of flowers and fruit she gathered in the forest for the children and him. However, she returns to self-blame and states that she must have "offended wandering ascetics somewhere in the world, Brahmins, virtuous and learned men, aiming for a life of restraint, for today I cannot see my children" (CG 71). Vessantara remains callous, continues to allow her to blame herself and stays silent as she wanders around looking for her children. However, his love for Maddī finally overwhelms his stoic resolve when he sees her collapse on the ground in grief. He "trembling at the thought that she was dead, the Great Being was filled with deep grief at the idea that Maddī had died ... when he placed his hand on her heart he felt warmth, and so he brought water in a jar, and although he had not touched her body for seven months, the strength of his anxiety forced all consideration for his ascetic state from him, and with eyes filled with tears he raised her head and held it on his lap, and sprinkled her with the water. So he sat, stroking her face and her heart. After a little while Maddī regained consciousness and rose" (CG 73).

Then Vessantara admitted to her what he had done. She forgives him when she hears about the miraculous act of generosity. She understood his need to perfect giving and non-attachment so much so that when Indra came the next day disguised as another Brahmin and asked Vessantara for his wife, he gave her and she freely agreed. The final act of generosity led to Indra giving Maddī back to Vessantara immediately stating "My lord, I give you back your wife Maddī, in whose every limb sits beauty. You belong with Maddī, and Maddī belongs with her husband. Just as milk and a conch-shell are alike in colour, so you and Maddī are alike in heart and thoughts" (CG 78). He grants the loving couple eight wishes and along with a long life, desires to be a just and charitable king, he wishes: "may I be faithful to my own [wife]."[31]

Obviously this is not a simple story about a king who turns ascetic and gives away his wealth, his power, his children, and his wife. Vessantara doesn't act without some regret. His wife does not easily accept his actions. They both struggle emotionally with their own decisions. They are apprehensive and unsure with how to act towards each other caught between uncontrollable love for each other and their children and the determination to be detached ascetics. They are bound to each other even though they both realize how much pain attachment can cause. Without this emotional struggle, which is emphasized in dramatic performances in Southeast Asia, the gifts of Vessantara and the understanding and loyalty of Maddī would not seem as difficult. Any parent or spouse understands the pain that love causes. This story is as much about marriage and children as it is about the importance of equanimity and giving. In the end, of course, Vessantara and Maddī live happily as a married couple and their children are returned to them. The value of the family, in the end, is celebrated. Indeed, it is celebrated in Southeast Asia in art, drama, and literature, as much as (if not, arguably more) the life of the Buddha, who, of course, does not return to his wife and son. Marriage is neither condemned nor seen as unproblematic, but the struggles that come with it, are acutely acknowledged and displayed.

Indeed, the struggles that occur in marriage are not simply shown between Maddī and Vessantara. Vessantara's parents, Queen Phusatī and King Sañjaya, are seen as struggling with their decisions as a couple to exile their son and daughter-in-law to protect the health of the kingdom and their own royal household. Jūjaka and Amittatāpanā also have marriage problems. Indeed, without them, Vessantara would not have been given the chance to make the ultimate gift of giving away his children and his wife. Jūjaka seems reluctant to look for servants for his wife, but she presses him because she is mocked by the other wives in the village for marrying a poor and ugly husband. To save face, she needs to have servants. The importance of this aspect of the story is emphasized in the Thai tradition. In the most common Thai vernacular telling of the *Vessantara Jātaka* the scene of the women mocking Jūjaka's wife is expanded extensively. In the Pali telling, this scene is quite short and simply contains 12 verses in which a group of women poke fun at Jūjaka's wife for being so obedient to an old man. There is only a subtle mention of the lack of romance and sex in their relationship. However, this scene in Thai tellings depicts the women as much more vicious in their verbal attacks.[32] This expanded scene is featured on murals and paintings. One notable addition is seen in a Thai cloth painting. The painting shows several women ridiculing the wife of the elderly Brahmin Jūjaka. The painting is quite bawdy. The women are depicted groping each other, dancing, and holding long wooden phalluses (dildos). Many are half-naked pretending to penetrate each other vaginally in various positions. This kind of explicit sexual display is not mentioned in the Pali text, but must have offered some shock and delight to the late nineteenth-century audiences of the painting, as well as showed the difficult social situation in which both Amittatāpanā and Jūjaka found themselves.[33] Indeed today there is a popular protective amulet in Thailand of Jūjaka (Thai: Chuchok). The amulet is usually in the form of a decrepit old man with a long beard hunched over and walking with a cane. This small wooden or metal amulet is supposed to bring much merit to his owners since, on the one hand, Jūjaka was able to get everything he asked for including a young and pretty wife, and on the other hand, without his requests, Vessantara would have never been able to perform his final acts of giving without Jūjaka.[34]

Conclusion

If we look at the *Vessantara Jātaka* as not simply a story about making merit and perfecting the art of giving and see it as part of a larger genre of stories about marriage, we can learn a lot about how an ascetic religion that promotes celibacy and monastic life communicates with a larger population who chooses to support the institutions and ideals of marriage and children. Murals, dramas, poems, and reliefs in Southeast Asia often celebrate love and loyalty between married couples. They depict the struggles couples go through to stay together and raise children. While women are often depicted in a submissive role, there are many stories in which husbands are devoted to their families. As we saw, religious quests for merit do not necessarily necessitate the abandonment of marriage and family. When the choice is made to no longer participate in family life and romantic love, this is not depicted as an easy decision anyway. One may not be able to realize enlightenment while married and attached to spouse and children, but this may not mean that they can't cultivate merit and Buddhist virtues. Indeed, in Southeast Asian's most popular narrative, the *Vessantara Jātaka*, it is described as the ultimate sacrifice, and without his family Vessantara would not have been able to perfect his practice of generosity. The study of marriage in its Buddhist context in Southeast Asia has not, to date, been a subject of much study or debate. When it is mentioned, marriage is described by scholars as something to be abandoned and marriage ceremonies are described as an irritating duty for monks to perform for the lay masses who haven't woken up the dangers of attachment. However, in narratives, both Pali and vernacular, marriage is not a problem to be ignored or an institution to be condemned, but a very worthy subject on which to write and ruminate. Indeed, as a popular Thai saying suggests, Buddhist monasticism is seen as not incompatible with marriage, but as a precondition for it. "Buat gon biat" loosely translates as "a man should be a monk in order to be fit for marriage" or more literally—"the experience ordination (and monastic life) is an appropriate precondition before pressing your body against another." Men in Thailand are often described as *dip* (raw) until they have ordained. Women should not trust a man to be a good husband if he has not been ordained for a short period (usually three months or one rainy season is an ideal) before getting married. Monkhood "cooks" a man and prepares him for the restraint and the dedication needed to be a good husband. Perhaps this is how we should think about reading Buddhist stories in which these two institutions, monkhood/asceticism and marriage/family are featured, not as foes, but complimentary, even necessary paths towards self- and other-awareness.

Notes

1 See Ja II 27. Note: I have geared the transcription system to a general audience without advanced skills in Pali, Thai, or Sanskrit. For Thai, I follow with a few exceptions the Royal Institute's *Romanization Guide for the Thai Script* (Bangkok, April 1968) which also elides most diacritical marks for easy reading. This closely follows international library standards. Pali transcription is now relatively consistent internationally. I follow the standard CPD (Helmer Smith, *Critical Pali Dictionary, Epilogomena to Vol. I*, Copenhagen, 1948) used by the Pali Text Society. I have not translated the title of most Pali texts I referred to into English because near every title is a personal name. For example, the *Nimi Jātaka* would translate as the "Birth Story of Nimi." This is also largely the case for the Tai Khoen and Thai texts titles I provide. Translating the titles would be redundant.

2 Ja I 190.

3 Ja IV 11. See also Ja I 61. The term, *rāga*, commonly translated as "passion," is universally an unskillful (*akusala*) quality in a person and is supposed to hamper spiritual advancement. It is often found in a triad with *dosa* (aversion) and *moha* (delusion).

4 Ja IV 314-325.

5 Ja III 250.

6 See for example the Pv-a VI 54-56.

7 Even though there have not been many publications to date and the subject is not covered in any major textbook on Buddhism, over the past few years there has been a growing interest in Buddhist monastic marriage and family life among Buddhist Studies scholars, especially in Japanese Buddhist Studies. Monastic marriage has a complicated and controversial history. While, institutional status and acceptance of marriage for some priests, nuns, and monks in Nepal, Korea, and Japan is beyond the scope of this chapter, for those interested in the subject of the acceptance of marriage as an institution permitted for monks, nuns, and priests, see Alan Cole, "Buddhism," in *Sex, Family, and Marriage in World Religion*, ed. Don Browning, Christian Green, and John Witte (New York: Columbia University Press, 2006), pp. 299–366; Stephen Covell, *Japanese Temple Buddhism* (Honolulu: University of Hawai'i Press, 2005); Richard Jaffe, *Neither Monk nor Layman: Clerical Marriage in Modern Japanese Buddhism* (Princeton: Princeton University Press, 2000). Shayne Clarke also discusses the issue of marriage, children, and family life in early Indian Buddhism extensively in his book *Family Matters in Indian Buddhist Monasticisms* (Honolulu: University of Hawai'i Press, 2013). I thank him for sending me an advanced copy of the book. Anne Hansen is presently working on a project about love and passion in Cambodian Buddhism and Southeast Asian Buddhist texts more broadly.

8 See Chutima Chunhacha, ed., *Chut chitakam faphanang nai prathet Thai Wat Khongkharam* (Bangkok: Muang Boran, 2537 [1994]) and Sanitsuda Ekachai, "Thailand's Gay Past," *Bangkok Post*, 23 February 2008, p. 1. See also No Na Paknam's historical introduction to the temple and the special issue on Wat Khongkaram in *ASA: Journal of the Association of Siamese Architects* 3, 1 (2517 [1974]: esp.

pp. 19–52), with contributions from Nit Ratanasanya among others. I thank Donald Swearer for giving me a copy of this last source. A very similar story is found in the *Dhammapada-Atthakathā* (Dhp-a 8.3). However, here the husband plots to kill his wife by throwing her off a cliff. She uses this treacherous plan against him and is able to throw him off the cliff. She is lauded for her actions and becomes a *bhikkhunī*.

9 Santi Phakdikham has shown that the walls of one monastic building can have paintings of a canonical *jātaka*, while the paintings on the doors of the room can have paintings from non-canonical *jātakas* and other local romance stories that have little to do with Buddhist teachings or religion in general like the romance story of *Sangthong*. Santi Phakdikham, "Chitakam wanakhadi Thai nai phra ubosot Wat Ratchaburana," *Muang boran* 33, 3 (2550 [2007]): 78–92. See also Stuart Robson and Prateep Changchit, "The Cave Scene or Bussaba Consults the Candle," *Bijdragen tot de Taal-, Land- en Volkenkunde* 155, 4 (1999): 585.

10 Dhp-a 8.12; 8.13. See also different versions of their stories along with 38 other female sages (*Therī*) in the *Paramatthadīpanī VI*. A partial English translation is available: William Pruitt, trans., *The Commentary on the Verses of the Therīs* (Oxford: Pali Text Society, 1998).

11 Dhp-a 3.9. For an English translation see Burlingame, *Buddhist Legends*, vol. 2, pp. 23–7.

12 Padmanabh Jaini, *Apocryphal Birth-Stories*, vol. II (London: Pali Text Society, 1986), p. 204.

13 Ibid., p. 205.

14 Ibid., p. 185.

15 Ibid.

16 See Anatole-Roger Peltier, ed., *Along Chao Sam Lo* (Chiang Mai-Paris: L'École française d'Extrême-Orient, 1988).

17 See Anatole-Roger Peltier, ed., *Chao Bun Hlong* (Chiang Mai-Paris: L'École française d'Extrême-Orient, 1992).

18 See Anatole-Roger Peltier, *La Litterature Tai Khoeun* (Chiang Mai: L'École française d'Extrême-Orient, 1989), pp. 227–8.

19 I discuss this story extensively in my "Creative Engagement: The *Sujavaṇṇa Wua Luang* and Its Contribution to Buddhist Literature," *Journal of the Siam Society* 88 (2000): 156–77.

20 Anatole-Roger Peltier, ed., *Sujavaṇṇa Wua Luang* (Chieng Tung: Wat Tha Kradas, 1993), p. 174.

21 See Anatole-Roger Peltier, *Kalasa Grua Dok* (Chiang Mai: L'École française d'Extrême-Orient, 1990), introduction. He notes that romance is one of the most dominant subjects of all Khoen literature.

22 Peltier, *Sujavaṇṇa*, p. 126.

23 Ibid., p. 128.

24 Peltier, *Sujavaṇṇa*, ch. 7.

25 Jaini, *Apocryphal Birth-Stories*, vol. I, pp. 100–28.

26 Ibid., vol. II, xviii and vol. I, pp. 129–59. See also Andrew Rotman's new translation of the *Divyāvadāna* [*Divine Stories: Translations from the Divyāvadāna, part 1* (Boston: Wisdom Publications, 2008)] which recounts many love stories popular in South Asian Buddhist literature.

27 Jaini also points out another story in the *Lokaneyyapakaraṇam* in which the author states that one of the main characters should not be faulted for being sexually promiscuous. See Jaini, *Apocryphal Birth-Stories*, vol. I, pp. 32–3.

28 We cannot say that monogamy was a value of the Khoen people in general. In fact there are numerous narratives in Khoen which mention men having two or more wives and they are not criticized for this practice. See manuscripts 16, 135, 188, and 202 of Peltier, *La Litterature Tai Khoeun*. Furthermore, there is no extensive ethnographic material available about Khoen marriage patterns.

29 Gombrich and Cone's translation of *sabbaṅgasohanā* is literally correct. *Aṅga* does mean "limb;" however, it might translate into contemporary English better as "whose beauty was flawless" or colloquially as "who was beautiful from head to toe."

[30] This section of the story is greatly expanded in several Thai versions. In those versions Maddī is confronted by ascetics and magicians in the forest and they try to rape her. However, she is saved by Indra who sends "fruit-maidens" to protect her. Fruit maidens or "makkaliphon" or "nariphon" are a well-known part of Thai folklore. The source of the story undoubtedly comes from a scene in the *Wessandon chadok*, in which, while in exile in the Himavanta Forest, Prince Vessantara's wife Maddī finds 16 Makkali Trees on which, instead of fruit, hang small beautiful women (Pali: *makkaliphala*). Scenes from the Himavanta forest are popular in Thai mural painting and many people I have spoken with seem to know this story both within the context of the Vessantara story and from other stories as well. It is believed that these trees were miraculously planted by Indra (Sakka) to distract men so that Maddī would be safe in the forest gathering water and food for her family. If a man, usually depicted as a Brahmin ascetic or Chinese medicine man in murals, picked and had sex with a fruit maiden, he would lose all of his magical and virile powers. Maddī is protected by the tree as she does not desire the female fruit. In Singburi Province there is another type of corpse display. Luang Pho Charan is the abbot of the large *vippassanā* meditation centre at Wat Ampawan. He is well-known as a person with the power to grant wishes in Central Thailand. He has put on display two corpses of "fruit maidens" at the nearby Wat Prangmuni. These fruit maidens are about eight inches long, have grayish leathering skin, and he claims that they were given to him by an ascetic in Sri Lanka in 1972. Luang Pho Charan claims that these fruit maidens are real and that when they fall to the earth and shrivel up, they can be collected by human beings. He claims that he was given two while on pilgrimage in Sri Lanka. Only ascetics of certain powers are able to enter the Himavanta Forest where the Makkali Trees grow. Today at Wat Prangmuni visitors can hold the dried up corpses which do indeed look like young girls with stems coming out of their heads; however, they certainly look like carved pieces rather than organic. They are kept on a small pillow and surrounded by gifts of flowers. Holding these corpses of mythical beings is believed to grant a person good luck, especially with love. In August 2011, I was able to acquire two fruit-maidens from an amulet dealer in Bangkok. Interestingly enough, male fruit "maidens" are also available now.

[31] Steven Collins has worked on the subject of adultery in Pali literature. He also makes a note in regards to monogamy, see particularly, note #3 from his article in the *Journal of the Pali Text Society* ("On the Third Precept: Adultery and Prostitution in Pali Texts," vol. XXVIII, Festschrift for K.R. Norman, 2007) where he writes: "Many texts praise monogamy for man and wife, in deed and thought, as a virtue; see, e.g., the *Suruci Jātaka* (Ja IV 314ff), which contains the very widespread motif that jealousy of one's co-wives (*sapattiyo*) is one of the sufferings particular to women. A man is urged not to visit other men's wives; women are encouraged not even to think of other men (e.g., D III 190 with Sv 955). See also DPPN s.v. for the story of Nakulapitā and his wife."

[32] See, for example, the *Mahawessandon chadok chabap 13 kan* published by the Department of Education in Thailand. It has gone through 15 printings to date and is easily found in Thai libraries. In this edition, the section on the mockery of Amittatāpanā by the other Brahmin wives takes up over 14 pages of text in the form of an extended *vohāra*-style gloss of the Pali verses.

[33] I appreciate Forrest McGill taking his time to show me this painting at the Asian Art Museum. See E.W. Cowell, ed., *The Jātaka or Stories of the Buddha's Former Births*, vol. VI (Cambridge: Cambridge University Press, 1907), p. 271. Naked women are not limited to cloth paintings and are found on prominent royal temple murals like those at Wat Pathumwanaram, Wat Rakhang, among others.

[34] Arthid Sheravanichakul recently gave a talk on the popularity of the Jūjaka amulets in Thailand at the European Association of Southeast Asian Studies Conference in Gothenburg, Sweden (28 August 2010). I thank him for the conversations about these amulets.

5

The Bird in the Corner of the Painting: Some Problems with the Use of Buddhist Texts to Study Buddhist Ornamental Art in Thailand*

Traditionally the study of Buddhist art tries to relate the sources of the art, whether it be a painting of a Bodhisattva or a statue of a hell being, to its source in a Buddhist text, preferably a really old text in a classical language. As a scholar trained in Pali and Sanskrit who works on Buddhist manuscripts in Laos and Thailand, I often get asked by art historians, usually friends and colleagues that I have met over the years and occasionally by a curator, student, or collector of Southeast Asian art, to provide them with some information on the textual origins for objects, characters, and ornamental features they have seen on pieces of Buddhist art. Sometimes they are figures in illuminated manuscripts or animals depicted on murals or particular characters on bas-reliefs or sculpted architraves. Sometimes I can identify the character or object in question with ease, other times I am stumped and consult texts at my disposal or ask others for help. Often times the art historian, curator, or collector has already identified the "main story" of the mural or relief, usually a *jātaka* or scene from the life of the/a Buddha but is bothered by certain elements in the particular piece that seems out of

* Originally appeared as "The Bird in the Corner of the Painting: Problems with the Use of Buddhist Texts to Study Buddhist Ornamental Art in Thailand," *Moussons: Recherches en sciences sociales sur l'Asie de Sud-Est* 23 (2014): 21–53.

Window shutters decorated with painted birds of various sorts at Wat Ratchaorot in the Phasi Chaloen Section of Bangkok/Thonburi. Photo by author.

place. The questions often go something like: "I think the green figure in the corner with the pointed crown is Indra and the figure sitting next to the Buddha is Ananda, but I can't figure out who the person peeking over the wall in the upper register is," or "I understand that this scene is probably drawn from the *Temiya-jātaka*, but why is there a kinnari in the scene?" or "why is a Chinese merchant painted in a scene that was supposed to take place in India?" or "does the tree carved behind the Buddha image indicate that this image is supposed to represent Siddhārtha Gautama or Dīpaṅkara?" or "what does this type of flower represent?" I love these types of questions. It is a gift of a mystery that arrives in my e-mail inbox when I get to my office. It usually leads to a fun back and forth with the questioner trying to decipher the story and identify all of its textual sources. In general, I think trying to discover what a piece of Thai art refers to textually, what message or lesson (whether historical and descriptive or ethical and didactic) is a productive exercise. These questions linking text to art have also given me the privilege of getting to know many art historians and art enthusiasts who have exposed me to an entire side of Buddhist Studies I neglected for far too long.

As I became interested in Buddhist art more seriously, soon roles reversed. I started being one of the many people trained in Buddhist texts, particularly Pali texts, that assisted specialists in art, but soon became a person trained in texts that was sending my own queries to art historians about the paintings I encountered while translating manuscripts or on the walls of the monasteries where I was conducting interviews with monks and nuns. More and more I encountered paintings, mosaics, and reliefs where I could not identify the exact textual source and I did not know where to turn. The best textual scholars, art historians, curators, and even long-term monastics were not able to help. Like a drinking problem, what used to be a fun pastime slowly turned towards anxiety and frustration. I couldn't just put the art down even though it wasn't giving me any answers or solving any of my problems. Texts were only taking me so far.

The problem became particularly acute when I started what I thought was a relatively harmless investigation into birds as depicted in Siamese/Thai Buddhist art. It all started when I was reading a short description of King Chulalongkorn's coronation in 1868. I learned that two books were published for that occasion and given to him as special gifts. One described the ten avatars of the God Vishnu, perhaps strange considering Chulalongkorn was a Buddhist king of a Buddhist kingdom; however, not strange if you realize that Thai kings are usually seen as both Buddhist Bodhisattvas and representatives of Vishnu on Earth. The other was about birds. This second book was apparently chosen above new editions of Buddhist canonical or commentarial texts, chronicles of past Siamese monarchs, royal law codes, great Sanskrit epics, stories of Indra, Śiva, or Avalokiteśvara, and important ethical and philosophical treatises. Printed books were still quite rare in 1868 in Siam and why would the efforts of printing one to present to a king be wasted on birds? There isn't much evidence that King Chulalongkorn was particularly fascinated with bird watching, ornithology or animal folklore. However, it started to dawn on me that if one takes a stroll around the great eighteenth- and nineteenth- century monasteries and palaces of Bangkok, s/he will find statues and paintings of birds virtually everywhere. They form a permanent backdrop for Thai religion, art, and literature. Indeed, throughout the history of mainland Southeast Asian culture we find stories of birds in manuscripts, murals, and reliefs. Stories of birds and human-bird hybrids abound in Buddhist and Hindu literature popular in Southeast Asia. Naturally, I resorted to my addiction and started looking for the textual sources of this bird art. Big mistake.

Why Ornamental Art?

Every monastery regardless of lineage, sect, or region has ornamental elements, but they have been ignored in favor of studies of ritual activity or institutional history. It is striking that the monks in the Theravada school of Buddhism, known for their orthodox attention to the Vinaya, eschewal of material luxury, and austerity of monastic practice, dress, and comportment, are also the purveyors and stewards of some of the most lavish (if not gaudy) monasteries in the Buddhist world. There is hardly a monastery, even a forest monastery in the region that could be called aesthetically austere. There are gold images, flowers, incense, posters, amulets, intricate murals, packed altars, signs nailed to trees with ethical maxims and advertisements, and large amounts of food, reading material, and paraphernalia found at thousands of Thai monasteries. Monks are neither hapless victims of the crude materialism of modern society nor the overwhelmed recipients of the arbitrary gifts of overzealous merit-makers too lazy or ignorant to meditate or read ethical and philosophical texts. Monks often promote, encourage, and explicitly advertise occasions to not only give gifts to their monasteries, but also distribute objects to their followers.[1] Part of the gifts ordered by patrons and monks are decorative elements added or restored on the monastic grounds. For example, Phra Thammakittiwong, the abbot of Wat Ratchaorot in Bangkok personally oversaw the restoration of the bird paintings on the window shutters between 2006 and 2011. My own abbot in rural Northeast Thailand along the Lao and Cambodia border, in 1995, personally drew the plans for a new chedi (reliquary) including its floral and bird decoration.[2] Whole committees of monks work with local artisans to add decoration to their monasteries on a daily basis. They might offer sermons, perform funerals, and meditate, but they are also often amateur interior designers and landscape architects.

The study of the ornament arts, dance, drama, and non-explicitly religious poetry, has not excited folks in Buddhist Studies even though, visually Buddhist monasteries are highly decorated throughout Asia, and have decoration (often depicting birds and other animals) that rivals, if not surpasses, the greatest palaces in the region.[3] Manuscript chests are often highly decorated with birds and other natural designs, the architraves, columns, murals, sermon chairs, platforms of Buddha statues, etc. abound with birds of various colors flying among trees and over oceans.[4] In the nineteenth and early twentieth centuries kings, poets, artists, dancers, and sculptors were interested in birds, foreign scholars of Southeast Asia were too. However, these studies dried up over the last 80 years and there have been few precious serious studies of Thai theatre, music, and non-explicitly Buddhist literature by anyone trained or teaching Buddhist Studies. What happened? In many ways, it is the nature of modern scholarly disciplines and the rise of the professional scholar of religious and Buddhist Studies. Many foreigners and local scholars who studied humanistic endeavors like art, literature, ritual, drama, or clothing were not writing dissertations, trying to earn tenure, earn research fellowships, and other standard activities of the academy. They were members of various noble families, dilettantes, collectors, amateur botanists, big game hunters, missionaries, tutors, colonial officials, Buddhist monks, surveyors, or translators. These producers and documenters of religion and culture are part of the missing history of Southeast Asian Buddhism.[5] Amateurs like James Audubon, often broke and desperate to earn a living, ran around the Southern United States capturing, drawing, and selling paintings of birds, were also running around Siam, Laos, Cambodia, and Burma in the nineteenth century, exploring, doing field sketches, and writing up what they saw. They were trying to make money, collecting, promoting, and observing. There was often little separation between Buddhist and non-Buddhist or secular and religious culture in these early documentary studies and reports. Professional scholars in established disciplines over the past few decades though have developed a habit of intentional selecting of evidence and ignoring of aesthetics, seeing certain parts of a monastery as "religious" and others as "cultural." Culture was left to the art historians and the ethnomusicologists, while scholars of religion believed they were the students of the texts and the "ideas." This is particularly acute in foreign studies of Buddhist life. Encyclopedias and survey texts, especially in the Thai and Indonesian languages for example, include much information on decorative and performative art and drama at monasteries. Indeed, the study of Southeast Asian religion, art, drama, and literature in non-Western languages, until recently, has made little separation between the Buddhist and non-Buddhist cultural expression. In Buddhist monasteries there was little separation, if any, of secular and religious manuscripts and stories—both were held and often together.[6] Now though it is entirely acceptable for a scholar of Southeast Asian Buddhism, especially one trained in the West to study Buddhist texts and admittedly know nothing about drama, decorative arts, music, or dance. On the other hand, art historians might never read extensively in Pali literature or vernacular poetry (although, in my experience, art historians are often trained in Buddhist texts, but textual specialists are not trained in art history). A student of local romance and adventure epics might never read the Abhidhamma and vice versa, even though these knowledge were rarely separated, even at Buddhist monasteries in the past. Indeed, the greatest composer of epic romance and adventure poems in Thai history, Sunthorn Phu, wrote some of his best work as a monk residing at Wat Thepdhitaram. The doyen of Lao Buddhist history and former monk, Mahasila Viravong, wrote actively about both what would be called "secular" and Buddhist art, literature, and drama without much need to separate their study.

This is one of the major reasons why birds and ornamental art in general have been seen but not studied by Buddhist Studies scholars. Birds are ignored, not because of their popularity or beauty or the fact that they are common in Buddhist art and literature, but because they no longer fall within the discipline of religion or religious history, but in Buddhist life they are everywhere, on lintels, as decorative elements in manuscripts (part of a class of images with the unfortunate name—"drolleries"—in European manuscript studies), on the edges of ceremonial skirts, on headdresses and crowns, on tattoos and belt buckles, and flying around the edges of murals. Being ordinary, they are unnoticed as if they were flying above us quickly and then, in a moment, out of sight. Birds are a normal part of European and American life, Buddhist monks are not. Monks are noticed by scholars and birds are not.

Problems

When noticed, the scholar of religious studies retreats to the tried-and-true methods of textual research and textual origins. There are several problems that a textual scholar or a specialist in art history or material culture encounters when trying to link Thai Buddhist art (sculpture, mural paintings, architectural facades and ornamental elements, and illuminated paintings and drawings in manuscripts) to their textual sources. The problems are particularly acute when one tries to decipher the meaning of ornamental art. Is there a meaning to ornamental art? Is there a message in it? Is there a purpose for decorating a manuscript or a mural or a lintel with a particular flower or particular bird over another? Since ornamental art is such a significant feature of Thai Buddhist art, I want to know if a scholar of texts can bring anything to its study. I will try, as systematically as possible to go through these problems briefly and then offer some possible solutions. As an organizing tool and in order to keep this relatively short, I will concentrate on birds in Thai ornamental art since they are features in every type of art and have been for a long time. Some of my comments will be specific to the study of ornamental art and texts, some will suggest broader approaches to Buddhist art in Thailand in general. Simply put, I hope this will help future students of Buddhist texts and/or Buddhist art in Thailand and Southeast Asia more broadly avoid some of the mistakes I have made in the linking of texts to ornament.

Problem One: When Texts aren't Whole Stories and Symbols aren't Referents

Textual scholars like to complain that art historians need their language skills and vast knowledge of Buddhist texts to know the sources of their art. However, this rhetorical (and condescending) move in guise of normative scholarly "due diligence" has the tendency to make art derivative of texts. In my investigation into the near ubiquitous presence of different types of birds in Thai Buddhist art, I initially went through my normal routine of one-by-one trying to associate different birds in Thai Buddhist ornamental art to particular birds found in different Buddhist texts. I also consulted ornithologists, field guides to birds in Thailand and Southeast Asia, and dictionaries of symbols in Buddhist art. I went looking for meaning. However, I quickly discovered that this tells us little about how the birds in art are actually encountered by occupants and visitors to monasteries. I have nearly never found in many years of observation, interviews, and interaction, Buddhist practitioners (including resident nuns and monks) who actually know these textual sources of these birds (and sometimes art in general) or think of them on a regular basis. Birds were seen as beautiful and normative ornamental art, not as something to be "sourced" or deciphered for symbolic meaning or textual origin. Knowing that a particular bird in the corner of a mural painting or on a bas-relief comes from a particular *jātaka* is no more telling that a "fun fact." Sure, some birds and half-human/half-bird hybrids like kinnari and garuda are probably drawn from the *Sudhana Jātaka*, an extra-canonical *jātaka* (*chadok nok nibat*) commonly found in the region.[7] Others are drawn from the *Sivijaya Jātaka*, the *Sussondī Jātaka*, and the Mora Paritta.[8] Most artists, monks, and laity did not and do not read these texts (although the Mora is chanted as a protective text) in the original Pali or Sanskrit, and many haven't encountered the story as a whole in the vernacular. The bird depicted in a particular painting might not be invoking the entire classical text. For example, kinnari are commonly depicted in Thai statuary, murals, framed paintings, and on ornamental door panels and window shutters. However, they are not depicted as characters in a particular story, whether it be the *Sudhana Jātaka* or the *Pakṣī-pakaraṇam*. They are not included in a particular narrative sequence (more on this below) or with other characters in the text. Rebecca Hall, a visiting curator of Thai art at the Walters Museum in Baltimore, sent me two examples of kinnari depicted in nineteenth-century Siamese art. One was a stunning framed painting (*phra bot*) of five kinnari in a forest.[9] The textual sources speak of seven kinnari sisters or a couple—female kinnari and male kinnara—not five. The painting is beautiful but does not point to any known text. The second is found on a gold and black lacquer manuscript chest. One panel features a kinnari and kinnara curled together in a loving embrace. So I thought this must refer to the *Sudhana Jātaka*, but then the other panels on other sides did not continue the story and moreover simply depict several other birds, not mythological hybrid birds, but actual thrushes, peacocks, and finches alongside lions, rabbits, and other animals. Examples like this started to accumulate in the image database on my computer's desktop and in piles of reference works stacked in the corner of my office.

I thought, maybe I shouldn't be looking for a particular text, but a textual trope. I began to assume that this whole manuscript chest might be referring to the Himaphan Forest (Pali: *Himavanta*). This mythical forest in the Himalayan Mountains is the backdrop of many Buddhist and non-Buddhist stories in both Pali and Sanskrit. Indeed, the Pali Dictionary of Proper Names (which is now conveniently online rendering my heavily appended and tattered copy that I lugged around from monastic library to monastic library for years obsolete!) shows how many references that there is to it:

> The name given to the Himālaya. It is one of the seven mountain ranges surrounding Gandhamādana (SNA.i.66).[10] It is 300 thousand leagues in extent (SNA.i.224), with 84 thousand peaks its highest peak being 500 yojanas (SNA.ii.443). In Himavā, are 7 great lakes, each 50 leagues in length, breadth and depth—Anotatta, Kannamunda, Rathakāra, Chaddanta, Kunāla, Mandākinī, and Sīhappapātaka; these lakes are never heated by the sun (A.iv.101; SNA.ii.407; cf. AA.ii.759). From Himavā flow 500 rivers. SNA.ii.437; but according to Mil.114, only ten of these are to be reckoned, the others flowing only intermittently [...].[11]

This definition goes on for another page with nearly 20 more references. I cite it for a reason. I have asked numerous scholars, monks, nuns, and lay people in Thailand if they can tell me which text they think is a particular scene from the Himaphan forest depicted on a door panel, mural, or manuscript painting comes from and they look at me like I'm crazy. The answer is usually (in Thai), "I don't know, it is just the Himaphan Forest, a beautiful place, it is just a place of beauty and many animals." They don't refer to the Manipabbata mountain peak or the *Kunāla Jātaka* or the various rivers that flow out of it. On two occasions, I was told it was the place Prince Vessantara went with his wife and children, but nothing more specific than that. The Himaphan forest is so common a background to paintings, stories, and is the abode to so many animals that it is disconnected from any specific text. It has become like the mysterious forests in medieval European folktales like Hansel and Gretel or Little Red Riding Hood. It is the place where action happens, but no longer tied to a specific forest or a specific textual source in the mind of a reader or an illustrator. A forest is a forest. Buddhist art in Thailand often invokes these backdrops set vaguely somewhere in India usually but the characters and the backdrops often invoke scenes and moments, not specific texts or narrative sequences.

They are not symbols or signs either. Symbols invoke meanings and concepts. They are specific referents to larger ideas. However, the kinnari, thrush or peacock in various settings do not invoke any specific concept as far as I have been able to determine besides the vague notion of beauty and love. Strange concepts to invoke, it might seem, for Buddhists, although I hope to challenge this below. They are also not signs pointing to specific references with specific meanings. They are not to be "read" and do not contain messages in Thailand to the same degree that they supposedly do in Chinese court and temple art, for example. This leads us to the next problem.

Problem Two: Buddhist Art doesn't Necessarily Teach Buddhist Lessons

While there are certainly hundreds of examples of art drawn from *jātakas* (either canonical or apocryphal Southeast Asian *jātakas*), and scenes from the life of the Buddha, often murals in Thailand do not attempt to represent Buddhist narratives or illustrate texts at all or provide symbols invoking Buddhist concepts.[12] This is how art historians working in Southeast Asia often talk about art though—either as visual representations of texts or pedagogical tools for the illiterate masses. Either way they are secondary to texts. They represent a lesser form of traditional learning. Moreover, the birds in art are generally not depicted in a narrative sequence and so the paintings or the sculpture is not an effective visual aid or cue for relating these narratives. I have never witnessed a teacher in a monastery use ornamental features in art to tell a textually-based story. There is also no ethnographic evidence or travel accounts from the past stating that monks ever did this on a regular basis in Thailand. Michael Baxandall and Henry Maguire have tried to show the problems with assuming that text and image are simply two different ways for depicting the same narrative. The former observed that "we [art historians] do not explain pictures, we explain remarks about pictures—or rather, we explain pictures only in so far as we have considered them under some verbal description or specification" (Baxandall 1985: 1, Maguire 2007).[13] Eugene Wang laments the way murals have been unimaginatively studied in China. He notes that modern scholarship on the subject is based on the premise that murals are "pictorial illustrations or derivatives of sutras. Therefore, to make sense of these tableaux is to match them with sutra texts. They are accordingly filed away in our mental cabinet according to the bibliographic taxonomy of sutra sources" (Wang 2005: xiii).[14] The same can be said for scholarship on Thai art.[15] Almost every introduction to a study of murals at a Thai monastery, especially in English, begins with the association of the mural with a particular text.[16] There are studies of Thai painting in particular which completely ignore the particular histories, local contexts, artist biographies of any one set of murals, choosing instead to offer a study which takes examples of murals from many monasteries that depict one text. These often neglect to mention that the particular sets of murals they are drawing evidence from contain scenes from several narratives, some of which are unknown, and may be the product of an artist's own imagination. For example, the doyen of Thai mural painting, Jean Boisselier, bases his analysis of some of the best known Thai mural paintings, almost solely on the way in which they depict Buddhist texts (Boisselier 1976). Uthong Prasatwinicchai's two-volume study of the murals of the last ten *jātakas* offers a long introduction on the texts, but very little on the artists who painted the murals. Furthermore, he draws examples of murals of the ten *jātakas* from monasteries like Wat Ban Takhu, Wat Khao Yisan, Wat Mahathat (Petchaburi), among many others whose histories and styles are not related. The only thing that links them is the choice of *jātaka* to represent. The grouping of these murals is the choice of Uthong, not the artists who painted these murals originally and may not have seen themselves as part of a movement to teach or represent this particular collection (Ringis 1990: 124).

Paintings, mosaics, and reliefs whether they be in frames, carved into lintels, or as wall murals are often not seen as the creators of their own narratives, as texts in themselves. However, some mural sets creatively combine elements from a number of oral and textual sources with the artist or artists' own imagination.[17] For example, in an illuminated manuscript from 1897 held in the Chester Beatty Library in Dublin, Ireland, there is a large manuscript of the Phra Malai story which contains a wide variety of paintings. Some are taken from specific scenes in specific texts, like the Phra Malai visiting two parents. However, in the background there is a ghostly child that is not usually found in the text and seems to suggest a local oral version or perhaps just the particular artist's addition. However, this is one of the only textual references in the entire manuscript. Other illuminated folios include decorative devas, flowers, *asubhakammaṭṭhana* meditation (meditation on human corpses), a scene with four men fighting with knives, a scene of a monk (not Phra Malai) speaking with a deva on a city street replete with European street lamps and other eclectic features. There are many other manuscripts like this which contain a seemingly haphazard set of images not connected to the text of the manuscript.[18] The murals in the ubosot of Wat Kongkaram (Ratchaburi Province) are a good example. It was originally a monastery used by the Mon ethnic community in the area and built in the eighteenth century. The murals on the interior walls are drawn from several sections of several different stories. There are scenes from the story of Prince Siddhattha's "Great Departure" into the ascetic life, the *Traibhūmikathā* cosmology, and scenes from various *jātakas*, some included in the last ten, like the *Temiya*, *Suvannasama*, and the *Nimi*. Among these more common *jātakas* is a rendering of erotic and violent parts of the *Cullapaduma* (the 193rd story in the canonical collection). This is a racy story of husbands hacking up their wives, roasting them on a fire, and feasting on their flesh, a Bodhisattva feeding his wife from the blood dripping out of a self-inflicted wound on his knee, and even an erotic scene of a woman having sex with an armless, legless, earless, noseless man. These are combined with scenes of Persian soldiers, the Buddha subduing the evil Mara, and naked, perhaps lesbian and gay, women and men embracing and fondling. These murals form a type of creative anthology. Not only are these stories loosely related, if at all, the choice of scenes to draw from the stories seemed to be based more on the unknown artist's penchant for depicting erotic sexuality than for choosing iconic narrative triggers from each story. Moreover, each scene does not attempt to "faithfully" depict the Indian stories, but sets these Indian characters in scenes with Persian, French, and Mon peoples, as well as cosmopolitan Ayutthayan architecture. The fact that Mon peoples often forbid women from entering their ubosots suggests that this room may have been a type of room for pornographic entertainment. It is not an isolated example though. The artist drew many of the building and dress styles, as well as some of the story choices, not from texts, but from murals at other monasteries like Wat Thong Noppakun (Thonburi), Wat Pakklongbangkaeo (Nakhon Chasi), among others. Therefore, the "texts" the artist was drawing from were not texts in the traditional sense. He was drawing from other murals at other places in Thailand.[19] These murals reference each other; they do not attempt to accurately depict Indic Buddhist stories.

Many muralists and sculptors in Thailand, past and present, are not concerned with teaching or representing a particular text, but instead with executing a vision, creating an atmosphere, and invoking a mood. In reality, although they certainly could have been in the past, they are rarely used today as visual pedagogical tools during sermons. The murals high on the walls are often hard to see and were much harder to see before the age of electric lights. Indeed, I have interviewed many monks and nuns who were unaware what texts or histories the murals at their own monasteries represented. They did not "study" these artworks, nor were they inspired to go and read the texts they supposedly represented or reproduced. Moreover, paintings and reliefs almost never present an entire history or visually executed set of teachings in total or in sequence. In fact, the physical space of the walls or the frame, the artist's own tastes and talents, and the possible lack of textual knowledge of the artists themselves may account for the fact that rarely can a story be reconstructed. There are also paintings seemingly based on texts which add elements not contained in those texts. Therefore, art could either be evidence of textual variants or sites of creative expansion of texts. It is likely that in many cases, the artist was not concerned with reproducing a text in a different medium. In this way, murals have limited value if a monk wants to use them as systematic and sequential visual aids during textual lessons. Thai Buddhist art is evidence of the individual repertoires of particular artists and patrons, they reveal the influences, texts, daily experiences, values, sociohistorical contexts, and teaching lineages unique to them rather than depictions of a known canon of Buddhist texts or Royal histories. Now if this is a problem for murals that depict narratives with human characters, how much more of a problem could it be for the ornamental features of paintings, reliefs, etc.? Can ornament be sourced? In some cases, yes, as we will see below, but in many cases, it is one of the places in art where an artist is free from the weight of direct prototypes and combine many disparate ornamental features into a single piece or even develop new types.

Problem Three: Performance not Text as a Source for Art

Another problem with looking for the textual "origins" of ornamental art that features birds (or trees or animals or particular flowers) is that even if they were at some point placed there by an artist who wanted to or was instructed to make reference to a particular text, the likely source for the text might very well not likely have been a Buddhist text in Pali and either orally delivered as a sermon or encountered in an actual physical manuscript or printed text. Most Buddhists in Thailand past and present did not encounter birds in stories in Pali texts, but through the live performance of vernacular dramas.[20] This is also true of well-known Buddhist characters in Thailand like Phra Malai, Maddi and Prince Vessantara, Phra Sangkhajai, Khun Paen, Sangtong, Phra Lo, and even the historical Buddha. Many of these performances are based on stories of birds and their costumes and sets feature trees, flowers, patterns, designs, and the like. The most popular bird dance is probably that of the female kinnari and male kinnara.[21] Living in the forest flying from tree to tree and delighting in themselves and nature, the couple, especially the kinnari, loved to play a lute and sing. The beauty of their song and dance seems to be the most common way people in Southeast Asia learn the story. Surely, Buddhists in the region, growing up, do not read entire Buddhist stories often, but witness parts of them in sermons, dances, dramas, and murals. Scholars often read whole texts and assume that is what is actually being received, copied, and learned by others. In my experience, it is obvious that certain scenes, characters, tropes, and images from stories are being accumulated over time. For example, Tai Yai/Shan Buddhists in Burma and Northern Thailand sponsor the Kan Fon Nok Kingkala or Kinnari Bird Dance. This dance is highly stylized with elaborate costumes and headdresses made of silk, feathers, gold leaf, and bamboo strips which support silk wings that project out from the dancers' backs. Besides the kinnara and kinnari there are other characters dressed in elaborate forest animal costumes. All of these costumes and the rehearsals for the annual performances take weeks to prepare and children are picked at a young age to learn the dance and become apprentices to masters. The dance which takes years to learn properly is precise in its movements as the dancers must act like two birds amusing and enticing each other. The lead dancer must master 37 poses that mimic the flight of a bird and can be executed at various speeds.[22] The Kan Fon Nok Kingkala dance of the Shan takes place most often at the end of the Buddhist rain retreat in (usually) October and is as large a festival as the ordination ritual which has been extensively studied by scholars. The dance ritual is referred to as Buddhist by Shan Buddhists.

The texts that guide the dance are referred to as *anisong* (Pali: *ānisaṃsa*) which is a Buddhist guide to the advantages or "blessings" of making merit by giving gifts (like the gift of dance) to Buddhist monks. These *anisong* texts are found as manuscripts in monastic libraries throughout the region alongside other Buddhist texts and are not seen as secular in any way. The dance is not only performed at monasteries but is part of a ritual which involves giving lit candles and incense, chanting Buddhist liturgical texts, and prostrating to Buddhist monks and Buddha images. Performers are instructed to meditate (*nang bhavana*) before their performance. Sermons at the beginning of the dance relate a story of the Buddha himself returning from preaching to his deceased mother in the 33rd level of heaven (similar to the story of the first preaching of the Abhidhamma). It is said in these sermons that the Buddha stopped to delight in the Himalayan forests among the kinnara and kinnari. Since the Buddha enjoyed the music and dance of the half-bird/half-humans, the Shan ritual involves not only prostrating to his image, but also to the instruments and costumes. Indeed, not only are Buddhist texts and images honored, but musical instruments, masks, silk wings, and costumes are placed on the altar and presented with gifts and words of gratitude. They are collectively called in "*sing saksit tang buang*" (part of a class of sacred objects) (Sangkham Changyot 2548 [2005]): 12). Moreover, the teachers of the dance and the craftspeople (*nak silipin*) who made the costumes receive prostration and words of praise.[23] The dance is fully part of a Buddhist ritual and not relegated to a "cultural" performance or entertainment. It is referred to as "*mongkhon*" (Pali: *maṇgala*) or auspicious by Sangkham Changyot who has written extensively about the dance in Thai and Shan but has been consulted by scholars of Buddhist Studies. Mongkhon here does not just mean karmically beneficial, but also beautiful and the Buddha is described as delighting in beauty and so the dance, costumes, and music should be beautiful to honor his presence. If ornamental art in a monastery, either in a mural or even on a costume of a dancer, is encountered, it does not invoke a Pali text, but a very different vernacular performance.

This does not merely happen in villages, but even on the stages of National Theatres or on the grounds of royal monasteries in the region, parts of the *Rāmāyaṇa*, *Arjuna Wiwaha*, or the *Romance of the Three Kingdoms* or the *Vessantara Jātaka* are being heard and seen. Indeed, some of the most important dances in Thailand, Laos, and Cambodia feature birds, the most common form being the Manora (often transliterated as Manohra) or the story of Sunthon and Manora. This dance drama is based in narrative form on the Buddhist *Sudhana Jātaka*. Like the Shan kinnari/kinnara dance, it is a love story. It depicts the great love between the Buddha in one of his past lives as the Bodhisattva Prince Sudhana and the most beautiful kinnari in the world—Manora. The dance is quite popular in Southern Thailand and parts of Cambodia and is known in Burma, and Laos as well.[24] Originally it was not considered an inner-court (*lakhon nai*) or royal play, but a play performed outside the palace (*lakhon nok*) often on the grounds of Buddhist monasteries. However, it became popular with the royal family and elite playwrights and choreographers in the 1830s and by the 1950s it was one of the most elaborate royally-sponsored dance dramas in Thailand (Mattani Mojdara Rutnin 1996: 175–9 and 235–9).[25]

Even though the non-elite story of Manora was taken up by the royal court and brought to the grand stage of the National Theatre, the play is still performed often at Buddhist monasteries throughout Laos, Cambodia, and especially Southern Thailand. There are nine forms of Manora (often called simply Nora or Chatri in Southern Thailand). Even though only one of the forms, the Ram Nora Klong Hong, closely follows the *Sudhana Jātaka*, they each involve a lead character as a female bird and all can be performed on the grounds of monasteries as these are often the cleanest and most spacious places to establish stages. The biggest performances, as among the Shan, are performed at the end of the rainy season (Chak Phra in the south or Ook Pansa in Central Thai), one of the biggest Buddhist celebrations in the region. Indeed, what needs to be emphasized here is that the costume designers and set builders and painters for these stages at these monasteries are often the same craftspeople (including Buddhist monks, nuns, and novices) who also help make Buddhist decorative banners, paint Buddhist reliquaries, build altars for Buddha images, and help prepare for a whole range of ritual celebrations. In rural areas, this decorative multi-tasking is normal. I once helped lift a wooden frame of a set for the Manora at Wat Kutithong in rural Ayutthaya and was amazed as to the degree in which the novices and monks and lay people visiting the monastery for religious purposes got involved in helping the dance troupe prepare. They also formed the audience that evening along with throngs of teenagers, food vendors, and dating couples showing off their new motorcycles or cell phones. Often times, public and Buddhist primary and secondary schools involve their students, in classes, decorating sets, sewing costumes, and practicing musical instruments to play at the performance. Many high school courses enlist teenage girls (and some boys) to perform dances at the monasteries. Indeed, when I was a teacher at an all-girls high school in Samut Sakhon in the early 1990s, my students often performed the Manora and other dance dramas at monasteries. They took class time in their "culture" and music courses to work on these performances and designs. Buddhist monks at these monasteries were active participants in staging these events and there seemed to be little notion that these were somehow non-Buddhist activities.[26] In fact, the Manora is drawn from one of the most popular Buddhist narratives in Southeast Asia and is not only the source for the dance performance, but also for sermons and monastic murals.[27] Marlene Guelden in her sadly unpublished PhD dissertation, provides a serious investigation of this performance. She notes the great degree to which Buddhist monks are involved in the ritualization of the performance and its arrangement and production (Guelden 2005).[28] However, this dance, like others, has not been a central subject of research for scholars of Buddhism and despite its appeal and familiarity to all classes and age groups in many parts of Southeast Asia, it remains largely unmentioned in the dozens of studies of monastic life and history in the region in Western languages.

Regardless of how or where it is performed and by whom, these performances do not usually replicate a text, but present iconic scenes like paintings or reliefs. The narrative sequence, the beginning and end of the story is much less important than the design of the costumes, the talent of the dancers, and the quality of the set and sound system. The story isn't presented in full. Moreover, for anyone who has spent anytime attending these performances, they know that the entire stories are far too long to present to a single audience at a single sitting. Even when abridged versions are performed, the stages are often outside, the acoustics are awful, there isn't a ticket counter or a barrier closing off the performance from other activities at the monastery or public park. People come in and out, children play, people talk on cellphones, eat, have picnics, leave in the middle, laugh and joke, and the like. Getting to a proper seat in time for the performance, silencing one's cellphone, listening attentively, is just not the culture of these performances. In murals and manuscript illustrations scenes of monastic festivals and performances are relatively easy to find. They show that this culture of performance was common in the pre-modern period as well. Moreover, many scenes and songs performed on stage take on the "medley" form. Students from particular schools form dance troupes that train in different regional dances that when combined on stage form a medley of northeastern style "ram wong," southern style "nora," dances etc. The best scenes, the favourite songs are taken from various traditions and combined in one performance. Narrative sequence, textual allegiance, ethical message, and historical lesson are either secondary to beauty and form or neglected altogether.

Problem Four: Monastic Art doesn't Always Draw from Buddhist Texts

Any tourist to the Grand Palace or the famous Wat Pho in Bangkok will see that non-Buddhist texts like the *Rāmāyaṇa* or the Javanese *Inao* are prominently featured in relief and mural painting on the walls of Buddhist monasteries. I have argued in a recent article that these Sanskrit "Hindu" stories are so common in Buddhist monasteries that they should be considered Buddhist in Southeast Asia (McDaniel 2013). However, here let me focus on birds. Birds are major and/or minor characters in many non-canonical and often non-Buddhist stories commonly known in Lao, Burmese, Thai, and Khmer like *Kakey* (*Story of the Crow*), *Kogan Pyo, Sangthong, Litlit Phra Lo, Xiang Miang*. These are taught in monastic and secular schools and featured in monastic art alongside *jātaka* tales, canonical suttas, or narratives from the Pali *aṭṭhakathā* collections. Manuscripts of these stories are also held together in monastic libraries, and sometimes painted together with Buddhist stories on monastic murals.[29]

This all leads back to the book I mentioned in the introduction that was given to King Chulalongkorn when he ascended his throne—the *Book of the Birds* (Thai: *Pakṣī-pakaraṇam*; Sanskrit: *Pakṣi-prakaraṇam*). The *Pakṣī-prakaraṇam* is part of a whole genre of *prakaraṇam* texts that have circulated in Southeast Asia since, according to manuscript evidence, the fifteenth century.[30] Some of the most important *prakaraṇam* texts include the *Vetāla-prakaraṇam* (*Collection of Stories of Zombies*), the *Nandaka-prakaraṇam* (*Collection of Stories of the Bullock*, but it is actually a tale which includes all manner of animals visiting a single bullock in Indian, Javanese, Tamil, and Lao tellings), the *Maṇḍūka-prakaraṇam* (*Collection of Stories of Frogs*), the *Piśāca-prakaraṇam* (*Collection of Stories of Ghosts*), and the *Pakṣī-prakaraṇam*, which is also titled the *Śakuna-prakaraṇam* in some tellings (both words mean bird in Sanskrit).[31] These are usually collections of short stories featuring monsters and animals. However, the term can also be used, at least in one case, for a historical collection of stories about the founding of certain cities or the travels of certain statues and relics.[32] They are similar in some ways to the *Setsuwa* tales of medieval Japan or the *Zhiguai* stories of China, but not beastiaries like we find in Europe. They are not descriptive guides to the worlds of fantastic or grotesque creatures, but stories in which the agents are animals and humanoid demons, ghosts, and hybrids. The *prakaraṇam* genre does not see collections of stories of birds as different in kind than collections of stories about other species or supernatural ghosts and monsters. In fact, 7 out of the 31 stories contained in the Central Thai versions of the *Piśācaprakaraṇam* (*Collection of Stories of Ghosts*) are about birds like peacocks, eagles, crows, and geese (another four involve kinnari and/or garuda). These stories differ from those found in the Thai telling of the *Pakṣī-prakaraṇam*. The longest story (out of a total of 25) in the *Vetāla-prakaraṇam* (*Collection of Stories of Zombies*) is about a parrot and a myna bird trying to decide whether women or men are more virtuous.[33] Many of these stories contained within individual *prakaraṇam* texts in Southeast Asia are drawn from Sanskrit stories in the *Pañcatantra*, *Hitopadeśa*, *Kathāsaritsāgara*, and other Indian collections. Like other Indian stories though, many telling in Southeast Asia are quite different from their Indian counterparts. The Lao and Thai *Pakṣī-prakaraṇam* in particular are drawn indirectly from different stories in the *Pañcatantra*, especially the third book, but a few are only known locally. Directly though, they were first introduced in Southeast Asia (especially Java, Northern Thailand, Shan region, and Cambodia) through the *Tantropākhyāna* (Lao: *Mun Tantai*; Thai: *Nithan Nang Tantrai*; Javanese: *Tantri Kāmandaka* or *Tantri Demung*).[34] Of course, more widely known tellings of these stories also appear in Central and Middle-Eastern languages.[35] For example, the Pahlavi, Persian, and Syriac tellings of the Kalilah and Dimnah story (also known as the Fables of Bidpai) share close similarities with several birds stories in the *Pakṣī* and the *Pañcatantra*.[36] Some of these stories were also translated in Greek, Arabic, Hebrew, and Spanish.[37] The very popular *Conference of the Birds* (Persian: *Manteq at-Tair*) by the twelfth-century poet Farid ud-Din Attar has similarities to the plot and bird characters of the *Pakṣī-prakaraṇam*.[38]

There are no Pali equivalents found and the Northern Thai manuscripts are in *nissaya* form which draw from Sanskrit texts and not Pali. In some cases the Sanskrit terms have been rendered into Pali, but there seems to have been no full Pali translation of these texts before the Northern Thai vernacular translations and glosses.[39] So what is the Southeast Asian *Book of the Birds* about?[40] Like the Sanskirt, Syriac, Tamil, Malayalam, Persian and other tellings, the basic story is about a group of birds, often 30, who meet together for the purpose of choosing a king. In the Sufi telling, the birds have the purpose of undertaking a journey to find a king. In Southeast Asia, this meeting is the setting to explain the different qualities of each bird and learn lessons on the differences in temperaments, physical qualities, tendencies, and virtues that make a good leader. There is a wide variety of birds mentioned, most of which can be found in naturalists' descriptions. Some of the birds include the myna, brahminy kite, peacock, partridge, pigeon, pheasant, hen kite, vulture, lapwing, stork, cuckoo, hoopoe, karawek, eagle, thrush, parrot, as well as the garuda and kinnari. Indeed, these supposedly mythical birds are mentioned right alongside birds that have been documented by ornithologists.

I offer this description of the *Book of the Birds* because I hope it shows the complexity of looking for textual sources for Buddhist art in Thailand. Many of the birds featured in monastic art whether it be on a wall or in a manuscript could be drawn from oral and written versions of these non-Buddhist stories just as scenes from the *Rāmāyaṇa* are depicted in Thai art. However, do viewers of a peacock on a lacquer cabinet in a sermon hall or readers of a manuscript that includes paintings of crows flying over a palace or a Brahminy Kite landing on a tree branch on a mural depicting the life of the Buddha think of these textual sources? Did the artists? There is no evidence whatsoever that Thai artists were trained in the past or the present to use certain birds as symbolic meanings or to convey certain messages. There is no evidence that any text, Buddhist or non-Buddhist, served as guide to painters of birds or other non-narrative elements in Buddhist art. The manuals that are found in pre-modern Japan and China for artists to use certain colors, flowers, birds, and the like to convey certain teachings or invoke certain stories are not found in Thai.[41]

Problem Five: What is Ornamental Art and does it Mean Anything?

In Burma and Northern Thailand anserine and gallinaceous bird weights were often used to measure opium, rice, and other commercial products. Although these metal weights were not used in Buddhist ceremonies as far as I know they do open connections through the study of symbolism and metallurgy that help reveal trade routes that existed between Yunnan, Chiang Mai, Tak, Moulmein, and Yangon. Not only does the metal probably come from Southwest China, but the birds, which look at first glance like a haṃsa (Thai: *hong*), a common bird symbol found in Thai and Mon art, are probably a Feng-Huang bird which is a symbol for longevity in Southwest China. However, this Feng-Huang bird may have been domesticized in a sense in Northern Thailand and Burma because on the weights we sometimes find the larger bird being led by two smaller birds which is the way Haṃsa birds are depicted often on the tympana of Buddhist monasteries in the region, especially those monasteries founded in the Mon ordination lineage tradition. A lineage based in the old Mon capital called "Hamsavati" (Hamsa Bird City).[42]

Bird-shaped weights are simply some of the types of ornamental art found in Buddhist Southeast Asia. Just as the bird weights help us make connections between trading partners, religious lineages, metal foundries, and artistic styles, birds found on tympana, lintels, doors, flags, the borders of skirts, murals, and jewelry help us open up connections to an under-studied world of Buddhist activity. Let me provide a few examples of the plethora of depictions of birds, the list could fill several books, but I will try to contain myself.

Reliefs, images, and murals in Southeast Asia depict birds. These are sometimes kinnari and garuda drawn from narrative texts and appear in the art of royal, commercial, Hindu and Buddhist buildings as either main images or as architectural and decorative elements. Some of the more striking examples include: the kinnari carved on the vantaux (door panels) of Wat Aram in Luang Phrabang (Laos) where they are, as in most cases, depicted frolicking among flowers and trees; the beautifully-executed garuda bas-relief on the so-called "Lacquer Pavillion" (a Ho Trai or library for monastic texts) which had been moved from Wat Ban Kling south of Ayutthaya to Bangkok by the royal family in 1959; the seventh–eighth century reliefs of dancing kinnari found at the Kok Maiten site in Nakhon Sawan, Central Thailand; the spectacular golden garuda on the central tympana of the uposatha at Wat Channasongkhram in Bangkok; and the wooden carvings of an entire garuda army on the tympana of Wat Mae Nang Plum (held at the Chao Sam Phraya National Museum in Ayutthaya).[43] Furthermore, carved garuda appear on Angkor Wat in Cambodia; carved images of garudas appear in the art of Pagan (Burma) from the eleventh century and in painted murals at the famous Ananda Temple in Burma (added in the Konbaung Period); and the dozens of iconic kinnari and garuda statues on the grounds on the Grand Palace and lining the base of the Temple of the Emerald Buddha (Thailand) that appear in most tourist photo albums. Indeed, kinnari and garuda have been such mainstays in Buddhist art in Southeast Asian art since at least the seventh century that a garuda is one of the symbols of the royal family of Thailand, the name of Indonesia's national airline is Garuda, and Thai Airways International's magazine is called Kinnari. For the last ten years there have been efforts in Bali (Indonesia) to construct what will be the largest statue in the world, a 146-meter image of Vishnu riding on the back of a garuda in the Garuda Wisnu Kencana Park.[44] Even the cover of the catalog from one of the most respected and largest exhibitions of Burmese and Thai art in history, "Emerald Cities: Arts of Siam and Burma, 1775–1950," is a wooden kinnari image (McGill 2009). A garuda was the symbol of the 2011 Southeast Asia games. The Buddha was a kinnara (male kinnari) in four of his previous lives. Kinnari and garuda also show up carved on royal insignia, banks, silk shops, and schools. As for murals, they are so common throughout Thailand and Laos (as well as Cambodia and Burma) that they are not worth mentioning. Indeed, it could be argued that the kinnari and the garuda rival the Buddha as the unifying artistic figure of Southeast Asia. South Asian, especially Tamil examples are beyond the scope of this chapter.

Besides the nearly ubiquitous and pan-Southeast Asian part-human, part-bird kinnari or the animal-hybrid garuda though, there are other birds that fly throughout Southeast Asian art and are more specific to certain ethnic groups, time periods, and monastic lineages. According to Sombhong Akharawong, royally designated as one of the leading instructors of art in Thailand, painting birds and forest vegetation is the basis of each artist's training (Sombhong Akharawong 2550 [2007]). These birds come in many types: peacocks, finches, hoopoes, parrots, swans, geese, kites, thrushes, among others. These birds often appear in murals, illuminated manuscripts, bas-reliefs, and other architecturally-dependent Buddhist monastic art. Most often they are depicted, as mentioned briefly above, as part of the scenes of the Himaphan/Himavanta forest, the mythical forest inaccessible to most humans that appears in many Buddhist and Hindu narratives and nearly every mural of the *Vessantara Jātaka* and other *jātakas* like the *Cullapaduma*, *Sudhana* (discussed below) and the more rare *Himavanta Sutta* (*Samyuttanikāya*). Other birds appear in the forest scenes of the *Rāmāyaṇa* or the *Aranyakaparvan* (or *Vana Parva*) of the *Mahābharata*. This is not surprising, of course, birds attract each other and they don't particularly follow one religious tradition and so appear in temples of various lineages and traditions in the region. Of course, it is well-known that many of the same artists worked on art in temples regardless of their religious affiliation, central images, patrons, or narrative program. Artists painted birds, not just "Buddhist" birds whatever they might be. The importance was, it seems, to create beautiful, lush, verdant, and evocative spaces that the central statues, as well as the human visitors and practitioners could passively take in.[45] I believe that this is not so different from the gifts offered to land and tree "spirits" (*thewada* or sometimes ghosts—*phi*) at small spirit houses in the region (Thai: *san phra phum*). The house for the Buddha and the house for land spirits are supposed to be beautiful and welcoming. Indeed, they should be much more beautiful than your own home. Beautiful decorative accents and gifts are everywhere in the region, many involve depictions of birds. This accumulative affect/effect of birds in the forest recreated spaces which matched or enhanced the stories of forested places where heroes learned magic and practiced asceticism, lovers secretly embraced, gods were exiled, and children and animals played.

These non-kinnari/garuda birds are rarely found though alone as the subjects of murals, bas-reliefs, and architectural elements in the region unless one looks closely at Sino-Thai Buddhist monastic art of the King Rama III period in Central Thailand in the early nineteenth century. Indeed, the Chinese influence in this period of Thai Buddhist art history shows clearly the problem for looking for meaning or linking textual sources to Buddhist ornamental art in Thailand. Under the direct patronage of Rama III several monasteries were constructed or renovated and renamed in the 1830s and 1840s. Of the more than 80 monasteries that he sponsored, some of the largest ones were built in honor of his family. Besides Rama III's affection for Chinese style architecture and his use of Chinese artisans (much of the growth in wealth under his reign was due to extensive trade with China and the influx of cheap Chinese labor into the Bangkok area), he also apparently had an affection for birds as they are one of the dominant artistic features of many of his monasteries. For example, the monastery, Wat Nang Nong, he dedicated to his Muslim mother, Queen Srisulalai (her family origins were in Southern Thailand, but she grew up in Nonthaburi near Bangkok) features gold and black lacquer birds, in the lai gamalo style, on every door and window shutter of northern (there are two at Wat Nang Nong) Wihan (Pali: *vihāra*).[46] These birds frolic in the forest reminiscent of murals of the Himaphan forest. However, unlike most murals of the Himaphan, there are no humans on these doors and the birds become the main focus.[47]

Birds are also the main focus of the murals at a monastery dedicated to Rama III's youngest daughter, Ying Wilat.[48] Wat Thepdhitaram's (which means "Monastery of the Divine Daughter") western Wihan features impressive murals populated only by a single type of bird, the so-called Chinese Phoenix (Chinese: Feng-Huang; Thai: *Nok Hong*), which in Thai is often associated with the haṃsa. Phra Wisuddhiwaraphon, one of the assistant abbots at the monastery and its primary historian who has written two books on the subject, believes that these birds are symbols of women. This is a symbolic association that he is unsure about and I have not been able to corroborate it with any other text or scholar.[49] The birds on this mural program may not be narrative murals describing the life of the Buddha, kings, or previous lives of the Buddha and arahats, but they are "decorative elements" that have taken center stage.

Rama III's first and most beloved monastery is Wat Ratchaorot (Wat Ratchaorosa Wararam).[50] Here birds are not simply featured on the doors of one of the buildings or on one set of murals, but fly around all of the buildings in lacquer, mother-of-pearl, on painted doors and shutters, and on murals. This monastery's design were so strikingly different from previous Central Thai examples that the author of Thailand's first major study of architecture, Prince Damrong Ratchanuphap, called this monastery "wat nok yang" (the monastery without precedence or literally "with outside style").[51] This monastery came to be the one of the models on which later "Silpa Racha Niyom" (the so-called "favored artistic style of the King") was based. In order to feature certain birds in this new style, he or at least the unrecorded architects and artists who worked on the monastery had to remove some birds. Therefore, what we do not find at Wat Ratchaorot which is common on most Thai monasteries are the distinctive roof ornaments: *cho fa* (distinctive golden finials that project off the corners of the upper and lower roof lines and can be in the shape of birds taking flight or dragons/nagas), *hang hong* (tails of swans or geese and sometimes nagas/snakes, usually made out of gold painting wood) which decorate monastic roofs, and *bai raka* (garuda designs on roofs, usually on the lower tiers of multi-tiered monastic and palace roofs). However, different birds were added. Despite having spent several years visiting Wat Ratchaorot and taking over 2,000 photographs of its art and architecture and examining every available document about its history and interviewing its abbot and many scholars I have not been able to determine exactly why these other, non-mythical, birds feature so prominently there.[52] Even though the style of the monastery's murals, tympana, architraves, columns, courtyards, tiles (*bhradab krabueang khleuab*), and much of its statuary is clearly influenced by Fuzhou, Quanzhou, Zhangzhou and Teochiu (or Chaozhou) architecture and decorative elements found in eighteenth-century Fujien, Taiwan, and parts of Guangdong monastery architecture and art, most of the birds that adorn its doors, window shutters, tympana, tiles, and other places are not particularly

"Chinese" and seem to be unique to Wat Ratchaorot.[53] These birds include kites, peacocks, cranes, something that looks close to a red summer tanager (although it is not native to Southern China or Southeast Asia and might actually be a Red-headed Trogon), and numerous birds with blue-tipped wings which I could not identify (and which the monks and laypeople who resided and worked at the monastery could not as well). For example, there are ceramic birds on nearly every tympana and architrave which are often depicted flying alone and not flying in the sky above Buddha images or characters from *jātakas*.[54] Painted on the interior of every pair of window shutters in the largest building on the monastic grounds, the Hall of the Great Reclining Buddha image (Wihan Phra Phuttha Saiyat) are pairs of mostly peacocks. These are very large paintings of birds, 46 in all. They feature the birds not as ancillary features, but as standing alone on rocks neither facing the Buddha image nor the viewer, but towards the other birds along the wall. Each bird is different in shape, color, and posture, and while most seem to be peacocks, there are no peacocks quite like these in color and plumage in nature. Published descriptions of the monastery by Prince Damrong, John Crawfurd, Phra Thammakittiwong, among others strangely hardly mention these prominent and striking paintings of peacock-like birds.[55] One could speculate that the peacocks symbolize death since these birds are on window shutters surrounding a nearly 100-feet long giant statue of the Buddha on his deathbed. However, as seen below, peacocks are usually symbols of the escape of death as they were believed to protect against poison. Painted on the window frames of this image hall are gold cranes standing in lotus ponds against black lacquer. These cranes in Southeast Asian and Indian Buddhist art can symbolize bad monks. Cranes, like monks, stay still in meditation. However, cranes stand in water and stay still because they are waiting for fish to let down their guard so that they can strike quickly and eat them. Bad monks can stay still but might have unfettered desire in their minds.

Even if a particular bird or flower was designated in texts as having a meaning, how do we know if the artist intended that meaning or the audience, if they knew the meaning, would somehow have their experience at the monastery changed in any significant way? Third, meanings shift over time and different meanings can be applied over time by different visitors, abbots, restorers, etc. Perhaps the crane and peacock in this instance mean nothing. This is especially true if these birds and flowers had specific (which they did) symbolic and representational meanings in Southern China, but these meanings were not communicated to audiences in Thailand. If these were Chinese artisans or Thai artisans guided by Chinese master craftsmen, then the meaning in Fuzhou or Sanming might be different from the meaning of the same bird in Thailand. Regardless, there were no texts and no evidence of sermons that explained the meanings of these ornamental features in any systematic way and if there was an artist, a patron, or a monk (of which I have not found evidence) that explained his or her interpretation of the meaning orally at some point in the past, that knowledge has not been passed down or recorded, which means it obviously was not that important.

Even if we had documents, which we do not, naming the individual artisans, the prices they were paid for their work, the detailed instructions from their patron King Rama III, diaries of craftspeople working daily on the monasteries, a guide to the use of birds in Thai art composed in 1836, or even knew what the artisans ate for lunch while they worked—who cares?[56] Yes, as an enthusiastic student of Thai monastic life, I would love such detail. All I have are some poetic descriptions of 37 of Rama III's monasteries by the poet, Sunthorn Phu, in his lovely *Ramphanphilap* and a few royal orders in Rama III's chronicle, and the *Phra Thammadesana Chaloem Phra kiat Rachatkan thi 3*, a long sermon delivered during the reign of King Rama V about the life of Rama III which talks about his building projects. This fascinating sermon was delivered on the 100th anniversary of Rama III's birth and is not an eyewitness account. It does not tell us anything about birds. But all the possible historical detail which I have patiently assembled is only useful for providing a richer description of these individual monasteries and works of art. This detail might eventually make it into a monastery brochure which would temporarily be examined by a visitor before ending up in a trashcan or wrinkled in the bottom of a backpack.

Following birds shows that art in Buddhist temples doesn't necessarily have to be Buddhist, teach Buddhist lessons, invoke Buddhist stories, or symbolize Buddhist truths. Monasteries are constructed and reconstructed over time for multiple reasons, for mothers and sons, to celebrate military victory, or to impress one's friends. Wat Ratchaorot became one of the two medical schools in Central Thailand in the nineteenth century for example. Birds lead us to think not about Buddhist texts, but at the lives of decorative artists, the ways in which local ethnicity and popular aesthetic trends impact monastic decoration and design. They show us that monasteries are not just repositories of tradition, but dynamic arenas of cultural, economic, and social life. If we followed birds further it would lead us to study the world of jewelry, textile production, kite-making, and bird-song imitation—all of which take place on the grounds of monasteries often and all of which feature bird designs.[57]

Conclusion

The controversial and world-famous Japanese novelist Yukio Mishima was obsessed with the tempting allure of beauty and the way the presence of beauty made him feel inadequate. This is one of the enduring themes of his best-known works, *The Temple of the Golden Pavilion*, *Confessions of a Mask*, and *Temple of the Dawn*. The *Temple of the Dawn* is named after the Buddhist monastery in Bangkok (Wat Arun). In that novel (part of a four-part series), the protagonist Honda travels to India, Thailand, and back to Japan and on the way spends much time discussing a Buddhist treatise that features a peacock.[58] He refers to it as "The Sutra of the Great Golden Peacock Wisdom King," which is his slightly incorrect translation of the *Mahāmāyūrī Vidyārājñī Sūtra*[59] or *Kujaku-myoo* in Japanese. The Peacock King (actually queen in this text) is a foundational dhāraṇī or protective text probably inspired by the Pali text, the Mora Paritta, which came to Japan via China where the text had been translated from Sanskrit by some of the most prominent translators including Kumārajīva, Saṅghavarman, Yijing, Amoghavajra, and others. Similar stories are also found in the Mora Jātaka and an important meditation training text by Dharmarākṣita (via Atiṣa)—The Wheel of Sharp Weapons.[60] For the frequency of its appearance alone, the peacock may be the most Buddhist of all birds. Both the female and male peacock are featured in several very popular texts and stories throughout East, South, and Southeast Asia. These texts have been studied by scholars interested in tantric ritual, sacred kingship, and ritual protection (especially against poison). However, despite the insights of these studies, I find myself still confused as to why peacocks? Why is the peacock figure so prominent in Buddhist stories when it seems another animal or human could easily substitute it for the text to make sense? I believe that Mishima, a twentieth-century novelist who committed ritual suicide in 1970 without any formal training in Buddhist Studies, might have had some insights into this text missed by us in Buddhist Studies. Mishima's character Honda states that the story of the peacock and its dhāraṇī were popular in Japan because they were used to protect the emperor in the Heian period (and certainly beyond) from poisoning and other attacks. He stated that it was the beauty of the peacock as a "gorgeous and sumptuous figure, and its song 'ka-ka-ka-ka-ka' [...]" its mantra "ma yu kitsu ra tei sha ka," and its majestic mūdra which impressed the emperor. This ritual and the story depicted displayed "a blue Indian sky trailed behind the Wisdom King on his golden peacock mount. A tropical sky with its impressive clouds, its afternoon ennui, and its evening breezes, all necessary for spinning a gorgeous and colorful illusion" (Mishima 1973: 141–3). He is enamored with the beauty of the peacock and ends the chapter not discussing the teachings of the text, just its beauty (unlike other sections of the novel where he discusses Yogācāra [Japanese: Yuishiki] notions of reality). For Mishima, the importance of the text and the peacock was its beauty. This is not just the uninformed opinion of a novelist though. This is certainly a legitimate reading of the story of the peacock.

In many cases the metaphor of the peacock transforming things of harm, whether they are selfish thoughts or actual poison, into beauty has developed far beyond the story of the bird. The text was used for royal protection and had little to do with birds. However, while the story has changed in different places at different times, the root of the story still emphasizes, like many Buddhist texts, the beauty of Bodhisattvas and Buddhas and their previous births as animals of various sorts. Mishima didn't analyze the Peacock Sutra, he simply describes the beauty of the Peacock King as reminding him of a beautiful woman he couldn't possess—Satoko and the goddess Kali whose beauty was both terrible and alluring:

> The Wisdom King posed with compassionate countenance, and his body was extremely fair. The skin visible under silk gauze was enhanced by such

> magnificent jewelry [...] a cool weariness lingered on the heavy lids of the half-open eyes as though the diety had just awakened from an afternoon nap [...] of the plumage of all birds, that of the peacock was closest to the hue of the evening clouds [...].

Mishima's description is actually close to the way these peacock texts are presented in Lao, Thai, Sanskrit, Pali, Tibetan, Chinese, and Japanese texts, as well as painting and drama. The beauty of the bird and the allure of passion, especially dangerous passions, are at the forefront of literary and artistic expressions of peacocks, kinnaris, and other birds.

Is it simply that beauty just is? Is it hard to write, analyze, explain? In mine and other textual scholars' efforts to find political messages, symbolic equivalences, psychological coping mechanisms, metaphors, class aspirations, philosophical positions, and the like, have we avoided the elephant, or perhaps beautiful bird, in the room? Buddhists produce beautiful things. These birds may not symbolize anything and be, like many features of Southeast Asian ornamental art, there for their beauty. And beauty does not have meaning but accumulative affect. What a child learns growing up playing cards in monastic courtyards, taking mathematics and writing lessons in monastic schools, and eating afternoon snacks under the eaves of monastic pavillions is different from what a student of Buddhist Studies learns through canonical and extra canonical texts and examining the main Buddha images or narrative murals in person or in catalogs. They learn through accumulating visual, auditory, olfactory, and tactile cues. The subtle affect of a monastery enhanced by not just the main images, but the decorative elements can lead a child to associate monasteries not only (or not necessarily) with the values of non-attachment, compassion, self-control, self-denial, or indifference, but with the values of beauty, abundance, and frivolity.

I do not want to leave the reader with the idea that there is no meaning to be derived from birds in Thai Buddhist art or that texts and art have nothing to do with each other in the study of ornamental art. I hope that the plethora of examples above has shown, what one of the very helpful anonymous reviewers of this article stated, was "the multi-vocality" and "fuzzy meanings" of this art and the jazz-like "improvisation" of its enactment. I am just concerned with the way art, especially ornamental art, is experienced in multiple contexts, more than what it "originally" meant (in whatever way we decide to attribute original meaning). All experience and interpretation is contingent, inconsistent, and partial. Of course, the kinnari or hamsa hybrids and birds have textual sources and these sources are known to many people, but when they are used in art it is not necessarily for the purpose of invoking "the" moral of a story or "the" symbolic meaning. The meaning shifts or gets lost over time, the connection with one or many texts becomes vague. Moreover, the viewer (usually experiencing the bird in the mural or relief as they pass by it or under it, not gazing at it) might possess numerous and conflicting interpretations of what the bird means or completely ignore it. The artists creating these theatrical sets and costumes, ornamental architraves, and decorative manuscript chests were not telling stories or designing elaborate coded messages through the deliberate employment of certain symbols, but drawing on a common and wide-ranging repertoire of sources of which they also had an incomplete knowledge. Some artists had a plan, a deep knowledge of texts, and message to offer. Most clearly did not. If we as scholars seek out the textual source or the symbolic meaning we miss the way the art is experienced.

My point is that by using a "thing" like a bird as a "organizing device" or "critical term" instead of languages, countries, regions, schools/sects, institutions, ethical or speculative teachings, textual lineages (i.e., studying a source text and its subsequent commentaries and sub-commentaries), in an exploration into Buddhist expression, we can undertake studies that depend less on the traits, great thinkers, and teachings of particular Buddhist schools and national or ethnic groups and more on the "aesthetics" which help shape Buddhist cultures. We can start to question the authority of texts. We can give more attention to affect than doctrine. We can start to design research projects that both value a close study of the historically and culturally specific aspects of local Buddhism while acknowledging the translocal history of Buddhism as a "world religion" which shares certain affective ways of presentation and certain material culture that is recognizable beyond the boundaries of language difference and sectarian affiliation. We can start studying not just the actors and scripts of Buddhism, but the sets, scores, and costumes as well.

Scholars often see widely distant communities bound together by their shared humanity—we all face death, need food, have the drive to procreate, experience gravity, and the like.[61] But perhaps it is more basic than that. We all share death, but we also all share birds. We all want to procreate, but we all also like beautiful or sensuous things— flowers on table, paintings on temples walls, jewels, insignia, theatre, music, comedy, etc. Beauty is fundamental to Buddhist literature and art whether it is found in a mandala, a ritual costume, or a sublime statue. Widely distant communities don't just share the ethical and ontological problems of death, sex, and children, they also share other universals—birds, trees, and water. Since all Buddhist communities are inhabited by birds, is there something Buddhists say about birds? If so, what can we learn from it? I would like to point out some resources for the study of birds by my field of Buddhist Studies and see where this takes us both historically and methodologically, and what, in the end this tells about the way we make categories and decide what counts as subjects of study. I draw most examples from my own field of Thai and Lao Buddhist Studies, but I trust that some of my comments and examples will have resonance for those working on other Buddhist repertoires in East and South Asia. Birds fly over the walls of royal courts, monastic complexes, rural theatres, rivers, and seas, landing where they wish and often not where we might expect. I have learned much from trying to catch up.

Notes

1 See McDaniel's *Lovelorn Ghost* (2011: chapter four).

2 Although it is not the focus of the article, for a comparative example of monks involved in decorative art at monasteries in Cambodia, see John Marston (2004). This is a well-documented phenomenon in Japan where monks are closely involved in artistic design at monasteries.

3 The study of ornament in Western and Islamic has become more developed recently. See for example the influential works by Oleg Grabar (1995), Michael Snodin and Maurice Howard (1996), and David Cannadine (2002). I also thank one of the anonymous reviewers of this article for her/his very helpful suggestion of looking at E.H. Gombrich's *The Sense of Order: A Study in the Psychology of Decorative Art* (Gombrich 1994) which discusses information theory with reference to patterns and ornaments in art. Most works on ornament in South and Southeast Asian art, like Henry Wilson's *Pattern and Ornament in the Arts of India* (Wilson 2011), have been largely descriptive works. Although largely descriptive as well, perhaps the most well-developed area of research on ornamental art, especially in symbolic meaning of ornamental elements is in the study of Chinese and Japanese court and temple art. See for example: Terese Tse Bartholomew (2006), C.A.S. Williams (2006), Motoji Niwa (2001), Li He and Michael Knight (2008), among many others. There are many studies of specifically "flower and bird" art of China and Japan as well, a few will be mentioned below.

4 Recently, Rebecca Hall sent me photographs of a wonderfully detailed manuscript chest decorated with birds in the Walters Art Museum Collection.

5 Although he did not focus on artists, collectors, restorers, choreographers, and the like, Craig Reynolds revolutionized the study of Southeast Asian history by studying thieves, traders, printers, and criminals, all people generally left out of court, state, and monastic histories. See particularly his *Seditious Histories: Contesting Thai and Southeast Asian Pasts* (Reynolds 2006).

6 For the ways Lao and Thai manuscripts were grouped in monastic libraries see my *Gathering Leaves and Lifting Words* (McDaniel 2008: chapter four).

7 It is also found in the Sanskrit *Divyāvadāna* and famously forms the main subjects of the reliefs of Borobodor in Java and in cave #1 of Ajanta. See Padmanabh Jaini (1966). See also Andrew Rotman's new translation of the *Divyāvadāna* [*Divine Stories: Translations from the Divyāvadāna,* part 1 (Boston: Wisdom Publications, 2008)] which recounts many love stories popular in South Asian Buddhist literature. Henry Ginsburg's PhD dissertation "The Sudhana-Manohara tale in Thai: a comparative study based on two texts from the National Library, Bangkok, and Wat Machimawat, Songkhla" (1971) provides a detailed look at early textual sources for the dance performance in Southeast Asia. See also his "The Manora dance-drama: an introduction," *Journal of the Siam Society* (Ginsburg 1972).

8 The *Sivijaya* is well-known in Laos and Thailand and is the subject of popular sermons where it is called the *Si Vixai* (Lao) and *Srīwijai* (Thai) today. Although there has not been any literary analysis of the story, thanks to the codicological research of Jacqueline Filliozat, Saveros Pou, and Harald Hundius, we now have evidence that it is also found both in Pali and in the bi-lingual sermon guide *nissaya* form as well as with many manuscripts going back to the sixteenth century at least. In Cambodia, this story was mentioned in inscriptions in Siemreap and was part of one of the several *Paññāsa-jātaka* collections.

9 See Walters Museum object report ID #2010.12.32 and James Bogle (2011).

10 An explanation of the text abbreviations are also now online at: http://what-buddha-said.net/library/Wheels/img/paliabbreviationsystem.html.

11 http://www.palikanon.com/english/pali_names/h/himava.htm.

12 At some new monasteries, especially among the immigrant Thai communities in the US, there are now framed cartoonish lithographs hanging on the walls with descriptions printed on them depicting the life of the Buddha. These are hung at US temples in place of traditional murals (which are often too expensive and finding qualified artists is difficult). They are similar to Catholic paintings of the "Stations of the Cross" popular in the 1950s. I thank Donald Swearer for reminding me of these new narrative paintings.

[13] See also James (2007).

[14] See also Fraser (2004) and Teiser (2007).

[15] A major exception to this is the last book written by the late Wyatt. See his *Reading Thai Murals* (2004).

[16] See particularly Zaleski (1997: 93–150); Ringis (1990); Matics (1992); Fickle (1979); Bhirasri (1959); Nidda Hongwiwat (2549 [2006]); Chuphon Euachuwong (2007); No Na Paknam (2538 [1995]). This last book by Na Paknam contains his collected articles on Thai art published between 1974 and 1991. He often refers to the texts that murals represent. However, in two articles, one on the murals of the partition wall of Wat Suthat ("Phap kian bon lap lae faprachan thi wat suthat thepwararam") and another on the murals at Wat Bangkhae Yai in Samut Songkhram ("Chitakam faphanang thi wat bangkhae yai changwat samut songkhram"), he notes that—probably because there was no clearly identifiable textual source—these murals are a creative interpretation of daily life scenes depicting Mon, Chinese, Shan, and other peoples who resided near the monasteries. In 2003 (Vol. 29.4), *Muang Boran Journal* dedicated a special issue to murals which depicted historical events.

[17] Narrative additions to well-known canonical texts were of course also common on murals and other forms of Thai painting. One notable addition is seen in a Thai cloth painting held by the Asian Art Museum. The painting depicting chapter five of the story shows several women ridiculing the wife of the elderly Brahmin Jūjaka. In the original Pali text, this scene is quite short and simply contains 12 verses in which a group of women poke fun at Jūjaka's wife for being so obedient to an old man. There is only a subtle mention of the lack of romance and sex in their relationship; however, the painting is quite bawdy. The women are depicted groping each other, dancing, and holding long wooden phalluses (dildos). Many are half-naked pretending to penetrate each other vaginally in various positions. This kind of explicit sexual display is not mentioned in the Pali text, but must have offered some shock and delight to the late nineteenth-century audiences of the painting. I appreciate Forrest McGill taking his time to show me this painting at the Asian Art Museum. See Cowell (1907: 271). Naked women are not limited to cloth paintings and are also found on prominent royal temple murals like those at Wat Pathumwanaram, Wat Rakhang, among others.

[18] Thai Ms. 1319 (Chester Beatty Library). I thank Sinead Ward for helping me locate this manuscript while in Dublin.

[19] See Chutima Chunhacha (2537 [1994]) and Sanitsuda Ekachai (2008: 1). See also No Na Paknam's historical introduction to the temple, *Wat Khongkaram: Moradok paen din bon lum nam mae khlong* (Bangkok: Muang Boran, 2537 [1994]) and the special issue on Wat Khongkaram, with contributions from Nit Ratanasanya among others (Nit Ratanasanya et al. 2517 [1974]: esp. 19–53). I thank Donald Swearer for giving me a copy of this last source.

[20] According to the Sekhiya (chapter ten, verses 5–6 of the Pali *Pāṭimokkha*), a monk should be "well-restrained" and this according to later commentaries emphasize that being restrained means not dancing. However, that should not suggest in any way that dancing has been absent from Buddhist monasteries. While monks and novices do not dance (well, at least not publicly), dance performances are frequent in their courtyards and open-air pavilions (sala) at monasteries.

[21] They are half-human/half-birds popular in South and Southeast Asian mythology. However, in the *Mahābharata* (in both the *Adi* and *Vana Parva*), the *Bhagavata Purāṇa* (see: Purnendu Narayana Sinha [1901: 26–7]), and the *Viṣṇu Purāṇa* (see: The *Vishnu Purana*, translated by Horace Hayman Wilson [1840], at http://www.sacred-texts.com/hin/vp/vp115.htm, accessed April 2, 2012), the male kinnara was a half-horse/half-human and they were one of the Himalayan tribes of superhumans. The horse changed to a bird in Southeast Asia.

[22] This is one of the biggest events of the annual monastic calendar in the Shan regions. Crowds are a mixture of novices, monks, and lay people at monasteries. However, it has hardly been mentioned in the plethora of excellent studies of Shan Buddhism that have come out over the past several years. This is not

strange and in no way the fault of scholars in this growing field. Dance has not been a part of Buddhist or Religious Studies and is one of the least studied parts of the field of ethnomusicology. However, this has more to do with these fields of study than what actually goes on "in the field." There has been a real efflorescence in the study of Shan Buddhism over the past decade. See particularly Eberhardt (2006) and Tanenbaum (2001). See also the special issue on Shan Buddhism in *Contemporary Buddhism* edited by Kate Crosby, Khammai Dhammasami, Jotika Khur-Yearn, and Andrew Skilton (2009). Unfortunately for the field of Shan Studies, performances like the Kinnari dance were rendered "non-Buddhist" by E. Paul Durrenberger in the early 1980s. See particularly Durrenberger (1980: 48–56; 1982: 16–26; 1983: 63–74).

23 See particularly Wong (2001). This is a rare study of non-ecclesiastical, lay Buddhist performances, particularly focused on the "wai khru" ritual and classical drama. Unfortunately, it has not been followed by other studies on the subject.

24 There is another, related, Sudhana in East Asian Art which is one of the main characters in the *Gaṇḍavyūha Sūtra*. See for example Jan Fontein's *The pilgrimage of Sudhana: a study of Gaṇḍavyūha illustrations in China, Japan and Java* (1967).

25 The doyen of Thai dance and former director of the Department of Fine Arts in Bangkok, Dhanit Yupho, even invited the famous costume designer and choreographer Mom Phaeo, who was married to Mom Sanitwongseni, to work on new Manora sets and costumes. Her husband held different high-rank positions in the foreign service in Europe. This enabled her to bring set and costume design ideas from France, Italy, and other places and combined them with classical royal dance forms for the staging of Manora. Her work was also enhanced by the set innovations of Mot Wongsawat who was the artistic director for stage design with the Department of Fine Arts between 1933 and 1967. Dhanit also designed most sets for the National Theatre of Thailand in the middle of the twentieth century. Wongsawat traveled to Japan with 36 Thai dancers, musicians, and artists in 1934 and brought Kabuki stage technology to Thai bird dances. Soon he had built a revolving set in Thailand replete with real trees, waving cloth mimicking flowing rivers, flowers, and mountain scenery, as well as bridges for his dancers which extended into the audience. The dancers dressed as birds could even fly around the audience suspended by ropes. In different ways, they added new dance styles to the play emphasizing the intimacy between Prince Sudhana and his half-bird/half-human lover in her elaborate winged dress. Some of these innovations were also applied to the Prasantha To Nok, a well-known scene from the epic royal poem, Inao (adapted from a Javanese romance) which involves a hunter chasing a female bird.

26 For more general information on festivals that take place at Buddhist monasteries that often include Chinese romance plays/operas, fashion shows, and dance performances, see my *Lovelorn Ghost* (McDaniel 2011: 132–9).

27 See especially Phitya Busararat (2553 [2010]: 211–45).

28 See especially chapters four and five.

29 The slim pickings include some of the chapters in David Symth's *The Canon in Southeast Asian Literature* (2000) and John Okell's "'Translation' and 'Embellishment' in an Early Burmese 'Jātaka' Poem," *The Journal of the Royal Asiatic Society of Great Britain and Ireland* (1967): 133–48.

30 Louis Finot first identified these types of texts in Laos in 1917. See his "Recherches sur la littérature laotienne," *Bulletin de l'École Française d'Extrême-Orient* (Finot 1917). Jean Brengues documented vernacular Lao telling of the stories in his "Une version laotienne du Pancatantra," *Journal Asiatique* (Brengues 1908). Henry Ginsburg helped identify the 20 manuscripts of the *Tantropākhyāna* in the National Library of Thailand (there are also many in Northern Thai collections).

31 The Royal Press in Bangkok published a printed copy of the *Nandaka-prakaraṇam* (Thai: *Nonthuk Pakaranam*) in 1876 and Ginsburg (1972) mentioned that there is a lost copy from 1870 (314).

32 Another northern Thai text with *p(r)akaraṇam* in its title is the *Jinakālamālī-pakaraṇam*. This text has been translated and studied by numerous scholars, including myself in 2002, as a chronicle or history. However, I now see that I might have missed something fundamental about the text even though it is right in the title. If we see it as a collection of stories instead of a chronicle it might permit different readings.

33 Skilling, writing on Indian and Tibetan Vinaya commentaries clarifies the meaning of vetala in Sanskrit. He shows that the oldest Sanskrit spelling of vetala was "vetāḍa" (Pali: *vetāla* or *vetāḷa*). He also believes that the closest English translation is zombie versus Burton's (see below) use of "vampire." See Skilling, "Zombies and Half-Zombies" (2007: 315fn7). See Ginsburg (1975: 279–314). Furthermore, Ginsburg wrote a fascinating Master's thesis in 1967 on the *Tantropākhyāna*, especially a collection of ghost stories called the *Piśācap(r)akaraṇam* (Ginsburg 1967). This vernacular Thai text, unlike the rest of the *Tantropākhyāna*, has little connection to any known Sanskrit text. It seems to be the creative work of Thai authors. It was quite popular in the mid-nineteenth century in Bangkok, there were several manuscript copies, and was actively studied by both Thai and foreign scholars in the late nineteenth century. Bishop Pallegoix, adviser to the Siamese king, included it in his list of important vernacular Thai "secular" texts in his 1850 Thai grammar. There were some English and German translations made of the stories in 1872 and 1894 respectively (this was a time in which there were very few translations of any Thai text available). Adolf Bastian hand copied these ghost stories in 1864. It was certainly seen as an important collection. These texts were copied and circulated among monks as well as lay people and clearly influenced modern Thai understandings of ghosts and the ritual needed to protect against them. See my "Encountering Corpses: Notes on Zombies and the Living Dead in Buddhist Southeast Asia," *Kyoto Review of Southeast Asia, Special Issue on Death and Funerary Cultures in Southeast Asia* (2013). There are many modern English and Sanskrit editions of this collection. See for example N.M. Penzer (ed.) and C.H. Tawney's translation *The Ocean of Streams of Story* in ten volumes (London: Chas Sawyer, 1926) or the more recent translation by Arshia Sattar, *Somadeva: Tales from the Kathāsaritsāgara* (New York: Penguin, 1994), and Riccardi (1968). This was later published in a slightly reduced form by the American Oriental Society (Riccardi 1971). The oldest manuscript of this collection in India was found in Mysore and dates from 1031 CE. Sanskritists and South Indian literary specialists Edgerton, Venkatasubbiah, and Artola have traced different versions of the Sanskrit text, as well as Tamil, Kanada, and Malayalam telling attributed to the Indian authors like Vasubhāga, Viṣṇuśarman, and Durgasiṃha. There are similarities with the stories about the Jain sage Pārçvanātha composed by Bhāvadevasūri. Burton's telling was published by Longmans, Green, and Co. (London, 1870) and Ryder's 1917 translation is now available online at http://www. sacred-texts.com/hin/ttg/.

34 Bloomfield (1920: 314–6).

35 The *Book of the Birds* is briefly circulated in Southeast Asia in the context of comparing it to examples from the Islamic and Indic world in Benfey (1864: 171–2). The first European to study these connections to Southeast Asia seems to be Adolf Bastian who traveled extensively in the region, especially Thailand, in the 1860s.

36 For Indian influences of Kalilah and Dimnah and information on the Syrian, Arabic, and other tellings, see Keith-Falconer (1970: introduction).

37 Syam Phathranuprawat and Kusuma Raksamani have undertaken extensive studies of these possible Indian progenitors, as well as comparing them to the Javanese telling. He shows that this text, as well as the Pakṣī, Maṇḍūka, and Piśāca, were introduced into Northern Thailand in the mid-1400s and probably came from the tradition of Vasubhāga, although much of the Pakṣī seems to come from the Viṣṇuśarman textual lineage. See Raksamani (1978: 12–15). See also studies of the Indic and Javanese manuscripts by Artola (1965); Sastri (1938); Hooykaas (1929); and three articles by Venkatasubbiah (1965: 74–142; 1966: 59–100; 1969: 195–283).

38 See Farid ud-Din Attar (1984 and 1954). Recently, a beautiful children's telling was published by Peter Sis (*The Conference of the Birds*, 2011). None of the numerous scholars of these texts which circulated widely in the Islamic world has undertaken a serious comparative study with the Sanskrit manuscripts nor the Southeast Asian tellings.

39 Some *Tantropākhyāna* manuscripts do not include the Maṇḍūka and most do not include the Vetala. Most manuscripts include the Nandaka, Pakṣī, and Piśāca. There are many northern Thai *Nithan Nang Tantrai* manuscripts available, including complete ones (with at least four of the *prakaraṇam* collections).

For example, there are four in Chiang Mai monasteries, one in Lampang, one in Phayom, two in Phrae, and one in Nan. In Laos, the National Library has collected two large manuscripts of the Mun Tantai and the National Library of Thailand has two as well, although both exclude the Maṇḍūka and seems to have come from a very different Indian source. For a relatively complete bibliography of manuscript and printed editions of the various *prakaraṇam* texts in the region, see Syam Phathranuprawat's three articles in different stages of publication: "Nithan bhisatbhakaranam: chak rueang phi lueak nai ma ben rueang bhisat taeng ngan kap manut," "Kan bhlaeng nithan sansakrit ben chatok nai rueang kalithat," and "Nithan rueang chao chai okatanna kap mi: rong roi nithan sansakrit nai lanna." I thank Syam for sending these articles and for his advice and guidance. For a general study that draws from this research, see his thesis "Bhaksibhakaranam: kan seuksa bhriaptiap chabap sansakrit lanna lae thai" (Bangkok: Silapakorn University, 2546 [2003]) and his "Lanna bhaksibhakarana," *Damrong Journal of the Faculty of Archaeology* 4, 1 (2005): 39–51. I also thank Jacqueline Filliozat for her kind help with this research. It should be noted that in Central Thailand (Siam) there was an entire other genre of manuscripts, many held at Buddhist monasteries, which depicted birds—Tamra nok (Bird Manuals). These colorful khoi paper manuscripts from the nineteenth century depict different type of birds, mostly roosters, cranes, and other birds, as well as garuda and kinnari. These are more descriptive like European beastiaries and document different species, as well as connect them to human types and astrological symbols [although they are different from the quite common zodiac (tamra horasat) manuscripts]. There are also elephant, horse, and cat manuals in these forms. Hiram Woodward is conducting a study of the elephant in Southeast Asia and looks at these manuscripts. I am cataloguing some of these manuscripts at the Chester Beatty Library in Dublin, Ireland.

40 A modern Thai translation of the text is found in Kriangkon Sambhacchalit (2553 [2010]: chapter two). I thank Arthid Sheravanichkul for providing me with a copy of this book. J. Crosby (1910) translated the Thai text into English based on a manuscript in the Wachirayan Royal Library in 1910. He noted that there were both metrical (khlon) and prose manuscripts available. He was unable to find another lilit (mixed measured classical Thai lyrical poetry) manuscript mentioned in the 1904 *Vachiranana Magazine* (n°113). I thank Peter Skilling for sending me a copy of this translation.

41 See for example: Arakawa, Hasebe, Imanaga and Okumura (1967); Baird (2001: esp. 101–23); Laumann (1991: 285–354). The numerous source books guiding artists in China discussed in Park's Art by the Book (2012) do not have an equivalent in pre-twentieth-century Thailand.

42 See Gear and Gear (2002).

43 See in order Parmentier (1988: planche 6); Griswold (1960); author unknown (2510 [1967]: 14); M.R. Naengnoi Saksit (2537 [1994]: 81); McGill (2005: 162).

44 See http://gwk-culturalpark.com/ (accessed March 22, 2012).

45 For a provocative study on the way murals were perhaps meant as visual gifts for Buddha images, see Brown (1997); and my "The Agency between Images: the relationships among ghosts, corpses, monks, and deities at a Buddhist monastery in Thailand" (2011b).

46 I am undertaking a study of her life and her connection not only to Buddhist monasteries, but also to the Ton Son Masjid (Mosque) in the Thonburi Section of Greater Bangkok.

47 Although not focused on the doors of the wihan, a good, highly detailed introduction to the decorative arts and architectural elements of Wat Nang Nong is in the cremation volume dedicated to Mrs. Suthin Bunbhan which is a collected study of three Rama III monasteries which were built around the same time along the same canal in Chomthong District of Thonburi/Bangkok—Wat Nang Nong, Wat Nang Ratchawihan, and Wat Ratchaorot. This impressive tome is simply titled *Wat Bhrawatisat* ([*The History of the Monasteries*], Bangkok: Published through Wat Nang Nong, 2552 [2009]). I also thank Phra Maha Wichan Chutibanno at Wat Nang Nong for all the time he spent with me and his detailed tours of the monastic grounds.

48 This monastery and the life of Ying Wilat, Queen Srisulalai, and the Thai poet Sunthorn Phu is the subject of another study I am presently completing.

[49] This monastery, as I argue in *Ethnicity and the Galactic Polity: Ideas and Actualities in the History of Bangkok* in this volume, was a monastery dedicated to women.

[50] Wat Ratchaorot was originally a monastery known as Wat Chomthong that was built during the late Ayutthayan period. It was a place in which Prince Jessada camped with his army in preparation for a planned battle with the Burmese near Kanchanaburi. At this monastery, Prince Jessada, who later became King Rama III, had the Brahmanic ceremony, Khon Thawan, performed to ensure his battle with the Burmese would be successful.

[51] Phra Thammakittiwong (2548 [2005]: 17). See also Prince Damrong Ratchanuphap's *Tamnan Nangseu Samkok* (reprint 2543 [2000]).

[52] Some of the documentation can be seen at my website for the Thai Digital Monastery Project. Wat Ratchaorot is one of the three monasteries featured on the site. See tdm.sas.upenn.edu.

[53] For example, see strikingly similar decorative birds at the Kaiyuan Temple in Chaozhou or the "White Pagoda" of Fuzhou which is nearly identical at its base to the chedi of Wat Nang Nong. The saddle-shaped roofline of the gates of Wat Ratchaorot is distinctly Hokkien in style.

[54] Christopher Adler, composer, ethnomusicologist and avid bird-watcher, helped me identify considerably the birds at Wat Ratchaorot. I cannot do justice to the details he provided, but he noted that some of the birds featured in the decorative art there included: the Indian Roller (Coracias benghalensis), a type of Laughing Thrush (perhaps the Spotted or the Yellow-throated Laughing Thrush), what look to be Green Peafowls (Pavo muticus) or Lady Amherst's Pheasants all of which can be found in Southern China and Southeast Asia. He also noted that bringing captive birds by wealthy people to the region was not an unknown practice and so often birds in art can be copied from other pieces of art or be the artist's favorite bird. See also the useful guide to the birds of Thailand by Bhrasit Chanserikon (2551 [2008]).

[55] John Crawfurd, a Scottish collector and traveler, described Wat Ratchaorot in his journal while serving in the embassy in Siam in the 1820 and 1830s. See excerpts from this description in Wat Ratchaorosara Ratchawirawihan (2541 [1998]), author unknown [it was composed by an unnamed committee working at the monastery] The full journal, *Journal of an Embassy from the Governor-General of India to the courts of Siam and Cochin China* was published in London in 1929 based on the original notes. Oxford University Press reprinted this in 1987. See also: *The Crawfurd papers: a collection of official records relating to the mission of Dr. John Crawfurd sent to Siam by the government of India in the year* (London: Gregg Books, 1915). The only description of the window shutters I have found in detail is in Phra Thammakittiwong's Wat Ratchaoroasaram Ratchaworawihan (2548 [2005]: 33). He neither speculates on their meaning nor origin.

[56] I recently came across a samut khoi (black) manuscript from 1831 in the University of Pennsylvania archives. It has several sections of handwritten notes by an unnamed adviser to Rama III. The section contains specific instructions on repairing a monastery in Bangkok. Giving instructions on monastery building and repair was obviously a regular part of the king's workday. The cataloguing and translating of this manuscript took place in Fall 2014.

[57] See for example work by Rebecca Hall on the very large bird-shaped Nok Hadsading funerary floats that carry corpses of important monks and laity through village streets before being ignited in huge bonfires.

[58] I thank Cecilia Segawa Siegle, one of the original translators of Mishima's *Temple of the Dawn* (Mishima 1973) into English, for her insights into this section and assistance with understanding the Japanese terms rendered into English. Honda's travels to India, especially scenes at Ajanta and along the ghats in Benares, are mirrored in the many ways in Shusaku Endo's *Deep River* (*Fukai Kawa*) in 1993.

[59] For more information see Orzech (2002: 55–83).

[60] The peacock is also mentioned as a beautiful bird in the popular *Amitābha Sūtra* (also known as the *Shorter Sukhāvatīvyūha Sūtra*). In Tamil poetry, like the *Tirukkōvaiyār*, the peacock can represent Śiva. I thank Leah Comeau for the conversations on this point.

[61] See particularly the work of Wendy Doniger, especially (1999).

6

The Material Turn: An Introduction to Thai Sources for the Study of Buddhist Amulets*

In June 2001, a police officer in Pattaya (central Thailand) was arrested and charged with attempted murder and grand theft. He was caught after he held up a 61-year-old wealthy man who was wearing a Buddhist amulet around his neck. The off-duty police officer drew a concealed pistol and pulled the trigger twice. The gun jammed and the wealthy man took off on foot. The police officer was later identified and arrested. The small clay amulet, worth approximately eight million baht (240,000 USD), was recovered. This story is one of many that have made headlines in the past few years regarding amulet theft, assault, and even murder. In fact, there are hundreds of miracle stories such as this published in amulet collectors' magazines and related between friends in the amulet markets or while relaxing at monasteries. Some stories tell of people who were protected from house fires because of amulets. Others tell of those who have successfully passed entrance examinations, and others who were cured of cancer.

The popularity of amulets has been generally approached by scholars as a reflection of a growing crisis in Thai Buddhism and the rise of religious commercialism.[1] Most of these critics have very little appreciation for the history of Buddhist material culture

* Originally appeared as "The Material Turn: An Introduction to Thai Sources for the Study of Buddhist Amulets," in *Material Culture and Asian Religions: Text, Image, Object*, ed. Benjamin Fleming and Richard Mann (London: Routledge, 2014), pp. 135–50.

Amulets. Photo by author.

and so are surprised by its apparent growth now. Critics are shocked by the prices of amulets, the excessive trading, the prominent display, the miracle stories, and the crime caused by the economics of the trade. They seem surprised by materialism in Buddhism, as if it were a new phenomenon. Critics have been shocked by amulets and in turn want to shock their readers. This shock is often characterized by anger at Thai society in general for being duped by duplicitous religious commercialism. Terms like *phuttha phanit* (Buddhist business), *sasana dalat* (the religion of the market), and *sasana phlom* (fake religion) are employed to separate true Buddhism from that which has been sullied by money and things. Some studies express shock in a different way. They explain it away. They reduce amulets to empty signifiers onto which those uneducated in Buddhist doctrine place their lower-class frustrations, their modern anxieties, their insecurities over the Islamic insurgency or the global economic downturn, their fears regarding health, and their petty aspirations for wealth (indeed, it is comfortably easy for elitist scholars born with wealth to criticize the poor masses for wanting to be wealthy). These are condescending studies on the one hand, and studíes of longing on the other—longing for a Buddhism that fits more in line with a certain Protestant rationality that eschews materiality in favor of an undefined spirituality. Scholars have not been studying amulets and other objects used in Thai religious ritual; they have been looking at these objects and seeing them as referents to something else.

Herein lies a tension. A minority of elite and vocal critics condemn the use of objects in Buddhist life for anything more than symbolic purposes. They see the amulet industry as somehow part of the globalization of Thai culture and amulet traders and enthusiasts as victims of this new global reality. This approach effectively marginalizes any serious historical or sociological study of amulets. The production, ritualization, and trade of Buddhist amulets are among the great contributions of Thai artisans and ritualists to global Buddhist culture. However, instead of studying amulets as part of a serious investigation into Thai art history and material culture, such critics reduce them to an economic phenomenon. Therefore, in this short chapter, I want to encourage a material and historical study of Thai amulets, as well as to cast the economy of amulets in a new light.[2]

The Materiality of Amulets

In Thai, amulets are alternatively called *phra khreuang* or *phra phim*. Even though they are made mostly of clay, oil, bits of copper, fruit, and flowers and often measure approximately 2.5 × 3.8 × 0.5 cm (one can hold five or six in the palm of one's hand), some can cost more than two million dollars. Phra Somdet amulets at Wat Rakhang and Wat Indrawihan, made by the famous Thai saint Somdet To or his disciples or followers, have consistently been some of the most valuable in the country. His amulets have also attained the most privileged place among the five highest-ranking amulets of the nation, the Benchaphakhi (League of Five).[3] Other valuable amulets include Phra Kring amulets connected to the present king and Luang Pho Doem's ivory-handled knives. There are thousands of articles in popular amulet collectors' magazines. These magazines contain stories about the value and beauty of these small objects. There is a regular section in the popular Thai-language newspaper *Thai rath* called "Sanam phra" that features new amulets on the market, stories of their production, and occasionally a miracle tale about how an amulet saved a person from drowning or helped his or her business. These amulets are usually connected to the monk who first made them.

What can we learn from amulets? The most cursory reading of Buddhist canonical texts or study of South and Southeast Asian archaeology reveals that objects have been integral to the spread of Buddhism since its inception 2,500 years ago, beginning with the relics of the Buddha himself. One could argue that buildings, images, stupas, and amulets—like the Phra Pathom Chedi, Emerald Buddha, Wat Sri Chum, the Sandalwood Buddha, the Mahamuni image, the Phra Bang, the image of Queen Suriyothai in Ayutthaya, the image of King Chulalongkorn in front of the parliament building, and so on—have inspired Buddhist practice and belief in Southeast Asia more than doctrine. Pilgrimages to images, the cherishing (not just the collecting) of amulets, the prostration to images, and the circumambulation of *stūpas* certainly occupy the days of more Buddhists than the close study of Pali texts.

Pattaratorn Chirapravati (1999) has traced the history of amulets in Thailand to the use of votive tablets made of clay and metal going back to the sixth century. Evidence suggests that they were more popular among religious communities on the Malay Peninsula and in southern Thailand as well as among the Khmer. Chalong Soontravanich (2005) has noted that archaeological evidence has uncovered the use of "locally available 'natural' objects, such as cowries, a certain kind of jackfruit seed, 'mai ruak' [a local species of small bamboo] and 'wan'."[4] There are also dozens of different types of phallic amulets, often worn on a man's belt, that can be acquired in virtually every amulet market. Chalong believes that Brahmanism and Buddhism brought the added ingredient of powerful words inscribed on these objects in Sanskrit and Pali in a variety of scripts. This led to the use of *takrut* (small metal scrolls), *yantra* cloth, and *mit mo* (small knives), as well as of *luk prakham* (string of beads), *si phung* (consecrated beeswax), and *sua* (ivory-carved tiger statuette). Tattoos can also be seen developing from this tradition of wearable and mobile objects of protection. Of course, amulets are part of Southeast Asian religions in general. In the Philippines and parts of Indonesia, objects known as *anting-anting* are held in the hand and are supposed to protect the possessor.

In Thailand, the ranking of these amulets into categories by the royal family began in the late nineteenth century. One of the earliest ranked amulets was the Phra Kamphaeng Thungsetthi, which became one among the prestigious League of Five after it was found in the 1850s in Kamphaengphet. King Chulalongkorn also went on amulet-hunting pilgrimages in the late nineteenth century and was given Phra

Nang Phraya, another member of that prestigious league, in Phitsanulok Province. When an old stupa collapsed in Suphanburi, it exposed a large number of Phra Phong Suphan votive tablets, also of the league, some of which were confiscated by the local authorities and presented to Rama VI. The amulets in the League of Five are prized royal gifts, thus showing that amulet trading and collection is not a pastime only of the masses. Chalong Soontravanich (2004; 2005) has also noted that this early amulet trade grew after World War II. He traces the rapid rise in the collection and trade of amulets in the 1950s and 1960s. At that time, magazines relating stories of brave police officers being protected by amulets while battling bandits in urban and rural Thailand became popular reading material in Thailand. These stories were popular because of the rise in the use of small arms and in crime in Thai society. These cheap and accessible texts, coupled with the growth in the publication of detailed studies of the materials and rituals used in the production of amulets, led to a greater desire among people to seek their own amulets. As more people became involved in such trade, the more the study of the history of particular amulets grew. Unlike in most studies of amulets, Chalong does not reduce the rise of amulets simply to socio-historical forces but instead emphasizes that the histories of individual amulets, individual sacred monks, and individual thieves and crime fighters need to be undertaken to explain why certain amulets are treasured and others fall into disuse.

Material objects are seen by some scholars and social critics as getting in the way of the simplicity, non-attachment, and quiet embracing of impermanence needed to achieve world peace and future enlightenment. I see them as something cherished by Buddhists that ought not to be ignored, reduced, or lamented as a product of commercialization of religion. I also see them as expanding the study of Thai religion beyond Theravada Buddhism. There are many amulets of Chinese deities and *Bodhisattvas.* In addition, there are hundreds of different types of amulets in Thailand that do not depict Buddha images or Buddhist monks, but rather Hindu deities, royal family members, and local goddesses and gods.[5] Therefore, any conversation about amulets needs to include these other important historical sources.

The study of the amulets of famous monks like Luang Pho Suk, Luang Pho Doem, Luang Pho Khian, and others is a major intellectual endeavor in Thailand.[6] Not only do local scholars closely investigate the history, material features, and authenticity of amulets before national auctions, museum exhibitions, and contests, but they also publish detailed studies of them. Soraphon Sophitkun (1997/2540; 2001/2544), Akadet Khrisanathilok (2006/2549), and Ram Watcharapradit (2004/2547), among others, have written extensive studies of amulets in Thai; they provide information on the ritual production and material composition, while also discussing the competing historical claims regarding the authenticity and origin of particular amulets.[7] Somsak Sakuntanat (2007/2550) has given basic biographical details of many monks (because an amulet is only as powerful as the person who originally forged and consecrated it) followed by a detailed catalog of the major amulets of individual monks. Somsak creates new lineages (or perhaps "halls of fame") by writing a book in which monks who had no connection in life are associated with one another in print. In his two-volume catalogue of monks and their amulets, he includes lesser-known monks like Luang Pho Khan of Wat Nok Krachap in Ayutthaya (1872–1944) and his Phra Pit Ta[8] amulets with nationally famous monks like Luang Pho Khun of Wat Ban Rai in Nakhon Ratchasima (b. 1923). He also makes a concerted effort to describe the biographies and amulets of monks from southern Thailand, like the lesser-known Luang Pho Klai of Wat Suan Khan in Nakhon Sri Thammarat (1876–1970) and Luang Pho Kham of Wat Prasatnikon in Chumphon (1852–1948). He even includes a monk from northern Malaysia, Luang Pho Khron of Wat Udommaram (n.d.), whose amulets are hard to find in Thailand. He elevates the prestige of Luang Pho Khron by telling the Thai reading audience that this monk is well respected in Malaysia and that his amulets, especially his own version of the Phra Pit Ta, with large ears, are treasured there.

Akadet Khrisanathilok's (2006/2549) three-volume study of Phra Somdet amulets is a good example of how local independent historians study amulets. They start with the object itself—the material and the methods of its production and design. Akadet makes a great effort to teach the reader how to spot fakes, and he warns against schemes. His concern is how the material qualities of Phra Somdet amulets reflect both local choices and the relation between material and worship. He refers to Phra Somdet as *buchaniyawatthu* (raw material for the purpose of worship). The famous monk, Somdet To, who made the original Phra Somdets, wanted—Akadet claims—to cause *aphinihan saksit* (sacred miracles) after his death (the amulets would act in his place) and to offer the Thai people *ekalak thang tham* (something that possessed the essence or "identity" of dharma). He emphasizes that people in Thailand today do not have the skills or proper substances, especially the *phong*, or powder of high enough sacred quality, to make these items anymore. This powder is the most important material needed to make an amulet. Somdet To used *phong khao suk* (fresh white powder) to make amulets and then distributed it to novices and monks to make their own amulets. At Wat Rakhang, one of the high-ranking monks, Phra Khru Platwichit Khantiko, guards a large stone that was used by Somdet To to grind powder (*bao khlot phong*) for making his amulets. Therefore, Somdet To saw himself not simply as the sole producer of amulets but as a person who helped others develop their own amulet lineages. One amulet is used to make others, like mothers bearing children. The powder Somdet To used could be seen as the raw material others could use to create their own material offspring. This is why Phra Somdet amulets can have multiple *rung* (generations). Phra Somdet of the first generation are considered the most valuable; however, those made by Somdet To's own students with raw material and techniques directly connected to Somdet To are also extremely valuable, like colts sired by famous thoroughbreds.

Somdet To did not only use *phong khao suk* but also *phong keson* (pollen-filled powder), *phong wan* (sweet powder), and *phong takrai bai sema* (lemongrass powder taken from the boundary stones of monasteries). The first was made from lotus, jasmine, plumeria, and other flower pollen (and pistils and stamens). The flowers were said to have been given to Somdet To during his alms rounds and, therefore, were already the products of merit. The second was made out of roots of sweet-smelling plants. These plant materials were used not only for their olfactory and visual aesthetics but also because they were medicine for curing headaches, fevers, and the like. The third is taken from lemongrass pollen, which often floats through the air. Somdet To was said to have scraped this pollen off the boundary stones of monasteries, where it is often collected. Therefore, these amulets possess direct medicinal value. Besides these three basic types of powder, there are also different mixtures, with names like *itthiche, patthamang, maharat,* among others, with different amounts of each petal, stamen, root, and the like. They could not only be used to hold and keep close to one's heart around a necklace but also soaked in holy water. The medicine in the powder would be absorbed by what was around it (that is, skin and water). Akadet does not discuss the importance of Nam Man Tang Yu, a rare herbal oil associated with the Sino-Thai community in Sampeng/Yaowarat section of Bangkok. This oil is still sold at a couple of small shops there and is used in the batches of many amulets.

Akadet is an important source not simply for what he reports, but also for what he does not. He emphasizes that Somdet To was a practical healer, but not a materialist or charlatan. While other scholars criticize the irrational collection of seemingly worthless trinkets (based on the fact that amulets do not usually contain rare and precious material like gems or gold), Akadet links the material the amulets are made of directly to their value. Akadet offers methods and photographs to train readers in the identification of the material in amulets. For example, *phong* is identifiable by color and can be seen with a small magnifying glass (jeweler's loop). Besides the color of *phong,* there are also other substances in amulets that are easy to spot if one is trained in what to look for: oyster and clam shell-flakes, lime, banana flower, ground jackfruit seeds, small scraps of monks' robes, and pieces of palm-leaf manuscripts.[9] Some of these ingredients are roasted before being added to the mixture, and each ingredient is chanted over with various incantations, including the *Nāmo buddhāya, Itipiso, Jinapañjara, Bahuṃ,* and various *parittas.* Since most amulets are barely one inch tall, correctly identifying these substances takes time, but this time is relaxing and social, as it is often interspersed with short conversations and snacks.

The Economy of Amulets

If we view the phenomenon of amulets in Thailand through the lens of economics as is the approach of most critics, we must study amulets in their broad socio-economic context—not just providing shocking stories about the cost of individual pieces. First, it is important to note that the income from amulet sales is widely distributed. The amulets produced at these ceremonies are rented or given as gifts, and the direct profits from their rentals are usually quite insignificant. These gifts are considered some of the most gracious ways of thanking another person for their friendship, because you are giving them the gift of merit making. They might not have been able to go to the monastery or ritual you attended, so by giving them a material object from the monastery, they share in the merit. For example, an amulet with the image Phra Phuttha Chinarat was made for the anniversary of a locally well-known monk in Phisanulok and sponsored by Naresuan University in 2008. This amulet was freely distributed at the consecration and then rented later for less than three dollars a piece. Considering the amulet was gold plated and presented in an inscribed plastic case, the profits were insignificant. Even a solid silver amulet stamped with Luang Pho Saeng's image was produced at Wat Manichonlakhan in Lopburi in 2000. The sales, I was told, did little to increase the coffers that year at this small monastery, even though each amulet cost 14 dollars. Many people who sponsor the production of amulets and the monks who host the consecration and later distribution or sale would not go through the trouble if they were interested simply in profits. However, the production and renting of some batches of amulets can be considerably profitable. The point is that the history and production of each amulet need to be investigated before reducing the motivation to pure commercialism.

Second, there needs to be a study of indirect profits of amulet sales. The consecrations of batches of amulets are rarely national events, as in the previous example, but are very popular local events often connected to annual monastic fairs or anniversaries. These events attract locals in various provinces, students, monks, as well as pilgrims and invited honorary guests. These people need places to eat, sleep, and shop. Therefore, there are hundreds, if not thousands, of people who profit from these events—food vendors, carnival-ride operators, astrologers, the renters of sound equipment, local shopkeepers, souvenir makers, candle and incense companies and vendors, florists, motel owners, charter-bus companies, dance troupes, and the like. Of course, the publishers of amulet magazines, commemorative volumes, cases, and necklaces also indirectly or directly profit from this industry. Even when amulets are distributed freely, most people who visit monasteries make small or large donations. There is a considerable amount of local revenue that is produced. For example, I have been to many amulet-consecration rituals and have gone on "pilgrimages" to see certain monasteries and certain monks. I nearly always rent a few amulets for myself and as gifts for friends and often purchase local products in whatever province I happen to be, such as silk, fruit, nuts, or handicrafts. I am one of millions in Thailand who participate in this practice regularly. Wat Phra That Lampang Luang, the site of the mixing of the ingredients in the Phra Kring amulet, is a fifteenth-century monastery situated in the middle of rice paddies and fruit orchards in rural northern Thailand. It is out of the way and not on most Western-tourist itineraries. However, it is very important historically and ritually in the north. It attracts mostly Thai pilgrims seeking to view its architecture, circumambulate its reliquary, and participate in ritual consecrations and other ceremonies. It is the single-most important moneymaker in the villages that surround it. There are hundreds of shopkeepers, students, carpenters, and truck drivers who depend on it. It is responsible for the most consistent local income stream, especially when the agricultural commodities markets change so frequently and the region fluctuates between flood seasons and droughts. The same can be said of Wat Ban Rai in northeastern Thailand, Wat Wangwiwek in Kanchanaburi, and Wat Chang Hai in Pattani, among many others. The economy of amulets is a desperately needed boost to the local economy. Moreover, it is not only the abbot of the monastery, local government officials, and members of local mafia families who are hoarding this revenue. People from all classes are profiting. Monks are not simply manipulating people into buying trinkets. They are participating in a microeconomic environment that is encouraged by many who have nothing to do with the monastery, some who may or may not be interested in collecting or believe in the power of amulets, and some who may not even self-identify as Buddhist. There certainly are problems with the amulet trade, as with any other: theft, fraud, obsession, and the like. These have been well discussed by others. However, in scholarly studies, the negative effects of the trade too often overshadow the benefits.

Third, the amulets, old or new, that make it to the amulet markets outside monasteries are a profitable business but not centrally controlled like a brewery, oil company, toy factory, or automobile producer. There is no centralized group of monks who produce amulets and who are hoarding the raw materials or secrets of production. Amulets are produced by many monks of different ranks in many different monasteries. Amulet sales do not require elaborate storefronts, access to foreign technology, heavy machinery, tech-repair specialists, lawyers, insurance, or a highly-trained staff with salaries and benefits. It is an industry that the uneducated and non-elite can break into and become experts. Most amulet dealers I know are not wealthy. For example, Sutachai, who runs a store in the Tha Phrachan amulet market, the most well-known one in the country, crowded with renters, traders, and the curious every day, states that she usually takes in 500 to 1,000 baht a day (14 to 28 dollars). Some days she hardly sees a customer. Other days she manages to rent a large image or a rare amulet. Since she employs two assistants and must stock her shelves, she does not see her shop as being very successful. However, she loves the friends she has in the market; she makes merit; and she learns much about different teachers and ancient things (*wattu boran*). Sutachai's shop is one of the larger ones in the market: she earns a living. The amulet dealers who set up shop by spreading a blanket on a folding table on the sidewalk are lucky, they tell me, if they rent one or two items a day for between 25 and 300 baht each (about 0.75–9.40 USD). In general, the shops and the temporary sidewalk dealers do not pay high rents. Owners of the shops in the market, some of whom have been in business over 40 years, can either occupy the space themselves or rent the space out to rotating temporary shops. These owners pay only 20 baht (80 cents) a day for upkeeping the market. However, a renter will need to pay the shop owner about 125 baht a day in rent (3 dollars). The shop spaces are tight and usually passed down from parent to child. If they are sold, which is rare, they can fetch up to 10,000 dollars. Nevertheless, this is a relatively low buy-in to own your own business. Since they are rarely sold, large conglomerates or chain stores have not infiltrated the market. Taxes are extremely low since no one reports their full income, and there are few receipts. Sidewalk vendors pay no taxes but pay the shopkeepers in the neighborhood low under-the-table fees.[10] There are certainly a few wealthy individuals who own a number of stalls in the larger amulet markets in the country, but for a large part, this is one of the few industries in Thailand, like the street-restaurant business, that help the lower and middle classes, as well as the rich.

Fourth, there are indeed many monasteries that get rich from amulet sales, but it is where the profits go that is worth noting. Let me provide a couple of examples. At Wat Srapathum, Phra Thawon organized a casting of Jatukham Ramathep amulets of various colors and sizes in 2006. This ceremony and its products raised 65 million baht (almost 2 million dollars). This money has been used to build a Buddhist school for poor children in rural Bangladesh and to help fund the building of a monastery in Australia. It also helped with the repairs and restoration of the nineteenth-century *ubosot* and *wihan* of Wat Srapathum itself. While Phra Thawon is certainly a self-promoter and effective marketer of amulets, in an interview with me in February 2008, he said that people who came to make merit and rent the Jatukham Ramathep amulets were well aware where this funding was going. Indeed, there are photographs of the construction of the school and monastery on large bulletin boards at the entrance of Wat Srapathum. The massive income brought in at Wat Indrawihan is generated from Phra Somdet, Jatukham Ramathep, and Phra Chiwok Koman amulet and image rentals, among other products like books, CDs, and holy-water containers. Much of these funds go to the Somdet To Foundation (Munitthi Somdet Phutthachan To Prahmarangsi), which to date has funded the building of 30 elementary schools in rural Thailand. It is not just cash that is generated, though; the people employed at monasteries (alongside the free labor of novices, *maechi*, and monks) are often the handicapped, destitute, or orphans. For example, a woman named Benchawan at Wat Rakhang lives at Wat Rakhang without paying rent. She told me that her husband abused her and she ran away. She lives at the monastery and spends her days sitting at a booth renting Phra Somdet amulets. She eats, largely for free, and participates in regular monastic events. She now has a large group of supportive friends. The new computers and reference desk in the library of Wat Rakhang—a place that provides free after-school tutoring programs and study space for children in this very dense and loud neighborhood of Bangkok—have been funded by the renting of Phra Somdet amulets. A young mentally-disabled boy at Wat Sateu in Ayutthaya, a site of one of Somdet To's residences, helps hand out candles, flowers, and incense sticks at the Somdet To shrine. I was told by a monk there that he was abandoned by his parents when he was a baby and is now being cared for by the monks at the monastery. He also attends the monastery's elementary school, eats in the cafeteria, and is given clothes and toys, all without charge. The funding for this child comes from the ability of Wat Sateu's monks and wider rural community to "commercialize" the amulets and legacy of Somdet To.[11] This is not just a new phenomenon. The funding of one of Thailand's premier Pali grammar schools came in 1939 through the sale of amulets (Newell 2008).

The Social Lives of Amulets

Besides these four economic considerations, amulets have more abstract and unforeseen dimensions that scholars would benefit from studying. Amulets create communities and texts. The wonderings, reflections, and visualizations that take place while looking at an image or walking around a monastery generate questions that can be posed to texts or help individuals develop new beliefs. The conversations that take place over the trading of amulets can be seen as emerging doctrine. Buddhist texts in Thailand are seen as having value, but amulets as being corrupting objects. This is because texts are not seen as objects but as voices. The material features of texts are often overlooked. Yet amulets are generated by texts. Many, if not most, amulets have inscribed in metal or clay *yantras* in Khom, Thai, or Lan Na script. Many also have information about the monastery, date, and name of the monk they were made by (or in honor of) inscribed on them. This information would go a long way in tracing local lineages and art history, but it has not been the subject of any serious non-Thai study.

Other amulets were actually texts originally. These are called *takrut*. They are amulets made of rolled metal (copper, gold, silver, or lead) or palm-leaf scrolls with an inscription. The rolled inscriptions are placed inside glass or metal tubes and sealed. Phra Oot Thamakamo of Wat Sai Mai in Nonthaburi Province has recently produced a set of two *takrut* that have metal scrolls inserted inside bullets that help protect soldiers (among others).[12] These inscriptions can be *yantras,* but more often they are short *paritta* texts. My abbot presented me with one with an abbreviated *Ratanasutta* inscribed on it. There are *takrut* with a full or abbreviated *Jinapañjara* inscription. These *takrut* are rolled and either placed inside small glass or clear-resin tubes and worn around the neck or rolled, bound with sacred string, and sealed with wax, molten metal, or tree sap. This sealing process makes the texts unreadable. One of the most famous *takrut* in Thailand was produced by Phra Khru Thammanukhun Cantakesaro of Wat Indrawihan. He was born in Tak Province in 2373 (1830) and was a *phra thudong* (*dhutaṅga*: "wandering forest monk"); later he moved to the forested area near Wat Indrawihan (along the riverbank where the National Bank of Thailand's offices are now located). This used to be a forested area used by Lao refugees and *thudong* monks traveling in from upcountry, often to visit Somdet To. This area became renowned for magically powerful Lao monks. Phra Khru Thammanukhun, who may have been of Lao ethnicity, resided here and later became the abbot at Wat Indrawihan, in 2435 (1892) at the age of 62. He died at age 103 (in 2476/1933). He created, it is believed under the tutelage of Phra Arannik and Somdet To, a *takrut* that was eight inches long. It was a short text, covered with a clay mixture used to make Phra Somdets (*phong*). The text inscribed on the metal sheet before being coiled, wrapped in string, and covered with powder and resin was the *Awut* (Pali: Āvudha) *phra phuttha chao* (The Weapon of the Buddha). It warded off *phi sat* (devils). His students continued this tradition and produced a number of shorter and different-colored *takrut* with the same incantation. All the *takrut* are sealed and unreadable.[13] Some clay amulets are actually made from texts. One of the more popular ingredients for amulets is the ground-up clay roof tiles from famous monasteries. The red, blue, orange, and other roof tiles of Thai monasteries are iconic. These clay tiles often need to be replaced. Men on scaffolding slowly replacing one tile after another is a common sight at Thai monasteries. The old tiles are taken down and smashed. The dust from the tiles is considered valuable because it has absorbed the chanting of the texts inside the monastery for years. It is believed that as the monks sit under the ceilings and chant, the sound drifts upward and is absorbed. The dust from the old clay tiles is mixed with other ingredients and shaped into amulets. When individuals donate (usually 10 baht [25 cents] each) new tiles to the monastery, they often write their names on the tiles using black, felt-tip pens. Therefore, eventually their names will be ground up and placed in amulets as well. In other cases, old palm-leaf manuscripts that have become tattered and unreadable are ground up into dust and mixed with water to form a paste. This paste is one of the ingredients that can go into an amulet. Obviously, the semantic meaning of the texts in question is not important. They are illegible. However, amulets are, in this way, textual practices and oral liturgies, and physical texts are needed to make them. Another way amulets are part of Buddhist textuality is through conversation. The stories and conversations generated from the trade, collection, and production of amulets can be seen to be as valuable as other Buddhist texts (McDaniel 2008: 119–60). When people chat in Internet blogs about amulets, meet in markets in and outside of monasteries, attend consecration rituals, amulet contests, monastic fairs, and auctions, they often talk about different Buddhist teachers, monasteries they have visited, and the material qualities and power of their own amulets.

Most of these conversations are ethereal and brief. However, they can be seen as Buddhist texts.

The most popular Buddhist texts in Thailand are *jātaka* tales (both canonical and non-canonical), and stories drawn directly or inspired by the *Dhammapada-atthakathā*. Local histories, such as relic chronicles, dynastic histories, and biographies of famous monks, are also popularly known (*tamnan, phongsawadan,* and the like). These are all found in manuscripts from various regions in Thailand, some dating back to the fifteenth century. They form the content of many sermons. These are all stories that relate miracles, the heroic acts of famous images, monks, and princes, and trace the mytho-historical legacy of Buddhism both locally and translocally. Conversations about amulets, especially their material composition, history, and powers, are part of this longer textual heritage of Thailand. The rituals, catalogs, detailed material analyses, stamps, photographs, museum displays, and amulet sets not only help collectors but they also attract amateurs to the field and inspire pilgrims, start conversations, and create new communities.

Conversations about amulets are a way of breaking the ice. They are also a way to commiserate and express fears. When my wife was pregnant with our second child, I had conversations with several pregnant couples at the Mae Nak shrine at Wat Mahabut regarding fears of miscarriage as we rented protective oil. I have overheard women *huang* (worry) about their husbands and sons serving in the military at the shrine while they purchased dresses and cosmetics to present to the image of Mae Nak. Students who have never met often strike up conversations about impending examinations as they stand waiting to pick up flowers or incense or rent an amulet near the image of Somdet To at Wat Rakhang. These conversations are taking place between people in Australia, Japan, Singapore, the United States, Thailand, Malaysia, and other places in online amulet trading and collecting blogs. Tour groups of amulet traders from Taiwan and Singapore are beginning to go to Wat Rakhang and Wat Indrawihan. One visitor to Wat Rakhang was so inspired by the story of Somdet To and the possible power of his amulets that he donated a painting he had done of Somdet To. This painting, executed in abstract calligraphic style with Somdet To's name in Chinese, now hangs prominently above the main door of the newly-designed library. These new communities sometimes formalize themselves into amulet-collecting clubs or charitable foundations. This social component and the conversations lead to the writing of new texts, the tracing of new histories, the recounting and reinterpreting (and exaggerating) of local biographies, and the increase of local pride.

Individuals not only feel protected wearing amulets around their necks but also can participate in an abundant material culture even if they are not wealthy themselves. For example, an ice-cream vendor, Batwat, whom I met at Wat Rakhang, proudly showed me the amulets hanging on his necklace. He had a Phra Somdet, a Jatukham Ramathep, a Luang Pho Tuat, and three *takrut,* one of which he stated helped him meet his future wife! Sopon Suptongthong, a taxi driver from Bangkok, is a devotee of Somdet To. He showed me the *yantra* made at the Hindu temple Wat Khaek in Bangkok, that he had placed above his head on the taxi's roof. It was placed next to two other *yantras,* one drawn in white powder and another one made of red cloth and sealed in a plastic sheath. These, he stated, protected him against accidents, and they were also drawn by a Phra Prahm (a Hindu priest). On the dashboard, he had glued a Phra Sangacchai because it brought happiness and money. He said this encouraged his passengers to give him money and *udom sombun* (abundance) for his family. Aesthetically, he also liked this image because it "*yim talot*" (smiled all the time). In the center of the dash, he had a Phra Somdet To amulet. Somdet To, he asserted, was important because he had *metta* for the people, just like the king. He elaborated that Somdet To was much like the monk-king to all the people of Thailand. Next to the Phra Somdet, he had a Kuan Im that, he said, reminded him not to get drunk and drive. He was unsure himself why Kuan Im was believed to protect against drunk driving. He had Chiwok Koman (Jivaka) hanging from the rear-view mirror because that protected him from catching colds from his passengers and getting sick. He had many Jatukham Ramatheps stuck to the wind-shield. He wasn't sure why he had those, he said. He just liked them.

Sathapon Sawamiwat from Chachoengsao Province was the driver of a taxi I took in Bangkok. He had only one image in his taxi, a Somdet To statue on his dashboard. He liked Somdet To because he practiced both *paṭipatti* and *pari-yatti*—he was a meditator and a scholar. He was *yot* (high ranking), like the king, but he loved the *chao ban* (villagers), like the king. Somdet To visited all the villages; he did not just stay in the city. Somdet To, he also stated, was an expert in Pali-Sanskrit but used simple words in his sermons. Sathapon admitted that he did not know much about history (he did get a few simple facts about Somdet To's life wrong) and could chant only a little, but he still loved Somdet To.

One of the most interesting conversations I have ever had about Thai Buddhism was with Pithipon, a coffee-shop owner in Chiang Rai (northern Thailand). As I was ordering a cup, I noticed that she was reading an English-language translation of the *Tibetan Book of the Dead*. She had received a master's degree in Bangkok and learned to read (although not speak) English. This led to a discussion about different religious traditions in Thailand. She showed me her extensive collection. She had a Chinese Jade Emperor image, a Kuan Im, statues and photographs and amulets with images of Somdet To, Luang Pho Khan, Khrupa Siwichai, Khrupa Nunchum (a Shan monk), King Chulalongkorn, and photographs from the shrine to Ṛṣi Bharata, a local famous Brahman sage in Nakhon Ratchasima Province. She did not believe that people needed to choose which religion to believe in; she valued sacred people and was drawn to their teachings and *barami* (a type of sacred power generated through specific virtuous practices). Amulets and images were not mere bricolage she had assembled from random trips. They defined her intellectual approach to religion in general.

Conclusion

Willa Cather (1949: 27) famously quipped that "religion and art spring from the same root and are close kin. Economics and art are strangers." I hope that I have shown that, despite Cather's quip, amulets are objects in which art, religion, and economics have come together in creative ways. Opening a discussion about amulets that takes history and materiality seriously exposes motivations and values for the production, display, and trade of amulets that cannot be reduced to mere modern commercialism, globalization, or Westernization. I see these famous monks and their amulets as simply creating new types of communities—communities of pilgrims, amulet traders, spiritual tourists, and online communities. Scholars so often separate culture and religion: Culture is something that "happens" to religion, and this happening is almost always negative. I am arguing that we cannot hope to learn from Thai Buddhism if we do not take seriously its material culture and the way individual agents incorporate objects into their personal religious repertoires.

Notes

1 See McDaniel's *Lovelorn Ghost* (2011: 189–212) for a more extended version of this argument, discussing the ways in which amulets have been studied and criticized as aspects of religious commercialism in Western scholarship and Thai elite social circles.

2 Chalong Soontravanich (2004) has noted that Phra Somdets may fetch the highest prices, but a Phra Pid Ta Luang Pho Kaew, Wat Khruawan of Chonburi, sold for 7 million baht. In June 2004, an amulet made by Luang Pu Iam of Wat Nang in Bangkhunthian was priced at 6 million baht. There are national conventions, online auctions, and contests where collectors show off and rate the "beauty and authenticity" of these amulets. There are also dozens of websites dedicated to the display and trade of amulets. The sale of old amulets adds about 1 billion baht a year to the Thai economy, and the production and sale of new amulets accounts for as much as 10 billion baht annually.

3 Although not an extensive historical study, Cœdès (1964/2507: 35–60) includes a short history of *phra phim.*

4 Chalong Soontravanich (2005: 31) describes *wan* as "a Thai term given to a group of plants, with or without roots, which are believed to have medicinal property as well as to give those who carry it or consume it the power of invulnerability. *Wan* remains to this day one of the major ingredients in making certain Buddhist amulets that contain the power to confer invulnerability." See also Soraphon Sophitkun (1994).

5 See, for example, the description of the amulets of Shiva, Vishnu, and Ganesha produced by the Thewasathan, the national Brahman training center under the supervision of Chiraphat Praphanwithya (2002/2545), which includes the liturgies (including the Sanskrit texts) and histories of these amulets. Often these amulets of Hindu deities are forged in rituals performed by both Buddhist monks and Brahman priests working together. For example, the Brahman expert Montri Chanthaphan, the physician Somneuk, and the monk Pho Than Somphong Thammasaro produced a set of Jatukham Ramathep amulets together at Wat Phrahmalok in Nakhon Sri Thammarat Province for the specific purpose of curing those who had been bitten by snakes.

6 Amulets are made almost exclusively by monks. However, there is one famous nun (*maechi*) named Mae Bunruean Tongbuntoem (1894–1964) who has been worshipped as an *arahant* (lit. "worthy one;" that is, "awakened one"), and it is believed that she realized the six *abhiññās* (higher knowledge); see Seeger (2009).

7 Also Phraya Sunthornphiphit (1972/2515), Triyampawai (1954/2492).

8 That is, a corpulent monk, often identified as Mahākaccāyana, covering his eyes with his hands as a sign of being uninfluenced by sensual desires.

9 See Akadet Khrisanathilok (2006/2549; esp. vol. 2, ch. 3, and 3.45–52).

10 I thank many shop owners in the market for their help in this research, as well as Thongchai Likhitphonsawan for all his advice and training in the amulet trade.

11 Somdet To money is also printed. There are reproductions of thousand-baht notes with Somdet To's image on them instead of the king's (King Rama IX's face is on every legal baht note). Other famous monks, like Luang Pho Khun, also have their own money.

12 This is not a particularly new phenomenon. There have been bullet amulets available in regional amulet markets for many years. These particular bullets (*takrut*) were no longer available at Wat Sai Mai in 2008, but I later rented one at the Wat Srapathum monastery for 240 baht (8 dollars).

13 The ritual that is used to concentrate this particular *takrut* is described in Somsak Sakuntanat (2007/2550: 33–6). I thank Vivian Nyitray for translating this inscription for me.

7

Strolling Through Temporary Temples: Modern Buddhist Art Installations in Thailand*

Most studies of Buddhist culture and history are rooted in the institution of the monastery. This is logical. Most Buddhist teachings, art, music and architecture emerge from monastic life. However, in modern Thailand, the presentation of Buddhist teaching, art and material culture are being found outside traditional monastic spaces. Modern Art in Thailand is thriving. New galleries, new exhibitions and new publications in Chiang Mai and Bangkok (and growing in other cities) have given artists in Thailand a stage on which to display their creations. Not surprisingly, considering that over 90 per cent of Thais are Buddhists, much of this modern art has Buddhist-inspired themes and explicit Buddhist messages. One of the more interesting developments in modern Thai art is the plethora of installation artists.[1] These installation artists have created new and mostly temporary temple-like spaces. Installation artists, like architects, create three-dimensional places. Their works are much more than moveable paintings, statues or mixed-media pieces. These installations cannot be purchased and taken home to hang on one's wall and rarely, because of their size and complexity, can they be parts of the permanent collections of museums. The artists are like architects of temporary Buddhism. Their pieces are seen by the public in

* Originally appeared in "Strolling through Temporary Temples: Modern Buddhist Art Installations in Thailand," *Contemporary Buddhism* 18, 1 (2017): 1–34.

"Shroud" created by contemporary Thai artist Jakkai Siributr. Displayed at several venues. Photo taken by the author at the Asian Civilizations Museum in Singapore (December 2012) as part of the "Exploring the Cosmos: The Stupa as a Buddhist Symbol."

museums and galleries for barely a few months at a time and then dismantled. Rarely are their shows big enough or long enough to produce printed exhibition volumes. After the show is over, their work exists only in photographs on online catalogues or inexpensive posters advertising the show. Since these installations sometimes include music, video and even live performance as part of the physical space, seeing them as still images or even short videos on the internet often cannot recreate the experience of the temporary live show.

The spaces I focus on below are run largely by the laity, with no connection to a single monastery. They do not ordain or train monks or nuns. In most cases, they are privately owned, but open to visitors from all walks of life (although they tend to attract the urban middle and upper classes). Oftentimes one finds very few monks or nuns in the spaces, and those that are there are not in roles of teachers or administrators and do not offer formal sermons, accept formal gifts or conduct specific rituals. These spaces in general are not affiliated with a specific lineage, sect or school of Buddhism (although most visitors might come from a certain sect) and the designers and directors of the space do not overtly promote a particular approach to Buddhist learning and practice.

I see these installation art exhibitions as a part of an emerging non-monastic, Buddhist public culture in Thailand. I am using the term "public" here for spaces that, using Michael Warner's expression "create a public" (Warner 2002: 66).[2] He sees a public, like a public for a novel or a film, as categorized by choice—"a public organizes itself independently of state institutions, laws, formal frameworks of citizenship, or preexisting institutions such as the church" (Warner 2002: 68). A public is self-organized and self-creating and often ephemeral and discontinuous. Warner poses a good question for those interested in religious studies to think about:

> Imagine how powerless people would feel if their commonality and participation were simply defined by pre-given frameworks, by institutions and laws, as in other social contexts through kinship. What would the world look like if all ways of being public were more like applying for a driver's license or subscribing to a professional group—if, that is, formally organized mediations replaced the self-organized public as the image of belonging and common activity? (Warner 2002: 69)

To better refine what counts as "public," and in an effort to look at the ways that installation artists can create publics in contemporary Thai Buddhist culture, I focus on leisure—what I like to call socially-disengaged Buddhism.[3] Scholars of Buddhist studies have always been very good at presenting research on obligation—paths (Pali: *magga*), sects (*nikāya*), ways (*yāna*), precepts and ascetic rules (that is, things that fall under the categories of *vinaya*), morals, and the like. The role of the laity, especially studies of what lay families do in or outside their homes at their leisure, and writings or art of lay Buddhist artists and scholars have been much less important to scholars, including myself.[4] Our primary subject—monasteries and monks and the art they create and books they write—are places defined by discipline and obligation. We have not been so good at studying leisure, the non-teleological and non-formal. In Western films, books, and art depicting and describing Buddhists, practitioners have been long associated with sobriety, discipline, shaven heads, and neatly folded robes. When speaking of leisure, I am not referring to very active debates in sociology and economics on the activities of the so-called leisure class or the vast literature on games and contests.[5] Instead, I simply am referring to the non-obligated parts of life in Johan Huizinga's sense of the term. Huizinga was concerned with, among other things, leisure as *licere*, or that which is permitted or unbound.[6] Although the field of religious studies has not concerned itself much with leisure, when it has, it has usually been with leisure as *otium* (retreat, meditation, spiritual exercises, contemplation, even monastic labora, like gardening and manuscript copying), as Petrarch did in his famous *On Religious Leisure* (*De otio religioso*)—not idleness (Latin: *accidia*), but an active reflection on theological conundrums and ultimate truths.[7] Some religious studies scholars have profitably learned from the approaches of Bakhtin or Turner and have seen religious festivals, plays or pilgrimages as alternative or liminal places for testing and then reaffirming the value and power of moral rules and social norms.[8] Leisure as otium is functionalist and goal-oriented. However, in these new Buddhist places, activity is not necessarily directed or designed to be overtly purposive. Now, one could say that anyone who visits a Buddhist museum, monument or park is purposefully "making-merit" or has an ulterior motive based on a vague sense of spiritual advancement. The same people might also want to impress members of their social circle with their wholesome activity or financial ability to travel and take time off from work. Others want to collect amulets, try new food or take photographs. Perhaps there is no such thing as purposeless or non-teleological action. I certainly grant that true freedom and choice might be illusions. Every choice we make is somewhat controlled by our socio-economic context and cultural and genetic background, and influenced constantly by the choices of others. However, unlike directly giving gifts to members of the sangha, chanting, performing rituals, participating in group meditation or taking on precepts in a monastic setting, the goals in these Buddhist public and leisure places is not often articulated or prescribed by the artists or curators. Buddhism is not presented as a series of systematic assignments on signs, pamphlets or mission statements. There are many social, economic, soteriological and ritual reasons for entering a monastery, studying a Buddhist treatise, or performing a ritual, but there are few easily definable reasons or articulated goals for going to a museum or art gallery, besides a vague sense of intellectual enrichment, artistic inspiration, to meet a possible romantic partner or friend, physical relaxation or the desire to just pass time.

Buddhist visitors in the spaces I describe below are not just lounging around passively. They are engaging in what Lauren Rabinovitz calls "energized relaxation," which is activity without having larger economic, social, religious or intellectual goals

(Rabinovitz 2012: 2).[9] These places are not necessary. Visiting them does not directly improve one's chances at a job promotion, earn credit towards a degree, contribute knowledge needed to pass monastic or secular examinations, provide a place for a life-cycle ritual like tonsure, ordination, marriage or cremation, or even provide karmic merit to improve one's present and future life. What Rabinovitz and Miriam Hansen see as one of the most important factors of success for amusement parks and movie theatres can be profitably applied to Buddhist installation art spaces: "[They] provide a space apart and a space in between . . . a site for the imaginative negotiation of the gaps between family, school, and workplace" (Hansen 1991: 90–118, as quoted in Rabinovitz 2012: 6). These are not places of didactic sermons, forced spirituality or ethical directives. I want to move out of the monastery and away from monk-centric teaching to see how the casual visitor experiences Buddhist history, art and ideals at their leisure. I am interested in the way this type of "on-the-way" experience happens in non-monastic or semi-monastic spaces. In other publications, I have discussed other leisure spaces like parks, monuments and gardens. Here, I limit myself to modern art installations. This experience isn't necessarily embedded in ritual, supported by texts, or part of a monastic training regimen, but is part of the total experience of contemporary Buddhism.

Buddhist Installation Artists in Thailand

Jakkai Siributr graciously met me for an interview at a coffee shop in the Emporium, a high-end shopping mall on Bangkok's famous Sukhumvit Road in September 2011. I had been following his work for a few years, and although we ended up talking about Philadelphia, my home and a place he spent a lot of time in as a student at Philadelphia University (previously known as Philadelphia Textile, one of the oldest industrial arts and fashion schools in the US), I was struck in our interview at his candidness about his struggle with belief in and scepticism over certain Thai Buddhist practices. He and I both spent a lot of time at Wat Mahabut in Bangkok. In 2011, I had written a book about ghosts and magic in Thai Buddhism which featured a long section on this monastery. He had gone there frequently to be inspired for his work called "Kuman Thong" (Golden Child).[10] *Kuman thong* are the mummified corpses of stillborn children, aborted foetuses and some are children who die in their first few days or even years of life. These corpses are mummified (bled, desiccated and stored in camphor oil) and then usually covered in gold or blackened by roasting them slowly. More often than not, *kuman thong* are actually not mummified foetus corpses, but small golden wooden or plastic statues of infants. They are held by some practitioners of Thai Buddhism (as well as Cambodian and Malaysian Buddhist) to be sources of protective power. They often fetch a great deal of money in the religious markets of the region. Jakkai's work generally looks at these seemingly superstitious and commercial practices. However, he does not simply condemn these specific practices as unfortunate products of modernity or religious greed but wants to make Thai Buddhists (his main audience) aware of the practices that they do every day, but rarely reflect upon. He does not believe that the use of *kuman thong* is merely superstitious. He believes that human aspirations, whether they are for money, fame, safety, a good next life, healthy children, etc., create a type of energy that pools around certain sacred sites or objects like *kuman thong*. He is not sure if that energy is just his imagination or is real, but he "feels" it and his art is about these practices that cannot be explained rationally, but that we feel compelled to do. He wants his audience to be aware and, in that awareness, learn to be honest with themselves and even occasionally laugh at themselves. He laughs at himself often because he engages in practices he is not sure he believes in, but does out of habit and a strange compulsion that he finds hard to explain.

Jakkai's agenda is not to change Buddhist practice, but encourage it to be reflected upon in a non-didactic and non-systematic way. For example, in one installation called "Temple Fair" (2008) at the Tyler Rollins Fine Art Gallery in New York City he made dozens of fabric animals that the audience could walk around, thus showing that Buddhist temple life was not merely about monastic training and ritual, but about festivals and leisure activities. Similarly, in Miami he told me of a show in which he made religious "lottery tickets" that gallery viewers could actually take away. In San Francisco, he had an interactive piece called "Reciprocity" in which viewers could write down their own aspirations as part of the exhibition. In a large solo show called "Karma Cash & Carry" in New York in 2010, he created large textile compositions alongside installation and video works. The exhibition was organized around his conception of a karmic convenience store, where merit can be bought and sold. He makes use of found objects associated with bringing good fortune, integrating them into his elaborate compositions of Thai fabrics, embroidery, and hand stitched sequined work.[11]

Here, as in his work shown in San Francisco alongside Sopheap Pich in the "Here/Not Here: Buddha Presence in Eight Recent Works" exhibition, there is an emphasis on the material objects that are presented as offerings to Buddhist monks, ghosts and land spirits in Thai monasteries. This piece features actual plastic yellow buckets with various toiletries and various commercial products in them including an electric fly swatter. These buckets are exactly the most common way gifts are offered in Thai monasteries, as the buckets are used by the monks to do their laundry.[12] In an exhibition at Chulalongkorn University in Bangkok, he made himself part of his installation by creating a statue of himself sitting in meditation in the center of the room while texting on his cell phone. There was also an elaborate piece called "Shroud" which the viewer can stand under and within. The shroud was made of dozens of small, hand-woven Buddha images. The fabric (crocheted hemp) and the way the installation was set up allowed the viewer to "wear" the Buddha-like clothes.[13] The installation also featured a statue of him as a walking Buddha statue holding a shopping bag. This is particularly poignant since the university's gallery is very close to the largest shopping complexes in the country. In one of his most provocative and personal exhibitions,

"Transient Shelter" (Tyler Rollins Fine Art, New York City, April 17–May 31, 2014), Jakkai presents a series of photographic self-portraits in various military uniforms. These uniforms are also displayed in an installation on mannequins in the gallery. In each photograph, Jakkai's uniform is ornamented with various Thai Buddhist amulets, phallic talismans and protective diagrams (Thai: *yan*; Sanskrit: yantra). The photographs are visually unsettling, but the viewer would need to be well versed in Thai protective talismanic practices and material culture to understand the local significance of the exhibition. Indeed, since actual Thai military personnel are famous for wearing a variety of religious objects, these photographs are much more than satire. Jakkai brilliantly shows the close connection between the military and religious culture in Thailand. Tyler Rollins further describes Jakkai's personal connection to the exhibition:

> With the photographs, Jakkai adopts poses taken from portraits of his ancestors, many of whom served as royal courtiers and in some cases had their lives cut short by the sometimes tragic vicissitudes of Thai political history. Wearing Thai civil service uniforms (ranked from C-11, the highest category, down to C-2) decked out with awards, he evokes the type of formal portrait photographs that are included in the funeral books that Thai families compile to commemorate the lives of relatives, and that typically emphasize the deceased person's social status. Jakkai has encrusted the actual uniforms with elaborate ornaments that are inspired by Buddhist amulets and animist talismans, hinting at the deep-seated beliefs that underlie current social conventions. With some of the portraits, Jakkai poses in front of dilapidated backgrounds, pointing to the process of decay and rebirth that alludes to the cycle of life and death ... [the exhibition includes a] short video work, in which a uniform jacket slowly moves under flowing water, accompanied by a soundtrack of a burning funeral pyre.[14]

Iola Lenzi, the curator of the exhibition, further notes how Jakkai's work is highly specific to local Thai practices:

> He enters his topic via a still-thriving Thai nineteenth-century tradition, the funeral book. This memorial publication, distributed to guests at cremation ceremonies, through anecdote, eulogy and snippets of biography, celebrates the life of the deceased. Such books also include Buddhist chants and more eclectic cultural information, with particular emphasis placed on photographs of the deceased clothed in medal-adorned uniforms that denote rank and social strata. In these publications the late person's achievements and honors are dwelled upon, while character flaws and set-backs are minimized or ignored. Not morbid, and preciously kept as mementos, cremation books, in their amplifications and deletions play with truth and fiction, so constituting the dead's personal mythology.[15]

Jakkai's art is indeed very local. For example, on two separate occasions, he set up a spirit house (Thai: *san phra phum*) on the street where he lives in Bangkok (Sukhumvit Soi 28) and wrapped the trees in monks' robes. It was designed to make the street sacred for the very specific reason to stop people throwing trash and parking illegally in his street. He also wanted to stop city officials from widening the street and cutting down the trees there. Simply put, he just wanted a more peaceful block on which to live. He said it has worked. However, now he worries that the spirit house will become popular and more crowds will come to his street to make offerings to it! Indeed, Jakkai is an artist that takes bold risks and sees himself as both a student and teacher of Buddhism in the modern period.[16]

Perhaps the most productive Thai Buddhist installation artist over the last 30 years was Montien Boonma. Unfortunately, he passed away at only 47 years old from cancer. In his short life, he created numerous temporary, but memorable Buddhist installations. Graduating from Silapakorn University in 1978, he was a classmate of Chalermchai Kositpipat who created the white temple (Wat Rong Khun) described below. While Chalermchai was what art historian and critic Apinan Poshyananda calls a Buddhist "neo-traditionalist," adding new elements to traditional Thai mural painting and monastic architecture, Montien radically departed from traditional Thai Buddhist art. However, this departure did not delocalize his work. Even though he had exhibitions in far off places such as Europe, the United States and Australia, his installations (he was also a painter and sculptor) used material, sounds, rituals, ideas and even smells that were very specific to Thai Buddhist practice. For example, in 1997, because of his terrible experience watching his wife, Chancham Mukdaprakorn, die from breast cancer a few years ago, he created the "House of Hope" installation in New York. The grief caused by her untimely death was compounded by the fact that when he became engaged, soon after his disrobing from the monkhood at Wat Cholaprathanrangsit near Bangkok (he ordained for three months as it is traditional for many Thai males), he was told by a Thai astrologer named Sombat Yanawaro at Wat Chamnihatthakan, that his marriage would be inauspicious and end in misery.[17] When this prophecy seems to have come to fruition, it increased his already-strong dedication to Thai Buddhist prognostication, healing and protective practices. Inspired by these practices, in this particular exhibition, he hung over 1,600 strings of Thai chanting beads (Thai: *luk brakham*) from the ceiling, creating the walls of a temple. He played recordings of Pali Buddhist chants and infused the entire room with a scent made from the mixture of herbal medicines (Thai: *ya tam duai samon prai*) that his wife and he had acquired while trying to fight her cancer after other treatments failed. Within the temporary temple of scent and sound, he built small red stools like Thai miniature altars that seemed to form a stairway. This was reminiscent of Thai notions of stairways to the heavenly realm of Indra (Phra In).[18] In 1994, a few months after Chancham's passing, he created "Room" which referred to both the hospital room where he had read Buddhist sermons (thet) to her and stuck chants to the walls and the small "rooms" made by tent-like umbrellas used by meditating Thammayut monks in Thai and Lao forests. His "Room" is a series of small structures in which a viewer can actually sit in meditation, made of pinewood slats on short stilts (Poshyananda 2003: 27). These references, scents and beads would be lost on a Buddhist from Korea or Tibet but are very easily understood by a person growing up among Thai monasteries. Similarly, in one of his earliest installations, 1983s "Shrine and Metal Door," he inverted the colors used on Sino-Thai spirit houses (san phra chao or san chao jin) that would only be noticed by someone intimate with household shrines used by certain members of the Chinese community in central Thailand (Poshyananda 2003: 14). Montien had also studied in Rome and Paris and had learned much from post-structuralism especially regarding the disruption between signifier and signified. Although he did not elucidate in writing to any great extent the way he incorporated these theoretical understandings, he did state, according to Poshyananda, that he was inspired by Donald Judd and Joseph Beuy's use of installation works to connect social and spiritual agendas. However, despite this theoretical inspiration, he created work specific to the Thai Buddhist context. For example, Beuy's use of found objects and simple forms like cardboard boxes and pieces of metal to create bricolage works influenced Montien to create works like "Pagodas in Boxes Construction" which was a Thai Buddhist chedi or stupa made out of wooden crates and detergent boxes (Poshyananda 2003: 16–17). After he had spent much time in monasteries in northern Thailand, he created the installation called "Lotus Sound" which is a large wall of stacked terracotta monastery bells made in Ban Muang Krung, a small village in Chiang Mai Province, inspired by the sounds he heard while in the actual monasteries.[19] Montien created installations that were rooms in which viewers could enter and in which they could walk around. These included the installations "Room," "Lotus Sound" (1992) and "House of Hope" (1997). Since some of his installations were displayed outside museums (because of their large size), they actually formed temporary buildings or even small monastic structures. Some of these many installations include "Inner Sky" (1990), "In Between (Tunnel)" (1994), "House of Breath" (1996), "Body Temple" (1996), "Temple of the Mind" (1995) and "Sala (English: pavilion) of the Mind" (1995). The last one he said was inspired by Prasat Hin Phimai, a famous Angkorian-era temple in northeast Thailand (Poshyananda 2003: 32–5). He believed that his installation could not only remind the viewer of a Thai Buddhist monastery, but also become a place of practice

> when audience visit this room ["Sala of the Mind"] with a dome top, they look like they are wearing a shada (classical headdress) ... this piece intends to provide a space for the audience to examine their beliefs, let them be in a "sala of mind," to rest their mind and thoughts. It could also be a space where people could probably ask some question, like whether God exists ... It's a kind of ritual space [sic]. (Poshyananda 2003: 31)

This concept is taken further in "Melting Void: Molds for the Mind" (1998) where he created large abstract Buddha heads on stilts in which a person can stand and place their head within the Buddha's head like a helmet. It was not just a vague reference for Montien, he wanted to recreate the Thai practice of commissioning statues of the Buddha to make merit. The viewer, by inserting their own head into a Buddha's head, could become the act of merit themselves. Since the ceremony of offering included incense, the inside of the heads were scented and painted red like the interiors of Wat Phra Singh and Wat Ton Guan monasteries in Chiang Mai (Poshyananda 2003: 35). Melissa Chiu in her essay "An Architecture of the Senses" compares Montien's use of scents in his sculptures to Chinese contemporary installation artists, like Chen Zen who used Chinese herbal medicines in installations like "Obsession of Longevity" (1995), or Huang Yong Ping's "The Pharmacy," referring not to Buddhist practices but Daoist-influenced medical practices in China. Cai Guo-Qiang's huge "Cultural Melting Bath" (1997) incorporates an actual jacuzzi filled with water and scented herbs big enough for five adults to soak (Poshyananda 2003: 40–7). Montien's installations, while certainly inspired by and inspiring these other artists, draw the viewers' senses to exact places and practices in the Thai context.

Before the popularity of Montien, modern art in Bangkok was largely confined to students working at Silapakorn University's Galleries (Thailand's oldest and premier university focusing on fine arts). After 1974, the National Gallery of Thailand also became a center for modern art.[20] Both museums are under royal patronage. These artists brought modern art to the far north of Thailand or to other gallery spaces in Bangkok. This is good, because before the 1990s, neither the National Gallery nor Silapakorn University's Art Centre received many international or local visitors, and modern art in Thailand was confined to a selected number of elite patrons and artists. The latter museum I used to call the quietest place in Bangkok, because every time I visited I was the only person besides the security guards in the entire museum! I am always shocked about how many Thai friends of mine do not even know the National Gallery exists.

Montien, Jakkai and other "neo-traditionalist" or "neo-Buddhist" installation artists have brought Buddhist art and architecture in Thailand out of its ritual and monastic setting and royally-approved museum setting.[21] They are part of a much larger wave of Thai installation artists whose work has been publicly displayed since the early 1990s (Boonma 1997). For example, Amrit Chusuwan's exhibition, called "Tuk" (English: Suffering) in February and March 2010 at the DOB Hualamphing Gallery in Bangkok, had a series of video and sculpted installations that the visitor could interact with, including a series of Buddha-like plaster heads projecting from the wall filled with small stones, giant uncomfortable stones to sit on to meditate, and sound and video projections of the four noble truths next to photographs of dogs devouring raw meat and an engraved dagger called "the End of Suffering" (Thai: *dap tuk*). These juxtapositions of well-known Buddhist terms and teachings next to scenes of modern urban decay were striking without being overly moralizing or didactic.[22] At the 2006 National Art Exhibition large installations dominated the galleries and grounds. Many were focused on Buddhist themes. Some notable ones were Khemrat Kongsuk's "Arunrung" (Morning) in 2006, which featured life-size, but armless and faceless Buddha images made out of roughly sculpted clay, holding real metal alms bowls, in which one could actually place offerings. Sriwan Janhattakankit's "Sangsanwat" (Cycle of Life) was simply a long robe ladder made out of resin femur bones. Pat Ponchai's "Raka haeng tua ton" (Sensuality) was a very large fibreglass and metal head consuming a pile of stones that the artist described as depicting the danger of *taṇhā* (a Pali term for "desire" or "thirst" common in Buddhist teaching). Hathairat Manirat's sculpted stupa covered with broken sticks and vines called "*Chedi khong mae mai lek song*" (My Mother's Reliquary/Stupa number Two) was made of several different tactile materials.[23] Although there are many more modern art exhibition spaces today in Thailand, especially in Bangkok, than there were 20 years ago, Silapakorn University Art Centre is still a major exhibition space of modern art in Thailand and should not be discounted even though there has been something of a growing movement away from what some people in the elite art circles of Bangkok call the "Silapakorn Mafia."[24] For example, the Thai Contemporary Art Exposition there in 2009 had a wonderful display of new installation works and paintings with Buddhist themes by Manit Kuwattanasilp, Manop Suwanpinta, Santi Thongsuk, Songdej Thipthong, Chalavit Soemprungsuk, Sittichai Pratchayaratikun, Chaiwut Thiampan and others.[25] It was also the center of one of the largest modern Buddhist art exhibitions in recent Thai history in 2001, called "Jintakab jak phraphutthasasana" (Images of Buddhism), which featured an installation by Wichai Sithirat of a glowing stupa surrounded by small statues of infant Buddhas called "Samadhi" (Meditation), and other installations by Wichok Mukdamani, Wibun Lisuwan, Saravut Duangjampa, Thanomjit Chumwong and Noppadon Wirunchatapun. Two of the most interactive installations were by Suti Kunawichayanon, called "Khon ha" (Searching), and Amrit Chusuwan's "Phra yu thi nai" (Where Are the monks?). The latter featured wrinkled and empty monks' robes hung on the wall, which the viewer could feel, and the former a pair of binoculars that could be picked up and used by the viewer to look closely at small objects around the room that invoked Buddhist teachings.[26] Sarawut Duangjampa is one of the most productive, but least internationally known of Buddhist installation artists in Thailand. He has had several large installations set up at various galleries. One of his most striking was at the Thai-India Art and Cultural Exchange exhibition in 2004 which featured large translucent white tubes, internally lit and made out of cotton with bamboo frames hanging from the ceiling of the gallery space which the viewer could walk around and under. Called "Phra Phut Phra Tham Phra Song" (Buddha, Dhamma, Sangha) and "Rup song khong khwam chaloen ngok ngam" (The Form of Growth), they seemed to make the room float.[27]

One of the only major installation projects at the National Gallery (with co-sponsorship from Silapakorn University) with Buddhist themes over the past decade was the "Mindfulness" show by Phatyot Phutthachaloen (whose last name means coincidentally "the Growth or Increasing Significance of the Buddha," also transliterated as Phatyos Buddhacharoen). Clearly inspired by Montien's work, Phatyot created large rooms like Montien in which the viewer could enter and meditate. He mastered the use of lighting in the gallery to create mysterious structures that glowed inside, but only cast strange shadows on the walls outside. In his "Chapel," the temporary room was circular with small text covering the inside of the walls with Buddhist quotations. Inside the room were two small Buddha images, one with its back to the viewer. Three other lotus-shaped altars in the room held sculpted body parts as if the viewer was only going through the physical motions of worship and left their mind outside the space. In "Crisis," the room looked like a traditional Buddhist pavilion but the roof was made out of a fabric net and covered a small altar that had dangling plaster arms and legs above it. In another installation called "Shed the Shells," which certainly reminds the viewer of Montien's "House of Hope," Phatyot strung hundreds of snake skins above a similarly large number of bamboo stalks topped by miniature brown masks used in traditional Thai *khon* dancing. One installation took the entire space of the National Gallery's largest room—"Way of Breath." In a very dark room, Phatyot, in collaboration with Supon Lohachitkun, created a low and wide floating wall of cardboard paper and welded metal that stood on thin stilts and was internally lit. Underneath the dome was a small lamp surrounded by eight pillows on which viewers of the exhibition could sit facing each other in meditation or watchful repose. Surrounding different rooms in the exhibition, Phatyot installed imitation chao fa, which are wing-like architectural features found on the corner eaves of most Thai monasteries. By bringing them into the gallery space, he made the entire public space a Thai monastery of his own creation.[28]

For artists who construct large installation pieces, gallery space is a serious and expensive concern. However, two artists/architects have worked around that problem by creating their own "monasteries" in which to display their creations. In the northernmost province of Thailand, Chiang Rai, there is a new monastery and sculpture garden that is the brainchild of a modern artist. When I visited Wat Rong Khun in March 2008, I knew immediately that I was at a monastery unlike any other in the world. It was still under construction, having only been in existence for a year. It is the creation of Chalermchai Kositpipat, one of the most well-known Thai artists who has had gallery shows in many different countries and has been the feature of numerous reviews. Recently Chalermchai has branched out into architecture. Although the *wihan* (image hall) of the monastery, similar in size and architectural structure to central Thai monasteries, is completely white with carved leaping flames, statuary of Brahmanic gods, and skulls—lots of skulls—there are dozens of small statues on the grounds as well. The front entrance to the monastery has a bridge over a wide pit.

Hundreds of sculpted hands are reaching up from the pit which is supposed to depict hell. The hands are asking for alms, for mercy. Inside the *wihan* there are murals hand-painted by Chalermchai. Most murals on the walls of Thai monasteries depict the life of the Buddha, the lives of famous monks and nuns, the previous lives of the Buddha (Pali: *jātaka*), as well as depictions of stories from Indian and South-east Asian epic poems like *Khun Chang Khun Paen*, the *Ramāyāṇa*, *Inao* and the like.[29] However, Chalermchai's are completely different. Among other phantasmagoric images on these murals, there is a depiction of the American actor Keanu Reeves dressed as his famous film character, Neo, from the "Matrix" Trilogy, wearing a black trench coat and dark sunglasses. He is standing in a macho Kungfu-like pose next to a "pod-racer" from Episode One of Star Wars. Near him is a painting of Ultraman, a well-known Japanese animated hero (and, by far, my young son's favorite mural character in Thailand!). Besides these fictional and randomly assembled heroes, there are also images of a demon holding a cell phone and the World Trade Center in New York City being hit by a commercial jet. Depictions of the terrorist attacks on September 11, 2001 and international pop culture heroes are interspersed with paintings of AK-47 machine guns, gas pumps, flaming skulls and satellites.

Chalermchai is a social critic who uses painting and sculpture to point out the dangers of global culture, materialism and greed. His work is very popular in Thailand, but he has not been critically well-received by critics or other artists. He is a business person who runs shops and a large gallery at the monastery selling his art. Life-size posters of him are hung in several places on the monastic grounds. This is neither a gimmick nor simply one man's obsession; Wat Rong Khun is a functioning monastery in the process of building dormitory rooms for novices and monks. For example, one day when I was there, over 200 monks from Pichet Province in central Thailand were visiting and chanting. People prostrate, offer alms and the like as they would at any other monastery, but it attracts more visitors who want to view its striking architectural features and who want to shop at the several tourist and handicrafts shops surrounding it or have a picnic on its grounds.[30]

Less than a ten-minute drive from Chalermchai's glowing white Wat Rong Khun is another "monastery" built by the modern Thai artist, Thawan Duchanee. Perhaps invoking the common rivalry between artists, it is named the "Black House" (Thai: *Ban Dam*). Thawan trained under the Italian artist Feroci and for four years in the Netherlands (Royal Academy of Visual Arts in Amsterdam). He juxtaposes modern and traditional Thai Buddhist art and has a particular focus on skeletons, insects and death. Like Chalermchai, he is a shameless self-promoter, and there is no shortage of photographs of him with his Tolstoy/Whitman-esque long white beard on his website or in the many Thai and English newspaper and Youtube videos that discuss him and his work.[31] For example, in Thai and English on his website one can read:

> Born in 1939 in Chiang Rai, one of the foremost Asian painters, Mr. Thawan Duchanee has pursued his career throughout the world. His paintings are in an original genre, rooted in a unique Buddhist perspective. These paintings depict the insanity, degeneration, violence, eroticism, and death lurking in the heart of modern man. The artist has shocked the world by creating a uniquely Asian artistic expression. Mr. Thawan is indeed worthy to be called a master of modern Asian art.

As well as this rather magnanimous call to the people who see his art:

> Do not seek for understanding, in the temple of mysterious. Feel them my friends from heart to heart. Do not ask the meaning of the stars in the constellation. Smile of the baby in the cradle of mothers. Sweet fragrance in the pollens of flowers. It is the work of art! My friends ... In the deepest of my mystic mind, come closer to my spirit. Listen to my heartbeat, without word.[32] [sic]

While the Thai original is more poetic, the self-indulgence is no less obvious. What concerns us here though is not his personality, but his architecture and the creation of a sculpture park similar to Lek and Braphai's. The Black House is a wonder to behold. It is not a monastery, but the artist's own residence and a collection of galleries holding his collection, much of it created by him. There are 40 separate structures spread out in a large campus-like setting. Most of the buildings are reminiscent of traditional northern Thai monastic architecture but painted black with some dark brown trim [with a few exceptions such as three small white stupas (Thai: *chedi*) with plain black doors]. These structures contain large collections of mostly abstract sculpture, as well as skeletons of elephants, oxen and water-buffalo, skins of various animals, found objects like old Thai canoes and canes. Much of the strangely shaped furniture was hand carved by Thawan. There is one building in the shape of an abstract boar and one of the bathrooms is filled with wooden monkey and bird carvings. There are sculpture gardens that consist largely of natural stone arranged in patterns. While the buildings certainly looked like largely unornamented Thai monasteries and monastic library buildings, the art in the buildings is a striking contrast. The visitor can walk around freely among the buildings like in a village, but there are no direct comparisons between the artist's ideas and Buddhist texts or well-known teachings. There are no ritual or liturgical services. Nuns and monks are not in residence. There is no direct pedagogy and seemingly no central "message." Indeed, many visitors just seem to walk around with their mouths slightly open in a state of wonder and bewilderment.[33]

Times have changed though. Exhibitions of modern art with a heavy emphasis on installation pieces have become more well-known since the opening of several new public and private gallery spaces in Bangkok over the past ten years and the success of artists like Thawan, Montien and others.[34] These include the H-Gallery, the Jamjuree Gallery at Chulalongkorn University, Tadu Gallery, the very popular multi-levelled and dynamic commercial and gallery space known as the Bangkok Art and Culture Center in the heart of Siam Square, among several others. In April 2012, the newest modern art museum opened in Bangkok. It is called the Museum of Contemporary Art (MOCA) (Thai: *Phipihithaphan Silapa Thai Ruam Samai*) on Vibhavadi-Rangsit Road. It is the brainchild of the very wealthy Bunchai Bencharongkul who has a massive personal collection of modern Thai art, especially the work of Thawan Duchanee, whose work occupies over 20 per cent of the entire museum. Except for Bunchai's new museum, which is a rather long bus or taxi ride through major traffic jams north of the Chatuchak/Mo Chit part of the city (although relatively close to a regional train line) and far from the fashionable districts of Bangkok, these spaces are located in central Bangkok and are quite convenient to visit.[35] Unlike Silapakorn University and the National Gallery, they are mostly located in the more modern and commercial sections of the city (Sukhumvit, Siam Square/Pathum Wan, Chitwan, Ploenchit, Lumbini and Sathorn Road) and most are easily reached by the sky train (Thai: Rotfai Fa/BTS) or subway which have been in operation since 1994 and have grown steadily in ridership and number of stations. This convenience combined with Thailand's growing urban, well-educated, cosmopolitan upper-middle class have created a market for modern art and gala affairs such as exhibition openings. People can leisurely swing by galleries (often while on dates) while out shopping, seeing movies and eating at fashionable restaurants. This modern art scene has long existed in the fashionable districts of Hong Kong, Tokyo, Osaka, Seoul, Singapore, and is similarly growing in Phnom Penh, Saigon and Shanghai. However, only in Bangkok is the modern art so focused on Buddhist concepts, symbols, messages and themes.

This can be seen in an exhibition at the Bangkok Art and Cultural Center (August–October 2011) which included numerous artists working on the theme "Koet, Kae, Cheb, Tai, Kin, Khi, Bhi, Non" (translated by the artists rather crudely as "Birth, Aging, Sickness, Death, Eating, Shitting, Humping, Sleeping"). They creatively interpreted the passage of life drawn from the narrative of the life of the Buddha, particularly the "Four Visions" of the Buddha (old age, sickness, death and ascetic life). This show—which was quite popular with Bangkok teenagers and young adults as it was directly across from one of the largest shopping malls in the capital—was a series of interactive installation pieces which forced the viewer to go through the process of birth to death, with sex and sleeping along the way. One installation, created by Surasi Kusolwong, filled an entire room (about 60 by 30 feet) with different colored yarn which visitors could climb in, bury themselves under, throw at one another or take a nap. It became like sickness when you tried to leave the room, because the yarn was easy to lay down in, but very difficult to walk through and so the visitors would have to slowly climb out of it, struggling and tripping. In another section, there were two types of beds, one was comfortable and invited visitors to nap (although I witnessed few that did since they had already been lounging in the yarn), but the other was made out of concrete and metal bars and was quite uninviting and the bars formed the shape of what seemed to be two corpses. In another section, an artist and playwright, named Pattarasuda Anuman Rajadhon, who had studied in London and Bangkok, created along with Millie Young a maze made of wood which had dead lotus flowers sticking out of it.[36] The lotus, she suggested, was dead, but still had the shape of a living flower. The maze took the visitors through a path representing the passage from life to death, which they called "disappearing." It was this in-between moment they wanted to force the visitor into. Along the way, besides the dead lotus flowers, were many quotations about death drawn from a wide variety of sources, none of which were properly cited, but which made the reader think of this act of disappearing. For example, one quote in Thai which they attributed to "the Buddha" (Phra Phutthachao) read "*Maw khwam tai ko mai chai ruang na wan klua samrap phu mi chiwit yu duai khwam teun ru*" ("Even death is not to be feared by one who has lived wisely") next to another quote attributed to an "Irish Saying" which read "A black cat crossing one's path by moonlight means death in an epidemic." These sometimes whimsical, sometimes profound, sometimes cryptic quotes slowed the visitor down as they walked through the maze and forced them to think about death along the way. Next to this section, along the wall, there were more painted quotes arranged by Lom Pengkaeo, which drew from Buddhist and other sources, including quotes by Plato, Schopenhauer and even Jean Cocteau—"Since the day of my birth, my death began its walk. It is walking toward me without hurrying." In another section, Pracha Suveeranont, presented an installation called "Aging" (labelled in Thai: *Kae*) which depicted a traditional Thai "hell mural," alongside hand-drawn commentary in Thai and English that made associations between traditional Thai depictions of hellscapes and modern politics, consumer habits and even watching television. In another invoking sex, visitors were given paper, pens and crayons to write their own love notes to each other and post them on a wall or write their ideas on sex and relationships. As you can imagine, with a lot of teenagers attending the show, the comments were often a humorous mixture of the bawdy and the sappy. Some were downright sweet. At the end of the long journey through the installations, I certainly felt differently than I would if I had only seen paintings on a wall or read quotes on plaques. I don't know if I was profoundly transformed, but I was certainly physically exhausted.

A second exhibition, in May 2012, was about 300 yards away in the Paragon Mall. The Paragon is one of the newest high-end malls in Thailand. This exhibition titled "Temple in the Clouds" was partly associated with the annual Buddhist celebrations on Visakha (Vesak) Day celebrating the Birth, Awakening, and Death of the Buddha.[37] It was a mix of temporary booths selling Buddhist products for the modern consumer, like environmentally sound meditation pillows, fashionable t-shirts with inspirational Buddhist sayings, children's books on Buddhism, CDs and MP3 recordings of chanting and relaxing music, and the like. There were dozens of different publishers of religious books, both scholarly and commercial. Alongside this commercial section were different exhibitions about Buddhist sites in different regions of Thailand and the activities of specific temples, meditation centers and charitable organizations, many focusing on children's education at schools in poor rural communities. Most booths were focused on projects, but some promoted the teaching of particular monks like Phra Mahasompong Talaputto and the activities of specific nunneries like the Song Dhammakalyani Bhikkhuniaram. Occasionally, there were small performances and speeches about meditation in the modern world or living as a modern urban spiritual person. The architecture of the large exhibition hall in the mall was decorated with large temporary architectural elements like wooden and plastic stupas, resin statues of monks and a series of white curtains and temporary rooms with white walls that you have to pass through like a maze mimicking a spiritual journey called Nitasat Trasaru (Exhibition on Awakening). As the visitor passed through this maze, inspirational large print words in Thai like "*phrasut*" (purity) greeted them. Near this installation was a very large wooden and metal Bodhi tree with gold and silver paper leaves with inspirational messages. In the large lecture hall adjacent to the exhibition, there were even talks by prominent international scholars of Buddhist Studies like Donald Swearer and Anil Sakya (Phra Sugandha).[38] This seamless combination of art, commerce, religious teaching and activities, education, and temporary installations is still relatively new, but certainly growing and becoming part of the way that Thai Buddhists are learning to be Buddhist. In many ways, though, it is not wholly different from the ways Thai have encountered Buddhism for centuries. Monasteries have long been a place for commercial, educational, leisurely, meditational and artistic activity, often happening at the same time. Urban and rural monastic festivals have also long included temporary shrines, sand stupas, scroll paintings, dance performances, puppet shows and sermons.[39]

Conclusion

While Buddhist themes might be the most common inspirations and messages for Thai modern artists, there are certainly many major modern installation artists in Asia who are inspired by Buddhist themes.[40] For example, South Korean artists like Choi Jeong Hwa installed a 24-foot air-filled red nylon balloon, with motorized moving petals, floated above the Civic Center Plaza for the entire summer of 2012 as part of the "Phantoms of Asia" exhibition at the Asian Art Museum of San Francisco. Chan-soo Park and Sooja Kim (who often goes by "kimsooja") have had major international installations in Paris, Vienna, New York, Berlin, Tokyo, Seoul, Rome and the like. Park's Moga-A garden and gallery is a major space to display his large installations and sculptures about two hours from Seoul.[41] Sooja Kim's most memorable installation based on a Buddhist theme has to be "Lotus: Zone of Zero" which has had many different reincarnations in places like the Samsung Museum in Seoul (2011), Galerie Ravenstein in Brussels (2008) and the Palais Rameau in Lille (2003). In Brussels, for example, she was able to hang over 2,000 red lanterns from the ceiling in circular patterns, which she refers to as Buddhist "mandalas," under which the viewer can walk and feel like they are suspended under a canopy of light, but there is also recorded Tibetan Buddhist chanting alongside Gregorian Christian and Islamic chanting played simultaneously. She wants the three "faiths" to have a "peaceful union" as the "exhibition space is transformed into a place of meditation and contemplation for viewers." On her own website it reads that she "questions the role of the individual within society and their purpose in a world that is chaotic and ephemeral. Her universe combines a subtle mixture of references drawn from Christianity, Zen Buddhism, Confucianism, Shamanism and Dao philosophy, but moves beyond these religious references to address the issues facing all of humanity."[42] Charwei Tsai, an artist from Taiwan who studied at the Rhode Island School of Design and L'École Nationale Supérieure des Beaux-Arts in Paris and who has had solo shows in Hong Kong, Bogata, Singapore, Taipei, Shanghai, Herzliya (Israel), Paris and many other places, created an installation of minimalist calligraphic paintings of the Heart Sūtra (Sanskrit: Prajñāpāramitā Hṛdaya), a sūtra she chanted as a child, on three-dimensional and non-traditional objects like mushrooms and pieces of tofu. In an interview, she stated that this exhibition emphasized the Buddhist notion of non-attachment and impermanence.[43] Hiroshi Sugimoto, a Japanese-American photographer and installation artist, who has also had major international shows has created installations drawing on "geometric symbols from thirteenth-century Buddhism" with the purpose to symbolize "the sea and air, origins of all life, [that] are seen through a prism of ancient Buddhist views of the universe."[44] Takayuki Yamamoto, who studied at Aichi University and later at the Chelsea College of Art and Design (United Kingdom), at the aforementioned "Phantoms of Asia" exhibition, created child-like, interactive sculptures for a video installation depicting his interacting with young school children in San Francisco. The exhibition description states that "after showing students the Kumano Kanjin Jikkai Mandala, a collection of traditional Japanese paintings depicting Buddhist notions of vice, virtue, and punishment, Yamamoto then encourages them to create and talk about cardboard dioramas representing their own ideas of hell. These dioramas are presented along with the video."[45] There is the Chinese artist, Tao Hongjing, whose installation simply called "Amitabha" is a series of angular and abstract gold, charcoal and white statues presented in a descending series of pedestals surrounded by multi-colored abstract mandalas.[46] Yoko Inoue offers a biting satire of modern Japanese Buddhism in her "Field Guide to Beautiful Monks." This is a book of her photographs of "hunky" monks, which sold over 10,000 copies in the first two months after its release in March 2012.[47]

One of the most successful of the modern installation artists that work on Buddhist themes is Sopheap Pich.[48] Pich was born in Cambodia in 1971 and moved to the US in 1984 as one of the hundreds of thousands of refugees escaping the Khmer Rouge and subsequent civil war. Therefore, he is better known internationally than in Cambodia where he did not have live shows or establish his own studio until recently. He earned his MFA at the Art Institute of Chicago in 1999. He is a sculptor working primarily in bamboo, rattan and wire. His pieces are often large, and even though they are made out of light material, tend to dominate (without bullying) gallery space. Although his first inspiration for making art came from a school trip to Guatemala in 1993, his work is about displacement and trauma from his personal experience, being forced to escape Cambodia. His work did not explicitly focus on Buddhist themes until long after he was established. One of his largest installations, called "Compound," is a large bamboo and wire sculpture shaped like bullets. It represented the cycle of destruction and rebuilding that characterizes modern Cambodia. It was made for the Singapore National Museum and was almost 15 feet high and 10 feet long. His references to Buddhism have been relatively vague, but his work has been very specific and speaks for itself. For example, in an interview with Boreth Ly in 2009, he states that "drawing [for him] is a Zen Buddhist process that requires meditative focus and concentration." Now, since Zen Buddhism is not practiced in Cambodia and the only way Pich would have come into contact with this vague and stereotypical view of Zen is from his education in the States, this statement tells us little about the Buddhist concepts behind his work. However, his individual pieces reveal a much more nuanced view of Buddhist concepts grounded in his experiences in Cambodia. For example, one of the sculptures, called "Buddha" in a larger series called "1979" is a striking half-constructed Buddha image made out of rattan and metal bolts.[49] He was so inspired from his memories of the road that he traveled back to his hometown of Battambang after the fall of the Khmer Rouge in 1979.[50] On that traumatic trip, he remembers seeing a half-destroyed Buddha on the side of the road that had human blood stains on it. This large sculpture is stunning and speaks more to Pich's own experience in a specific time and specific place than to broad Buddhist concepts.

Like Thai artists discussed in this article, modern art installations across Asia (and increasingly Australia, Europe and North America) are creating new types of Buddhist spaces. They can be touched, circumambulated and occupied, but they are often quite temporary, many lasting for less than three or six months in a public space, a commercial gallery or a private or public museum. Installation art usually attracts large crowds for short periods. These crowds are often experiencing these installations "on the way," on the way to dinner and a show, on the way to shopping, or on the way to see other exhibitions in other galleries. These are not, for most, pilgrimages (although the dedication by some art fans to certain artists can seem quite obsessive) to sacred places, but places for leisure repose, hushed conversations, social networking and the occasional first date. There is little to no practice, Buddhist ritual, ecclesiastical training, sermons, and the like, and they are usually completely disconnected physically from monastic places. These places are similar to other modern Buddhist architectural creations though, in that some of the artists or architects attempt to use particularly local symbols, materials and arrangements to speak to local concerns and while others attempt to speak to what they imagine are universal concerns. Regardless, they show the freedom many Buddhist enthusiasts feel they have to, what James Fernandez would call, "play with tropes." Fernandez argued that culture was never static. Cultural symbols are enacted by different people at different times (or even by the same person in different contexts with different audiences in mind) in a wide variety of tropic manners (synecdoche, metaphor, metonym, taxonomy, schema, irony, assertion, juxtaposition and so on). Individuals are polytropic and context-dependent. These artists show that there are many ways to express these unstable Buddhist symbols; whether it be enabling a visitor to a gallery to place their own head inside a Buddha image to make a metonymic "part-to-whole" connection between the viewer's body and the transformative body of a fully awakened being, or juxtaposing images from pop culture and traditional Buddhist mural art. This does not make these installation artists particularly unique. Buddhist artists have been playing with symbols and tropes for centuries, but it does reveal an effort to, in many cases, dislodge these symbols from well-worn analogous and contiguous relations on the one hand, and from certain ethnic and geographic relations on the other—just as the art is being dislodged from traditional monastic spaces. Buddhism is seen then by these artists as an ongoing project, not a resource that needs to be rediscovered, reformed or rejected. Even though installation art is still the leisure and public activity of the upper and urban classes and not encountered as frequently by large swathes of local and international communities, many times these large pieces are seen publicly (because they can't fit indoors). Moreover, they, circulate and often do, between galleries in Europe, Asia and the Americas. After the installations are closed and removed, they often maintain an active multi-media web-presence.

Its role in offering a diverse and polytropic way of teaching aspects of Buddhist symbols, actions and concepts is growing more and more prevalent and showing another way that Buddhists (and non-Buddhists) are learning what it means to be Buddhist in non-monastic spaces in their leisure time.

Notes

1 Many installation artists in Thailand also produce paintings and sculptures. I will be looking primarily at their installations. Some painters, like Surasit Saokong, have also created series of large paintings that creatively combine modern and traditional Buddhist monastic interiors inspired by temples in northern Thailand and Fatehpur (Uttar Pradesh, India). See Surasit Saokong, *Khwam sangob nai lanna lae rajasthan* (Bangkok: Surapon Gallery, 2553 [2010]). Other prominent Thai painters who work on modern Buddhist themes include Preecha Thaothong, Prating Emcharoen, Pichai Naran, Chakrabhand Posayakrit, Prasan Chandrasupa, among many others.

2 See Michael Warner's *Publics and Counterpublics* (2002). See also Charles Hirschkind's *The Ethical Soundscape: Cassette Sermons and Islamic Counterpublics* (2009); and Thomas Csordas, ed., *Transnational Transcendence: Essays on Religion and Globalization* (2009).

3 For a broader discussion of Buddhist public culture across Asia, see McDaniel, *Architects of Buddhist Leisure* (2016).

[4] Exceptions include the recent work of Jamie Hubbard, a project called "The Yamaguchi Story: Buddhism and the Family in Contemporary Japan" (BBC/Education Communication Inc., 2009 [1988]). Vanessa Sasson has edited a volume, *Little Buddhas: Children and Childhoods in Buddhist Texts and Traditions* (2012). Ingrid Jordt's work, *Burma's Mass Lay Meditation Movement: Buddhism and the Cultural Construction of Power* (2007), is a good example of a number of recent works on lay Buddhist political movements. See also Sarah Pike 2009 where she looks at the popularity of Princess Mononoke and the Spirited Away films by Hiyao Miyazaki. For example, whereas US children in the 1950s and 1960s often were presented with a picture of Japanese Buddhism as austere and aesthetically clean and plain, American children today are learning about Buddhism through the Miyazaki films, comic books (manga) and anime, and for example the eight-volume life of the Buddha comic book by Osamu Tezuka.

[5] See, among many others, the classic by Thorstein Veblen's *The Theory of the Leisure Class* (1899); and, more recently, see Chris Rojek, *Ways of Escape, and his Leisure and Culture* (2000); Roger Mannell and Douglas Kleiber, *A Social Psychology of Leisure* (1997); Heather Mair, Susan Arai, and Donald Reid, eds., *Decentering Work* (2010); Karl Spracklen, *Constructing Leisure* (2011), and his *The Meaning and Purpose of Leisure* (2009); Tom Winnifrith and Cyril Barrett, *The Philosophy of Leisure* (1989); Chris Rojek, Susan Shaw, and A.J. Veal, eds., *A Handbook of Leisure Studies* (2006).

[6] Johan Huizinga, *Homo Ludens: A Study of the Play-Element in Culture* (1955). See a good introduction to Huizinga's work in Thomas Henricks, *Play Reconsidered* (2006): chapter 1.

[7] Susan Schearer, ed. and trans., *Petrarch: On Religious Leisure* (2002). See Bakhtin, Rabelais and his World ([1968] 1984); Rojek, *Decentering Leisure* (1995: 85–7); a good comparison with the work of Victor Turner is found in Rojek, *Leisure and Culture* (2000: 148–50). For Turner, see his *Image and Pilgrimage in Christian Culture: Anthropological Perspectives* (1978), and *Process, Performance, and Pilgrimage: A Study in Comparative Symbology* (1979).

[8] This is, of course, similar to the argument Ray Oldenburg makes about spaces like barbershops and bars—they are "third spaces," being neither work nor home. Oldenburg did not see religious places as "leisure" spaces, or "hangouts," as he calls them. However, installation pieces could easily fit his definition of "third places." See his *The Great Good Place: Cafes, Coffee Shops, Community Centers, Beauty Parlors, General Stores, Bars, Hangouts, and How They Get You Through the Day* (1989).

[9] The display of infant corpses is a well-known practice in Thailand. See McDaniel, *The Lovelorn Ghost and the Magical Monk* (2011): chapter four, for a study of their history and use in Thailand.

[10] http://www.luxartasia.com/2010/04/opening-jakkai-siributr-tyler-rollins.html

[11] Two other interviews with Jakkai can be seen here: http://www.youtube.com/ watch?v=aIq2zbcput8, http://www.asianart.org/blog/index.php/2011/05/23/ herenot-here-jakkai-siributr/, and a video of a lengthy talk by Jakkai in San Francisco which features his photographs of daily Buddhist practice here: http:// www.youtube.com/watch?v=SddFJrdIHlg. I should note that in my interview with him he contrasted some of his statements with those he made in his talk in San Francisco. In that talk he criticized the commercial and superstitious nature of many modern Thai practices. In our interview he explained that he actually struggles with this issue more than he could express in a public talk with an audience comprised mostly of Americans not familiar with Thai practices. He struggles with respect for practices he grew up with in Thailand and study of Buddhism he actually learned by reading books and in conversations in the US. He does admit in his talk that he is "the biggest animist ever" and he feels compelled to believe in what others think is superstitious. I thank Jakkai for this interview and for answering questions of mine online.

[12] http://www.facebook.com/events/250493721657991/. I thank Jakkai for explaining these pieces to me. Parts of this exhibition was also installed at the "H Gallery" in Bangkok and the Chongqing Youth Biennial Art Exhibition.

[13] From the catalog to the show published by Tyler Rollins Fine Art (2014). See it online here: Tyler Rollins Fine Art - Jakkai Siributr: Transient Shelter (trfineart.com).

[14] Published on the occasion of the exhibition. I thank Jakkai for sending me a copy of the catalog.

[15] In Spring 2014 Jakkai has taken on the politically, religiously and ethically charged mass killing of Thai Muslims in Tak Bai (southern Thailand). It is important to note here that Jakkai focused on this local issue and created an installation that incorporated both Buddhist and Islamic symbols. The exhibition was simply called "78" referencing the 78 Muslim protestors that suffocated to death in Thai military trucks on October 25, 2004. I thank him for sending me the catalog and description of the exhibition from the Yavuz Fine Art Gallery (51 Waterloo Street, #03–01, Singapore 187969).

[16] Apinan Poshyananda, *Montien Boonma: Temple of the Mind* (2003: 15). Apinan also published the very influential (largely because it was the first major study of modern Thai art in English) *Modern Art in Thailand* (1992). While it does not focus on Buddhist themes in modern art specifically, many of the examples he chooses are explicitly works on Buddhist themes.

[17] http://www.artseensoho.com/Art/DEITCH/boonma97/boonma1.html and http:// www.deitch.com/projects/sub.php?projId=84

[18] The Kenneth and Yasuko Myer Collection of Contemporary Asian Art. Purchased 1993 with funds from The Myer Foundation and Michael Sidney Myer through the Queensland Art Gallery Foundation | Collection: Queensland Art Gallery. See http://qagoma.qld.gov.au/collection/contemporary_asian_art/montien_ boonma This is similar to two other installations he made called "Rock Bell Garden" and "Vessel Meditation."

[19] For more information on Thawan and Chalermchai's work, see Sandra Cate's groundbreaking book on modern Thai art in the 1990s, *Making Merit, Making Art: A Thai Temple in Wimbledon* (2003). A well-researched history of Silapakorn University is still a desideratum in the field.

[20] http://www.bangkokpost.com/lifestyle/family/246308/sculpting-emptiness

[21] Amrit Chusuwan, *Khwam tuk* (*Suffering*) (Bangkok: DOB Hualamphong Gallery, 2553 [2010]).

[22] Author unknown, *Kansadaeng silpakam haeng chat krang thi 53* (Bangkok: Silapakorn University Art Centre, 2550 [2007]). See especially pp. 30, 34, 114.

[23] In the past ten years there also has been a growing modern art scene in Chiang Mai with several excellent galleries opening throughout the city. I had a chance to visit a number of them in December 2014. While there have not been as many modern artists in the north of the country working on Buddhist themes (and that have gained a wide audience), the creation of these new galleries will undoubtedly lead to more artists finding a place to gain public recognition. I thank Anthony Irwin for recommending two of these galleries to me and for the conversations on modern Thai art in the north.

[24] See Punyawi Iamsakun, *Sati: Mahakamsilpakam wan silpa bhirasri* (Bangkok: Silapakorn University Art Centre, 2552 [2009]).

[25] See Wichok Mukdamani, *Jintakab jak phraphutthasasana* (Bangkok: Silapakorn University Art Centre, 2545 [2001]).

[26] Wichok Mukdamani and Nirmalendu Das, *Thai-India Art and Cultural Exchange 2003–2004* (Bangkok: Silapakorn University Art Centre), pp. 32–7.

[27] Phatyot Phutthachaloen, *Mindfulness* (Bangkok: Amarin, 2003).

[28] For a longer description and bibliographic references for the study of Thai murals, see my *Lovelorn Ghost and the Magical Monk*, chapter four (McDaniel 2011). See also Uab Sanasen's *Ten Contemporary Thai Artists* (1984): 144–61.

[29] See Chalermchai Kositpipat, Wat Rongkhun (no date); Chalermchai Kositpipat, *Roi ruang rao khong Wat Rongkhun* [DVD Video] (Chiang Rai: Wat Rongkhun, no date).

[30] There are dozens of available sites easily found online in Thai and English. See, for example: http://www.youtube.com/watch?v=y456xcuXDUU, http:// www.thawan-duchanee.com/index-eng.htm, http://www.photodharma.net/ Thailand/Black-House/Black-House.htm http://www.neverendingvoyage.com/ black-house-chiang-rai-thailand/, http://www.nationmultimedia.com/top40/detail/7058, http://www.sombatpermpoongallery.com/thawan-duchanee/, http://www.rama9art.org/

artisan/2004/october/trinity/index.html. There are dozens of individual exhibition catalogs, in Thai and English. See also Uab Sanasen's *Ten Contemporary Thai Artists* (1984), pp. 58–79 for some of his early work.

31 http://www.thawanduchanee.com/ See also the recent book on Thawan by Russell Marcus, *Thawan Duchanee: Modern Buddhist Artist* (2013).

32 Thawan has become so famous among international modern art circles that his works are selling for several thousands of US dollars at international auctions. For example, at a recent Sloane and Kenyon auction, one of his paintings sold for over 7,000 US dollars.

33 It is not only Buddhist artists who are creating large installation pieces in Bangkok. At the "Emerging Patterns" exhibition at the Bangkok Art and Cultural Center in the fall of 2011, Islamic artists from southern Thailand had numerous installations. For example, Charungrat Rotkuen created three "mosques" [labeled "Peunthi haeng Khwam Ngam" (Places of Beauty)]. They were made of string and paper and hung from the ceiling. The visitor could walk around and underneath them. Another artist named Chusak Srikwan created large hanging Javanese-style shadow puppets which the visitor could touch and spin around. They depicted scenes of Islamic buildings from southern Thailand as well as highly-politicized images of Buddhist monks using cellphones while riding in military tanks.

34 The Chatuchak/Mo Chit area of the city is popular during the weekends because of the Children's Museum and Weekend Market located there. Therefore, on Saturday and Sunday Bunchai's cool, quiet, and hyper-modern MOCA Museum and gardens are relaxing distractions from the crowds in the markets. A new history of Bunchai's collection and the founding of the museum can be seen in Bunchai Bencharongkul, Phipihithaphan, *Silapa Thai Ruam Samai* (Bangkok: Borisat Phipihithaphan Silapa Thai Chamgat, 2555 [2012]). In his collection, there are several pieces that are explicitly based on Buddhist history scenes, narratives, and teachings. See especially work by Surasit Saowakong, Wichai Sithirat, Chamnan Thongupakan, Siongdet Thipthong, Panya Wijinthanasan, among others.

35 Pattarasuda is related to the famous Thai scholar and noble Phraya Anuman Rajadhon (1888–1969). A bust of him and gratitude for his inspiration was also in the exhibition.

36 This show also helped promote the first International Buddhist Film Festival at the SF Cinema at Central World, a few hundred yards from the Paragon Mall. At this film festival, 30 films with Buddhist-related themes were screened. For more information on modern Thai Buddhist films, see my article "From Slapstick to Superheroes," *Journal of Religion and Film* (2011).

37 I thank Phra Sugandha (Dr. Anil Sakya) for his help in understanding this exhibition and his role in it.

38 For example see: Wichok Mukdamani, et al., *Chintaphap chak phra phutthasasana* (Bangkok: Mahawithayalai Silapakorn, 2545 [2002]). Between 2001 and 2003, Silapakorn University put on several shows of Buddhist-themed modern art at their art gallery, or helped sponsor shows at other universities, museums, and galleries including the Art Gallery at California Polytechnic State University, the Art Gallery of Kunstwerk, Cologne, Germany, the Art Gallery of Won Kwang University in Seoul, and the Molen van Sloten in Amsterdam. In 2004–05 there were other shows focusing on new developments in Thai Buddhist painting (Phra Bot) at Silapakorn, Khonkaen University, and Thaksin University called the Withi Thai nai Phap Phra Bot—see the catalog of the shows by Wichok Mukdamani et al., *Withi Thai nai Phap Phra Bot* (Bangkok: Mahawithayalai Silapakorn, 2546 [2004]). See also the exhibition catalogs for other modern Buddhist art shows many of them taking place at Ardel's Gallery in Taling Chan (Bangkok). For example: Panya Vijinthanasarn and Andrew Stahl, *Anywhere Anytime Anyhow* (Bangkok: Amarin Printing, 2009); Baan Lae Suan, *Young Female Artists of the Year curated by Thavorn Ko-udomvit* (Bangkok: Amarin Printing, 2009), a few of these female artists featured in this catalog worked on Buddhist themes in their art; Panya Vijinthanasarn, Thongchai Srisukprasert, and Anupong Chantorn, *Buddha, Dharma, Ecclesiastic* (Bangkok: Amarin Printing, 2012); Phatyos Buddhacharoen, *Namo Buddhaya: A Path Toward Divine Light* (Bangkok: Amarin Printing, 2010); Thongchai Srisukprasert, *Logiyadharma* (Bangkok: Amarin Printing, 2012); Anupong Chantorn, *Hope in the Dark* (Bangkok:

Amarin Printing, 2010). The Thai magazine, *Fine Art: The Art News of Thailand*, often features stories about modern artists working on Buddhist themes. One particularly creative show was by Thudong Sukasem, whose large sculpture called "Emptiness" consists of huge plaster Buddha-like heads that are actually supposed to reflect the emotional states of people who have been emotionally hurt in romantic relationships.

39 Another place that has seen a great deal of growth in modern Buddhist art in recent years is Kathmandu. Kathmandu has long been a center for the production of inexpensive Buddhist thangkhas and souvenirs for the tourist market, but recently there have been some galleries that have sponsored the exposition of modern and non-mass-produced Buddhist art. For example, the second international biennale of modern art took place in December 2012 and at the Kathmandu Contemporary Art Centre. Also, at the Planet Nepal Contemporary Art Exhibition some works with Buddhist themes by international artist Karl Knapp and Nepali artists Sujan Chitrakar, Ashmina Ranjit, Sajana Joshi, and Nayantara Kakshyapati were displayed. This is a slowly emerging center of modern Buddhist art, but it is still in its infancy in terms of funding, gallery space and patronage.

40 For more on Chan-soo Park, see my *Architects of Buddhist Leisure*, chapter three.

41 See http://www.kimsooja.com/projects/Brussels_Lotus_2008.html For detailed studies of her earlier work, see Julian Zugazagoitia, Nicolas Bourriaud, and Thieery Raspall, *Kim Sooja: Conditions of Humanity* (Milan: 5Continents Books, 2004) and two books she wrote with collaborators on specific exhibitions: Kim Sooja, Tae Hyunsun, and Ra Hee Hong Lee, *Kim Sooja: a Needle Woman* (Seoul: Rodin Gallery, 2000) and Kim Sooja and Oliva Maria Rubio Sooja, *Kim Sooja: To Breathe* (Madrid: Museo Nacional Centro de Arte Reina Sofia, 2006). I thank Charlotte Kim for her assistance while I was in Seoul visiting Sooja Kim's work. I also thank Sooja Kim for her assistance in answering my questions and sending me information about her installations.

42 http://www.charwei.com/index.html

43 For more work examples and short descriptions of some of his most prominent work, see: http://www.sugimotohiroshi.com/, http://www.pbs.org/art21/artists/ hiroshi-sugimoto, http://www.hirshhorn.si.edu/collection/sugimoto/#collection= sugimoto, and for a short critical study of his work, see Parveen Adams (2006). Palden Weinreb, a Tibetan-American artist, created light-boxes to serve as "meditations on existence and the universe" which "parallels the sublime emptiness of Buddhism."

44 See http://1995–2015.undo.net/it/mostra/140221. For more information: http://residencyunlimited.org/residencies/takayuki-yamamoto/

45 http://www.taohongjing.net/album/amithaba?p=1&s=UA-31097205-1#9

46 See "Buddhist Monks are Getting All the Love" in http://www.spoon-tamago. com/2012/06/12/buddhist-monks-are-getting-all-the-love/. Yoko Inoue also had a recent show at Five Myles, an art space in Crown Heights in Brooklyn. There she offers a commentary on the Mizuko-kuyo rituals in Japan for aborted foetuses. In "Liquidation" she dresses up empty water jugs as infants with ceramic heads, bibs, and the like. See: http://nymag.com/nymetro/arts/art/reviews/n_8660/ Of course, in Japan there is the recent phenomenon of the hip-hop monk Kansho Tagai, and punk rock monks are depicted in two Japanese films, Abraxas and Fanshi Dansa (Fancy Dancer) which are satirical, as well as efforts to connect Buddhist teachings to the youth.

47 See http://blog.asianart.org/blog/index.php/category/exhibitions/page/6/ for more information on the show, which was in the Tateuchi Thematic Gallery of the Asian Art Museum. I thank Forrest McGill for his invitation to the museum to give a talk and see this show among others.

48 This was originally displayed at the Queensland Art Gallery in Australia.

49 See the very informative article on Pich's work by Boreth Ly (2012). I thank Ly for sending it to me.

50 See Jerry Moore, ed., *Visions of Culture* (2009), p. 362; James Fernandez, ed., *Beyond Metaphor* (1991): introduction; and Emiko Ohnuki-Tierney, "Embedding and Transforming Polytrope: The Monkey as self in Japanese Culture," in *Beyond Metaphor*.

8

This Hindu Holy Man is a Thai Buddhist*

I have just turned 40 and have spent nearly my entire adult life conducting both ethnographic and textual research in Thai monasteries, museums, manuscript archives, amulet markets, historical parks and universities. One of my ongoing side-projects has been the study of Hinduism in Thailand. In the course of conducting research on other projects, on days off or breaks while at monasteries or libraries, I have taken hundreds of photographs, chatted to dozens of people, visited shrines and read what I hope is almost everything published on the subject. This was all done in an unsystematic but cumulative way—research by accretion, if you will. I finally decided I should sit down and start thinking about this material systematically. When reflecting on field and book notes, I noticed something—I could hardly find Hinduism anywhere in Thailand. Then the thought that pops into every 40-year-old's mind finally popped into mine—was this all just a waste of time?

At first the answer was a deafening "yes." Apart from a few small Hindu temples actually staffed by Brahmin (usually Tamil) priests such as Wat Umadewi (Sri Mariammam), which was founded in the early twentieth century, a few small shrines near Siyaekban Khaek, the Punjabi community's Wat Thepmontian, the small Visnu temple serving northern Indians on Soi Wat Prok, and the Thewasathan (discussed

---

* Originally appeared as "This Hindu Holy Man is a Thai Buddhist," *Southeast Asia Research* 21, 2 (2013): 191–210. I thank Craig Reynolds, Thomas Borchert and the anonymous readers at *Southeast Asia Research* for their thoughtful and valuable comments on an earlier draft of this article. Their comments much improved its content; however, I am to be blamed for all errors and inconsistencies.

Shopkeeper in front of small shop selling religious products in Bangkok. Photo by author.

below), virtually no "Hinduism" is practiced in Bangkok and very little anywhere else in Thailand. There are very few Hindu temples outside Bangkok and only one in Thailand's second largest city, Chiang Mai.[1]

The study of Hindu texts in Thailand is a rarity. In the manuscript archives, there are few, if any, copies of manuscripts composed in Sanskrit, Tamil, Hindi, Bengali, Malayalam, Telegu, Gujarati or other languages spoken by Hindu practitioners in India. While there are many Buddhist *jātakas* and folk tales providing alternate tellings of stories from the *Pañcatantra* and *Hitopadeśa* (well-known collections of fantastic, romance and adventure narratives composed in classical Sanskrit), they were not written in Thailand by Hindu pundits, sadhus or swamis, used as the foundation for Hindu practices or liturgies or read as distinctly Hindu tales.[2] They were copied and read by Buddhist monks and lay people as part of monastic education and Buddhist sermons. Tellings of the *Rāmāyaṇa* are well known in Thai art and theatre, but there are no regular and sustained concomitant religious rituals associated with them. There are virtually no examples of Hindu religious texts in *nissaya*, *vohāra*, or *nāmasadda* pedagogical manuscripts used actively to teach religion in Thailand. Printed material in the Thai language shows almost no evidence of guidebooks or handbooks [*khu meu*, *wohan*, *tamra*] that explain to Thai nuns, monks or laypeople how to perform a Hindu ritual. I used to tutor Sanskrit grammar at Mahachulalongkorn University in Bangkok (one of the major Buddhist monastic universities in the country) and had a number of students who were Thai nuns and monks very interested in the study of Sanskrit. However, not one of them was familiar with a Hindu Sanskrit chant or understood the basics of Hindu ritual sequences. I have interviewed dozens of Thai people who offer gifts to supposedly "Hindu" shrines in Bangkok and other places. I have not met one who could tell me any solid or detailed information about the place of these Hindu deities in Hindu ritual, liturgy or mythology. There are very few courses in Thai universities on the subject of Hinduism, and the ones that are taught do not attract many students. There are almost no teachers on television, in magazines or in popular books that teach Hindu ethics, Indian history or philosophy. There are no major books on the philosophical arguments proposed by Abhinavagupta, Śankhara, Madhvacharya, Vallabhacharya or Chaitanya in Thai and no major courses taught on their work. The teachings of the various major schools of Hindu religious and philosophical thought, such as Sāṃkhya or Vaiśesika, are present hardly anywhere in Thai religious or scholarly life. The Vedas are not translated into Thai. The individual texts of the Vedas are equally unknown by name or content by the vast majority of serious Thai Buddhists.

Although Thai Buddhists will occasionally visit a Brahmin ritualist, as I describe briefly below, there are very few public occasions on which the average Thai will see a Brahmin priest, apart from some large royal rituals shown on television, and at none of these few occasions are Hindu teachings relayed or sermons offered.[3] Thai

Buddhists do visit these mostly small temples, but they primarily serve ethnic Indians, and Bangkok's "Little India" [Phahurat] neighborhood's only major temple is Sikh.

Ethnic Indians (who, in my experience, are sometimes mistaken by ethnic Thais for Nepalis, Bangladeshis, Pakistanis, Sri Lankans and other South Asian peoples) are commonly referred to as *khaek*, which is explained as "guest" and "foreigner" in dictionaries. It is an ethnic term, not a religious term *per se*. This can be seen in the fact that individual shrines with images of Indra, Lakṣmī, etc., are not referred to as *thewadakhaek* [South Asian goddesses/gods], but neighborhoods where ethnic South Asians live, and temples that attract ethnic South Asians are referred to as *ban khaek* or *wat khaek*. Regardless of this, the ethnic *khaek* population of Thailand is quite low.[4] Since *khaek* can also refer to Sikhs, Zoroastrians or Muslims from Malaysia and Indonesia, the population of ethnic South Asian Hindu practitioners is even lower (less than 3 per cent of the population).

The problem was me. For so many years I had bracketed the study of "Hinduism" in Thailand as something separate and foreign—an anomaly that needed to be explained or explained away. I designated "Hinduism in Thailand" as a side project, as a discernible subject that I could research and write up in a descriptive study.[5] I might have wasted a long time looking for Hinduism in Thailand, but I had been spending my time well studying an integral part of Thai Buddhism. Hinduism as an intellectual, religious and philosophical system in Thailand hardly exists. Serious (or even amateur) knowledge of caste rules, ritual procedures and Sanskrit formulae is equally absent. However, visually speaking, Hindu influence seems to be everywhere.

The lack of knowledge of Hindu ethics and philosophy, Puja rites or the history of Vedic ritual and thought is only a problem if we assume, as I did, that Hinduism is actually a discernible set of beliefs and practices in Thailand (whether or not Hinduism is a discernible and distinct set of practices in India is entirely another problem). This is simply not the case. Thai people who visit these sites are not woefully ignorant Hindus. They simply see these supposedly "Hindu" statues and rituals as part of the practice of Thai Buddhism. No knowledge of their "Hinduness" is necessary. Hindu gods, goddesses and ascetics need to be studied as a legitimate part of Thai Buddhism. In this way, terms and phrases such as "Hinduization," "Hinduism in Thailand," and "Brahmanism in Thailand," which connote something wholly different from Buddhism, are detrimental to the study of Thai religion. First, these terms reify the idea that Hinduism in India is one religion, when in reality it is a convenient rubric for a panoply of practices, ethical rationales and transformative narratives. If it is difficult to define the boundaries of Hinduism in India, how could I expect to in Thailand? Second, it assumes that different ethnic, language, regional and sectarian groups such as Tamils, Punjabis, Bengalis, Vaiśnavites, Śaivites or the followers of Sūrya, Kriṣṇa or Kāli are all practicing more or less the same thing in India and in Thailand. Third, since Hindu gods and goddesses are seen as something separate from Buddhism in Thailand, something foreign, they are not included in most major studies of Thai

Buddhism, even though gods such as Gaṇeśa and Indra are a common part of Thai ritual, artistic and narrative traditions. This means that a significant part of a Thai Buddhist's religious life is ignored. There have been hundreds of articles and dozens of books on Thai Buddhism. Very few have included the serious study of supposedly Hindu figures alongside Buddhas and Bodhisattas, even though they have, from available evidence, clearly been part of Buddhist practice in Thailand for centuries. Indeed, there is barely any actual "Hinduism" in Thailand at all. "Hindu" figures are part of the Buddhist pantheon. Obviously, a full study of the role of Hindu deities such as Gaṇeśa, Brahma, Garuda, or Indra would require much more space than a short article can provide. Therefore, the remainder of this short study attempts to offer a description of the hermit and Brahmin as part of a study of Thai Buddhism. Indeed, the hermit should not be seen as a side-project under the rubric of Hinduism in Thailand, but central to the study of Thai Buddhism itself.

My Brahmin is Buddhist

The best place to study the role of the Brahmin in Thai life is the Thewasathan [Place of the Gods/Devas]. This is the royally-sponsored temple founded in 1784, which houses offices of the Brahmins of Thailand. However, it is a small center and, after three visits and interviews with different staff members (and a reading of their internally produced, but unpublished, history of the center), I have established that there are fewer than 15 actual Brahmins (ordained Phra Phram) in the whole of Thailand, and few intact Brahmin families left.[6]

The most useful information I gained was from Phra Maharatchakhru Phithisriwisutthikhun, the chief royal Brahmin in Thailand and teacher to many of the present Brahmins. He granted me a rare interview in January 2012.[7] In this very informative session, I learned that there were no exceptions to the rule that to become a Brahmin in Thailand one must come from one of the Brahmanic blood lines [*pen luk-lankhong Phra Phram*], which he claimed stretched back over 1,200 years in Thailand and were invited to come from the Nakhon Sri Thammarat area in southern Thailand to serve the Siamese royal family. These lines were originally from the Tamil region of India, but only oral records exist. Many of these families have long intermarried with local Thai Buddhists and are at this point ethnically Thai. None of the Brahmins was born in India and none spoke a modern Indian language well. Most had either never visited India or had gone there on a short tourist trip. He admitted that he last went to India seven years ago, when he stayed for two weeks. He also admitted that they used primarily Thai-language books and some Thai-Sanskrit glosses in their study. He had in his possession (but I was not able to examine them) some Sanskrit ritual manuscripts—even though I did not open them, from their outward appearance they were central Thai-style *samutkhoi* manuscripts from the mid-nineteenth century)—which were composed in what he called *akson thamin boran* [Old Tamil Script]. He emphasized that none of the Brahmins knew Sanskrit grammar, but they were trained to chant Sanskrit mantras during rituals. There is no school at the Thewasathan and no formal curriculum. Instruction and ordination are done on a one-to-one basis, and over his whole life (he is near retirement age) he has trained fewer than 25 people in total (he has been the primary trainer for the last couple of decades) and has had the most students. Clearly, he is treated with great deference by all the other Brahmins and staff. Training does not take place in any serious way anywhere else in the country or in Bangkok. Several of the Brahmins in present-day Thailand are in fact from his own bloodline, and I had a chance to meet one of his cousins, who also serves in the royal rituals. They do not produce books, hold regular classes, seek converts, promote the building of Hindu temples, have regular publicized visits from famous Brahmins from India or have a public lecture series.

However, this does not mean that the Thewasathan or Phra Maharatchakhru Phithisriwisutthikhun is not busy. He is in high demand for his services because he serves the larger Buddhist community. Although he was never ordained as a Buddhist monk, many of the other Brahmins had been ordained as young men, and all worked closely with Buddhist monks. On each visit I made there were several Buddhist monks visiting. One whom I interviewed was very helpful in explaining why monks were often seen at the Thewasathan. Phra Sompong Santikaro, a Buddhist monk from the Chomthong section of Bangkok, was there one evening to invite Phra Maharatchakhru Phithisriwisutthikhun to assist in the ritual to open a new building at the Buddhist practice centre, Samnak Batibat Tham Wat Phatham Phaisan. The new pillars for the building were going to be ritually consecrated by both the Brahmin and Buddhist monks on 4 March 2012 and he needed to make sure everything was ready for the ceremony. Phra Maharatchakhru Phithisriwisutthikhun also noted that he often performed rituals with Buddhist monks. In fact, while I waited three hours to meet Phra Maharatchakhru Phithisriwisutthikhun I met several others in the queue, all Buddhists, who were there for a variety of reasons. One couple were there to have their new baby consecrated and her astrological chart read. Another family was starting a new business and was arranging a time for Phra Maharatchakhru Phithisriwisutthikhun to come to their home for a ceremony. A young couple who were planning their wedding visited to gain merit from the statues of Viṣṇu, Śiva and Gaṇeśa. Another woman was there to attend a Brahmanic ritual for the new year. As I waited I also helped to carry about four hundred 25-foot-long bamboo stalks and several hundred coconuts (for decoration at the next large temple ceremony) from a truck to the storeroom of the Thewasathan, and chatted to several temple assistants, all of whom stressed that they were Buddhists and that they saw no problem at all with working at a Brahmanic temple. The ritual I attended in the evening had an audience of about 60 people and, although I had a chance to speak to only a few, all were Buddhists.

The biggest ceremony the Brahmins help to perform is the annual ploughing ritual, designed to ensure good crops for the kingdom. They are also involved in some weddings (but usually nine Buddhist monks chant at weddings today) and, perhaps surprisingly, at consecrations of new images of the Buddha [*phutthaaphisek*] and the seasonal changing of the Emerald Buddha's [Phra Phuttha Moradok] clothes. The occasional large construction project and planting of a spirit house [*sanphraphum*] involve Brahmin priests offering gifts to local spirits (although this is becoming a rarity).

The "Hindu" Hermit in Thailand

Among my notes and photographs was another "Hindu" figure that was much more pervasive in conducting rituals, who was a lot more common than the Brahmin—the hermit. The hermit, or seer (Sanskrit: ṛṣi/Thai: *phra reusi*), is the perfect example of a very common Hindu figure in Thai Buddhism. Although many Thai Buddhists might never meet a Brahmin priest and certainly very few will ever read a Hindu text or listen to a Hindu sermon, most will be familiar with the Hindu hermit. However, there are no major studies in Western languages of the hermit's role in Thai Buddhist ritual and narrative. I think one of the reasons this pervasive figure has been ignored is that he is seen as a Hindu instead of part of Thai Buddhist life.

Just like Śiva, Brahma, Indra (Sakka), Lakṣmī, the Buddha, Avalokiteśvara, Nārāyaṇa (Viṣṇu), Maitreya/Metteya, Ganeṣa, Rama, and other Indie powerful beings, the figure of the Indic-looking hermit or ascetic has long been present in the statuary of what is known today as Thailand. Indeed, these enlightened beings and deities, like Śiva and the Buddha (before he realized awakening), are often depicted as ascetics or hermits living in the forest, dressed in animal skins, engaged in meditation. The ascetic path and the time of training in the wilderness is one of the dominant narrative sequences in Asian religious biographies and stories from India to Burma and Japan since at least 1500 BCE. The hermit is not a character limited to the "Hindu" religion and is not always from the Brahmin caste.[8]

In Southeast Asia, images of these hermits are sometimes identified by art historians as the famous ṛṣi Agastya, a sage often connected, but not exclusive to Saivism. However, most art historical studies which mention ṛṣi do so only in reference to photographs of ṛṣi statues in Cambodia, Thailand or Java. They do not speculate on their personal name and they are known, because of lack of evidence, as simply hermits/seers/ṛṣi. There have been no extensive studies of their history or role in religious practice in the region.[9] In Southeast Asia, Agastya, like many hermit figures, usually has a pot belly, beard and moustache. More specifically, he is often identified as different from other sages because he carries a water jar and a large set of chanting beads. Fly whisks and tridents also occasionally accompany these statues.

In Thailand, Agastya is known as Akkhot, but statues of hermits are not very commonly identified as Akkhot specifically. Instead, the more general terms *nakphrot* [person who takes vows; from the Sanskrit *vrata*], *muni* [sage], *dabot* [hermit], *nakbuat* [ordained one], *yokhi* [yogi], *phram* [Brahmin sage], and most commonly *phra reusi* [ṛṣi; English, seer] are used. It should be noted that these names, except for *phram* and *phra reusi*, can be used for Buddhist monks as well, as they connote anyone who goes into the wilderness to meditate, chant *mantras*, and undertake physical austerities. Brahmin sages (although they do not actually have to be of the Brahmin caste to be called this) and *phra reusi* usually have beards and do not take the 227 *Patimokkha* precepts like bhikkhu [those who live by alms: that is, monks]. Women are almost never identified as hermits.[10] These hermits are defined in various Thai dictionaries and art encyclopaedias as *phra hen* [seers], *phu taeng phra wet* [writers of Vedic mantras],[11] and *phu miphonsawan* [those with heavenly gifts]. In Thailand, the slightly bent, conical hat, pot belly, goatee, animal skin (usually a leopard, jaguar or tiger skin) shawl, walking stick and chanting beads are the usual possessions and attributes of the hermit. When painted, these figures often have a black or yellow face and white beard.[12] Early examples are seen on votive tablets and miniature statues from Kanchanaburi known as Phra Thakradan, which is sometimes associated with Narada or Phra Reusi Narot.[13] Phra Reusi Narot is probably the most commonly depicted pre-modern hermit in Thailand as he was associated with teaching divine mantras, medicinal concoctions and music. Since at least the late Ayutthayan period, Phra Reusi Narot has been a type of patron saint of Thai classical music and is often imaged with a tiger skin shawl and holding a *phin* [type of sitar]. On "Teacher's Day" [*wan waikhru*] in many music schools, a mask of Phra Reusi Narot is ceremoniously placed on the head of each student one at a time to represent their path on the way to knowledge. He is even popularly considered to be the author of the *Ramakian* [Rāmāyaṇa]. These figures may have some iconic connection to Akkhot but should not be seen as direct descendants or corruptions of some more ideal named Indian itinerant ascetic.

There are many examples in pre-modern Thailand of art depicting hermits. For example, at the Angkorian site of Prasat Hin Phanom Rung in present-day Buriram Province (north-east Thailand), there are two large, sculpted hermits walking side by side on a pillar relief, probably carved sometime in the eleventh century. One holds chanting beads and a walking staff, and the other grips a trident in two hands. They are both bearded and with conical hats (the statue is badly damaged).[14] The floral designs around them may indicate that they are walking in the forest. Since there are only two of them, it is not likely that the relief is depicting a royal ritual or formal procession of any type, as ritual and royal processions are depicted differently in Angkorian reliefs. Nearby at Prasat Muang Tarn, there is a well-preserved stone *kuṭirṣi* [hermit's quarters or hut], one of three preserved in the north-east from the time of King Jayavarman VII. In Chiang Saen, there is a fine statue from 1604 of a hermit engaged in seated meditation. Although he does not sport the iconic beard, he is seated next to a fly whisk, water jar, bowl and fire pit (this indicates that it is not a Buddhist monk's alms bowl, as Buddhist monks are not permitted to cook or start fires) and a walking stick.[15] The famous reliefs telling the story of the *Ramakian* at Wat Phra Chetuphon (Wat Pho), one of the oldest monasteries in Bangkok, contain a prominent carving of Phra Reusi Narot, who offers advice to Hanuman seated on the verandah of his lush forest hermitage.[16] Wat Pho was the earliest monastic "hospital" in Bangkok from the late eighteenth century onwards. In its grounds today is a popular massage [*nuat*] school, and statues of hermits in various yogic poses are found built on a man-made stone "mountain" in the center of the monastic grounds. There is a list of 80 yogic poses and accompanying images in the inscriptions of Wat Pho.[17] Here most of the *phra reusi* remain nameless, but have been associated with hermits mentioned in the epics *Ramakian* and *Inao*, as well as in the commentaries of the *Vacchanakha-Jātaka* (No. 235), the local *Nemirāja-Jātaka*, *Indriya-Jātaka* (No. 423) in which Narada features prominently, *Mahājanaka-Jātaka* (No. 539), *Mahāpalobhana-Jātaka* (No. 507) and *Guṇa-Jātaka* (No. 157) and local stories such as the *Phra Rathameri*, *Camadevīvaṃsa* and *Unarut*.[18] Indeed, most sources for Thai hermits, as we will see below, are not "Hindu" epics, the Vedas or *Purāṇas*, but canonical or non-canonical *Jātakas* or vernacular Thai texts. Mural paintings, monastic banner paintings and illuminated manuscripts in Thailand also frequently feature hermits. In most cases, these hermits represent either Prince Vessantara (Thai: Wessandon), the Buddha in his final life before becoming Gotama Siddattha, or the sinister and lecherous forest Brahmin Jūjaka (Thai: Chuchok).[19] Usually Prince Vessantara is depicted as a dedicated forest ascetic who, although living with his wife and children, takes a vow of celibacy. Jūjaka, on the other hand, is a bearded Brahmin who lives in the forest like a hermit. However, he does not follow an ascetic path. Instead he is a lecherous creep (for lack of a better word). His creepiness is best seen in a set of Thai cloth paintings held by the Asian Art Museum. In one painting, several women ridiculing the beautiful young wife of the ugly and elderly Brahmin Jūjaka are shown. The painting is quite bawdy. The women are depicted groping each other, dancing and holding long wooden phalluses. Many are half-naked, pretending to penetrate each other vaginally in various positions. This kind of explicit sexual display is not mentioned in the Pali text, but must have offered some shock and delight to the late nineteenth-century audiences of the painting, as well as showing the difficult social situation in which both Jūjaka and his wife Amittatāpanā found themselves.[20] Indeed, today there is a popular protective amulet in Thailand of Jūjaka, usually in the form of a decrepit old man with a long beard, hunched over and walking with a cane. This small wooden or metal amulet is supposed to bring much merit to its owners, since Jūjaka, despite his age and poverty, was able to obtain everything he asked for, including a young and pretty wife.[21] Other not so complimentary depictions of hermits are seen on the walls of Wat Khongkaram, where hermits dressed in animal skin shawls attempt to rape Vessantara's wife Maddi.[22] The point here is that hermits are not necessarily "Hindu" or from the Brahmin caste in Thai art. They are Bodhisattas or local healers without Brahmin caste status.

In twentieth-century statuary, paintings, book illustrations and posters, the figure of the hermit is very common. Statues of Phra Reusi Narot, Phra Chiwok Goman, generic hermits simply called *phra reusi* or *nakphrot*, are found in nearly every store selling religious art and offerings (see particularly the shops along Thanon Mahachai, Thanon Arun Amarin, and surrounding Tha Phrachan in Bangkok). Posters are found in many monastic markets at the Loha Prasat, Wat Indrawihan, Wat Rakhang, Wat Pathum Wannaram, several popular shrines along the road to Wat Mahabut, and near the base of the Phu Khao Thong at Wat Srakhet (in Bangkok) and at many prominent rural temples.[23] There are dozens of shrines to hermits throughout Thailand. Some of the most frequently visited are the *tham* [cave] *phra reusi* at Somdet Pra Sri Nakarin Park (Phangnga Province), the shrine to the image of Suthewa Reusi in Lamphun Province, and the *phra reusi* shrine on the road to Wat Doi Suthep in Chiang Mai.

In the modern period, there are also various lists of *phra reusi* found in Thailand which do not overlap with Indie (Vedic or Puranic) lists. For example, at Wat Muang in rural Angthong, we find statues with the names of 15 *phra reusi*. Each is in a different pose and has different ritual implements. They are united in the fact that they all wear tiger fur/skin robes, have long white beards and sit in meditative positions.[24] Another very different list is found in *Tamnān Phra Reusi*, which is a series of stories, photos of statues and shrines, plus descriptions of *phra reusi* compiled by the lay scholar, KonthepThepyothin, advised by four Buddhist monks—Phra Khru Wimollilaphon, Phra Khru Phichanawiharakit, Phra Khru Sunthathammaghosit and Phra Khru Phisalathammanuwat.[25] Descriptions of 31 *phra reusi* are here with only Phra Reusi Narot (Narada), Phra Reusi Isuan (Śiva) and Phra Reusi Phrohmalok (Brahma) overlapping with the previous list from Wat Muang in Angthong and having almost no overlapping *phra reusi* with Indic lists.[26] However, their depictions do not closely overlap with Indic depictions, and most Thai enthusiasts I have met do not immediately equate these Thai hermits with Hindu deities or sages.[27] The important point for the purposes of this study is that these lists are almost completely local and idiosyncratic. There have been no efforts by monks, Brahmins, scholars or living hermits in Thailand to standardize the pantheon of famous *phra reusi* and no efforts to trace their origins to Indie sources. The various lineages, textual traditions and ritual technologies of Hinduism are ignored and the vast majority of Thai followers and scholars of these *phra reusi* are practicing Buddhists with no knowledge of Sanskrit or Hindu theologies.

Protective magical practices often involve the character of the hermit. Amulets, tattoos and warrior shirts with protective incantation drawings [*phrayan*] written on them often depict hermits.[28] Achan Nu Kanphai, a very popular magician (*mowiset/ mo phi*: wizard or ghost doctor) and tattoo artist in Pathum Thani Province (central Thailand) is often referred to as a living *phra reusi*. He has tattooed many Thai politicians and movie stars (even Angelina Jolie) using *mon khatha sek sak* [*mantra* verses for the empowering of tattoos] or the *mahawet* [Great Veda]. These chants are a mixture of Sanskritized Thai and Pali interspersed with rhythmic abbreviated syllables. At these ceremonies, which are held once or twice a year, monks also chant Buddhist Pali *parittas* while stirring pots of holy water.[29] At the end of the ceremony, all the lay people in attendance have their heads tied together with sacred string, which is also tied around Buddha images and monks in the room. Achan Nu Kanphai is assisted in his tattoo ceremonies (which also include spirit possession) by two senior monks from Ayutthaya. During these ceremonies, many lay people in the audience start dancing uncontrollably because they supposedly become possessed by spirits. He and the monks are all referred to as *kechiachan*, which is a specialized title for teachers, lay ordained, who have special knowledge of protective incantations like *phra reusi*. Achan Nu Kanphai is neither a Brahmin nor ethnically Indian. He does not know Sanskrit and does not practice Hinduism of any branch known in India. However, he promotes supposedly Hindu symbols, technology and the ideal of the powerful hermit.

Phra Chiwok Goman: The Buddha's Physician

Perhaps the most common hermit in Thai culture is Jīvaka Komārabhacca (usually pronounced in Thai: Phra Chiwok Goman). He is referred to as a *phra reusi* and a Brahmin. Although his statues depict him as a hermit, he was not famous for being a forest ascetic, but as the physician of the Buddha. He has been worshipped in Thailand for at least two centuries and appears in Pali texts (including three texts that figure him prominently: the *Jīvakasutta* in the *Aṅguttara Nikāya* 8.26, in the famous defence of vegetarianism in the *Majjhima Nikāya* 55, and an entire biography of Jīvaka in chapter eight of the *Mahāvagga* section of the *Vinaya Piṭaka*).[30] His story is well known to any Thai who is interested in "traditional" medicine or who has to spend time in amulet markets, at any major hospital or at monasteries connected with healing practices.[31]

I have encountered Jīvaka images and seen his likeness on herbal medicine bottles and have even offered flowers and incense to a statue of him while visiting a friend in hospital in Bangkok. One of the largest images of Jīvaka in the country is located in the grounds of Wat Indrawihan next to a famous holy water pool.[32] Not only do people offer flowers, incense and chants to the image; they also often request (usually for a 10-baht donation) a bottle of healing oil, said to be made by Thai physicians trained in Jīvaka's methodology. Some obtain small images of Jīvaka that come in several sizes and materials ranging in price from US$3 to US$75. The same monks who are in charge of making amulets of Buddhas and famous Buddhist monks at Wat Indrawihan are also involved in the making of Jīvaka images and amulets.[33] The group of Buddhist monks led by Phra Ratchratanaphon (Luang Pho Thong Seup) forged seven different types of Jīvaka images in gold, bronze and marble, as well as a copper amulet for (as advertised) helping "those afflicted by diseases" [*bukkhon thi mi rok*].[34] They hold seminars, advertise in amulet magazines and newspapers, and claim to be preserving the methods of the "Father of Medicine" [*Phra bida haeng kan phaet*].[35]

In the amulet market around Tha Phra Chan in Bangkok there are several Thai traditional medicine stores and clinics, three of them with images of Jīvaka. In fact, one physician [*mo*] named Parinya Uthichalanon, who runs the Sathanphyaban Phaet Phaen Boran Tha Phra Chan [Traditional Medical Institute of Tha Phra Chan], proudly showed me the amulets around his neck, which included one for Jīvaka. He was trained by Buddhist monks at Wat Chetuphon and handed his degree by none other than the Sangharat of the entire Thai Buddhist Sangha, although he also trained with those whom he called "Brahman" [Phra Phrom] teachers.[36] Not only did he recommend certain medicines he made, but also, like other physicians in the area, a particular chant that, although in Pali, is not found in any known canonical or commentarial Pali text from South Asia.[37]

Dr. Parinya saw no difference between Buddhist and Brahmin medicine and did not think I should either. He gave me an annotated list of 247 different medicines that he had mixed himself and said they could cure diseases regardless of my religion.[38] When I asked exactly what the Jīvaka method was, he replied that they were simply principles of anatomy, botany and physiology, but each physician developed her or his own method. This statement explains a great deal about Thai ritual practice. There were principles, tools, tropes and aesthetics, but not prescriptions. They were cultural tools which allowed, even encouraged, a modicum of individual agency when using them to solve practical problems. These ritual practices, like these herbal recipes, are never identical for each individual; however, they need at least to gesture towards or selectively employ known embodiments of power such as famous heroes (Jīvaka, the Sangharat, Gaṇeśa, etc.), powerful languages and scripts (Sanskrit, Pali, Khom, Lanna), common aesthetics and tools (Buddhas, Brahmans, or monks seated in the half-lotus position, small amulets, yantras, chanting meters, incense, certain flowers, candles) and the like.[39]

Perhaps the best place to see the rituals and hear the liturgies connected with Jīvaka is at the national monks' hospital in Bangkok [*rongphayaban song*]. This is not a traditional medicine hospital, but a thoroughly modern one with ambulances, surgical amphitheatres, MRI/CAT scanning machines and, of course, one sees monks in the waiting rooms, in observation rooms hooked up to intravenous drips and standing in line for prescriptions. The physicians are, however, dressed in white lab coats and the pharmacy is filled with synthetic medicines produced largely in Japan, Europe and North America. Behind the hospital stands a small Buddhist *vihāra* [sermon hall] staffed by one monk who receives gifts from lay relatives of the sick, and the hall contains both an image of the Buddha and one of Jīvaka.

In addition, at the edge of the parking lot stands a large shrine dedicated primarily to Jīvaka, with a chant to him carved in marble, where people offer incense, flowers, candles and small sums of money, just as they would to any image of the Buddha. The chant is identical to the one translated in note 37 but is introduced by the common clause that starts almost every Buddhist ceremony in Thailand: "namo tassa bhagavato arahato sammasambuddhassa" [Praise to the most perfectly enlightened arahant lord Buddha]. The Hindu hermit Jīvaka is praised with a chant followed by a praise to the Buddha. The statue of Jīvaka is seated in the half-lotus position like most Buddha images, and the altar decorations, candle holders, etc. are close to those of Buddha altars throughout the country. The sign above him reads: *asarahm phra achan phaet phra chiwok komanabhat* [Ashram of the great physician Jīvaka Komārabhacca] and a sign next to the shrine has an inscription of his *mantra*. In an interview with a nurse at the hospital in August 2010, I was told that some patients held an amulet of Jīvaka while monks chanted Pali Buddhist texts over them. This was not part of the modern medical practices at the hospital but was a request from some patients and their families.

What seems evident throughout the hospital is that people seem to move between the secular medical technological and Buddhist ritual spaces with ease. Even the small convenience store in the grounds of the hospital stocks Buddhist ritual items such as holy water holders, robes, ceremonial fans, candles and incense, as well as ice cream, soft drinks, instant noodles and fashion magazines. The symbol of the entire hospital on a sign above the entrance depicts the Buddha seated in meditation in the middle of a green cross. The cross is seen as a symbol of Western medicine since it often appears on the side of Western ambulances. Just as there seems to be no real boundary between those seeking protection and healing from Jīvaka and those seeking it from the Buddha, there seems to be no boundary between the use of Western and Thai traditional medicine. Buddhism has not been reified, nationalized, centralized and regulated to a distinct and separate part of social life.[40]

Conclusion

The conclusion to be drawn from the array of empirical evidence above is that statues of Hindu hermits, deities and some rituals that involve Brahmin priests (usually accompanied by Buddhist monks) are widespread in Thailand and have existed for hundreds of years; but the sum total of these images and rituals does not equal a "religion" and their presence has not led to an interest in Hindu eschatology, soteriology, ethics or metaphysics. Rather, Hindu images in Thailand are part of Buddhist culture. And while it can be stated that these images invoke vague ideas of "Indianness" or exoticism, they do not indicate a widespread motivation for people to follow Hindu caste, diet, gender, appearance, ritual or astrological guidelines for practice or to learn Hindu ethics or philosophy. Statues represent figures, either historical or divine; they do not represent religion.

Thai Buddhists have long been open to honoring and imaging a panoply of religious figures, regardless of religious affiliation. Buddhist shrines in Thailand commonly mix Hindu and Buddhist deities. Thai Buddhists offer gifts and prostrate themselves to both of them, regardless of their religious beliefs. Small workshops in Bangkok produce images of Buddhas, famous monks, Hindu deities, spirits, Taoist immortals, *ṛṣi* and jade emperors (made of resin, bronze, wood, copper and plastic).[41] Artisans churn out hundreds of images a month, some made to order and some for mass consumption. From my many interviews in these workshops, I have learned that images of famous monks rival the sales of Buddha images, and Gaṇeśa images in particular have become extremely popular. Images of past kings, of Kwan Yin and of Nang Kwak (a popular female image used for bringing profits into small businesses) are also big sellers. Occasionally, although this is not as popular as it was in the early 1990s, Greek and Roman deities or dolphins are also seen. The Hindu, Buddhist, Taoist, Animist and Greco-Roman all compete for space in the shop fronts on these streets with other items for sale such as robes, umbrellas, toiletry kits and pillows offered to monks. Buddha images are no more expensive than Hindu ones. Shopkeepers never inquire as to the purchaser's religious beliefs. One might assume that the gaggle of images found in these shops would not be replicated in more sacred environs. However, many monasteries in Thailand possess the same variety of objects. The belief that a particular image can protect, heal, serve as a nice gift or bring luck is more important than the specific religion that image supposedly represents.

Hermits have been part of Buddhist practice in Thailand for centuries, but despite the presence, prominence and popularity of these supposedly Hindu figures, there is barely any actual "Hinduism" in Thailand at all. These so-called "Hindu" figures instead constitute part of the Buddhist pantheon and should therefore be studied as a part of Thai Buddhism. In my search for Hinduism I had, rather, found figures, roles and individuals in Thai Buddhism. I needed to look very hard to find any evidence of Hindu teachings, but Hindu gods and persons are ubiquitous in Thai religious life. This study aims to encourage others to look at other supposedly "Hindu" figures in Thai Buddhism, leading to fruitful examinations of the role of the deva in Thai religions.[42] By not reading *phra reusi* as evidence of a Hindu substrate or a pre-Buddhist Khmer-Brahmanic influence in Thai culture, we can compare his figure more easily with Chiwok Goman, a *mowiset* [Thai wizard, protector or magician], a *mo phi* [expert at contacting, attracting or protesting against ghosts] or famous Buddhist saints. We can see "Hindu" hermits as part of Buddhist life. Prince Vessantara and the Buddha himself lived as "Hindu" hermits or *reusi*/*ṛṣi* themselves and they were occasionally referred to in Pali as "*isi*." And so these *reusi* are not simply evidence of "Hindu" influence in Thailand, but can be seen as part and parcel of Buddhism.

Notes

1 Hindi is still taught at the secondary school, Rongrian Bharat Witthayalai (Indian High School); however, besides this subject (which is not taken by all students) and some Indian cultural events and instruction, this is a matrathan [standard] Thai high school with a government-approved public curriculum. Indeed, most students are either Thai Buddhist or Muslim, and there are some Thai-born/

ethnic Indian high school students. Instruction is in Thai. Funerals for the small ethnic Indian community take place near Wat Yannawa in Bangkok. Child blessings usually take place at the Dewasathan or are performed by Brahmins invited to private homes.

2 For more information on Sanskrit literary tales prevalent in Thailand, see "Encountering Corpses: Notes on Zombies and the Living Dead in Buddhist Southeast Asia," in this volume.

3 There are fewer than ten Hindu temples, in comparison with 33,000 Buddhist monasteries, 3,500 Islamic mosques and over 300 Christian churches. Brahmin priests play a small role in the Thai film *Chomkhamang wet* (English title: Necromancer, RS Films, directed by Piyapat Chupetch, 2005) and Nonzee Nimibutr's version of *Nang Nak* (Buddy Film and Video Production Co, directed by Nonzee Nimibutr, 1999).

4 Several Thai dictionaries note that *khaek* means people from Nepal, Bangladesh, India, Afghanistan, Pakistan, Sri Lanka and central Asia who come to Thailand "looking for work" [*ma ha ngantham*] or "come to help [Thais] work" [*ma chuaithamngan*]. Dictionary definitions often note that *khaek* can also refer to Melayu [Malaysians and Indonesians], but should not refer to Jews, North Africans and *Nigro* [black Africans]. It is, however, extended to Arabs in the term *khaekarap*. Obviously, this is a term with which many ethnic Indians would rather not be associated.

5 Of course, I am not the only person to have done this. Scholars such as Majupuria and Chakravarti, for example, state that Hinduism is popular in Thailand and that Hindu gods are worshipped with "utter devotion" in Thailand (Chakravarti 1996: 17). However, they provide examples of Hindu statues on Buddhist shrines or the tellings of the *Rāmāyaṇa* in Thai murals and theatre to prove their point about the presence of Hinduism. Then they describe in different ways what the teachings of karma, the purva and uttara-Mīmāṃsā schools, the teachings of Śaṅkara are, but provide no evidence that any of these teachings are found in the Thai language or are actually known and commented on by scholars or practitioners in Thailand beyond the very small ethnic Indian community (indeed, they do not even provide evidence that Brahman ritualists in Thailand actually learn and teach these texts and traditions). They do not provide evidence of actual teaching of classical Hindu ethical or ritual texts, the Vedas, or the presence of established schools of Hindu thought in Thailand. See Majupuria's *Erawan Shrine and Brahma Worship in Thailand* (1987), especially chapters three and nine; and Chakravarti's (1996),"Brahmanism and Buddhism in Thailand," in the *Proceedings of the International Seminar on Brahmanism and Buddhism in Thailand* (Bangkok: Silpakorn University Press), pp. 16–25.

6 They are (in order of rank): Phra Maharatchakhru Phithisriwisutthikhun (family name: Khawin Rangsiphrahmanakhun), Phra Ratchakhru Siwachan (Thawon Bhavangkhanan), Phra Khru Sathanathamuni (Arun Sayomaphop), Phra Khru Yananasayambhu (Khachon Nakhanawethin), Phra Khru Sitthikhayabadi (Khon Komonwethin), Phram Sombat Ratanaphrahm, Phram Sisonphan Rangsiphrahmanakhun, Phram Phisana Rangsiphrahmanakhun, Phram Bhatihari Sayomaphop, Phram Bharikhawut Nakhanawethin, Phram Khawankhat Ratanaphrahm, Phram Phathan Wuthiphrahm, Phram Kharan Buransiri, and Phram Thawutthi Komonwethin. From this list, you can see that these positions are often a father-brother-uncle-son affair.

7 I thank Arthid Sheravanichkul for helping me arrange this interview and the Buddhist monk Phra Sompong Santikaro for his help at the Thewasathan.

8 In Vedic and Puranic literature there are multiple lists of ṛṣi. The earliest list is found in the Jaiminīya Brāhmaṇa (2.218), the Bṛhadāraṇyaka Upaniṣad (2.2.6). Quite a different list of seven seers is found in the southern Indian Puranic tradition and includes: Aṅgiras, Atri, Vasiṣṭha, Marīcī, Pulastya, Pulaha and Kratu. However, these ṛṣi, besides Agastya (see below) and Kaśyapa, are almost never found in Southeast Asian lists.

9 In Indonesia I have noticed that the name Agastya is written on labels of statues of ṛṣi, but I have not been able to ascertain why the name Agasyta, as opposed to other Indian ṛṣi, is applied to these images. In India, Agastya is believed to be one of the great teachers of the Ṛg Veda and son of the deities Urvaṣī

and Varuṇa. He conquered demons, held secrets of healing potions, and was adept at yogic poses and meditation. Agastya statues are mostly found in Java. Agastya usually guards the southern entrances to Śaivite shrines (see, for example, the statues at the Cand Sambisari or the Prambanan in Java). Girard-Geslan, Maud, et al., eds., *Art of Southeast Asia* (Paris: Harry Abrams, 1997), p. 350.

10 For a study of the categories of female professional religious teachers and ascetics in Thailand, see my article with Steven Collins (2010), "Buddhist 'Nuns' (*mae chi*) and the Teaching of Pali in Contemporary Thailand," in this volume. See also Collins's *Civilisation et femmes célibataires dans le bouddhismeen Asie du Sud et du Sud-Est: uneétude de genre* (Paris: Les Éditions de Cerf, 2011).

11 In Southeast Asia, *weda* and *wet* are common terms in Burma, Indonesia, Malaysia, Cambodia, Laos and Thailand to refer to protective magical practices or astrological rituals associated with prognostication. While there are no translations of the Sanskrit Vedas in Southeast Asian languages and the term *weda* does not directly refer to sections of the four Sanskrit Vedas and their commentaries, there are loose similarities with some of these practices and practices in various tellings of the *Artharva Veda* (AV). In particular, the Vidhaṇa and Pariśiṣṭa textual traditions, which describe how protective and healing mantras in the *Atharva Veda* were employed in ritual long after the original oral compiling of the AV, offer fascinating South Asian comparative examples. This is the type of detailed textual work that would make Indie comparisons useful. For amulets in particular, Hymns 11.4—5, II.9, VI.81, VI.85, VIII.5, X.3, X.6, XIX.34-35, among others from the Śaunakīya school of the AV, describe amulets of different materials (usually different types of wood) and their function in curing diseases, protecting pregnancies or protecting against curses. What should be noted here is that Thai practitioners do not seem to have any direct 'influence' from the *Atharva Veda,* and although the term *Phra Wet* [Vedas] is commonly used to refer to protective mantras in Thai, there is no one-to-one correspondence to particular hymns of the AV. The Pariśiṣṭa tradition is another story that is part of an ongoing study of mine.

12 One scholar, Pornthip Wongnisanakuson, provides (without citation) a *mantra* in a mixture of Sanskrit and Thai that worshippers are supposed to chant in front of an image of a *phra reusi,* which reads: "om imasmim phra prakhonthap phra munithewa hitatumhe pariphunchantu" followed by a list of 13 verses praising the qualities of the *Reusi* as a great mediator, teacher and father. This is followed by a list of different famous *reusi* teachers from India, such as Phra Witit, Phra Chamathakhani, Phra Atri, Phra Wayat and, interestingly enough, Phra Khaotama (Gotama, who after awakening became the one who is known as the historical Buddha) and Phra Chiwok (Jīvaka). The importance of Jīvaka will be seen below. The fact that the Buddha is considered a *phra reusi* by Pornthip is also supported by my comments in the conclusion. See her (undated) *Satsana Phram-Hindu* (Bangkok: S.V. Soluchan), pp. 59–60.

13 Phuchong Chanthawit, "Phra khreuang samkhan bang rung chakborankhadi" [A selection of important amulets from the ancient past], *Sinlapa watthanatham Thai lemthi 4* (Bangkok: Krom Sinlapakon, 2525 [1982]), pp. 21–63.

14 No Na Paknam, *Sinlapa boran nai sayam* [Ancient Art in Siam] (Bangkok: Muang Boran, 2537 [1994]), p. 258.

15 Theodore Bowie, M.C. Subradradis Diskul, and A.B. Griswold, eds., *The Sculpture of Thailand* (New York: The Asia Society, 1972), p. 117.

16 Niyada Laosunthon, *Silachamlak reuang ramakian: Wat Phra Chetuphon Wimalamongkhonaram* [Collection of the Inscriptions of Phra Chetuphon Monastery] (Bangkok: Chonniyom, 2539 [1996]), pp. 54–5.

17 I thank Hiram Woodward for reminding me of this source and for his guidance on *tamra* manuscripts in general.

18 See Niyada Laosunthon, ed., *Prachum chareuk Wat Phra Chetuphon* [Collection of the Inscriptions of Phra Chetuphon Monastery] (Bangkok: Amarin Press, 2544 [2001]), pp. 720–809. This is a new edition, which was published on the occasion ofthe cremation of Phra Thammapannati (Thawon Thillanukaro).

[19] There are too many examples to list, but some prominent ones can be seen on the walls of Wat Ban Takhu (Nakhon Ratchasima), Wat Hua Wiangrangsi (Nakhon Pathom), Wat Khao Yisan (Samut Songkhram), Wat Suwannaram (Thonburi) and Wat Mahathat (Petchaburi).

[20] I appreciate Forrest McGill taking the time to show me this painting at the Asian Art Museum. See E.W. Cowell, ed., *The Jataka or Stories of the Buddha's Former Births*, Vol. 6 (Cambridge: Cambridge University Press, 1907), p. 271. Naked women are not limited to cloth paintings and are found in prominent royal temple murals like those at Wat Pathumwanaram, Wat Rakhang, among others.

[21] Arthid Sheravanichakul recently gave a talk on the popularity of the Jūjaka amulets in Thailand at the European Association of Southeast Asian Studies Conference in Gothenburg, Sweden, 28 August 2010. I thank him for the conversations about these amulets.

[22] No Na Paknam, *Mural Paintings of Thailand Series: Wat Khongkaram* (Bangkok: Muang Boran, 2538 [1995]).

[23] These include Wat Ban Rai (Nakhon Ratchasima Province), Wat Kaeo Fa (Nonthaburi Province), Wat Tham Seua (Kanchanaburi Province), Wat Rai King (Nakhon Chaisi), Wat That Phanom (Nakhon Phanom), Wat Kao Thakiap (Hua Hin) and Wat Mahathat (Nakhon Sri Thammarat), among others.

[24] I briefly mention their notable features here: Pho Pu Reusi Phrohmalok (seated deep in meditation), Pho Pu Reusi Isuan (cobra around neck), Pho Pu Reusi Thosamungkhon (conical hat), Pho Pu Reusi Palaigot (wearing a crown), Pho Pu Reusi Ta Fai (third eye), Pho Pu Reusi Ta Wua (large "cow" eyes), Pho Pu Reusi Narai (Indra holding a conch shell and lotus flower), Pho Pu Reusi Narot (Narada, very long beard), Pho Pu Reusi Borom Kru Horasat (writing on a scroll depicting, I imagine, his calculations of astrological charts or "Horaśāstra"), Pho Pu Reusi Kru Wan Ya (using a mortar and pestle to crush herbs into medicine or "ya"), Pho Pu Reusi Borom Kru Phra Wet (reading a manuscript, I imagine, representing the "Vedas/Phra Wet"), Pho Pu Reusi Kassapa (Kaśyapa seated deep in meditation), Pho Pu Reusi Uchu (wearing beads), Pho Pu Reusi Muni Tapasa (holding a walking stick), Pho Pu Reusi Chiwok (Jīvaka, unlike the others he is dressed in white and does not wear a hat).

[25] Konthep Thepyothin, compiler, *Tamnān Phra Reusi* [History of the Rishi] (Bangkok: Sayampanyakanphim, n.d.). Note that the same drawings of the yogic poses found at Wat Pho mentioned above are found in a short descriptive epilogue on pp. 207–11 of *Tamnān Phra Reusi*.

[26] These include: Phra Reusi Sitthikhodom Borom Rachakru, Phra Reusi Phrohmabut, Phra Reusi Phrohm Bhrathan, Phra Reusi Phrohm Bhramet, Phra Reusi Phrohm Nimit, Phra Reusi Bhrasit, Phra Reusi Phrohm Loka, Phra Reusi Phrohmachak, Phra Reusi Phrohmamit, Phra Reusi Phrohmalok (different from Phrohm Loka), Phra Reusi Phrohmachuli, Phra Reusi Phrohmari, Phra Reusi Phrohm Ta Thip, Phra Reusi Phrohm Phangtru, Phra Reusi Na Phae, Phra Reusi Ling, Phra Reusi Neua, Phra Reusi Seua, Phra Reusi Philap, Phra Reusi Bhralaikothi, Phra Reusi Khobut, Phra Reusi Khotama (Gotama), Phra Reusi Sukhawattana, Phra Reusi Nonthi, Phra Reusi Satyaphrot, Phra Reusi Bhrasuram, Phra Reusi Thorawat, Phra Reusi Himaphan and Phra Reusi Thulasithat. Many of these Phra Reusi have the same names as Hindu deities, like Brahma and Parashurama (Bhrasuram).

[27] Others, such as Phra Reusi Ling, are hermits with animal faces, in this case a "monkey" [ling], as well as a tiger-faced hermit, a goat-faced hermit among others. Others have generic names such as Phra Reusi Himaphan (because he wanders in the Himalayan Mountains).

[28] Examples can be seen in amulet catalogues such as Ram Watcharapradit's (2547 [2004]) *Phap phra chanaloet* [Types of Powerful Amulets]; Soraphon Sophitkun's (2540 [1997]) *Sut-yotrianphra-khreuang* [The Ultimate Guide to Amulets], Triyampawai's (pseud) (2492–2508 [1954–65]) three-volume *Pari-atthathibai haeng phra-khreuang* [The Foundational Meanings and Explanations of Amulets] or can be found prominently displayed in amulet markets. There are hundreds of different types of amulets in Thailand that depict Hindu deities. See, for example, the description of the amulets of the gods Śiva, Viṣṇu and Gaṇeśa produced by the Thewasathan national Brahmin training center under the supervision of Chiraphat Praphanwithya. This book includes the liturgies (including the Sanskrit texts) and histories

of these amulets. Chiraphat Praphanwithya (2545 [2002]), *Phra Siwa Phra Wisanu Phra Phikhanesuan* [Śiva, Viṣṇu, and Gaṇeśa]. These amulets of Hindu deities are often forged in rituals by both Buddhist monks and Brahmin priests working together. For example, the Brahmin expert Montri Chanthaphan, the physician Somneuk and the monk Pho Than Somphong Thammasaro produced a set of Jatukham Ramathep amulets together in 2551 [2008] at Wat Phrahmalok in Nakhon Sri Thammarat Province for the specific purpose of curing those who had been bitten by snakes.

29 For more background on *parittas*, see Peter Skilling, "The Raksa literature of the Sravakayana," *Journal of the Pali Text Society* XVI (1992): 109–82; and McDaniel, "Paritta and Raksa texts," in *Encyclopedia of Buddhism*, ed. Robert Buswell (New York: Macmillan, 2004), pp. 634–5.

30 In one canonical Pali text, he is mentioned as being both a child of wealth and a low-class woman. In fact, his mother was a prostitute who became pregnant. After she gave birth, she threw her infant son on a rubbish heap because she did not want her clients to be disgusted by the fact that she had already given birth to a child. He was found by the king's son and was raised as a royal child. When he came of age, his father had him trained in Brahmanic science (even though he was not of the Brahmin caste by blood). He studied at the Buddhist "university" at Taxila in north-west India under masters of healing and anatomy. He took up his practice back in his father's kingdom of Rajagaha, curing anal fistulas, seven-year-long headaches and brain parasites. There are descriptions of him cutting skulls open, unknotting intestines with his hands and making patients snort clarified butter. He even cured the Buddha by making him ingest and later snort a mixture of oil, flowers and herbs, which caused him to vomit 30 times and thus relieved him of his illness. King Rama V compiled a collection of various Thai traditional medical texts in the late nineteenth century, published in a collection edited by unnamed staff at Ayurawet University: (2541 [1998]), *Tamrakanphaet Thai* [Manual of Thai Medical Practice]. Earlier references to Jīvaka are found in the inscriptions at Wat Ratchaorot (Thonburi) built in 1836. I documented the 50 individual medical inscription panels at Wat Ratchaorot (see some photographs at my website: tdm.sas.upenn.edu). See also Krom Silapakon (Department of Fine Arts editorial team) (2545 [2002]), *Chareuktamraya* [Inscriptions of Medical Manuals]. There is also a new edition of a Thai medical manuscript recovered from Ayutthaya by Chayan Phichiansunthon et al. (2544 [2001]), *Kham atthibaitamra Phra Osot Phra Narai* [An Explanation of the Documents about Phra Osot Phra Narai]. The most famous monasteries that had medical schools and hospitals in the early Bangkok (Ratanakosin) period were Wat Chetuphon (Pho) and Wat Mahathat.

31 For more information on Jīvaka and the stories that circulate in Thailand, see Tha Prian, *Mo Chiwok Komanphat* [Jīvaka Kumārabhacca: The Royal Physician] (Bangkok: Duang Kaeo, Bangkok, n.d.); and Kaisit Phisanakha's] *Chiwaprawat Borom Khru Phaet Komanphat* [The Biography of the Traditional Doctor: Jīvaka Kumārabhacca] (Bangkok: Saradi, (2545 [2002]).

32 Because of construction at Wat Indrawihan, the image was moved about 100 meters away from the holy water pool in early 2008 and now sits next to an image of Gaṇeśa.

33 This group also includes the senior monks Phra Ratchasitthiwimon (Luang Pho Sutchai) and Phra Sunthathamaphon (Luang Pho Bamnet), among 17 other monks from Ayutthaya, Lopburi, Ratchaburi, Rayong and other central provinces. Jīvaka is also known in other regions and is especially honored by the teachers at the Jīvaka Komārabhacca Traditional Medicine Hospital in Chiang Mai.

34 Descriptions of these images can be found on glossy flyers distributed free at Wat Indrawihan. There are also other studies of Thai health and medicine incorporating meditation and nutrition practices written by prominent Thai Buddhist scholars such as Phra Maha Sompong Mudito's *Kai khatasatikammatthan* [The Practice of Awareness Meditation], 3rd ed. (Bangkok: Thipwisut, (2543 [2000]) and Phanphen Kreuathai's *Mahaphon tamra ya* [The Wonderfully Beneficial Guide to Traditional Medicine] (Chiang Mai: Sathan wichai sangkhom Mahawitthayalai Chiang Mai, (2543 [2000]). The latter depicts a *phra reusi* hermit on the cover.

[35] I interviewed a number of monks involved in making these images and in advertising the oil between 2005 and 2010.

[36] He resisted offering me specific information about these teachers. A Sangharat (or Sangharaja) is the administrative and ritual leader of the entire Thai community of monks and nuns. He is appointed by the King and approved by a council of senior monks called the Mahatherasamakhom.

[37] "Oma [Om] namo jivako sirasa aham karuniko sabbasattanam osadhadibbamantam pabhaso suriyacandam komarabhacco pabhasesi vandami pandito sumedha so arokhasumana homi" [sic]:

> "Oh, Praise to Jīvaka, the wise one, the intelligent one, the one caring of all beings, the one who reveals the divine mantra [thus making] the medicine, he is the physician, he causes the sun and moon to shine. I praise him with my head [down], I am [thus] free of disease and my mind is at ease."

Some of the Pali spellings and grammatical forms may seem rather unorthodox to Pali scholars. This is based on a direct transliteration of this verse found in many published editions, including the edition inscribed in marble at the Monk's hospital. The translation is my own.

[38] An annotated litany of these recipes is available upon request, complete with a short biography of Dr. Parinya and his methods: Parinya Uthichalanon, *Khu-meu prakop kan chai ya* [Handbook for the Use of Traditional Medicine], n.d. Prathip Phayakkhaphon's classic medical manual *Tamra ya mo Thai* [Manual of Traditional Medicine for Thai Doctors] (2476 [1933]) was reprinted by Bukkhonanoe Printing in 2008. For a comprehensive text with drawings of recommended yogic postures and summaries of over 200 herbal ingredients and medical treatments supposedly taught by Chiwok Goman, see Mo Nakhon Bangyikan's (2546 [2003]) *Phra Borom Khru Phaet Chiwok Komarabhat* [The Traditional Doctor Jīvaka Kumārabhacca].

[39] There is a small, but seemingly growing, interest in Tibetan religions among the intellectual elite of Bangkok. Part of this interest involves the "Medicine Buddha" Bhaisyaguru. The Phandara Foundation has produced a biography and explanation of Bhaisajyaguru's teachings, and a translation of the Bhaisajyaguru Sutra for readers of Thai by Sorat Hongladarom, Phra Phaisachayakhuru (2548 [2005]).

[40] For medical traditions in the region, see Richard Pottier's (2007) comprehensive tome on traditional Lao medicine, Yu Di Mi Heng, especially pp. 357–75; Mulholland (1979), "Thai traditional medicine," pp. 80–115; and Mulholland's two books *Medicine, Magic, and Evil Spirits* (1987) and *Herbal Medicine* (1989). A physician at the hospital also gave me a rare book about Jīvaka and his methods: Phennapha Sapchaloen et al., *Prawat Mo Chiwok Gomanabhat* [The History of Jivaka Kumarabhacca] (Bangkok: Wat Thepsarin, 2481 [1938]). This large tome offers the most detailed account in Thai I have found on Jīvaka's biography and a long list of his methods. It was printed in 1938 and distributed at a Buddhist funeral/cremation at Wat Chakrawathiratchawat for a high-ranking noble named Phraya Aphai Ratchamahayutithamthon. It seems that many later smaller books in Thai on Chiwok Goman came from the contents of this larger book (which was reprinted once in 2537 [1994] under the auspices of the Sathaban kan phaet phaen Thai [Centre for Thai Medicine].

[41] These are mostly centered near the intersection of Thanon Phran Nok and Thanon Arun Amarin, and in the tight network of lanes and alleys near Wat Suthat.

[42] For example, a very good productive research topic could include the study of Indra/Sakka, a figure present in dozens of Buddhist narratives, and connected to Hinduism. Indra is not just a "Hindu" or "Vedic" god that happens to show up in Thai Buddhism. By disconnecting Indra from Hinduism, he can be profitably compared to a Bodhisatta, ghost or a local deity that also appears in Thai religious stories.

9

Encountering Corpses: Notes on Zombies and the Living Dead in Buddhist Southeast Asia*

Corpses are frequently encountered in the Christian religious cultures of Europe and the Americas. Without the need for a quick burial and restrictions on dismemberment in Judaism and Islam, Christians have spent a lot of time viewing corpses, handling corpses, depicting corpses, dissecting them in medical school, employing them in vehicle impact safety tests, and writing and relating both Christian and non-Christian stories about reanimated corpses like Lazarus, Jesus Christ, Achilles, Osiris, and Dr. Frankenstein's monster. People in Christian-dominated cultures mummify or embalm, dress and present corpses in coffins, put coins on corpses' eyes, or prop them up in front of fortresses to warn potential enemies. Writers in modern Christian-dominated cultures (influenced in many ways by West African heritage) have related stories of reanimated corpses often controlled by evil-masterminds or powerful wizards. These have become popular lore as seen in perennially popular stories and films about zombies and other members of the "living dead" like vampires, some types of goblins, and even Tolkien's orcs. Popular American television programs like Bones, Crime Scene Investigators (CSI), and Quincy, and recent books like the best-selling Stiff have brought corpses into the realm of everyday experience. Corpses are

* Originally appeared as "Encountering Corpses: Notes on Zombies and the Living Dead in Buddhist Southeast Asia," *Kyoto Review of Southeast Asia*, Special Issue on Death and Dying (2012) [translated into Japanese, Bahasa Indonesian, and French].

Monk meditating on corpse from a Phra Malai Klon Suat Manuscript in the Fogg Collection of Siamese Manuscripts. Photo by author.

common agents. Whether reanimated or merely displayed, they act in the world as symbols, decaying statues, messengers, members of mindless armies, and depositories of clues. These aren't the spirits of the dead, they are physical, but dead, bodies acting in the world.

One might assume that the reason corpses are such a part of cultural experience in the Christian West is because Christians embalm, encoffin, and bury their dead. They write what they know. However, in the Buddhist and Hindu cremation cultures of South and Southeast Asia, where bodies are burned and only bits of teeth, hair, or bones are kept as relics, corpses play a role in religion, literature, and art as well. They play important roles in protective rituals, religious art, and popular books and films. In this very short article I will introduce some sources for the study of corpses looking especially at Buddhist cultures in Southeast Asia and the stories of animated corpses or "zombies" popular among Buddhists in the region.

Corpse Meditation

Employing corpses in protective rituals and meditative exercises is a wide-spread Buddhist activity in Southeast Asia. Let me provide just a few brief examples. Corpses of the recently deceased are used by some advanced trained monks as objects for *asubhakammaṭṭhāna* meditation. Monks in Cambodia, Laos, and Thailand are known for meditating while staring at naked corpses. This is still a practice at some Thai monasteries like Wat Khao Yai in Pichit and Wat Hualompong in Bangkok. Here a donated corpse is either hung on a hook in front of meditating nuns and monks who have been given permission to enter into this meditation or meditators sit in charnel grounds viewing corpses before, during, and after they are cremated. These practices have been depicted on mural paintings and told in stories in the biographies of prominent Thai monks like Luang Phu Man, Than Achan Taeng, and Somdet To. These sources depict in detail the stages of *asubhakammaṭṭhāna* meditation including the stages of *lohitaka* (meditation on a bleeding corpse), *puḷavaka* (meditation on a worm-infested corpse), *vipubbaka* (meditation on a festering corpse), *vicchiddaka* (meditation on a corpse cut into two), *vikkhāyitaka* (meditation on a gnawed corpse), *hata-vikkhittaka* (meditation on a scattered corpse), among others. However, one does not need an actual corpse to practice this meditation. There is also a tradition of meditation on one's own decaying body. Some monks and nuns are instructed to imagine themselves dissecting their own body in meditation in order to examine the different organs, and especially the fact that the body also contains feces, bile, and urine. When I was ordained in the mid-1990s, my own abbot suggested that we could even imagine piercing our own flesh with a knife. Meditators in this practice are supposed to focus on both the "disgust" of the body, as well as the impermanence of the flesh, fluids, and bones. These are not only rites restricted to ordained specialists. Indeed, in nineteenth-century Bangkok along the Lot Canal, the bodies of prisoners who died in prison were left out for vultures to consume and for the public to watch. The bodies were deposited at a large monastery, Wat Sraket. Erik Davis, Pattaratorn Chirapravati, Patrice Ladwig, Ian Harris, and François Bizot have discussed the use of corpses in Cambodian, Lao, and Thai *paṅsukūl* rites which not only invite the practitioners to reflect on impermanence and the inevitable decay of the body, but also conduct rituals to either transfer the consciousness from a dying body to a new body or even to reanimate the body of the recently deceased.[1]

Protection and Luck

Corpses are not just used for meditation, but also for protective rituals. For example, at Wat Mahabut in Bangkok there is a corpse of an infant named Sirirot Phibunsin (affectionately known as "Ae" or "Dek Chai Sirirot") who died when he was only 39 days old. Since he died an unnatural death he was buried instead of cremated. Many Buddhists in Southeast Asia customarily bury those who die of murder, suicide, childhood diseases, starvation, car accidents, snake-bites, execution, or other unnatural deaths. Their corpses are bound with protective white string, their eyes, nose, ears, and mouth are either sewn or waxed shut, and they are wrapped tightly and buried in, often, unmarked graves. This is to prevent their ghosts from wandering free and bringing misfortune to the living. If you die a "natural" death you are generally cremated if you are a Buddhist in the region. Since "Ae" died unnaturally as a new-born, he was buried. Not long after he was buried there was a terrible flood in Phrakhanong district and the coffin of the infant resurfaced. His distressed parents, Pramot (a local police officer) and Sirilak (a nurse), brought his skeletal remains, which still had dried leathery flesh clinging to them, to the abbot of Wat Mahabut. The abbot agreed to take care of the infant (*du laeluk*) in order to avoid upsetting Baby Ae's ghost. He ordered a glass coffin, placed the coffin in a small wooden freestanding house built specifically for the coffin, and opened the doors to the public. Although not given a monthly re-funeral like Mae Nak, Baby Ae nevertheless receives a lot of visitors.

Baby Ae's coffin is filled with toy airplanes, spacecraft, trucks, boats, several teddy bears, a giant stuffed "Hello Kitty" doll, a cell phone (supposedly if he wakes up and can make a call), and lots of cash. In fact, Baby Ae's entire skeletal corpse (dressed in children's pajamas) is covered in a blanket of cash that drops down on him from donors who slip 20, 50, and 100 baht bills into a small slot on top of the coffin (as well as US and Singapore dollars occasionally). Only Baby Ae's eyeless head, covered with a thin layer of grayish leathery skin with blondish/white hair on top, is clearly visible through the glass. Next to the coffin is a place to give more offerings. One of the more popular gifts, besides toys, is excessively sugary children's fruit punch. A 76-year-old woman named Khun Somwong who keeps the shrine clean and generally manages the place sat with me for a long time on several occasions talking with me about visitors and activities at Baby Ae's house. She and her son would even unlock the doors in the evenings for me (as I could often not get there before 6:00 pm). Khun Somwong clearly was very attached to Baby Ae and I suspected it was not just for the cash she generated for the shrine and her family. She spoke of him as her own child. She spoke of Baby Ae's parents who would come once a year to the shrine, about the troop of about 12 to 16 *Kae Bon* (a traditional type of dancer) who would dance in front of Baby Ae for a fee upon request, and the school children and mothers who would visit the coffin. Baby Ae was said to give people who visited him dreams and in those dreams winning lottery numbers would be revealed. Most of Baby Ae's visitors were sports teams though. Local high school and technical school teams would visit Baby Ae to give offerings before or after big soccer, *takraw*, or volleyball matches. They either asked Baby Ae to help them win the game or thanked him when they won. I only observed this twice, but Khun Somwong and the assistant abbot assured me that this was the most common activity. I asked several people, including most of the monks in residence at Wat Mahabut why an infant corpse could help sports teams.

The display of infant corpses is well-known practice in Thailand. The display of Baby Ae is loosely related to the honoring of *kuman thong* and the collection of corpse oil. There are several groups which employ a staff of "corpse gatherers." The most well-known of these societies is the Poh Teck Tung, also called the Potek Xiangteng. They are a Teochiu-speaking Chinese group originally from Guangdong founded in Thailand in 1909 with members in Thailand and Malaysia. Many of the members who moved to Bangkok in the early twentieth century obtained permission from King Rama V to practice "second burials" for those who had died without relatives. This practice would ensure that these people who didn't have ancestors and children to honor them, would not turn into menacing ghosts. The ones performing the second burial—involving digging up corpses, drying their bones, and rearranging them in a mass grave after cleaning them and chanting over them—would become their adopted ancestors. Originally there is not much evidence that corpse oil was gathered from the corpses. However, Francis Giles observed the practice as early as 1937 and the Teochiu word for a corpse that is mummified when dug up is "kim thong" which is translated in Thai as "kuman thong" (a combination of Chinese and Sanskrit). There is a high likelihood that corpse oil was part of the early ceremonies in Bangkok and seems to be a custom added locally as it is not found in mainland Chinese burial practices. Today this group runs a large temple in Bangkok, a 44-hectare cemetery in the Bangkok suburbs, and a large number of private ambulances whose drivers listen to radio and police bands and show up suddenly at the scene of motorcycle and car accidents to collect any dead body. They also visit hospitals requesting that the family members of a newly-deceased child, sister, or husband, donate the corpse to their society.[2] Some families donate the corpse of their relative, other corpses are given to the society if no family member claims them. Sometimes these corpses are used for *asubhakammaṭṭhāna* meditation. Sometimes they are buried, as the Poh Teck Tung Foundation does, in mass graves, only to be dug up as a group once a year to gather corpse oil (*nam man phrai*) and bone relics from them. Then they are cremated en masse. This mass cremation not only creates merit for the foundation and those who attend, but also allows for the easy centralized collection of auspicious and protective ashes, bones, and oils.

Kuman thong are the mummified corpses of stillborn children, aborted fetuses, and some are children who die in their first few days or even years of life. These corpses are mummified (bled, desiccated, and stored in camphor oil) and then usually covered in gold or blackened by roasting them slowly.[3] Erik Davis has studied the use of these *kuman thong* in Cambodia extensively, as well as provided details on the binding of corpses in Khmer ritual.[4] These practices are mentioned in the most famous premodern Thai adventure and romantic poem, *Khun Chang Khun Paen*. Here, the clever, but devious and lecherous warrior Khun Paen is mentioned as cutting the fetus out of a woman and roasting it while chanting secret verses. Wat Tham Mongkhon in Kanchanuburi Province (Thailand) has a gruesome mural of this scene from the epic poem. He uses the corpse to give him invulnerability in battle.[5] One of the more famous monks of the twentieth century, Luang Pho Te Khongthong (1892–1981) of Wat Samngan in Nakhon Pathom Province (Thailand), produced a great number of these *kuman thong*.[6] He had audiences with the present king, was put in charge of five monasteries in central Thailand, took on the task of restoring abandoned monasteries, and is much loved among dog owners today because of his care for and training of a little white poodle named Chao Nuat. He is often pictured with this dog, who was said to go to the post office and pick up letters for his master and accompany him on alms rounds. He was well known for encouraging his followers to share their wealth with the poor and he famously refused to live in a brand new monastic cell built especially for him. He gave it to one of the youngest novice students in the monastery instead.[7]

Corpse oil is the prized substance in these ceremonies. Unlike statues of saints, Buddha images, or bas-reliefs, the importance of a mummified person is less in its aesthetic beauty or calming meditative affect/effect than in its ability to be harvested for oil, bones, ash, and wax. *Nam man phrai*, is an oily and fatty substance that is obtained by magicians, including monks, who either dig up corpses, or in the case of Baby Ae, find corpses, to melt. The magician holds a candle or magnifying glass up to the chin, elbows, forehead of the corpse and melts the dried skin. The drippings are collected and are believed to have the power to be transformed through incantations into love potion, protective oil, or even diluted into tattooing ink.[8]

Mummification

Displaying corpses for auspicious purposes, even though according to most books on Thai culture corpses are generally considered inauspicious, is not limited to infants. In fact, the display of mummified corpses of monks is spread throughout central and southern Thailand, perhaps the most famous being that of Luang Pho Daeng on the island of Koh Samui. Wat Nang Chi, a historically important monastery in Thonburi, has a small, relatively unkempt shrine, with the mummified corpse of a *maechi* (nun) laying in a glass coffin next to the mummified corpse of a young child. The nun, Maechi Nopparat, died in 1944 when she was only 19 years old after ordaining for three years with the famous Luang Pho Sot of Wat Phak Nam. Even though she came from a family of poor salt farmers, she was born with great merit and compassion (*chai bun mi mettatham*) and this preserved her body.[9] Luang Pho Poon and Luang Pho Din of Nakhon Pathom and Chainat Provinces respectively have also been mummified.[10] These mummies are held in glass coffins for people to view and offer gifts. In front of Luang Pho Din's mummy is a life-size bronze image of him that even depicts him wearing his glasses. When famous monks die they are not cremated like normal Thais. Instead the corpses of the highest-ranking monks are propped up in seated position (I have been told that a surgically inserted metal or wooden rod is sometimes used). The seated body is encased in thin gold leaf and plaster so that the wrinkles of the skin, the facial features, and muscle tone are frozen. The corpse is made into a living statue to freeze the body in time. These are not old lifeless statues or artificial representations. A dedicated patron or person seeking protection and guidance can visit and prostrate to the image at any time. It can be said that this type of hypostatization has been a regular practice of central Thai Buddhist image makers over the past century.[11]

One does not necessarily have to spend a great deal of money commissioning a resin image from Duangkaeo. Indeed, the idea of making an image of a powerful person for the purpose of asking that image to act ritually as if alive is an old Thai practice. The making of "hun phi" (ghost dolls) by sculpting clay into small human figures or creating warriors made out of grass to contain their spirits (so that their ghosts don't move on to the next life) is mentioned in *Khun Chang Khun Paen*.[12] These images are found in many amulet markets today and are usually black, terracotta, or yellowish-gray. They can be placed inside glass or clear plastic lockets and worn around the neck serving as a type of guardian angel. These images are not representations, symbols, or simulacra then, they are tools in an individual protective arsenal. They are powerful despite the fact that they are copies of the supposed original. They are to be held, honored, and respected as powerful in themselves. The normative Buddhist values of non-attachment and impermanence are forgotten in this process of hypostatization. Indeed, even the mummies of Luang Pho Pun, Maechi Nopparat, Baby Ae, and *kuman thong* are not less powerful because they are lifeless. They are not empty shells or mnemonic devices. They are objects worthy of gifts and givers of merit. Just as the Buddha has not been permitted to pass quietly onto nirvana, these nuns, monks, women and children are held in this life psychologically and even physically. They do not foreground the Buddhist values of non-attachment and impermanence, as well as compassion and the belief in transmigration or rebirth.

These bodies, whether simulacra or actual corpses, are useful and powerful. They bring security and promote the value of abundance. They do not participate in what

Marina Warner has identified as the "aesthetics of shock" or gory verisimilitude.[13] She examined the European fascination with horrific images in wax museums and exhibitions of medical curiosities which were meant to both scare and fascinate. She compared them in some ways to the Catholic display of martyrs being flayed, Mary with bleeding stigmata, or Christ hanging on a crucifix. Although there are Thai museums of torture and medical oddities, Thai Buddhist monastic shrines do not generally attempt to present visceral gore. Even the mummies (of children, nuns, or monks) or statues of ghosts are not meant to frighten. They are covered in gold and wearing dresses, monastic robes, or pajamas. They are surrounded by toys, cash, incense, and candles. They are not display items. They are objects of worship and sites of memory. They invoke the values of love, dedication, and loyalty. They mark historical events of triumph over death.

The Book of the Zombies

Examining the wide variety of rituals that employ corpses in Buddhist Southeast Asia begs the question—why? Why would there be so many religious uses of corpses by a culture that promotes cremation? Certainly some customs, especially regarding the particular ways of sealing and binding the body after death are indigenous. One source is the influence on burial rites and the *kuman thong* were most likely brought by from Fuzhou, Quanzhou, Zhangzhou and Teochiu (or Chaozhou) laborers, and merchants from Fujian, Taiwan, and parts of Guangdong in the eighteenth and nineteenth centuries as we saw above. Corpse meditation was documented in early Indian and Sri Lankan Buddhism. However, another source may be Indic, but not Buddhist. Most often scholars of Southeast Asian Buddhism are trained in Pali and the Indic origins of Buddhism. However, Pali literature and Theravada Buddhist lineages are not the only Indic source for religious narrative and practices in Southeast Asia. Non-Buddhist Sanskrit literature like the *Rāmāyaṇa*, the *Mahābharata*, the *Hitopadeśa*, and the *Pañcatantra* are all well known in manuscript libraries, the dramatic performance, in mural art, and in oral culture in the region. Speaking specifically of zombies and corpses, one of the least studied, but best-known local sources is the *Vetāla-prakaraṇam* (*Collection of Stories of Zombies*).[14]

The *Vetāla-prakaraṇam* is part of a whole genre of *prakaraṇam* texts that have circulated in Southeast Asia since, according to manuscript evidence, the fifteenth century.[15] Some of the most important *prakaraṇam* texts include the *Vetāla-prakaraṇam* (*Collection of Stories of Zombies*), the *Nandaka-prakaraṇam* (*Collection of Stories of the Bullock*, but it is actually a tale which includes all manner of animals visiting a single bullock in Indian, Javanese, Tamil, and Lao tellings), the *Maṇḍūka-prakaraṇam* (*Collection of Stories of Frogs*), the *Piśāca-prakaraṇam* (*Collection of Stories of Ghosts*), and the *Pakṣī-prakaraṇam* (*Collection of Stories of Birds*) which is also titled the *Śakuna-prakaraṇam* in some tellings (both words mean bird in

Sanskrit). These are usually collections of short stories featuring monsters and animals. However, the term can also be used, at least in one case, for a historical collection of stories about the founding of certain cities or the travels of certain statues and relics. They are similar in some ways to the *Setsuwa* tales of medieval Japan or the *Zhiguai* stories of China, but not beastiaries like we find in Europe. They are not descriptive guides to the worlds of fantastic or grotesque creatures, but stories in which the agents are animals and humanoid demons, ghosts, and hybrids. The prakaraṇam genre does not see collections of stories of birds or frogs as different in kind than collections of stories about other species or supernatural ghosts and monsters. Many of these stories contained within individual prakaraṇam texts in Southeast Asia are drawn from Sanskrit stories in the *Pañcatantra*, *Hitopadeśa*, *Kathāsaritsāgara*, and other Indian collections. Like other Indian stories though, many telling in Southeast Asia are quite different from their Indian counterparts. The Lao and Thai *Pakṣī-prakaraṇam* in particular are drawn indirectly from different stories in the *Pañcatantra*, especially the third book. Directly though, they were first introduced in Southeast Asia (especially Java, northern Thailand, Shan region, and Cambodia) through the *Tantropākhyāna* (Lao: Mun Tantai; Thai: Nithan Nang Tantrai; Javanese: Tantri Kāmandaka or Tantri Demung).

The oldest manuscript of this collection in India was found in Mysore and dates from 1031 CE. Sanskritists and South Indian literary specialists Edgerton, Venkatasubbiah, and Artola have traced different versions of the Sanskrit text, as well as Tamil, Kanada, and Malayalam telling attributed to the Indian authors like Vasubhāga, Viṣṇuśarman, and Durgasiṃha. There are similarities with the stories about the Jain sage Pçāvranātha composed by Bhāvadevasūri.[16] Of course, more widely known telling of these stories also appear in central and middle-Eastern languages.[17] For example, the Pahlavi, Persian, and Syriac tellings of the *Kalilah and Dimnah* story (also known as the *Fables of Bidpai*) shares close similarities with several birds stories in the *Pakṣī* and the *Pañcatantra*.[18] Some of these stories were also translated in Greek, Arabic, Hebrew, and Spanish. The very popular *Conference of the Birds* (Persian: *Manteq at-Tair*) by the twelfth-century poet Farid ud-Din Attar is extremely close to the plot and bird characters of the *Pakṣī-prakaraṇam*.[19]

Syam Phathranuprawat and Kusuma Raksamani have undertaken extensive studies of these possible Indian progenitors, as well as comparing them to the Javanese telling (although they do not compare them to Buddhist texts). Although Kusuma concentrates on the *Nandakaprakaraṇam*, he shows that this text, as well as the *Pakṣī*, *Maṇḍūka*, and *Piśāca*, were introduced into northern Thailand in the mid-1400s and probably came from the tradition of Vasubhāga, although much of the *Pakṣī* seems to come from the Viṣṇuśarman textual lineage.[20] There are no Pali equivalents found and the northern Thai manuscripts are in *nissaya* form which draw from Sanskrit texts and not Pali. In some cases the Sanskrit terms have been rendered into Pali, but there seems to have been no full Pali translation of these texts before the northern Thai vernacular translations and glosses. Syam emphasizes that the northern Thai, Lao, and central Thai tellings of the *Tantropākhyāna* are quite different.[21] The *Tantropākhyāna*'s title comes from the name of the woman, Tantrī or Tantrū in Sanskrit and Nang Tantai or Nang Tantrai or Tantri in Lao, Thai, and Javanese traditions, who tells the various stories to a king and this initiates ideally almost 360 stories, although there are usually only 80–90 stories in Southeast Asian collections.[22]

The *Vetāla-prakaraṇam* or more commonly in Thai—*Nithan Wetan*—is well-known in Thailand and over the past few years there have been several modern editions of the 20–25 stories in the Sanskrit collection that have circulated in Lao and Thai over the last four centuries.[23] The collection is found in various tellings in Sanskrit and some modern South Asian languages. The oldest collection most likely contained 25 stories and was titled the *Vetālapañcaviṃśati* from approximately the tenth century. It was later incorporated in the *Kathāsaritsāgara* compiled by Somadeva.[24] Theodore Riccardi wrote his dissertation on another telling by Jambhaladatta known in Nepal.[25] A popular telling of 11 of the stories was made by Richard Burton called *Vikram and the Vampire* and Arthur Rider's *Twenty-Two Goblins* is another incomplete translation.[26] The text claims that the stories were originally told by a king named Vikramāditya and this is the author acknowledged by Southeast Asian manuscript copies.[27]

In the Southeast Asian tellings, *Vikramāditya* is a king who has a series of conversations with a corpse hanging in a tree. This is a living corpse or a zombie known as a *vetāla* (Thai: *wetan*). The king wants to capture the zombie, carry *him* on his shoulders and bring *it* to a Brahman seer (Sanskrit: *ṛṣi*/Thai: *phra reusi*) in order to gain magical powers from the seer. The zombie continually escapes by tricking the king with riddles involving extensive and often quite funny stories of various creatures. After he tricks the king (strangely, by allowing the king to guess the right answer) he jumps off his shoulders and climbs back up the tree. For example, in one story there are a parrot and a myna who are arguing over who are more ignorant—women or men. The myna tells a story about an ungrateful man who despite being loved by a beautiful and wealthy woman continually stole from her and abandoned her. The parrot tells the story of a woman who despite being married carried on a long-term affair with a Brahman. However, one day the Brahman was mistaken for a thief sneaking into her room. He was struck in the head by a servant of the woman and as he lay dying the woman tried to revive him by breathing into his mouth. However, in his death throes he accidently bit her nose off! She blamed her disfigurement on her husband who, if not for her guilt, would have been executed by the king. The zombie asked the king who was indeed more wicked, the man or the woman. The king answered "woman," which was deemed, for no objective reason, correct by the zombie. In another story a Brahman mother and father are lamenting the sudden death of their young son. They took him to a cemetery where an old yogi first cried when he saw the child, but then jumped up and danced and used his magic to spiritually possess the child's corpse. The parents were delighted when their child seemed to come back to life. The child decided to practice as an ascetic yogi for the rest of his life though! The zombie asked the king why the yogi first cried and then danced. The king answered correctly again that the yogi was sad for losing his old body, but happy to now have a new, young, Brahman body. There are many other stories of riddles involving love affairs, poisonings, harlots, and magical sex-changes. In the end of these stories of the king and the zombie, the zombie uses his insight into the ways of humans and beasts to warn the king about the ascetic's intentions to kill the king and use the zombie's power for himself. The zombie doesn't frighten the king, but, in the end, saves his life and becomes his magical ally.

As seen from the stories of (or perhaps "conversations with") the zombie from Sanskrit, there has been a certain level of comfort with the notion of the living dead giving advice, being a source of protective power, and serving as a source of auspiciousness or luck. These stories which were circulating throughout most of mainland Southeast Asia, as well as Java, are sources for rituals and story-telling today. Indeed, they are also sources for the hugely successful horror film industry especially in Thailand (the film industry of Burma, Laos, and Cambodia is still in its infancy). Many of these films involve the use of zombies, corpses, ghosts, and other members of the world of the living dead. Films including *Maha-Ut*, *Arahant Summer*, *The Coffin*, *Eternity*, *Uncle Boonmee Who Can Remember his Past Lives*, *Nang Nak*, *Nak*, *Chom Khamang Wet*, *Ahimsa*, and many others have included corpses or ghosts that can provide power and knowledge or can torture and kill. These films often feature Buddhist monks and lay people as characters as well. It is time to start investigating the multiple sources for these cultural features so distinctive in the region.

Conclusion

Even though most Buddhists in Southeast Asia practice cremation, stories, and rituals involving corpses and animated corpses abound in the region, I hope that I have provided some possible sources, both textual and ethnographic, for these relatively widespread aspects of Buddhist religious repertoires in the region. What should be emphasized in the end is that scholars of Buddhist history and practice in Southeast Asia need to pay more attention to both southern Chinese and Sanskrit literary sources for supposedly the Pali-based Theravada Buddhist history instead of labeling those non-Theravada/non-Pali elements of Buddhist culture in the region simply "local" or indigenous or even animist. The binary between "Indic" and "local" in the region needs to be completely reimagined or perhaps re-animated.

Notes

[1] See particularly the edited volume by Patrice Ladwig and Paul Williams, *Buddhist Funeral Cultures of Southeast Asia and China* (Cambridge: Cambridge University Press, 2012); Ian Harris, *Cambodian Buddhism* (Honolulu: University of Hawai'i Press, 2005), chapter four; François Bizot, *Le don soi-même* (Paris: École Française d'Extrême-Orient, 1981), pp. 20–30. I describe these rites briefly in *The Lovelorn Ghost and the Magical Monk* (New York: Columbia University Press, 2011), pp. 126–8.

[2] Photographs and recent stories of PohTeck Tung's collection of corpses from accident scenes can be found at these three websites (last accessed 29 December 2009) among many others: http://www.bangkokpost.com/091108_Spectrum/09Nov2008_spec20.php, http://pohtecktung.org/, http://www.bangkoksvildeveje.dk/pohtecktung.html.

[3] This is not to be confused with the practice of "roasting" the mother after she gives birth. See Jane Richardson Hanks, "Maternity and Its Rituals in Bang Chan." Southeast Asia Program Data Paper no. 51, Cornell Thailand Project, Interim Reports Series no. 6. Ithaca: Southeast Asia Program, Cornell University (1963: 41–57); and Lauren Dundes, ed., *The Manner Born: Birth Rites in Cross-Cultural Perspective* (Baltimore: AltaMira Press, 2003), p. 134.

[4] See especially Davis, "Treasures of the Buddha: Imagining Death and Life in Contemporary Cambodia" (PhD dissertation, University of Chicago, 2009), chapter three.

[5] I thank Christopher Baker and Pasuk Phongpaichit for their advice on this scene. The making of a *kuman thong* is mentioned in chapter 35 in two different versions of the poem. They note that the use of corpse or spirit oil (*nam man phrai*) is mentioned in four different parts of the poem. Baker and Phongphaichit, *Khun Chang Khun Paen* (Chiang Mai: Silkworm Books, 2010), chapter 35.

[6] Kamala Tiyavanich also mentions stories of *kuman thong* practice done by Buddhist monks in southern Thailand—*Sons of the Buddha* (2007: 195). This practice seems to be particularly popular in southern Thailand and is one in which Muslims and Buddhist participate together. These practices may be related to the Malaysian practice of using *toyol* (stillborn fetuses used to make protective oils) or *guigia*, a southern Chinese belief in the protective powers of fetuses. For Cambodian practices, I rely on Erik Davis (personal communication). See also his PhD dissertation: *Treasures of the Buddha* (2009).

[7] The use of *kuman thong* is not without controversy. In 1995 there was a high-profile case in which a Buddhist novice, Samanen Han Raksachit, was arrested after he released a video tape of himself piercing, bleeding, roasting, chanting, and collecting the drippings from a baby at Wat Nong Rakam in Saraburi Province (central Thailand). These drippings, which he called "*ya sane*" (lust medicine); he sold to visitors to the monastery. Although he was disrobed and arrested, he did not serve jail time and was arrested again in 2005 for tricking several women into sexual acts and defrauding them of money in exchange for dubious claims that he could help them attract their true loves. He is serving time now for a sentence of 23 counts of rape, in addition to other charges. Richard Erhlich, "Baby Roasting Monk Caught Tricking Women Into Sex," posted on http://www.scoop.co.nz/stories/HL0507/S00277.htm (last accessed Wednesday, 20 July 2005); James Austin Farrell, "The Hex, The Monk, and the Exorcist," http://www.chiangmainews.com/ecmn/viewfa.php?id=2206.

[8] Francis Giles witnessed a corpse oil collection ritual in the early twentieth century: "About a Love Philtre" (1938: 24–8). Published online in *Scoop* (New Zealand) and the *Chiang Mai News* (Thailand).

[9] I thank the keepers of the shrine (mostly local homeless men supervised by the monks in residence) for guiding me around the monastery on three occasions in 2008 and 2009.

[10] I thank Peter Skilling for calling these mummies to my attention.

[11] Drawing on Gell's idea of "technologies of enchantment," Jessica Rawson has shown that creating identical portraits of emperors in early China would allow a follower to perpetually give gifts as an emperor was made to be always present in the world. "The Agency of, and the Agency for, the Wanli Emperor," in *Art's Agency and Art History*, ed. Robin Osborne and Jeremy Tanner (London: Blackwell, 2007), chapter four.

[12] See Baker and Phongphaichit, *Khun Chang Khun Paen*. The popular Thai horror film, *Chom Khamang Wet* (English title: Necromancer, RS Films, directed by Piyapat Chupetch, 2005), features an ascetic magician who creates a particularly fierce spiritual child to protect him.

[13] Marina Warner, *Phantasmagoria* (Oxford: Oxford University Press, 2006), pp. 31–46.

[14] Skilling, writing on Indian and Tibetan Vinaya commentaries clarifies the meaning of vetala in Sanskrit. He shows that the oldest Sanskrit spelling of vetāla was "vetāḍa" (Pali: vetāla or vetāḷa). He also believes that the closest English translation is zombie versus Burton's (see below) use of "vampire." See Skilling, "Zombies and Half-Zombies: Mahāsūtras and Other Protective Measures," *Journal of the Pali Text Society* 29 (2007): 315fn7.

[15] Louis Finot first identified these types of texts in Laos in 1917. See his "Recherches sur la Litterature Laotienne," *Bulletin de l'École Française d'Extrême-Orient* 17, 5 (1917): 5–224. Jean Brengues documented vernacular Lao telling of the stories in his "Une version laotienne du Pancatantra," *Journal Asiatique* 10, 12 (1908): 361–2. Henry Ginsburg helped identify the 20 manuscripts of the *Tantropākhyāna* in the National Library of Thailand (there are also many in northern Thai collections). See Ginsburg, "The Thai Tales of Nang Tantrai and the Pisaca Tales," *Journal of the Siam Society* 63, 2 (1975): 279–314. Furthermore, Ginsburg wrote a fascinating Master's thesis in 1967 on the *Tantropākhyāna*, especially collection of ghost stories called the *Piśācap(r)akaraṇam* (Ginsburg, "The Literary Tales Derived from the Sanskrit *Tantropākhyāna*," Master's Thesis, University of Hawai'i, 1967). This vernacular Thai text, unlike the rest of the *Tantropākhyāna*, has little connection to any known Sanskrit text. It seems to be the creative work of Thai authors. It was quite popular in the mid-nineteenth century in Bangkok, there were several manuscript copies, and was actively studied by both Thai and foreign scholars in the late nineteenth century. Bishop Pallegoix, adviser to the Siamese king, included it in his list of important vernacular Thai "secular" texts in his 1850 Thai grammar. There were some English and German translations made of the stories in 1872 and 1894 respectively (this was a time in which there were very few translations of any Thai text available).

Adolf Bastian hand copied these ghost stories in 1864. It was certainly seen as an important collection. These texts were copied and circulated among monks as well as lay people and clearly influenced modern Thai understandings of ghosts and the ritual needed to protect against them. They also are the precursor to modern Thai films and novels that depict ghosts and the practice of protective magic that are extremely popular among Buddhists (Ginsburg, p. 40, see examples of magical ritual in the Piśāca, especially on pp. 54, 61, 64, 65, 69). The manuscripts include both "common" *samutthai dam* (blackened khoi tree bark paper) and expensive and elite *samutthai khao* (unblackened white khoi paper) (Ginsburg, pp. 24–34). From the colophons we can see that these manuscripts were copied by monks and have Pali blessings written at the end. These manuscripts are not just found in rural homes, they are kept in royal libraries and museums. For example, on one Piśācapakaraṇam manuscript, a monk named Phra Phimontham, pays homage to the triple gem (Buddha, Dhamma, Sangha) in his colophon (ibid., p. 40). The Piśācapakaraṇam is one of many vernacular narrative collections (not to mention the vernacular ritual and astrological manuals) that have not been studied by scholars working in Buddhist and Religious Studies. Ginsburg, who was one of those rare scholars who felt comfortable in both fields, realized this as a very young man in 1967 when he translated this colophon in one of the manuscripts he was studying: "you who have heard these tales, honor them well and make your hearts pure and clear from vice and in the future you will have happiness in the heavenly city of Nirvana" (ibid., pp. 79–80). I thank Henry Ginsburg for his advice and conversations on these stories and sundry. I discuss the importance of studying vernacular and Sanskrit literary tales in Southeast Asian Buddhist Studies in McDaniel, *The Lovelorn Ghost*, pp. 117–9.

[16] Maurice Bloomfield, "On Overhearing as a Motif of Hindu Fiction," *American Journal of Philology* 41, 4 (1920): 301–35. See particularly pp. 314–6.

[17] The *Book of the Birds* is briefly circulated in Southeast Asia in the context of comparing it to examples from the Islamic and Indic world in Theodor Benfey, ed., *Orient und Occident*, Vol. 3 (Göttingen: Verlag der Dieterichschen Buchhandlung, 1864), pp. 171–2. The first European to study these connections to Southeast Asia seems to be Adolf Bastian who traveled extensively in the region, especially Thailand, in the 1860s.

[18] For Indian influences of Kalilah and Dimnah and information on the Syrian, Arabic, and other tellings, see Ion G.N. Keith-Falconer, *Kalilah and Dimnah or the Fables of Bidpai: An English translation of the late Syriac version of the text*, originally edited by William Wright with critical notes and variant readings preceded by an introduction, being an account of their literary and philological history (Amsterdam: Philo Press, 1970), introduction.

[19] See Farid ud-Din Attar, *The Conference of the Birds*, translated by Afkham Darbandi and Dick Davis (New York: Penguin, 1984) and Farid ud-Din Attar, *The Conference of the Birds*, translated by S.C. Nott (London: Cirwen Press, 1954). Recently, a beautiful children's telling was published by Peter Sis (*The Conference of the Birds*, New York: Penguin Books, 2011). None of the numerous scholars of these texts which circulated widely in the Islamic world has undertaken a serious comparative study with the Sanskrit manuscripts nor the Southeast Asian tellings.

[20] See Kusuma Raksamani, "Nandakapakarana attributed to Vasubhaga: A Comparative Study of Sanskrit, Lao, and Thai Texts" (PhD Dissertation, University of Toronto, 1978), pp. 12–15. See also studies of the Indic and Javanese manuscripts by George Artola, *Ten Tales from the Tantropakhyana* (Madras: The Vasanta Press, 1965); Sivasamba Sastri, *The Tantropākhayāna* (Trivandrum: Government Press, 1938); Christian Hooykaas, "Tantri de Mittel-javaansche Pancatantra – beworking" (PhD Dissertation, Leiden University, 1929); and three articles by A. Venkatasubbiah, "A Javanese version of the Pañcatantra," *Annals of the Bhandarkar Oriental Research Institute* 46 (1966): 59–100, "A Tamil version of the *Pañcatantra*," *The Adyar Library Bulletin* 29 (1965): 74–142, and "The *Pañcatantra* version of Laos," *The Adyar Library Bulletin* 33, 1–4 (1969): 195–283.

[21] Some *Tantropākhyāna* manuscripts do not include the *Maṇḍūka* and most do not include the Vetala. Most manuscripts include the *Nandaka*, *Pakṣī*, and *Piśāca*. There are many northern Thai *Nithan Nang Tantrai* manuscripts available, including complete ones (with at least four of the *prakaraṇam* collections). For example, there are four in Chiang Mai monasteries, one in Lampang, one in Phayom, two in Phrae, and one in Nan. In Laos, the National Library has collected two large manuscripts of the Mun Tantai and the National Library of Thailand has two as well, although both exclude the Maṇḍūka and seems to have come from a very different Indian source. For a relatively complete bibliography of manuscript and printed editions of the various *prakaraṇam* texts in the region see Syam Phathranuprawat's three articles in different stages of publication: "Nithan bhisatbhakaranam: chak rueang phi lueak nai ma ben rueang bhisat taeng ngan kap manut," "Kan bhlaeng nithan sansakrit ben chatok nai rueang kalithat," and "Nithan rueang chao chai okatanna kap mi: rong roi nithan sansakrit nai lanna." I thank Syam for sending these articles and for his advice and guidance. For a general study that draws from this research see his thesis "Bhaksibhakaranam: kan seuksa bhriaptiap chabap sansakrit lanna lae thai" (Bangkok: Silapakorn University, 2546 [2003]) and his "Lanna bhaksibhakarana," *Damrong Journal of the Faculty of Archaeology* 4, 1 (2005): 39–51. I also thank Jacqueline Filliozat for her kind help with this research. There are a large number of vernacular Thai editions including comic book tellings.

[22] The South Indian telling of the text often include an initial six verses dedicated to Śiva, but these are not always present in the Southeast Asian manuscripts.

[23] See especially the seventh printing of Phrarajaworawongthoe Korommuenphitayalongkaran, *Nithan Wetala* (Bangkok: Amarin, 2554 [2011]) and the book published in honor of the cremation of Mom Chao Winita Raphipha, ed. Kriangkrai Sambhacchalit, *Brachum pakaranam* (Vols. 1–5) (Bangkok: Saengdao, 2537 [2003]), chapter 4. A modern Thai translation of the text is found in Kriangkon Sambhacchalit, ed., *Bhrachum bhakaranam bhak thi* 1–6 (Bangkok: Saengdao, 2553 [2010]), chapter

two. I thank Arthid Sheravanichkul for providing me with a copy of this book. The original edition was published in six volumes between 1922–27 as cremation books. J. Crosby [*Journal of the Siam Society* 7 (1910): 1–90] translated the Thai text into English based off a manuscript in the Wachirayan Royal Library in 1910. He noted that there were both metrical (*khlon*) and prose manuscripts available. He was unable to find another *lilit* (mixed measured classical Thai lyrical poetry) manuscript mentioned in the 1904 *Vachiranana Magazine* (no. 113). I thank Peter Skilling for sending me a copy of this translation. The Royal Press in Bangkok published a printed copy of the *Nandaka-prakaraṇam* (Thai: *Nonthuk Pakaranam*) in 1876 and Ginsburg mentioned that there is a lost copy from 1870 (314). A copy of the *Pakṣī-prakaraṇam* was given to King Chulalongkorn on the occasion of his coronation in 1868 (Crosby, *Book of the Birds*, introduction).

[24] There are many modern English and Sanskrit editions of this collection. See for example N.M. Penzer (ed.) and C.H. Tawney's translation *The Ocean of Streams of Story* in ten volumes (London: Chas Sawyer, 1926) or the more recent translation by Arshia Sattar, *Somadeva: Tales from the Kathāsaritsāgara* (New York: Penguin, 1994).

[25] Riccardi, "A Nepali Version of the Vetālapañcaviṃśati Nepali Text and English Translation" (Dissertation, University of Pennsylvania, 1968). This was later published in a slightly reduced form by the American Oriental Society, Vol. 54 (New Haven, 1971).

[26] Burton's telling were published by Longmans, Green, and Co. (London, 1870) and Ryder's 1917 translation is now available online at http://www.sacred-texts.com/hin/ttg/.

[27] Kusuma Raksamani, *Pakaranam-nithan* (Bangkok: Mae khamphang, 2547 [2004]), pp. 70–5.

10

Buddhist "Nuns" (*mae chi*) and the Teaching of Pali in Contemporary Thailand*

Introduction

This article has two main purposes: first, it presents an account of Buddhist "nuns" involved in the teaching of Pali language, and in a form of Buddhist Higher Education (*Abhidhamma*—term explained below), in Bangkok in the early 2000s, phenomena which seem to have gone unnoticed in the western ethnographic record.[1] Second, it reflects in a deliberately open-ended manner on both the emic Buddhist and etic interpretative vocabularies which have been used to describe these women and their social role(s) and status(es). Readers who are familiar with the topic will understand the need for inverted commas around the word nuns; others will not, and we explain what is involved briefly below. We hope that our discussion of both emic and etic terminologies will help in making sense of the sociological complexities involved, and also in providing an orderly way to progress beyond the simple binary opposition between laity and members of the Buddhist monastic Order (the *saṅgha*), especially as it has been used in the study of Buddhism under the influence of Weberian

* Originally appeared as "Buddhist 'nuns' (*mae chi*) and the teaching of Pali in contemporary Thailand," Steven Collins and Justin McDaniel, *Modern Asian Studies* 44 (2010): 1373–1408.

| *Rare statues of Bhikkhuni (nuns) in Wat Thepdhitaram in Bangkok. Photo by author.*

comparativism. We aim to go beyond the lens of victimizers/victimized in thinking about "nuns," and to celebrate the large and increasing numbers of Pali-scholar "nuns" in modern Thailand.

"Nuns" have existed, for example, since at least the nineteenth century in Burma and Sri Lanka, and in Thailand for much longer.[2] But a striking characteristic of the twentieth century, especially in its second half, has been the greatly increased number of women adopting this role, and in particular the greatly increased number of younger women doing so.[3] Previous scholarship on this phenomenon in Sri Lanka and Burma has adopted a Weberian approach: Gombrich and Obeyesekere saw such women as an example of the more general phenomenon of the "laicization" of modern (and modernist) Buddhism;[4] Houtman on Burma, Holt on Sri Lanka, and Cook on Thailand have turned the tables and referred rather to "monasticization," in relation to the increasing practice of meditation by laity and "nuns."[5] The use of both terms can be defended: but perhaps we need not simply choose between one or the other term from a Weberian binary opposition, but rather speak of the pluralization of practice(s) and status(es).[6]

It is not our intention to criticize Weber overall: his writings on Buddhism were and still are incisive and thought-provoking, indeed awe-inspiring given the quantity and quality of materials available to him. But were he alive now, a century later, he would not give the same account: our knowledge of Buddhism and our forms of interpretation have moved on. The authors of this article cannot hope to match his genius, but we would like to offer some ethnographic *reportage* and some terminological precision which might facilitate the work of a latter-day Weber, should we be blessed with one. An overall assessment of Weber is impossible here.[7] In relation to our present concerns, the most important notion of which we need to rid ourselves is that of "the world," and the idea that Buddhist monastic life "rejects" it, as in Weber's very influential "Religious Rejections of the World and their Directions."[8] This concept of "the world" is, like so much of his vocabulary, taken from Christian theology and—seemingly but in fact insufficiently—secularized as a term of comparativist description and analysis. It is impossible to extricate a sociologically descriptive sense of this word from its theological context: as a technical term it is irredeemably ambiguous.[9] One so often reads, given the ubiquitous involvement of Buddhist (and, indeed Hindu and Christian) monastics with all or part(s) of the rest of society, and in wording borrowed from St Paul, that they are "in" the world but not "of" it—a mystifying phrase which serves in effect to preclude rather than facilitate further analysis of the very many social roles and statuses which monastics have, and have always had. It is true that there does exist an analogous Buddhist dichotomy, between *lokiya* and *lokuttara*,[10] which can be translated as "worldly" and "super-worldly"—but these terms are not standardly given a sociological sense in Buddhism: they are used for a number of different soteriological evaluations, and refer to Buddhist cosmology and related individual behaviors in relation to it (and to what is beyond it) rather than to society.

Lay and Monastic Statuses

The basic distinction between lay and monastic statuses is, certainly, a fundamental and ubiquitous division in Buddhist thought, although equally it has always had complex and varying relations to practice throughout the Buddhist world. On the level of thought and imagination it is implicated, conceptually and metaphorically, in the most basic structure of Buddhism, as both an analogy to and a part of the dichotomy between *saṃsāra*, the world(s) of rebirth, and *nirvāṇa* (Pali *nibbāna*), the timeless beatitude which constitutes the transcendence of suffering and rebirth. To use the widespread imagery of dwelling in a house ("householder," *gihi*, *gahapati*, etc., is a standard binary opposite of "monastic"): the monastic leaves his or her home physically, by going to live with the Monastic Community; but the individual, though of necessity still living in the house of the body, aims not to produce another such body-house so that at death he leaves the household-world of *saṃsāra* forever.[11] Two verses of the *Dhammapada* (153–54), attributed to the Buddha on achieving Enlightenment, put it thus:

> I have wandered through many births, seeking but not finding the house-builder; repeated birth is full of suffering. Housebuilder! You are seen, you will not build a house again.... My mind is beyond conditioning and has reached the end of desire.[12]

When this basic dichotomy is enlarged to include gender, there are said, again standardly and ubiquitously, to be four "Assemblies" (*parisa*): monks, nuns, laymen, and laywomen.[13] But already we are in the thick of translation issues: the English words "monk" and "nun," which are firmly established now and are quite acceptable, translate *bhikkhu* and *bhikkhunī* (Sanskrit *bhikṣu* and *bhikṣuṇī*), which are desiderative adjectives from the root *bhaj*, to *have a share*: monks and nuns are in this sense those who do not produce their own means of sustenance but wish to share in those provided by others. "Monk" does not come, as is often said in popular books, from Greek *monos* = alone, but from *monachos* = single (unmarried); "nun" comes from medieval Latin *nonna*, which like the masculine *nonnus* was an honorific used for older people, both in general and in monasticism. This is true of most modern terms used in the Theravāda world for what we will call "professionally celibate women" (see Appendix 2). Laity, male and female, are referred to in this four-fold division as *upāsaka-s* and *upāsikā-s*, from the root *upa-ās*, to *serve*, *show respect to*: a lay follower takes The Three Refuges, in the Buddha, the Teaching (dhamma) and the Monastic Order (*saṅgha*), and standardly also undertakes to observe the Five Precepts, repeating this undertaking on numerous ritual occasions, and sometimes Eight (see Table 1). Sometimes the terms *upāsaka* or *upāsikā* are used of laity with some special status in the Buddhist world generally: modern women meditation teachers, for example, to be discussed briefly below, often have *upāsikā* as a kind of special title. It is also often used in relation to older people who spend more time at temples than others, notably on ritually special days and in the rainy season: for example those among the Shan also called "temple-sleepers."[14]

The binary opposition between monastic and lay statuses, widened to a quartet with gender included, is further elaborated in Pali texts in terms of the Buddhist Precepts (*sikkhāpada*-s, see Table 1). Entry into the monastic Order requires one preliminary stage for men, and two for women. Both can become novices (*sāmaṇera-s, sāmaṇeri-s*)[15] at any time from mid-childhood,[16] preceded by a specific ritual, *pabbajjā*, "Going Forth." (This term can also be used in a general sense for what South Asian traditions of all kinds call "Going Forth from Home to Homelessness.") There is also another status for women, little-studied: a woman must spend two years as a trainee (*sikkhamānā*, from the same root as *sikkhāpada*), keeping to Six Precepts, before initiation as a nun.[17] Initiation to become a *bhikkhu* or *bhikkhunī* is called *upasampadā*: candidates have to be, inter alia, 20 years old. The *Vinaya* for monks has 227 rules; that for nuns 311. The titles *thera*, *theri*, *mahāthera*, and *mahātheri*, can be accorded after 10 and 30 years, respectively, in the robe.

The single question which has dominated study of this issue in what are now called "Theravāda countries," as also in relation to the Tibetan tradition, is that the female statuses of novice and nun (and therefore trainee) have either died out or, in some areas, seem never to have been established (see "The History of the Order of Nuns" below). A great deal of energy has been spent, even more in the international, globalized Buddhist world than within Asian countries, on the question of re-establishing the Order of Nuns, culminating in the summer of 2007 with a large-scale International Conference in Hamburg, attended by the Dalai Lama.[18] The issue is simple to state, but not easy to solve: in Buddhist monastic law, ordaining *bhikkhunī-s* requires five already fully-ordained ones: if none exists, then it seems that the order cannot be revived. The majority opinion in Asian countries, among women as much as men, which is supported by our data, is that indeed the Order of Nuns cannot be revived before the arrival of the next Buddha Metteyya (Maitreya), and so is simply out of the question. Indeed, the majority of professionally celibate women explicitly oppose the idea of Ordination, on various grounds, amongst which perhaps the most obvious is that such Ordination would put them according to the *Vinaya* under the direct legal control of Monks, which many regard as undesirable.[19] However, here our concern is not to contribute to this debate, although we will revert to it occasionally. The issue will be resolved by Buddhists, making their own history. From an academic perspective now what is needed, inter alia, is much more ethnography, to describe what such Buddhist women actually do; and perhaps also some discussion and possible clarification of categories to help situate this activity socially.

TABLE 1

Lay and monastic statuses in regard to the Precepts (*sīla*)

1. Laity: male and female lay followers, *upāsakā* and *upāsikā*.

The precepts are to refrain from:

killing stealing non-celibacy lying drinking liquor which causes intoxication and heedlessness	Five Precepts (1–5 *pañca-sīla*) are taken by all laypeople on repeated occasions, ideally though not automatically as a permanent lifestyle. When only five Precepts are taken, number 3 is taken to be against adultery.
eating after noon dancing, singing, music and shows using garlands, perfumes, unguents, adornments using high and luxurious beds	Eight Precepts (1–9 but called Eight, *aṭṭha-sīla*, because 7 + 8 are seen here as a single Precept) are taken by laypeople on special days, and permanently by some older people and most modern "nuns."
handling gold and silver (= money)	Ten Precepts (*dasa-sīla*) are taken permanently by male and female novices, some older people and some modern "nuns."

2. Monastics: male and female Novices, female Trainees, Monks, Nuns.

Age	*Ritual initation*	*Designation*	*Rules undertaken*
from mid-childhood for women (any age after 8)	*pabbajjā*, Going Forth a necessary preliminary to Full Ordination	*sāmaṇera*, *sāmaṇerī*, Novice *sikkhāmānā*, Trainee	Ten Precepts Six Precepts (1–6)
20 years and above	*upasampadā*, Full Ordination	*bhikkhu*, Monk *bhikkhunī*, Nun	227 Vinaya rules for monks 311 Vinaya rules for nuns

Some Etic Categories

Some reflection on etic categories: we think it useful to speak of *professional (female) celibates*, who practice, in a general sense, *asceticism*. In this phrase the term *celibate*, as in Latin *caelebs* and French *célibataire* (but not in modern English) refers not, or not merely, to the practice of chastity, for any length of time, but to the permanent or at least long-term social status of being single, unmarried.[20] The word *professional* is not meant ironically: The *Oxford English Dictionary* (OED) has *proper to, or connected with a profession or calling*; it gives the sense *pertaining to or marking entrance into a religious order*, before giving the modern sense of doing something as a livelihood, for money, rather than as a pastime, as an amateur. A *professional* has a vocation; in most cases with a particular form of dress and a recognizable form of deportment undertaken as a continuing, often lifelong, way of life. Greek *askēsis*, from *askeō*, *practice*, means primarily *training*, the *practice of self-discipline*, where *self-discipline* means self-fashioning; Sanskrit and Pali *sādhanā*, *bhāvanā* are much the same. Our usage of the word does not imply what OED refers to as *the exercise of extremely rigorous self-discipline, severe abstinence, austerity*. In many cases where there is an aspect of educating or training others, in meditation, scholarship, or any other métier, teachers of either gender, ascetic or not, can be referred to by the vernacular equivalents of words for "teacher," such as Pali ācariya, Sanskrit ācārya = Thai *ajaan*; *guru* = Thai *khru*, Cambodian *grü*,[21] etc. For our purposes, the *mae chi* on whom we report are *professional (female) celibates* following an *ascetic vocation*, with a distinct social status (or a number of fluctuating statuses) concomitant with that role and with their activity as teachers. As will be seen, their lifestyles, their vocations, can be many and various.

Appendices 1 and 2 offer an introductory survey of terms for such professional celibates, male and female, in Pali texts and in modern vernaculars. Here, before coming to the history and present position of Buddhist nuns and "nuns," we must turn to something any conceptual binary seems inevitably to entail: what of individuals who do not fall easily into one or another category? One possible option would be to categorize those who do not have straightforward one or another status as occupying a *third* status, or grouping of such statuses. In the history of Christianity, especially Catholic monasticism, for example, there has been for many centuries a standard category of Third or Tertiary Orders, which refer to men and women with a status and lifestyle which is in varying ways partially, though not fully, monastic.[22]

In cross-cultural Gender studies, an influential book edited by Gilbert Herdt in 1994 introduced the category *Third Sex/Third Gender*:[23] Adopting this approach we might speak in the Buddhist case of *Third Status(es)*. Herdt's project was not to reduce the multiform varieties of human sexuality and gender, of behaviors and identities, to three instead of two. Rather, for him and for us, the *Third* category is provisional and heterogeneous, aiming not at comprehensiveness in description or analysis, but simply at breaking down a previously assumed dimorphism. In this area of study an important distinction is made between sexual and/or gendered *acts* and *identities*: often non-western vocabularies contain words for the former but not for the latter, and introducing a western discourse of permanent or semi-permanent *identities* creates a need for corresponding terms in indigenous lexicons.[24] For us, *acts* and *identities* are two ends of a continuum: we will be concerned with women who have chosen *professional celibacy* as a permanent or semi-permanent *identity*. For a final example, see: Patricia A. McBroom's (1986) anthropological study of women in business *The Third Sex: The New Professional Woman*.[25]

The History of the Order of Nuns

But why, historically, have we arrived at circumstances where women cannot, according to the majority opinion, become novices or nuns? The history of *bhikkhunī-s* is reasonably clear but in various ways puzzling.[26] They existed in India and Sri Lanka from at least the time of Aśoka's reign in the third century BC, until the start of the second millennium AD. Inscriptions show that they were often as numerous as monks, and that they often had sufficient wealth to make large donations, have monuments erected, and so forth. Epithets and titles used for them indicate significant achievements in asceticism, scholarship, and the formation and maintenance of lineages. Evidence for their existence starts to diminish from the mid-first millennium AD, with a last (possible) reference from Nepal in the early eleventh century: this is part of the general mystery of the disappearance of Buddhism in India. In Sri Lanka it seems that by the eleventh century the number of *bhikkhunī-s* available became less than the five necessary for Ordinations, and no kings could or did have *bhikkhunī-s* come from elsewhere to resuscitate the Order, as happened often with *bhikkhu-s*. From the middle of the first millennium, elites throughout Southeast Asia adopted different kinds of Buddhism, along with other elements of Indie civilization arriving from Northeast and South India, and Sri Lanka,[27] but there is no certain evidence for ordained *bhikkhunī-s* anywhere in Southeast Asia at any time.[28]

So, it is clear that nuns existed in India and Sri Lanka, and just possibly, briefly, in some parts of Southeast Asia, until the end of the first millennium AD. Evidence suggests that many of them were highly educated and were involved in textual learning and teaching. But despite these achievements we have no evidence, with a very few possible exceptions, for *bhikkhunī-s* composing texts in Pali, as opposed to memorizing and transmitting them.[29] Historians may one day determine why the order of *bhikkhunī-s* died out in some parts of the Buddhist world, and seems never to have appeared in others, and also why there seems to have been such a clearly gendered division of labor in relation to composing versus transmitting texts. *Mae chi* in the early-modern and modern worlds seem to have been involved in neither, but contemporary *mae chi* in Thailand are very often involved in education at all levels, albeit that like their earlier premodern forebears they do not compose Pali texts—but then scarcely anyone does nowadays.

Mae chi in Thailand

In the term *mae chi* (sometimes romanized as *ji*) the word *chi/ji* is an honorific derived from Khmer, used for any person who occupies a position of respect, including both male and female ascetics;[30] *mae* is mother, often used as an honorific for hierarchical as well as familial relationships. It can also be used as a pronoun, in the first, second and third persons.[31] There exist many different portraits of *mae chi*, and certainly many more remain to be drawn. In accounts by pre-modern European travelers, and in much ethnographic literature, *mae chi* are described as older women, dressed in white and living in or near temples, acting as cooks and maidservants to monks, an often denigratory perception of them which still continues today.[32] More recently *mae chi*, especially the increased numbers of younger women who have adopted that lifestyle, have been described in various roles: as participants and sometimes teachers of meditation;[33] as involved in many kinds of social and psychological work, often subsumed in the category of Engaged Buddhism:[34] perhaps the best-known is Mae Chi Sansanee, whose institution in Bangkok, the Sathira-Dhammasathan, has been the subject of much media attention;[35] as involved in teaching, notably at the Dhammajarinee Witthaya Schools founded by Khun Mae Prathin,[36] and at the tertiary level Mahapajāpati Therī College, which was initiated by Khun Ying Kanittha though not started until after her death in 2002.[37] From a social-historical perspective, this increase in the number of younger *mae chi* is to be seen as part of the broader expansion of education, vocations and lifestyles for single, and also for married women in modern Thailand, for example in many different kinds of business (including, alas, prostitution)[38] and politics.[39]

Case Studies: Mae chi Teaching Pali

We know of no studies devoted to Buddhist *mae chi* studying and teaching Pali and *Abhidhamma*, nor of the institutional contexts in which they do so. The *Abhidhamma* is the third of the three "Baskets" (*piṭaka*) of the Pali Canon and is regarded by its followers and practitioners as the most profound aspect of the Buddha's teachings, both in itself and in connection with the practice of meditation. For the most part it consists of lists and analyses of the momentary Existents (*dhamma-s*) which make up the world and experience of it.[40]

Although we talked with many *mae chi*, formal interviews were only conducted with those who had either passed higher level Pali examinations or who held advanced degrees in Buddhist studies. We developed a questionnaire (four pages of detailed questions in Thai), handed it out and then conducted formal interviews based on the answers: there was no shortage in eligible *mae chi* to take part in both. The formal interviews were mostly conducted in July and August 2006;[41] nearly all were recorded digitally and all interviewees agreed to be photographed and used their real names, although they were told that they need not do so. Questions included the place, date and reason for ordaining as *mae chi*, and experience of Pali study, along with such questions as: is the study of Pali necessary to the practice and teaching of Buddhism? Is Pali necessary for *mae chi*? Why? Why not? Are you satisfied with opportunities to study Pali? What do you think of the textbooks used? Do you think there should be fully ordained *bhikkhunī-s* in Thailand? We interviewed and collected questionnaires from a lot more nuns than we can include in this short study.

The institutions studied are specifically monastic, where sometimes "studying" or "knowing" Pali refers primarily to the memorization of texts used in chanting; in monastic scholarly training, where Pali is usually studied without Sanskrit, there are nine levels of attainment, called *prayōg*;[42] monks who attain the 9th level receive a stipend of 3,000 baht ($100) a month;[43] *mae chi*, who can (though not all do) receive 800 baht a month stipend, also receive a bonus of 900 baht a month for passing the 9th-level exams. So, a 9th-level scholar-*mae chi* can only make 1,700 baht ($56) a month. This was, unsurprisingly, a bone of some contention among the *mae chi* who were interviewed, who feel that it is insufficient for their needs.

Undoubtedly the doyenne of all Pali scholars, male and female, in Thailand, has published under her lay name, Supaphan Na Bangchang, but is now known as Ajaan Mae Chi Vimuttiyā, sometimes with the epithet anagārikā, "homeless" (see Appendix 2 for this term in Nepal). She made an edition of a Pali commentary for her PhD thesis in Sri Lanka in 1978, and has since published and edited many books on Pali grammar, language and literature in Thai, being considered one of the leading scholars of Pali literature, not only in Southeast Asia but also in the world.[44] She lived for some years in a forest temple outside Chiang Mai, but is now director of the prestigious International Tripitaka Hall, at Chulalongkorn University (secular) in Bangkok, a library of rare and valuable Pali texts. She is responsible for developing education programs for advanced students of Pali and for greeting foreign guests and VIPs at the hall. She commands a great deal of respect and has been honored with awards from the Thai royal family. Despite holding a PhD she recently earned a master's degree at Abhidhamma Jotika College (see below). In our interview, she thought the fact that she was a scholar and a *mae chi* should be of no surprise. She expressed no desire to become a *bhikkhunī* even if it was possible, because now she is free to live in her own apartment, control her own schedule, write, work, and meditate, and also interact freely with students and colleagues. She encouraged us to visit and speak with *mae chi* throughout the city and see for ourselves how Pali scholarship was flourishing.

Abhidhamma Jotika College, in the grounds of Wat Mahathat in Bangkok, is the premier school of *Abhidhamma* studies in Thailand, and now has five branches nationally. Many, if not most of its professors are *mae chi*; some of the very highest scores in the royally-sponsored Pali examinations are achieved by its students, and many of the highest-ranking students at the college are *mae chi*.[45] Many of the Pali teachers we met at other institutions graduated from there. Mae Chi Bunchuai Sriprem, a 9th-level Pali scholar who received the title "Abhidhamma Pandit" from Abhidhamma Jotika College, is, at 39 years old, one of the most well-respected teachers of Pali grammar and dissertation advisors at the elite central campus of Mahamakut Monastic University, in the grounds of Wat Bowornniwet in Bangkok. One of the top two monastic universities in the country, this royally-sponsored institution has traditionally produced the brightest monks and *mae chi* of the Thammayut lineage, drawing students from Europe, Japan, China, Australia, Indonesia, Cambodia, Sri Lanka, Laos, Malaysia,

Nepal, Korea, and elsewhere. Mae Chi Bunchuai, like many highly-educated *mae chi*, resides at nearby Wat Chanasongkhram. She is originally from Suphanburi province, a farming region two hours' drive north of the capital. At the time of our interview, she had been in the white robes for 19 years; she is "determined to be a *mae chi* for the duration [of her life]." She ordained to have the time to study Buddhism until she understood it correctly and could lead others in practice and study, in order to make her heart and mind pure according to the fundamental words of the Buddha. At that time, she was studying *Abhidhamma*. Therefore, it was necessary to study Pali in order to understand the *Abhidhamma*.

This relationship between studying Pali grammar and the *Abhidhamma*, stated in our first interview, was consistently invoked by other educated *mae chi*, including those who had not studied at the Abhidhamma Jotika College. Although she stated that she did not teach courses in Pali, simply tutoring monks and other *mae chi* and advising dissertations and master's theses, we believe Mae Chi Bunchuai was being self-deprecating: McDaniel observed her teaching a formal Pali class in which all but one of the 17 students were monks. When asked about this, she jokingly said, "well, sure, I teach monks, but they are not 'my students,' they are above me." She nonetheless took the teaching of Pali very seriously: "teachers of Pali should possess the qualities of a true expert. They should have the ability to transfer their knowledge of Pali and allow their students [to] understand easily and memorize correctly." She described the Pali skills of monks and *mae chi* as most likely not different, but the lecture style and the pedagogical method are different. This is due to the fact that teachers are people who have studied hard to understand the meaning deeply. The only reason for doing this is to teach.

So, despite denying the ability to teach Pali formally, Mae Chi Bunchuai does so and considers herself, rightly, an expert. She emphasized that her intellectual focus as a *mae chi* was a good model, because "people who ordain in Buddhism (besides those who ordain for a short time or only to perform morning and evening liturgies or just practice meditation) should pass on the teaching of the Buddha;" she saw no barrier to *mae chi* who wanted to study for advanced degrees in Pali and other Buddhist studies subjects: there are resources for *mae chi* who want to study Pali. Furthermore, householders also get to study in the Pali curriculum just like monks and novices do. It [the Thai system] is a good system if you want to learn Pali.

Like most *mae chi* we interviewed Mae Chi Bunchuai also stated that the opportunities for them to acquire a Pali education would not increase or even be affected if Thai women could become *bhikkhunī-s*. In fact, she spoke directly about the subject: I do not think there should be *bhikkhunī-s*, because the lineage of *bhikkhunī-s* in Theravāda has been lost in India already, because *mae chi* are able to study and be part of the Buddhist community.

Mae Chi Bunchuai is far from being the only accomplished nun at Mahamakut University. There are dozens of *mae chi* studying for master's and doctoral degrees in Buddhist studies there; master's theses and doctoral dissertations by *mae chi* are available in their library, and any visitor will notice *mae chi* prevalent on campus. This is in part due to the fact that the headquarters of the Sathaban Mae Chi Haeng Chat (National Office of Mae Chi) is located there. Mae Chi Ladda Komalasing, a 38-year-old, 9th-level Pali scholar who holds a PhD in *Dhamma* studies and a post-doctoral degree in *Abhidhamma* studies, had first ordained in Chonburi Province, 30 kilometers southeast of Bangkok, at age 18, and moved to the city for higher education (in secular subjects also). She gave straightforward answers to our questions, saying that she studied to spread the *Dhamma* and was determined to remain ordained for the rest of her life because of this mission. She felt that the study of Pali is extremely necessary for studying and teaching *pariyatti-dhamma*[46] ... in order to give us the ability to understand the Pali vocabulary word-by-word. It allows us to understand the roots of words. It helps us understand the meaning of the vocabulary—every single word in the Buddhavacana. Therefore, we can translate the dhamma in a profound way. It allows us the ability to review the *Dhamma* perfectly.

Although Mae Chi Ladda Komalasing was qualified after more than a decade of formal Pali study, she chose not to teach Pali and instead concentrated on teaching *Abhidhamma* and meditation to mostly lay groups: every part of the *Dhamma* in the curriculum and outside the curriculum should be part of education. This education should focus on the details and analysis [of the mind while meditating and going about daily work].

In response to our question if it mattered if a Pali teacher was a monk or a *mae chi*, she stated emphatically (in fact this was the only time she became animated during the interview) that whether a person is a monk or *mae chi* has nothing to do with it. It depends on the teacher. Do they have an objective when they teach? Do they care for their students? Are they hardworking and focused? These are the important qualities of a teacher.

She did, however, unlike almost every other person we interviewed, complain about the lack of resources for *mae chi* studying Pali. She thought that better dormitories and stipends were needed, although the textbooks and pedagogical methods were fine. The problem she believed had nothing to do with gender, but with Thai people's support for Pali. The general populace did not sympathize and had no respect for how hard it is to study Pali: monks were the only members of society to support *mae chi*-s' studies. Although she was highly critical of the state of Pali study (for monks, *mae chi*, and laity), she did not believe that the ability to ordain as a *bhikkhunī* would help. She did not see how being a *bhikkhunī* would increase the resources to study Pali or any other Buddhist subject. She had no problem with what she saw as Mahāyāna *bhikkhunī-s* coming to Thailand, but she did not think that status was necessary for Theravadins.[47] The possibility of ordaining as a *bhikkhunī*, she stressed, had ended. There was no need to talk about it anymore.

Mae Chi Ladda's bluntness was softened and complicated by Mae Chi Wanpen Anuson, a 39-year-old woman who ordained at 15 years old in the northern province of Kampaengphet, and who attained 9th-level status in Pali. She also believed that *bhikkhunī* ordination is unnecessary, pausing between answers to reflect that it would not have helped her in her studies. She changed the focus of the questioning and asked us why it is important to study Buddhism. Before we could answer, she stated that it was "to end suffering." Suffering was most acute in the householder's life. *Mae chi* were not householders, they were working to end suffering for themselves. They had the time to meditate, study, and serve the monastery. Even though she had studied Pali seriously for over ten years, she did not, unlike most others, see Pali as essential. In fact, she said, it was useless without practice (*paṭipatti*). Nonetheless *mae chi* could and should teach Pali (she had been a teacher for one year at that point). She said that teachers should know the roots of words and grammar in great detail. They should care when teaching are the basis of the *Dhamma*. The teachings of the Buddha are the foundation.

This ability to teach and care for students "has nothing to do with gender. It depends on the education and training of the teacher, as well as the quality of their work." She did not answer questions regarding *bhikkhunī* on the questionnaire and found them silly when we asked them in person. Mae Chi Wanpen's friend and colleague, Mae Chi Wannana Rungriang, age 40, from Angthong Province 120 kilometers north of Bangkok, had been an agricultural student before getting a doctorate in Buddhist studies and a master's in *Abhidhamma* studies, as well as passing 8th-level Pali examinations. She was reticent with us. She was planning to ordain for life because of her faith and to free herself from suffering. She thought the study of Pali is necessary for Buddhists because Pali is the language of the Traipitok, that is the *Vinaya*, *Sutta*, and *Abhidhamma*. It leads us to practice *samatha-kammaṭṭhāna* [concentration meditation] and *vipassanā-kammaṭṭhāna* [insight meditation] correctly.

In this regard, she saw no difference between monks and *mae chi*. She referred to them as "two children in the same basket." They both have the same ability. In a surprisingly bold answer, she stated that *bhikkhunī* ordination was fine and good for Mahāyāna Buddhists, but not for Thai Buddhists, since "our Buddhism is better:" there was no need for *bhikkhunī* ordination. As the interview progressed, she became more and more heated about the subject, stating that the life of a *mae chi* was difficult, but it could lead to liberation. "Foreign women," she asserted, "are interested in Buddhism in Thailand, but when they see the lives of *mae chi* they run away." She stated that if Thai Buddhism had *bhikkhunī-s*, then she might ordain if it led to liberation, but if not, then "it didn't matter ... my life as a *mae chi* has allowed me to study the *Dhamma* and *Vinaya*. It has allowed me to practice meditation. I can die satisfied."

The other top university for Pali studies is Mahachulalongkorn (not to be confused with the non-monastic university mentioned above), the largest monastic university in the country with five colleges and nine regional campuses. The main campus is located on the banks of the Chao Phraya River and is surrounded by the Grand Palace, Thammasat University (secular), the amulet and herbal medicine markets, and a number of bookstores. Hundreds of *mae chi* study there, especially in the evenings and at weekends. Some of them are students, many are meditators who attend weekend sitting sessions, and others are regular students in the Buddhist studies college, the Pali studies program is run by Phra Sompong, or in the Abhidhamma Jotika College which occupies the same grounds. The best-known scholar *mae chi* in residence at the monastery on campus (Wat Mahathat) is Mae Chi Kritsana, from Ubon Ratchathani Province in the northeast. She was very comfortable with foreigners and had studied English for several years.[48] She comes from a very poor farming family, and has been ordained 26 years, earning a master's degree in Buddhist studies at Mahachulalongkorn and becoming a 9th-level Pali scholar. She is finishing a dissertation on the history of *bhikkhunī-s* in India. She had wanted to study Pali to learn the meaning of the chanting she heard as a young child, and is now a full-time professor of Pali syntax, Pali grammar level three, and 1st- and 2nd-level Pali-Thai translation. She also teaches classes in the mornings at Wat Chanasongkhram and in the evenings at Wat Sampraya. On Sundays she teaches a special 8th-level advanced Pali course. Almost all of her students are monks and novices, although she denied, with a self-deprecating air like that of Mae Chi Bunchuai, that she could actually "teach monks anything." She claimed that the only discrimination she has experienced as a woman at the university was when one monk from a rural area thought it was strange that a *mae chi* was teaching Pali, and teaching him. He was upset, but most of the city monks told him that this was normal in the city, and that she was the best teacher of syntax. He apologized and took several courses with her. She too connected Pali studies with *Abhidhamma* and meditation: the four fundamental concepts of the *Abhidhammatthasaṅgaha* (*citta*, *cetasika*, *rūpa*, and*nibbāna*) were essential to understanding the inner workings of the mind when meditating.[49] She believes that women might be better suited for *Abhidhamma* and advanced Pali and meditation training because of their patience. Women, she stated, like details. Monks gravitated towards *Sutta* and *Vinaya* studies.

As well as these colleges and universities (and the Mahāpajāpati College for Nuns, which we were not able to visit), and in addition to living at wats, nuns live and study in various kinds of institution, one of which is called a *samnak*. Of the 20–30 such institutions, one of the most important is Samnak Santisuk, the oldest nunnery in Thailand, about 45 minutes drive northwest of Bangkok,[50] which was established in 1898, has its own museum of *mae chi* history, a library of Pali and Thai Buddhist materials, several classrooms, a meditation pond and garden, and is completely operated by *mae chi*, who provide all the Pali and Buddhist studies instruction. It houses *mae chi* (42 in 2006–07), as well as many temporary *dhammacārinī*-s (white-robed female students who take ten precepts) and *nang dam* (women who take eight precepts, but do not shave their heads, and who wear black pants and a white blouse instead of white robes). The abbot of Samnak Santisuk is Mae Chi Pranom Wingmat.

At 58, she is a 9th-level Pali scholar, and has been ordained since she was a teenager in Ratchburi Province in central Thailand. She entered into the nunhood originally not for herself but for her mother. As she grew into a young woman, she realized that the teachings of the Buddha made sense and gave her confidence, and so knowing them in detail, in Pali, became more and more important to her:

> Pali is extremely necessary because it permits us to study and teach students. From the very first sentence to the very last sentence, there is meaning in each word of the Buddha. From the lowest level up until the highest level there is [a teaching that will help] surpass suffering. Furthermore, Pali is useful and can be used for scholarly reference. The spoken words [of the Buddha] are clear and direct. [Pali] helps us preserve the teachings.

She has taught Pali grammar for over 20 years at Wat Chanasongkhram and Samnak Santisuk, and has never felt discriminated against in her teaching or studies. She states that:

> the curriculum is similar and the basic concepts behind the teaching are largely the same. In terms of lecture style and pedagogical method, it really depends on the personality [of the teacher]. Therefore, [women and men] are most likely not the same [because they have different personality types].

However, if they both use Prince Wachirayan's Pali curriculum, she argued, women and men would teach the same ways. She regarded the question of *bhikkhunī* ordination in Thailand as "simply not an important issue."

Other highly-educated *mae chi* at Samnak Santisuk, such as Mae Chi Oom Chanphaeng and Mae Chi Chaemchit Klat, gave similar answers. The former, who had been ordained for 21 years, saw no significant difference in the way monks and *mae chi* approached their teaching or practice, but she believed that women are better teachers than men because of their compassion towards students. They also have a better sense of humor. The latter stated that Pali was very important to study "because Pali is the language of every Buddha. It is the language that is beautiful and gentle. It carries deep meaning." *Bhikkhunī* ordination was not one of her goals. She thought it would not change the way women could study and practice openly in Thailand. She was happy and *bhikkhunī* ordination would not make her happier. Mae Chi Sūrathā Udomwarakhun, a 9th-level Pali scholar, who had spent 11 months studying in Nepal and taught Pali grammar at the Samnak Santisuk, emphasized that she joined the order of *mae chi* for advanced Pali study.

The final institution we shall discuss is, in some ways, the most interesting. Wat Paknam, in Thonburi, is the temple where the Dhammakaya (Thammakai) movement began, with the monk Luang Pho Wat Paknam (Phra Thepmuni) and his star pupil, the laywoman Khun Yay, who went on to found the huge Thammakai temple at Pathum Thani north of Bangkok.[51] Khun Yay was illiterate, so the movement, a controversial group popular with university students, which practices a form of unusual meditation (at least in modern times) and which, according to some opponents, teaches unacceptable doctrines, tends to downplay textual and linguistic learning in its rhetoric and advertising. At Wat Paknam, however, this is not the case. It does house a very large number of kitchen *mae chi* (*mae chi krua*) who wear dark skirts and a distinctive dark sash over their white blouses. They are somewhat looked down upon as well as pitied by *mae chi* who concentrate on meditation and/or study, because they spend all their time cooking, serving and cleaning up after monks. *Mae chi* from all over Thailand have flocked to live at Wat Paknam for a number of reasons: the meditation system emphasizes that anyone of any rank, gender, and background can achieve enlightenment through visualization and breathing exercises; there is free dormitory housing for *mae chi* (approximately 300 rooms); they receive free courses in Buddhist studies, Pali grammar, and secular subjects, along with a stipend of 800 baht a month.

The Thammakai is often criticized for its overt commercialism, modern marketing campaigns, missionary zeal, and "new age" approach to science and meditation. Despite these criticisms, monks and *mae chi* from the Thammakai do very well on royally-sponsored Pali examinations and many of their monks occupy powerful positions in the national ecclesiastical councils. *Mae chi* attracted to the Thammakai generally are less traditional in their attitudes towards religion and have more favorable attitudes to modern uses of technology, rationality, and science in education and meditation. Although a *mae chi* does not have to associate herself with the Thammakai lineage in order to study and reside at Wat Paknam, many *mae chi* we interviewed were intrigued by the teaching of the Thammakai. One of these was Mae Chi Nathathai Chatninwat. Unlike many of the *mae chi* we interviewed, she had a strictly secular educational training: a BA in Sociology from Chiang Mai University and an MA in Women's Studies from Thammasat University. She is now a PhD student in Buddhist Studies at Mahamakut University. Her brother received a master's degree in Engineering from the University of Oregon (US) and she had travelled broadly—an unusually cosmopolitan background. She had already passed her 6th-level Pali examinations and planned to continue until she achieved 9th level. Although she was reluctant to tell us details of what led her to make such a switch from a successful secular education to a religious one, she did speak broadly about the need for women in Thailand to work hard in all aspects of education and for them to study Pali in order to understand the intricacies of meditation. She saw it as her mission "to continue my studies in the Dhamma and to apply my education in Women's Studies in the service of women's development." Although many nuns focus on Pali in order to meditate and be able to teach meditation, she studies Pali in order to spread the teachings of the Buddha. Therefore, she was what she called a *mae chi pariyatti*, "a scholar *mae chi*" and not a *mae chi thammakai* who concentrated on meditation and for whom studies are secondary. This learning-for-learning's-sake approach was a great source of pride for her. In fact, at one point in our interview, she stopped a young monk from interrupting us. She told him directly that the foreigners wanted to interview her because of her high level of Pali scholarship. They did not want to interview him, she subtly suggested, because he wasn't a student of Pali. The monk, mildly insulted, walked away without arguing. This incident led to Mae Chi Nathathai telling us that she was upset with the Sangha policy of giving monks a monthly bonus of 3,000 baht for passing 9th-level examinations when *mae chi* could only receive a total of 1,700 baht a month. Still, this injustice did not make her think *bhikkhunī* ordination was a good idea. She was proud to be a *mae chi* and did not want to become a *bhikkhunī* even if it was an option. Mae chi were not lesser *bhikkhunī* but a particular career choice for women that permitted them a chance to study and advance psychologically; *mae chi* were not below monks, but *bhikkhunī* would be. However, she would support *bhikkhunī* ordination if it actually helped women get more opportunities to study. She said that she had little difficulty in finding good textbooks at *mae chi* educational centers such as Wat Paknam, Wat Chanasongkhram, and Wat Thammakai, but that many *mae chi* in rural areas had very little. She doubts having a *bhikkhunī* education would change that; she would prefer improved funding opportunities to form more schools that would provide free food and education to *mae chi* who wanted to study Pali at a high level. There are many monasteries like Wat Paknam, she said, which simply did not have enough space for all of the *mae chi* who wanted to study. She stated that she enjoyed the freedom to enter and leave the monastery at her leisure and to study and interact with other like-minded *mae chi* on her own terms. She worried about *mae chi* without this network of family and colleague support.

Mae Chi Nathathai introduced us to several like-minded *mae chi pariyatti*, who were later interviewed more formally. The author was also able to sit in on classes at Wat Paknam where *mae chi* students were present in large numbers. One of Mae Chi Nathathai's mentors was a Pali teacher named Mae Chi Sunantha Rianglaem, originally from the seaside city of Mahachai south of Bangkok. She is a 9th-level Pali scholar and was studying for a master's degree in Buddhist studies from Mahachulalongkorn. Presently she teaches Pali grammar and translation at Samnak Santisuk and Mahachulalongkorn. She had experienced few obstacles in her career as a student and teacher and her main complaint was that the 1,700 baht a month stipend was not enough to live on, even with free housing. *Mae chi* had to pay about 50 baht a day for food, although some went on morning alms rounds.[52] However, she had little problem with the system and lauded the National Mae Chi Office for providing for her while she studied. She could not receive any support if she was a layperson. Mae Chi Rachata Hophet, a 51-year-old 6th-level Pali scholar from Suratthani in the south, sat in on our interview; she was shy, but occasionally chimed in, especially when discussing the issue of *bhikkhunī* ordination. She stated quite vigorously that *bhikkhunī* ordination was a terrible idea. She believed that women fighting for this right were simply looking for fame (*cheusiang*). All human beings, she said, were simply external "form" (*rūp*, referring to the body and to appearance in general). The way a person dressed or what color robes they wore was unimportant. An honest student and focused meditator could achieve great merit even if he or she were a layperson. Finally, Mae Chi Yupa Thongbhut, a 36-year-old 8th-level Pali scholar from Chantaburi province, about five hours drive east of Bangkok, was very quiet in the formal interview, but needed several sheets of extra paper to fill out her questionnaire. She felt more comfortable expressing herself on paper. Using terms similar to those Mae Chi Oom Chanphaeng of Samnak Santisuk had used about the Buddha's teaching, she wrote that the life of a *mae chi* was a beautiful life that gave her the opportunity to make merit for herself and all women. She was now living in peace and had little stress. This peaceful lifestyle gave her opportunities to study (she had been studying Pali formally for 14 years) and she enjoyed studying with teachers, who, when qualified, "spoke beautifully."

The idea of a *mae chi*'s life as "beautiful," with meticulous and inspiring pedagogy, sophisticated learning and meditative expertise as goals and values per se, with intrinsic virtue as well as instrumental value in reducing suffering and leading to nirvana, has not been emphasized enough in the existing literature, which tends too often to concentrate on the issue of *bhikkhunī* ordination, and more generally to focus on *mae chi*-s' hardships (which are often many), and on discrimination in the Thai ecclesia. Our interviews with a small number of the many highly-educated *mae chi* show that, despite inequality and discrimination, there are many opportunities for women to study and teach the two subjects, Pali grammar and *Abhidhamma*, considered to be the most difficult and therefore the most prestigious to pursue in Thailand.

It seems clear to us that the scholarly ethnographic record and sociological analysis of *mae chi* in Thailand, of "nuns" in the Buddhism of South/Southeast Asia and Tibet, and indeed the "status" of women in Buddhism generally, needs to get out of the cul-de-sac into which the dominant concern with *bhikkunī/bhikṣunī* ordination has driven it. This is, of course, a vital and dominant concern for many Buddhist women (albeit that this is more, as mentioned above, on the international, global stage than in the lived worlds of women in those parts of Asia). But the academic description of women's lives and the many and various social positions they occupy needs far more detailed ethnography than we currently have, despite some very good studies. It needs an expanded ethnography which leaves the issue of ordination aside, and which also goes beyond the Weberian dichotomy of "the world" and "renouncing" it, and the resultant question (for example) of whether to use the terms "laicization" or "monasticization" to understand what is happening before our eyes. The lives and aspirations of the educated women we have described, the hopes and aims they have for themselves and their pupils, are not in any way usefully understood as matters of "the world" and what is "inside" or "outside" it: we have suggested that the category of *professionally celibate* women (and men), in the sense in which we use the terms, locates them in society quite accurately; and we have suggested, as a preliminary category at this stage of our understanding, that the various terms in Pali texts and contemporary vernaculars which refer to those who occupy such a social position might be gathered together under the heading of *Third Status(es)*, following existing models in the history of Christianity and modern Gender studies. Further ethnography, and further academic study of women in Buddhism, past and present, will one day need to go beyond that also.

Appendix 1: Terms for Non-monastic Ascetics in Pali Texts

Mae chi and almost all other Buddhists in Thailand look to the heritage of Pali texts as the centrally authoritative account of Buddhist teaching and history. It is for that reason that we collect data here from Pali, not because we regard the Pali tradition as uniquely privileged as a source of Buddhist history. Most modern scholars see the Pali Canon as the only one amongst probably a number which circulated, in various forms of Indo-Aryan language, in ancient India; but it is the only complete Buddhist Canon to survive. Later Pali literature was written in South and Southeast Asia. Pali texts are therefore only one of a number of resources, textual, epigraphical, archeological, etc., with which we might attempt to write Buddhist history. They have many terms translatable as *ascetic, celibate, renouncer, religieux* (*religieuse*), etc. They are often used grammatically in the unmarked masculine; sometimes the context shows that men or women are being specifically referred to. They can all also, on occasions, be used as synonyms for Buddhist *bhikkhu-s* and *bhikkhunī-s*. But often there are contexts in which a specifically Buddhist identity is either irrelevant or impossible; the latter is the case most obviously in *Jātaka* stories of previous lives of Gotama, set at times when there was no institution of Buddhism. They give a sense of the wider range of ascetic statuses within which Buddhists have situated their own *bhikkhu-s* and *bhikkhunī-s*. Here as everywhere in Pali more research is necessary. Feminine forms are noted where they occur.

brahmacariya often translated *celibacy* (*brahmacārin/brahmacārinī, celibate*), literally means *living as a Brahma* in one of the Brahma realms, located above the heavens where gods and goddesses, *deva-s* and *devī-s* live.[53] Unlike the gods and goddesses, these beings are ungendered, in the sense that they have no genitals (*liṅga*); they do, however, have the outward shape and physical form (*saṇṭhāna*) of men. The terms are applied metaphorically to all humans, of both genders, who live on earth a life of chastity.[54]

isi/isinī (Skt. *ṛṣi*), for which the standard translation is *seer*. In cases where the Buddhist *sāsana* does not exist, or is not relevant, the term *isi-pabbajjā* is used, for the act of renunciation.

muni, is often rendered silent sage, though it does not necessarily involve silence; lay and monastic forms are specifically differentiated; this word, and *yati*, are both used very widely as terms for ascetics, Buddhist and non-Buddhist.

muṇḍa(ka), bald, shaved, shaveling, is often used in a pejorative sense of male or female ascetics.

pabbajjā, going forth (from home to homelessness), *paribbājjaka/paribbājjikā, one who has gone forth.* These words are derived from the root *vraj*, which is simply a verb of motion, to *go*, *proceed*, etc., and which with the prefixes *pra* [*pa-* in Pali] or *pari-* have come to have a specific meaning indicating the act, or less often the state, of renunciation. It is also used, as noted above, in a narrower sense as a technical term for entry into the monastic order, as a novice.

samaṇa/samaṇī, it is perhaps best to render these words by the (deliberately vague) French terms current in English, *religieux/religieuse*. *Recluse*, *wanderer*, and other such terms are often used, but they are hardly self-explanatory. The word is from the root *śram* (thus Sanskrit *śramaṇa*), *to make an effort, to exert oneself.*

tapas, asceticism, ***tāpasa/tapasī***, ascetic. These terms need no exegesis for Asianists. Occasionally they refer to the extreme asceticism rejected by Gotama on his way to Buddhahood.

yogin/yoginī, the well-known pan-Asian term for *practitioner of yoga*, is found, in both general and specific senses (depending on the denotation of the concept of *yoga*); it can refer specifically to the practice of Buddhist meditation rather than having the general sense of "religious practice."

yogāvacara, also *practitioner of yoga*, is a term especially in need of research: it can refer to lay or monastic practitioners, male and female, and it seems to have had a special connection with the meditational and ritual practices which have recently led some scholars to refer to "tantric Theravāda."[55] The existence of such forms of Theravāda practice has been known at least since the text called "The Yogāvacara's Manual," and the translation entitled "The Manual of a Mystic" were published in 1896 and 1916 respectively by the Pali Text Society.[56]

Other terms also specify, as sub-categories, particular kinds of non-Buddhist ascetics, who can sometimes be identified as Jains or other historically-evidenced groups: ***acelaka-s*** are naked ascetics, ***jaṭila-s*** are matted-hair ascetics, ***ājīvika***, "one who lives a (specific, i.e. ascetic) lifestyle," can be a general term or a proper name.

Appendix 2: Vernacular Terms for Modern Professionally Celibate Women—"Third Status(es)"

The terms given here, culled from the ethnographic and other secondary literature available to us, can be nothing but an opening overview of work done mostly in relation to specific places. Much more work is needed. Our intention is to collect together in one place as many of this kind of name and status as we can, with accompanying bibliographical footnotes, as a source for future scholars to use and add to.

Nepal: "nuns", central to the twentieth-century revival of Theravāda, have been influenced by Burma (as, for example, in dress-style); they are called *anagārikā*, "homeless," or *gurumā*, "teacher-mother."[57]

Bangladesh: very little has been written on women and Buddhism.[58] The Insight Meditation (*vipassana*) teacher, Dipa Ma Barua, was born there, but after the age of 14 lived in Burma and later moved to Calcutta.[59]

Maharashtra: in **Dalit** Buddhism, feminist concerns are often very important, emerging especially in literature; anecdotal accounts tell of older women living in temples, but there have been no reports of specific institutional arrangements for celibate women, although some individual cases are reported, and some women were involved in the mass ordination of *bhikkhunī-s* at Bodh Gaya in 1998.[60] In the group known in Maharashtra as Trailokya Bauddha Mahāsangha Sahāyaka Gana (TBMSG), and elsewhere as the Friends of the Western Buddhist Order (FWBO), women of a certain status, who may be celibate, are called *dharmacārinī* (practitioner of Dharma).[61]

Sri Lanka: the most common term is *dasasilmātā* (10 Precept mother), although other terms, including *upāsikā*, are used; there are women seen, by themselves and others, as *bhikkhunī-s*.[62]

Burma: the most common term for nuns is *thilashin*, those who practice *sīla*, where the latter term refers specifically to the taking of the Eight or Ten Precepts.[63] There are very many such women in Burma, usually living in their own institutions and apart from monks. A smaller-scale male analogy is the *pothudaw*, males who wear white and live at monasteries serving monks and novices.[64] Contemporary practitioners of Vipassanā meditation, male and female, monastic and lay, are called *yogi*-s.[65] Some men (monastic or lay, but not women) are called *weikza*, from Pali *vijjā* (Sanskrit *vidyā*), "knowledge," meaning "magician" or "wizard" (the term is a shortening of *vijjādhara/vidyādhara*). They are defined by their aim to remain alive, often in the Himalayas, until the coming of the next Buddha Metteyya when they will attain final nirvana. Their practices can include standard Buddhist meditations, but they can also practice alchemy, inter aliaas a means to affect the necessary physical prolongation of their bodies.[66]

Thailand has been discussed the most, both in the western academy and within Thailand, where work on *mae chi* and others is often blended with feminism.[67] Much of the public awareness of "women and Buddhism" in Thailand has concerned the issue of ordination of women, from a previous status as *mae chi* or directly, as *sāmaṇerī-s* or *bhikkhunī-s*, and much of that has concerned the former professor of philosophy, Chatsumarn Kabilsingh, now known as Ven. Dhammananda, and her group at Wat Songdhammakalyani.[68] There are some reports of other claims to *samanerï* status.[69] As noted above, the word *chi/ji* can also be used of men; nuns have in the past also been called *nangjī*, but the term seems to have gone out of fashion. *Mae chi* art also called *maekhaw* (mother in white), which is a gender sub-category of *phakhaw*, "ascetic in white."[70] The figure of the *reusi* (Sanskrit *ṛṣi*, Pali *isī*), is very common, in stories and in paintings (where they are marked by their leopard-skin "uniform"), and is sometimes used of contemporary people (always male).[71] A range of what Hayashi calls "Ritual Specialists" (*mo*) are almost exclusively male and often ex-monks: thus a *motham* is a "secular (lay) monk."[72] The highly publicly-visible Dhammakaya (Thammakai) group, very modernist and very wealthy, was strongly influenced by the lay woman, Khun Yay; their publications refer to her as either Upāsikā or Ācariya (or both).[73] She taught a distinctive form of meditation adapted from that developed by the monk Luang Pho Wat Paknam (Phra Thepmuni).[74] Thammakai is often paired with a strikingly different group (both together as "sects" or "new Buddhist movements"), the Santi Asok, whose celibate and non-celibate followers have very strict, austere lifestyles, and are increasingly involved in sustainable-agriculture ecology projects.[75] Some women are called *sikkhamāt-s*, "Precept Mothers." They dress in brown robes, take 8 Precepts, and it is said that were it not for the Santi Asok rule that there must be at least one monk (ordained according to their own ritual) for each *sikkhamāt*, the women professional celibates in the movement would be far more numerous than men.[76]

Laos: where *mae chi* are also referred to as *maexin* or *mae khao*, "women in white," very little ethnography is available.[77]

Cambodia: the devastations of the twentieth century, especially during the Khmer Rouge years 1975–79, have caused great changes to the practices of everyday life, as also to the academic study of them. Some male ascetics are known by the word *tāpas(a)*; there is a type of spirit medium known as *grūpāramī* who can be male or female, monastic or lay.[78] Nuns are called *don chi (ṭūn ji), mae/nān ji or yāy ji.*[79] Before the Khmer Rouge era there were mostly older women, living and working in temples, who were not accorded great respect; there were a few younger women, sometimes called *silavati*, "Women (who have taken the) Precepts."[80] After the revival of Buddhism in 1979, there have been many older women in this role because of economic necessity; but there is also a movement of younger *don chee*, who look for legitimation not only to Buddhism but also to the international discourse of women's rights and to NGOs: the Heinrich Boll Foundation, for example, has sponsored the main *don chee* organization, the Association of Nuns and Lay Women of Cambodia (ANWLC), the younger nuns in which are focused on meditation, social work or both.[81]

Vietnam:[82] there is a small community of Theravāda Buddhists among the Khmer Khrom in the south; there are nuns, mostly it seems older women, in the traditional roles.

England: in the Theravāda group deriving from the Thai teacher Ajahn Chah (whose monks live in monasteries at Chithurst and Amaravati in the UK, women have the status of *anagārika* and *siladhārā*.[83]

Notes

[1] We are very grateful to Peter Skilling for comments on and criticism of an earlier draft. The article is based on fieldwork done by McDaniel between 1993 and 2007 (especially in 2006–07); he was accompanied in the summer of 2006 by Collins. The writing of thisarticle is a joint effort. Some themes were developed in Steven Collins, "Civilisation et la femmecélibataire," Series of (four) lectures at École pratique des hautes études, Paris (2006). We hope the article, the appendices, and the fairly comprehensive references within the notes, are intended to be an opening exploration into what is a complex and always-changing field.

[2] Rawe Htun, *The Modern Buddhist Nun* (Yangon: Parami Bookshop, 2001). Tessa Bartholomeusz, *Women under the Bo Tree: Buddhist Nuns in Sri Lanka* (Cambridge: Cambridge University Press, 1994). Peter Skilling, "Female Renunciants (nang chi) in Siam According to Early Travellers' Accounts," *Journal of the Siam Society* 83, nos. 1–2 (1995): 55–61.

[3] On Nepal, see Sarah Levine and David Gellner, *Rebuilding Buddhism: the Theravada Movement in Twentieth-Century Nepal* (Harvard: Harvard University Press, 2005).

[4] Richard F. Gombrich and Gananath Obeyesekere, *Buddhism Transformed: Religious Change in Sri Lanka* (Princeton: Princeton University Press, 1988). In earlier works, both these scholars explicitly used their interpretation of Weber in referring to this as "Protestant Buddhism" [see the critique of this term in John Holt, "Protestant Buddhism?," *Religious Studies Review* 17, no. 4 (1991): 307–12], but this has not been generalized beyond Sri Lanka and has now, rightly in our view, more or less disappeared from scholarly analysis.

[5] Gustaaf Houtman, "How a Foreigner invented 'Buddhendom' in Burmese: From Tha-Tha-Na to Bok-da' Ba-Tha," *Journal of the Anthropological Society of Oxford* 21, no. 2 (1990):113–28; Holt, "Protestant Buddhism?;" Joanne Cook, *Meditation and Monasticism: Making the Ascetic Self in Thailand* (Cambridge: Cambridge University Press, 2010).

[6] Historical research in this area could look to various kinds of "restraint" (*saṃvara*) which can be practiced by laity and monastics alike, and which would not map directly on to that dichotomy.

[7] On Weber, Buddhism and anthropology, see David Gellner, *The Anthropology of Buddhism and Hinduism: Weberian Themes* (New York: Oxford University Press, 2001); Charles Keyes, "Weber and Anthropology," *Annual Review of Anthropology* 31 (2002): 233–55.

[8] Max Weber, *From Max Weber: Essays in Sociology*, ed. H.H. Gerth and C. Wright Mills (London: Routledge and Kegan Paul, 1948).

[9] Steven Collins, "Monasticism, Utopias and Comparative Social Theory," *Religion* 18, no. 5 (1988): 103–6. Justin McDaniel, *The Lovelorn Ghost and the Magical Monk: Practicing Buddhism in Modern Thailand* (New York: Columbia University Press, 2011).

[10] We give the Pali forms; see the opening remarks in Appendix 1.

[11] Steven Collins, *Selfless Persons: Imagery and Thought in Theravada Buddhism* (Cambridge: Cambridge University Press, 1982), pp. 167–76.

[12] O. von Hinüber and K.R. Norman, eds., *Dhammapada* (Oxford: Pali Text Society, 1995). Translation has been done on our own.

[13] On these and other Buddhist terms, many in gendered pairs, see Peter Skilling, "Nuns, Laywomen, Donors, Goddesses: Female Roles in Early Indian Buddhism," *Journal of the International Association of Buddhist Studies* 24, no. 2 (2001): 241–74.

[14] Nancy Eberhardt, *Imagining the Course of Life: Self-transformation in a Shan Buddhist Community* (Honolulu: University of Hawaii Press, 2006).

[15] These terms are from *samaṇa*: see Appendix 1.

[16] The Monastic Rule (*Vinaya*) specifies that male novices should be 15-years-old, and females 12; but there is an exception for boys younger than 15 who are "able to scare crows" (*Vinaya* I 79). This may be a reference to the importunate behavior of crows in South Asia; or it might refer to a boy who is old

enough to be employed as a field-watcher (*khettagopaka*) . In any case, boys younger than 15 are standardly initiated as novices in contemporary South and Southeast Asia.

[17]   It is possible that this stage was meant to ensure that no pregnant women could become nuns by subterfuge, but texts seem not to give explicit reasons why the status was necessary.

[18]   See http://www.congress-on-buddhist-women.org/ [accessed 4 March 2010]. On Thailand, see Martin Seeger, "The Bhikkhunï-ordination controversy in Thailand," *Journal of the International Association of Buddhist Studies* 29, no. 1 (2006): 155–83.

[19]   This was reported very clearly in one of the earliest treatments of modern "nuns," on Sri Lanka: Lowell Bloss, "The Female Renunciants of Sri Lanka: the Dasasilmattawa," *Journal of the International Association of Buddhist Studies* 10, no. 1 (1987): 1–31; see on Thailand, Barbara Kameniar, "Rurality, Ordination Debates and Thai Mae Chi." Paper presented at the Hamburg International Congress on Buddhist Women's Role in the Sangha (2007); on Burma, Hiroko Kawanami, "The Bhikkhunï Ordination Debate: Global Aspirations, Local Concerns, with special emphasis on the views of the monastic community in Burma," *Buddhist Studies Review* 24, no. 2 (2007): 226–44.

[20]   Thus, a phrase cited in one French dictionary (http://atilf.atilf.fr/tlf.htm, accessed 4 March 2010) calls a previously married man, with children, *un vieuxcélibataire coureur*, "an old celibate womanizer," which is self-contradictory in modern English; conversely in English one can speak of a married couple *practicing celibacy*, which makes no sense in French.

[21]   Deborah Wong, *Sounding the Center: History and Aesthetics in Thai Buddhist Performance* (Chicago: University of Chicago Press, 2001); Teri Schaeffer Yamada, "The Spirit Cult of KhlaengMoeung in Long Beach, California," in *History, Buddhism and New Religious Movements in Cambodia*, ed. John Marston and Elizabeth Guthrie (Honolulu: University of Hawaii Press, 2004).

[22]   Standard reference works are: *Encyclopedia Britannica* s.v. monasticism; Catholic Encyclopedia (e.g. http://www.newadvent.org/cathen/14637b.htm, accessed 4 March 2010) s.v. Third Orders and Tertiaries; W. Johnston, ed., *Encyclopedia of Monasticism* (London: Routledge, 2000) s.v. Lay Brothers and Lay Sisters.

[23]   Gilbert Herdt, *Third Sex, third Gender: Beyond Sexual Dimorphism in Culture and History* (New York: Zone Books, 1994).

[24]   For Thailand, see Peter Jackson and Nerida Cook, eds., *Genders and Sexualities in Modern Thailand* (Chiang Mai: Silkworm Books, 1999); Peter Jackson, "Performative Genders, Perverse Desires: A Bio-History of Thailand's Same-Sex and Transgender Cultures,"*Intersections: Gender, History and Culture in the Asian Context*, Vol. 9 (August 2003) (http://intersections.anu. edu.au/issue9/jacks0n. html, accessed 4 March 2010); Megan J. Sinnott, *Toms and Dees: Transgender Identity and Female Same-sex Relationships in Thailand* (Honolulu: University of Hawaii Press, 2004).

[25]   Patricia A. McBroom, *The Third Sex: The New Professional Woman* (New York: W. Morrow, 1986).

[26]   For India, see Gregory Schopen, "On Monks, Nuns and 'Vulgar' Practices: The Introduction of the Image Cult into Indian Buddhism," in *Bones, Stones, and Buddhist Monks: Collected Papers on the Archaeology, Epigraphy, and Texts of Monastic Buddhism in India* (Honolulu: University of Hawaii Press, 1997 [1989]); "The Suppression of Nuns and the Ritual Murder of their Special Dead," in *Buddhist Monks and Business Matters: Still More Papers on Monastic Buddhism in India* (Honolulu: University of Hawaii Press, 2004 [1996]); Peter Skilling, "Nuns, Laywomen, Donors, Goddesses;" "A Note on the History of the Bhikkhunï-sangha (I): Nuns at the Time of the Buddha," *World Fellowship of Buddhists Review* XXX, no. 4 and XXXI, no. 1 (1993–94 double issue): 47–55; "A Note on the History of the Bhikkhunï-sangha (II): The Order of Nuns after the Parinirvana," *World Fellowship of Buddhists Review* XXXI, no. 1 (1994): 29–49. For Sri Lanka, see R.A.L.H. Gunawardana, *Robe and Plough: Monasticism and Economic Interest in Early Medieval Sri Lanka* (Tucson: University of Arizona Press, 1979); "Subtile Silk of Ferreous Firmness: Buddhist Nuns in Ancient and Early Medieval Sri Lanka and their Role in the Propagation of Buddhism," *Sri Lanka Journal of the Humanities* 14, nos. 1–2 (1990): 1–59.

[27] For archaeology see, for example, J. Stargardt, "The Oldest Known Pali Texts, 5th–6th century; Results of the Cambridge Symposium on the Pyu Golden Pali Text from Sri Ksetra,"*Journal of the Pali Text Society* XXI (1995): 199–214; Peter Skilling, "The Advent of Theravāda Buddhism to Mainland Southeast Asia,"*Journal of the International Association of Buddhist Studies* 20, no. 1 (1997): 93–108; Ian Harris, *Cambodian Buddhism: History and Practice* (Honolulu: University of Hawaii Press, 2005) reconsiders the evidence from Cambodia. John Strong, *The Legend and Cult of Upagupta: Sanskrit Buddhism in North India and Southeast Asia* (Princeton: Princeton University Press, 1992); François Lagirarde, "Gavampati-Kaccäyana: le culte et la légende du disciple ventripotent dans le Bouddhisme des Thaïs," Thèsedoctorat (2 vols.), Paris, Ecole Pratique des Hautes Etudes, La Sorbonne, 2001; and Elizabeth Guthrie, "A Study of the History and the Cult of the Buddhist Earth Deity in Mainland Southeast Asia" (2 vols.), PhD thesis, University of Canterbury, New Zealand, 2003, together prove incontrovertibly that there was a cultural conduit from the Sanskritic traditions of northern India to Southeast Asia, quite separate from the textual and monastic lineage traditions which brought "Theravāda" from Sri Lanka in the second millennium AD.

[28] Nuns are said to have existed in Burma, but this is probably a mistake; there is evidence for female asceticism from Cambodia (an inscription and some Chinese travel accounts), but it is not clear what the institutional arrangements might have been: see Skilling, "A Note on the History of the Bhikkhunī-saṅgha (II)."

[29] For example, the *Thengathā* and *Therī-apadana* contain verses attributed to nuns at the time of the Buddha; the Pali historical work *Dīpavaṃsa*, written in Sri Lanka, refers a great deal to nuns, and has been thought to have been written by one or more of them. But these attributions are based solely on internal evidence from the texts themselves. For surveys of what is known about these and other Pali texts, see K.R. Norman, "Pali Literature," in *A History of Indian Literature*, ed. J. Gonda, vol. VII, fasc. 2 (Wiesbaden: Harrasowitz, 1983); and Oskar von Hinüber, *A Handbook of Pali Literature* (Berlin: de Gruyter, 1996).

[30] Olivier de Bernon, "Chi (jī), un mot d'originekhmèreen usage dans la langue thaïe, consideré à tort commed'originesanskrite," *Journal of the Siam Society* 84, no. 1 (1996): 87–90.

[31] One very important desideratum in the study of language used in this context is the kinds of pronoun used, and related forms of self- and other denotation, which vary according to the statuses of speaker and/or hearer; and also what do the lexicons drawn on: in Thai there is an extensive range of words used specifically of monks. Are they (ever) used of *mae chi*? We cannot enter into this issue here; and it is almost wholly lacking in the existing ethnographies: but see Hiroko Kawanami, "The Religious Standing of Burmese Nuns (*thilá-shin*): The Ten Precepts and Religious Respect Words," *Journal of the International Association of Buddhist Studies* 13, no. 1 (1990): 17–40.

[32] For example, reporting from the early 1990s, Stephen Sparkes, *Spirits and Souls: Gender and Cosmology in an Isan Village in Northeast Thailand* (Bangkok: White Lotus Press, 2005), esp. pp. 144–50; cf. Penny van Esterik, "Laywomen in Theravāda Buddhism," pp. 44–5, in *Women of Southeast Asia*, ed. P. van Esterik (Northern Illinois University, Center for Southeast Asian Studies, Monograph Series on Southeast Asia, Occasional Paper no. 17, 2 ed., 1996).

[33] Nerida Cook, "The Position of Nuns in Thai Buddhism: The Parameters of Religious Recognition." MA Thesis, Australian National University, 1981 is often cited, and is very useful, but unfortunately it is not widely available; likewise difficult to access are Anne Radcliffe, "Les femmes dans le Bouddhisme Thailandais: une étude sur la communauté des nonnes de Wat Chaina à Nakhon Sri Thammarat" (Paris: École pratique des hautes études, IVe section, Science Historiques et Philologiques, 1985), and Barbara Kameniar, "Shifting the Focus: a small group of Thai maechii in a semi-rural wat." Master of Education thesis, University of South Australia, 1993, both of which are unusual in describing the South, Nakhon Sri Thammarat and a village near Hua Hin respectively; Faith Adiele, *Meeting Faith: The Forest Journals of A Black Buddhist Nun* (New York: Norton, 2004, reprinted as a paperback in 2005 with the new sub-title *An Inward Odyssey*, with an author's statement); Sid Brown, *The Journey of One Buddhist Nun:*

Even Against the Wind (New York: State University of New York Press, 2001); J. Cook, *Meditation and Monasticism*; John van Esterik, "Women Meditation Teachers in Thailand", in *Women in Southeast Asia*, ed. P. van Esterik; Monika Lindberg Falk, *Making Fields of Merit: Buddhist Nuns and Gendered Orders in Thailand* (Critical Dialogues in Southeast Asian Studies, University of Washington Press, 2007); Marjorie Muecke, "Female Sexuality in Thai Discourses about Maechii ('lay nuns')," *Culture, Health & Sexuality* 6, no. 3 (2004): 221–38; Tomomi Ito, "Dhammamātā: Buddhadāsa Bhikkhu's notion of motherhood in Buddhist women practitioners," *Journal of Southeast Asian Studies* 38, no. 3 (2007): 409–32. On the lay teacher Khun Mae Siri Krinchai, see Donald K. Swearer, *The Buddhist World of Southeast Asia* (New York: State University Press of New York, 1995), pp. 143–4; and on Upasika Lee Nanayon, seeThanissaro Bhikkhu, "Upasika Lee Nanayon and the Social Dynamic of Theravādin Buddhist Practice" (1995), www.accesstoinsight.org/lib/thai/kee/dynamic.html [accessed 4 March 2010]; and Upasika Lee Nanayon, *Pure and Simple: The Buddhist Teachings of a Thai Laywoman* (Boston: Wisdom Publications, 2005).

34 For example, David Gosling, "Thai monks and lay Nuns (maechii) in urban health care,"*Anthropology & Medicine* 5, no. 1 (1998): 5–21; cf. various essays in Ellison Banks Findly, ed., *Women's Buddhism, Buddhism's Women: Tradition, Revision, Renewal* (Boston: Wisdom Publications, 2000); and Karma LeksheTsomo, ed., *Innovative Buddhist Women: Swimming Against the Stream* (Richmond: Curzon, 2000); Karma Lekshe Tsomo, ed., *Buddhist Women and Social Justice: Ideals, Challenges and Achievements* (New York: State University of New York Press, 2004); Karma Lekshe Tsomo, ed., *Out of the Shadows: Socially Engaged Buddhist Women* (Delhi: Sri Satguru, 2006).

35 Searching the web will find many sites, and there is a 2004 DVD: Victoria Holt, *A Walk of Wisdom: True Beauty Comes from the Heart* (www.walkofwisdom.com, accessed 4 March 2010), but there seems to be no article-length academic treatment in English; brief notes are given in Findly, ed., *Women's Buddhism, Buddhism's Women*, pp. 300–1; in Seeger, "The Bhikkhunī-ordination controversy in Thailand;" and in Tsomo, ed., *Buddhist Women and Social Justice*, pp. 186–8.

36 Brown, *The Journey of One Buddhist Nun*; Monika Lindberg Falk, "Thammacarini Witthaya: The First Buddhist School for Girls in Thailand," in *Innovative Buddhist women*, ed. Tsomo; Falk, *Making Fields of Merit*.

37 Tomomi Ito, "Buddhist Women in Dhamma Practice in Contemporary Thailand: Movements regarding their Status as World Renouncers," *The Journal of Sophia Asian Studies* 17 (1999): 147–81; Karma Lekshe Tsomo, "Khunying Kanittha: Thailand's Advocate for Women," in *Buddhist Women and Social Justice,* ed. Tsomo.

38 Penny van Esterik, "Laywomen in Theravāda Buddhism;" also her *Materializing Thailand* (Oxford: Berg, 2000); Khin Thitsa, "Nuns, Mediums and prostitutes in Chiengmai," *Women and Development in Southeast Asia*, Paper No. 1 (University of Kent, Canterbury, 1983); Mary Beth Mills, *Thai Women in the Global Labor Force: Consuming Desires, Contested Selves* (New Jersey: Rutgers University Press, 1999); Sinith Sittirak, *The Daughters of Development* (London: Zed Books, 1998); Susanne Thorbek, *Gender and Slum Culture in Urban Asia* (London: Zed Books, 1994); Ara Wilson, *The Intimate Economies of Bangkok: Tomboys, Tycoons, and Avon Ladies in the Global City* (Oakland: University of California Press, 2004); Virada Somswadi and Alycia Nicholas (n.d. but post-2003), *A Collation of Articles on Thai Women and Buddhism* (Thailand: Chiang Mai University, Women's Studies Center, cmu_wsc@hotmail.com); Sanitsuda Ekachai, *Keeping the Faith: Thai Buddhism at the Crossroads* (Bangkok: Post Publishing, 2001).

39 James Ockey, *Making Democracy: Leadership, Class, Gender, and Political Participation in Thailand* (Honolulu: University of Hawaii Press, 2005); Kazuki Iwanaga, ed., *Women and Politics in Thailand. Continuity and Change* (Denmark: Nordic Institute of Asian Studies, 2008). As both cause and effect of this, marriage patterns are changing, with the mean age at marriage later and more women remaining single: see Tan JooEan, "Living Arrangements of Never-Married Thai Women in a Time of Rapid Social Change," *Sojourn* 17, no. 1 (2002): 24–51; Gavin W. Jones, "The 'Flight From Marriage' in South-East and East Asia," *Journal of Comparative Family Studies* 36, no. 1 (2005): 93–119. A brief comparative note:

whereas in Europe and North America the numbers of Catholic nuns have been steadily falling in the modern world, and especially since Vatican II in the 1960s, they have to the contrary been rising in other parts of the world: see Helen Rose Ebaugh, Jon Laurence and Janet Saltzman Chafetz, "The Growth and Decline of the Population of Catholic Nuns Cross-Nationally, 1960–1990: A Case of Secularization as Social Structural Change," *Journal for the Scientific Study of Religion* 35, no. 2 (1996): 171–83; Rebecca Lester, *Jesus in our Wombs: Embodying Modernity in a Mexican Convent* (Oakland: University of California Press, 2005) on Mexican Catholics; and Pieternella van Doorn-Harder, *Contemporary Coptic Nuns* (Columbia: University of South Carolina Press, 1995) on Coptic Christians in Egypt, provide evidence that the increased number of vocations are in part at least due to an articulated desire to find another vocation apart from the two alternatives of traditional mother and homemaker versus modern business-woman.

[40] Steven Collins, *Nirvana and other Buddhist Felicities: utopias of the Pali imaginaire* (Cambridge: Cambridge University Press, 1998), chapter 1; Rupert Gethin, *The Foundations of Buddhism* (Oxford: Oxford University Press, 1998), Chapter 8.

[41] In Thai by McDaniel, with Collins present; they were followed up or conducted by McDaniel later in 2006 and in 2007.

[42] Yoneo Ishii, *Sangha, State and Society: Thai Buddhism in History* (Honolulu: University of Hawaii Press, 1986); cf. Ven. Khammai Dhammasami, "Idealism and Pragmatism: A dilemma in the current monastic education systems of Burma and Thailand," in *Buddhism, Power and Political Order*, ed. Ian Harris (London: Routledge, 2007).

[43] According to national statistics, less than one per cent monks achieve even level seven or eight.

[44] Her only publication in English is Supaphan Na Bangchang, "A Pali letter sent by the Aggamahāsenāpati of Siam to the Royal Court at Kandy in 1756" [with English summary], *Journal of the Pali Text Society* XII (1988): 185–212; just one example of her extensive work in Thai and/or Thai script is the very fine grammar, using material from pre-modern grammarians in Southeast Asia, *Waiyakon Pali: Tarn naeo Kaccāyanavyākaraṇa Moggalānavyākaraṇa Saddanītipakaraṇa* (Bangkok: Mahamakut Ratchwithyalai, 2534 = 1991).

[45] 2006 statistics show: *Bachelors*: 201 students, of whom some of the top *mae chi* are: M.C. Kannikar Ruamchit (Wat Khao Bo Nam Sap), 99.2 per cent; M.C. Duangchai Kanchanachan (no wat), 98.4 per cent; M.C. Anumak Bunloi (no wat), 97.6 per cent; M.C. Rochanani Bhotranan (Wat Rampoeng, Chiang Mai), 91.2 per cent; M.C. Somchai Pueangkaeo (Wat Khao Bo Nam Sap,) 89 per cent. *Master's*: (1st in class) M.C. Narumol Wothiphatphisal (no wat), 100 per cent; (2nd in class) M.C. Manimakhonkhon (Wat Nong Lamduan), 100 per cent; (3rd in class) Suphaphan Na Bang Chang (no wat), 99.2 per cent; M.C. Kanchaphon Srinatha (Wat Nong Lamduan), 98.4 per cent. There were not many *mae chi* in the PhD program, but some of them were among the best, such as (3rd in her class) M.C. Paphanakon Lohanimit (Hong Rian Phra That Sri), 100 per cent. From a total number of 760 students, 405 completed the course and took the examination: 98 monks, 51 *mae chi*, 32 novices, 224 lay people (of whom 80 per cent were women).

[46] This is a term for the scholarly approach to the *Dhamma*, in the standard sequence *pariyatti* (study), *paṭipatti* (practice) and *paṭivedha* (understanding).

[47] Historically there is in fact no such thing as a Mahāyāna monk or Vinaya lineages in Buddhism derived from Indian, "Hīnayāna" initiation in so-called Mahāyāna countries is complexly related to those of a Bodhisattva, which are taken by laity, monks and nuns."Mahāyāna" is standard in contemporary Thai discussions of the issue.

[48] Mae Chi Kritsana and McDaniel already had a working relationship because he had lived in her home village and they spoke Thai with similar Isan accents. An abstract of her paper "The Thai Buddhist Nuns Institute and its Work in Thailand" (2006, 9th International Conference of Sakyadhita) is at http://www.sakyadhita.0rg/9th/schedule.html [accessed 4 March 2010].

[49] This text is translated in Bhikkhu Bodhi (gen. ed.), *A Comprehensive Manual of Abhidhamma* (Seattle: BPS Pariyatti Editions, 2000); and R.P. Wijeratne andRupert Gethin, *Summary of the Topics of Abhidhamma and Exposition of the Topics of Abhidhamma* (Oxford: Pali Text Society, 2002).

[50] In 2006 and 2007, McDaniel visited Samnak Santisuk four times, and interviewed several *mae chi* who had passed higher level Pali examinations.

[51] Bibliography on the Dhammakaya (Thammakai) can be found in the remarks on Thailand in Appendix 2.

[52] In fact throughout Thailand the practical possibility as well as the legitimacy of *mae chi* going on the traditional morning alms-round is much disputed, as is the related issue of whether giving (*dana*) to them produces merit. Cook, *Meditation and Monasticism*, deals with the position of the *mae chi* she studied in networks and hierarchies of giving and merit-making.

[53] Collins, *Nirvana and other Buddhist Felicities*, pp. 297ff.

[54] Buddhadatta, *English-Pali Dictionary* (London: Pali Text Society, 1955), gives this term for "celibate," and also coins the neologism *avivahakattā*, "the state of non-marriage."

[55] For criticism of this phrase see McDaniel, *The Lovelorn Ghost and the Magical Monk*, Chapter 3.

[56] The main work, with Khmer and Pali materials, is by François Bizot and his associates; a good guide is Kate Crosby, "Tantric Theravāda: A Bibliographic Essay on the Writings of François Bizot and Others on the Yogāvacara Tradition," *Contemporary Buddhism* 1, no. 2 (2000): 141–98.

[57] Sarah Levine, "At the Cutting Edge: Theravāda Nuns in the Kathmandu Valley," in *Innovative Buddhist Women*, ed. K.L. Tsomo; and Levine and Gellner, *Rebuilding Buddhism*.

[58] Karma LeksheTsomo, "Factions and Fortitude: Buddhist Women in Bangladesh," in *Innovative Buddhist Women*, ed. Tsomo; see also http://www.congress-on-buddhist-women.org/index. php?id=44 [accessed 4 March 2010].

[59] Amy Schmidt, "Transformation of a Housewife: Dipa Ma Barua and her Teachings to Theravāda Women," in *Women's Buddhism, Buddhism's Women*, ed. Findly; Schmidt, *Dipa Ma: The Life and Legacy of a Buddhist Master* (New York: Bluebridge, 2005).

[60] Johannes Beltz, *Mahar, Buddhist, and Dalit: Religious Conversion and Socio-political Emancipation* (New Delhi: Manohar, 2005), pp. 199–203; Yuchen Li, "Ordination, Legitimacy, and Sisterhood: The International Full Ordination Ceremony in Bodhgaya," in *Innovative Buddhist Women*, ed. Tsomo; Owen M. Lynch, "Sujāta's Army: Dalit Buddhist Women and Self-Emancipation," in *Women's Buddhism, Buddhism's Women*, ed. Findly; and Eleanor Zelliott, "Religious Leadership Among Maharashtrian Women," in *Women's Buddhism, Buddhism's Women*, ed. Findly.

[61] Alan Sponberg, "TBMSG: A Dhamma Revolution in Contemporary India," in *Engaged Buddhism: Buddhist Liberation Movements in Asia*, ed. Christopher S. Queen and Sallie B. King (New York: State University of New York Press, 1996); Padmasuri, *But Little Dust: Life amongst the "Ex-untouchable" Buddhists of India* (Birmingham: Windhorse Publications, 1997) is an autobiography by an FWBO woman. In the TBMSG the Pali form *dhammacārinī* is preferred. Both words are often used without diacritics.

[62] Two articles by Nirmala Salgado discuss terms and give references to earlier work: "Religious Identities of Buddhist Nuns: Training Precepts, Renunciant Attire and Nomenclature in Theravāda Buddhism," *Journal of the American Academy of Religion* 72, no. 4 (2004): 935–53, and "Eight Revered Conditions: Ideological Complicity, Contemporary Reflections and Practical Realities," *Journal of Buddhist Ethics* 15 (2008): 177–213. See also Suzanne Mrozik, "A Robed Revolution: The Contemporary Buddhist Nun's (*Bhikkhunī*) Movement," *Religion Compass* 3, no. 3 (2009): 360–78. Significant earlier treatments are Bloss, "The Female Renunciants of Sri Lanka;" and Elisabeth Nissan, "Recovering Practice: Buddhist Nuns in Sri Lanka," *South Asia Research* 4, no. 1 (1984): 32–49; George Bond, *The Buddhist Revival in Sri Lanka: Religious Tradition, Reinterpretation and Response* (Columbia: University of South Carolina Press, 1988), pp. 67–8, 178–87; Nirmala Salgado, "Ways of Knowing and Transmitting Knowledge: Case

Studies of Theravāda Buddhist Nuns," *Journal of the International Association of Buddhist Studies* 19, no. 1 (1996): 61–80, and "Sickness, healing, and religious vocation: Alternative choices at a Theravāda Buddhist nunnery," *Ethnology* 36, no. 3 (1997): 212–27; Helle Snell, *Buddhist Women Meditators of Sri Lanka* (Kandy: Buddhist Publication Society, 2001). Book-length treatments are found in Bartholomeusz, *Women Under the Bo Tree;* and in Wei-yu Cheng, *Buddhist Nuns in Taiwan and Sri Lanka, Critical Studies in Buddhism* (London: Routledge Curzon, 2007).

63 See Ingrid Jordt, "Bhikkhuni, Thilashin, Mae-chii: Women who Renounce the World in Burma, Thailand and Classical Pali Buddhist Texts," *Crossroads: An Interdisciplinary Journal of Southeast Asian Studies* 4, no. 1 (1988): 31–9; Jordt, "Women's Practices of Renunciation in the Age of Säsana Revival," in *Burma at the Turn of the 21st Century*, ed. Monique Skidmore (Honolulu: University of Hawaii Press, 2005); Hiroko Kawanami, *Worldly Renunciation: the World of Burmese Buddhist Nuns* (ms.), "The Religious Standing of Burmese Buddhist Nuns," *Journal of the International Association of Buddhist Studies*13, no. 1 (1990): 17–40; "Kawanami/Patterns of Renunciation: the Changing World of Burmese Nuns", in *Women's Buddhism, Buddhism's Women*, ed. Findly and "Can Women be Celibate?: Sexuality and Abstinence in Theravāda Buddhism," in *Celibacy, Culture and Society*, ed. E.J. Sobo and S. Bell (Madison: University of Wisconsin Press, 2001); Htun, *The Modern Buddhist Nun*, was a limited-edition pamphlet—we are grateful to Alicia Turner for supplying a copy.

64 E. Michael Mendelson (ed. John P. Ferguson), *Sangha and state in Burma: a study of monastic sectarianism and leadership* (Ithaca: Cornell University Press, 1975), p. 120.

65 Ingrid Jordt, "Women's Practices of Renunciation," and *Burma's Mass Lay Meditation Movement: Buddhism and the Cultural Construction of Power* (Athens: Ohio University Press, 2007).

66 Patrick Pranke, "On Becoming a Buddhist Wizard," in *Buddhism in Practice*, ed. Donald Lopez (Princeton: Princeton University Press, 1995), pp. 343–58; Guillaume Rozenberg, *Renoncement et puissance: la quête de la sainteté dans la Birmaniecontemporaine* (Geneva: Editions Olizane, 2005).

67 For example: various essays in *Women's Buddhism, Buddhism's Women*, ed. Findly; and in *Innovative Buddhist Women*, ed. Tsomo; Thitsa, "Nuns, Mediums and Prostitutes in Chiengmai;" "Ekachai Keeping the Faith;" Somswadiand Nicholas, *A Collation of Articles on Thai Women and Buddhism.*

68 See the website www.thaibhikkhunis.org [accessed 4 March 2010]. Bhikkhum Dhammananda, *Bhikkhuni: The Reflection of Gender in Thai Society* (Chiang Mai: University of Chiang Mai Women's Study Center, 2004). Under her former lay name, Chatsumarn Kabilsingh, she published the influential *Thai Women in Buddhism* (Berkeley: Parallex Press, 1991). Her wat was first owned by Voramai Kabilsingh, Chatsumarn's mother, the first modern Thai woman to claim ordained status: see Martine Batchelor, "Voramai Kabilsingh: the First Thai Bhikkhum, and Chatsumarn Kabilsingh: Advocate for a Bhikkhum Sangha in Thailand," in *Women's Buddhism, Buddhism's Women*, ed. Findly.

69 Rachelle Scott, in *Nirvana for Sale?: Buddhism, Wealth and the Dhammakaya Templein Contemporary Thailand* (New York: State University of New York Press, 2009), and pers. comm., recounts an apparently short-lived attempt to use the status of *samaṇerī*, and the word "ordain" (*buat*) at the Dhammakaya temple in 1999; see also Bangkok Post Homepage: Phra Dhammakaya Temple Controversy, 9 February 1999. Ayako Itoh (pers. comm.) has told us of an event at a temple near Chiang Mai at which apparently quite a number of women received *sāmaneri* initiation in 2008; this was done, she says, given a promise by the women never to ask for *bhikkhuni* initiation. We await Ms Itoh's ethnography and further reports.

70 Kamala Tiyanavich, *Forest Recollections: Wandering Monks in Twentieth-Century Thailand* (Chiang Mai: Silkworm Press, 1997); and *The Buddha in the Jungle* (Chiang Mai: Silkworm Press, 2003).

71 Paul Cohen, "Buddhism Unshackled: The Yuan 'Holy Man' Tradition and the Nation-State in the Tai World," *Journal of Southeast Asian Studies* 32, no. 2 (2001): 227–47.

72 Yukio Hayashi, *Practical Buddhism among the Thai-Lao: Religion in the Making of a Region* (Kyoto Studies on Asia, Center for Southeast Asian Studies, Kyoto University, vol. 5, 2003); Barend J. Terwiel,

Monks and Magic: An Analysis of Religious Ceremonies in Central Thailand (3rd edition) (Bangkok: White Lotus, 1994).

73 Marja-Leena Heikkilä-Horn, "Two Paths to Revivalism in Thai Buddhism: The Dhammakaya and Santi Asoke Movements," *Témenos* 32 (1996): 93–111, calls her a *mae chi*, though here one should perhaps use quotes, as in "nun."

74 Scott, *Nirvana for Sale?*; Rachelle Scott, "'First Among Disciples - Second to None': Khun Yay and the Re-envisioning of Buddhist Nuns in Thailand," University of Tennessee Inaugural Lecture, February 2004; Catherine Newell, "Monks, Meditation and Missing links: continuity and authority in the Thai Sangha" (DPhil thesis, SOAS, University of London, 2008).

75 Peter Jackson, *Buddhism, Legitimation and Conflict: The Political Functions of Urban Thai Buddhism* (Singapore: Institute of Southeast Asian Studies, 1989); James Taylor, "New Buddhist Movements in Thailand: An 'individualistic revolution', reform and political dissonance," *Journal of Southeast Asian Studies* 21, no. 1 (1990): 135–54; Donald K. Swearer, "Fundamentalists Movements in Theravāda Buddhism," in *Fundamentalisms Observed*, ed. M. Marty and R.S. Appleby (Chicago: University of Chicago Press, 1991); Apinya Fuengfusakul, "Empire of Crystal and Utopian Commune: Two Types of contemporary Theravāda reform in Thailand," *Sojourn* 8 (1993): 153–83; Rory Mackenzie, *New Buddhist Movements in Thailand: Towards an understanding of Wat Phra Dhammakāya and Santi Asoke* (London: Routledge, 2007).

76 Marja-Leena Heikkilä-Horn, *Santi Asok Buddhism and Thai State Response* (Abo Akademis Forlag, 1996), pp. 154–8 gives a biography of one *sikkhamāt*. See also Juliana Essen, *Right Development: The Santi Asoke Buddhist Reform Movement of Thailand* (Lanham: Lexington Books, 2005).

77 Ruth M. Krulfeld, "Buddhism, Maintenance and Change: Reinterpreting Gender in a Lao refugee Community," in *Reconstructing Lives, Recapturing Meaning: Refugee Identity, Gender, and Culture Change*, ed. Linda A. Camino and Ruth M. Krulfeld (Basel: Gordon and Breach, 1994) depicts an unconventional nun (whom she calls a *mei khaw*) in the US Lao community, referred to by some as a "lady-monk." Male novices in Thailand are sometimes called "boy-monks."

78 John Marston, "Clay into Stone: A Modern-Day Tapas," in *History, Buddhism and New Religious Movements*, ed. Marston and Guthrie; and Didier Bertrand, "A Medium Possession Practice and Its Relationship with Cambodian Buddhism: The Gru Parami," in *History, Buddhism and New Religious Movements*, ed. Marston and Guthrie.

79 Hema Goonatilleke, "Rediscovering Cambodian Buddhist Women of the Past," in *Innovative Buddhist Women*, ed. Tsomo; and Heike Löschmann, "The Revival of the Don Chee Movement in Cambodia," in *Innovative Buddhist Women*, ed. Tsomo; Elizabeth Guthrie, "Khmer Buddhism, Female Asceticism, and Salvation," in *History, Buddhism and New Religious Movements*, ed. Marston and Guthrie.

80 André Bareau, "Quelquesermitages et centres de méditation Bouddhiques au Cambodge," *Bulletin de l'écolefrançaise d'extreme-orient*, tome 56 (1969): 11–28.

81 Aing Songkreun, "Defining Difference: Don Chee and Mae Chee in Cambodia and Thailand," *Siksācakr* 8 (2006): 1–14. There are various websites: for example, http//www.hbfasia.org/southeastasia/thailand/projects/anlwc.htm [accessed 4 March 2010]. The Khmer-Buddhist Educational Assistance project includes nuns: see http//www.keap-net.org/project/education.htm [accessed 4 March 2010].

82 http:/www.buddhismtoday.com/english/vietnam/figure/ooi -bhikkhuni.htm [accessed 4 March 2010] describes both Theravāda and "Mendicant" nuns (*tu nu*); cf. http://www.parami.org/duta/vietnam.htm [accessed 4 March 2010].

83 Sandra Bell, "Being Creative With Tradition: Rooting Theravāda Buddhism in Britain," *Global Buddhism* 1 (2000): 1–30 (http://www. globalbuddhism.org/toc.html, accessed 4 March 2010). Jane Anne Sarah Angeli, "Women in Brown: A history of the order of siladhārā, nuns of the English Forest Sangha" (MA, Buddhist Studies, University of Sunderland, 2005).

Bibliography

Abbreviations for the titles of Pali texts are from the Epilegomena of the Critical Pali Dictionary (CPD).

Adams, Parveen. 2006. "Out of Sight, Out of Body: The Sugimoto/Demand Effect." *Grey Room* 22 (Winter): 86–104. doi: 10.1162/152638106775434422.

Akadet Khrisanathilok. 2006/2549. *Phra Somdet: Nangseu phra kruang thi mi neua ha sara lae wichakan.* 3 vols. Bangkok.

Akiko Iij ima. 2002. "The Nyuan in Xayabury and cross-border links to Nan." In *Contesting Visions of the Lao Past*, ed. Christopher Goscha and Søren Ivarsson. Copenhagen: Nordic Institute of Asian Studies.

Allott, Anna J. 2000. "Continuity and Change in the Burmese Literary Canon." In *The Canon in Southeast Asian Literatures*, ed. David Smyth. London: Curzon, pp. 21–40.

Alsdorf, L. 1974. "The Akhyana Theory Reconsidered." In *Kleine Schriften Herausgegeben von Albrecht Wezler*. Wiesbaden, Germany: Franz Steiner Verla GMBH.

Anderson, Benedict. 1983. *Imagined Communities: Reflections on the Origins and Spread of Nationalism*. London: Verso.

Anil Sakya [Phra Sugandha]. 2004. *Suat Mon*. Bangkok: Mahamakut University Press.

(Phya) Anuman Rajadhon. 1961. *Life and Ritual in Old Siam: Three Studies of Thai Life and Customs*. Trans. by W. Gedney. New Haven, Conn: HRAF Press.

Anuson Bhuribhiwatanakun. *Abhidhamma-Atthasan˙gahādipakaran.a, lem thi 3.* Bangkok: Mahachulalongkorn Mahavidayalai, 2001.

Appleton, Naomi, Sarah Shaw, and Toshiya Unebe. 2013. *Illuminating the Life of the Buddha: An Illustrated Chanting Book from Eighteenth-century Siam*. Oxford: Bodleian Library.

Arakawa, Hirikazu, Gakuji Hasebe, Seiji Imanaga, and Hideo Okumura. 1967. *Traditions in Japanese Design: Kachō Bird and Flower Motifs*, vol. 1. Tokyo: Kodansha.

Archaimbault, Charles. 1980. *Contribution à l'étude d'un cycle de legendes Lao*. Paris: École Française D'Extrême-Orient.

(Phra) Ariyamuni [Chaem]. 1913. *Suat mon blae*. Bangkok: Rong phim phisalapanani.

Artola, George. 1965. *Ten Tales from the Tantropakhyana*. Madras: The Vasanta Press.

Baird, Merrily. 2001. *Symbols of Japan*. New York: Rizzoli International.

(Phra Khru) Baithikathep Singrak. 2551 [2008]. *Tamra Phetrat Mahayan* [Manual to Mahayana Medical Care]. Bangkok: Sripanya.

Bakhtin, Mikhail. [1968] 1984. *Rabelais and his World*. Cambridge, MA: MIT Press.

Balee Buddharaksa. 2543 [2000]. *Pali literature in Lan Na: Catalogie of 89 manuscripts with summaries*. [In Thai]. Chiang Mai: Social Research Institute.

________. 2545 [2002]. *Mahāvamsamālinivilāsinī: Kān sob chāmra choeng wikro wannakam buddhasāsanā phāsā pālī chāk ekasān tua khian blae ton chabap ben phāsā thai*. Chiang Mai: Social Research Institute.

Bartholomew, Terese Tse. 2006. *Hidden Meanings in Chinese Art*. San Francisco: Asian Art Museum.

Baxandall, Michael. 1985. *Patterns of Intention*. New Haven: Yale University Press.

Beasley, W.G. 1959. "Traditions of Historical writing in China and Japan." *Transactions of the Asiatic Society of Japan* 7: 169–86.

Becchetti, C. 1991. *Le mystere dans les lettres*. Bangkok: Editions des cahiers de France.

Bender, Ross. 1979. "The Hachiman Cult and the Dōkyō Incident." *Monumenta Nipponica* 34, 2: 125–54.

Benfey, Theodor, ed. 1864. *Orient und Occident*. Göttingen: Verlag der Dieterichschen Buchhandlung, 3: 171–2.

Bhassorn Limanonda. 1995. "Families in Thailand: beliefs and realities." *Journal of Comparative Family Studies*, vol. 26.

Bhirasri, Silpa. 1959. *The Origin and Evolution of Thai Murals: Edifices Containing Murals, catalogue of murals in the Silpakorn Gallery*. Bangkok: Fine Arts Department.

Bhrasit Chanserikon. 2551 [2008]. *Phapthai nok nai mueang thai*. Bangkok: Mahachon.

Bizot, François. 1976. *Le figuier à cinq branches*. Paris: École française d'Extrême-Orient.

________. 1980. "La grotte de la naissance." *Recherches sur le bouddhisme khmer II, Bulletin de L'École français de Extrême-Orient* 67.

________. 1981. *Le donne de soi-même*. Publications de École français de Extrême-Orient Monographies 130. Paris.

________. 1981. "Notes sur les yantra bouddhiques d'Indochine." In *Tantric and Taoist Studies in honour of R.A. Stein. Melanges chinois et bouddhiques XX*, vol. 1, ed. M. Strickmann. Brussels, Belgium: Institut Belge des Hautes Etudes Chinoises.

________. 1992. *Le chemin de Lankâ*. Paris: École français de Extrême-Orient.

________. 1994. "La consecration des statues et le culte des morts." In *Recherches nouvelles sur le Cambodge*. Paris: École français de Extrême-Orient.

Bizot, François and François LaGirarde. 1996. *La Pureté par les mots*. Paris: École française d'Extrême-Orient.

Blackburn, Anne. 2001. *Learning and Textual Practice in Sri Lanka*. Princeton: Princeton University Press.

Bloomfield, Maurice. 1920. "On Overhearing as a Motif of Hindu Fiction." *American Journal of Philology* 41, 4: 301–35.

Bode, Mabel. 1966. *The Pali Literature of Burma*. London: Royal Asiastic Society.

Bodhi [Bhikkhu], general editor. 1993. *A Comprehensive Manual of Abhidhamma: The Abhidammattha Sangaha of Ācariya Anuraddha*. Pali text originally ed. and trans. by Mahāthera Nārada. Translation revised by Bhikkhu Bodhi. Introduction and explanatory guide by U. Rewata Dhamma and Bhikkhu Bodhi. Abhidhamma tables by U. Sīlānanda. Kandy, Sri Lanka: Buddhist Publication Society.

Bogle, James. 2011. *Thai and Southeast Asian Painting: 18th through 20th Century*. Atglen, PA: Schiffer.

Boisselier, Jean. 2511 [1968]. *Khwam ru mai thang borannakhadi chak meuang Uthong: Nouvelles connaissances archeologiques de la Ville d'Uthong* [New Archaeological Information from Uthong]. Trans. by Subhadradis Diskul. Bangkok: Krom Sinlapakon.

________. 1976. *Thai Painting*. Tokyo: Kodansha International.

Boonma, Montien. 1992. *Lotus Sound, Installation*. Kenneth and Yasuko Myer Collection of Contemporary Asian Art. Purchased 1993 with funds from The Myer Foundation and Michael Sidney Myer through the Queensland Art Gallery Foundation Collection, Queensland Art Gallery.

________. 1997. *House of Hope, Installation at 76 Grand Street Gallery*. New York.

Bosaengkham Vongthālā et al. 1987. *Vannakhadi Lao*. Vientiane: Kaxuang Seuksa.

______. 1991. *Meuang Luang Phrabang*. Vientiane: Toyota Foundation.

Bowie, Katherine. 2000. "Ethnic heterogeneity and elephants in nineteenth-century Lanna statecraft." In *Civility and savagery: Social identity in Tai states*, ed. Andrew Turton. Richmond, Surrey: Curzon.

Bowie, Theodore, Griswold, A.B., and Subhadradis Diskul, M.C. 1977. *The Sculpture of Thailand*. Visual Arts Board, Sydney.

Brengues, Jean. 1908. "Une version laotienne du Pancatantra." *Journal Asiatique* 10, 12: 361–2.

Brereton, Bonnie. 1995. *Thai tellings of Phra Malai: Texts and rituals concerning a popular Buddhist saint*. Tempe, AZ: Arizona State University, Program for Southeast Asian Studies.

Breuilly, John. 1996. "Approaches to Nationalism." In *Mapping the Nation*, ed. Gopal Balakrishnan. New York: Verso.

Brown, Robert. 1997. "Narrative as Icon: The Jataka Stories in Ancient Indian and Southeast Asian Architecture." In *Sacred Biography in the Buddhist Traditions of*

South and Southeast Asia, ed. Juliane Schober. Honolulu: University of Hawai'i Press, pp. 64–112.

________. 1996. *The Dvaravati Wheels of the Law and the Indianization of South East Asia*. Leiden: Brill.

Buddhacharoen, Phatyos. 2010. *Namo Buddhaya: A Path Towards Divine Light*. Ardel Gallery of Modern Art, Bangkok.

Buddhadatta, A.B., trans. 1962. *Jinakālamālī*. London: PTS.

Buddhaghosa Acariya. 1982. *Atthasālinī-atthayojanā*. Edition of the Munidhi Bhumiphalobhikkhu. Bangkok: Wat Srakhet.

Bunroeng, Buasisaengbasoet. 1995. *Pavatsāt silapa lae sathābatt hayakamsin Lao*. Vientiane: n.p.

Bunsopha Chaloenniphonwanit. 2525 [1982]. "Chitrakam baep prapheni khong Thai nai yuk Ratanakosin [Traditional Thai mural painting in the Ratanakosin Period]." *Sinlpa watthanatham Thai 6*. Bangkok: Krom Silapakon, pp. 1–12.

Ca Brian. 1966. *Anisong 108 Kan chabab poem toem mai*. Bangkok: Amnuisasana.

Callinicos. Alex. 1989. *Against Postmodernism: A Marxist Critique*. Cambridge: Polity.

Cannadine, David. 2002. *Ornamentalism: How the British Saw Their Empire*. Oxford: Oxford University Press.

Cate, Sandra. 2003. *Making Merit, Making Art: A Thai Temple in Wimbledon*. Honolulu: University of Hawai'i Press.

Cather, W. 1949. *On Writing*. Omaha.

Chaloemphon Somin. 2004. *Itthiphon khong satsana Phram-Hindu lae Sik thi mi itthiphon to sangkhom Thai lae bukkhon* [Influence of Brahmanism and Sikhism on Thai Society and People]. Chiang Mai: Nai Chaloemphon Somin.

Chalong Soontravanich. 2004. "The Regionalization of Local Buddhist Saints." In *Proceedings of the Japan Society for the Promotion of Science and National Research Council of Thailand Core University Program Workshop on Flows and Movements in East Asia.* Kyoto, pp. 115–39.

Chalong Soontravanich. 2005. "Small Arms, Romance, and Crime and Violence in Post WWII Thai Society." *Southeast Asian Studies* 43, 1: 26–46.

Chandra, L. 1987. *Erawan Shrine and Brahma Worship in Thailand*. Bangkok: Craftsman Press.

Chang Noi. 2008. "PAD saves the nation from supernatural attack." *The Nation*, 10 November.

Chantorn, Anupong. 2010. *Hope in the Dark*. Bangkok: Amarin Printing.

Chatterjee, Partha. 1993. *Nationalist Thought and the Colonial World: A Derivative Discourse*. Minneapolis: University of Minnesota Press.

Chawalee Na Thalang. 2541 [1998]. *Prathetrācha khong siam nai samai phrabātsomdet phra chulachom Klao Chao Yū Hua*. Bangkok: Chulalongkorn University Press.

Chayan Phichiansunthon, Maenmat Chawalit, and Wichiang Chiruang. (2544 [2001]). *Kham atthibaitamra Phra Osot Phra Narai* [An Explanation of the Documents about Phra Osot Phra Narai]. Bangkok: Amarin Printing.

Chiraphat Praphanwithya. 2545 [2002]. *Phra Siwa Phra Wisanu Phra Phikhanesuan* [Śiva, Viṣṇu, and Gaṇeśa]. Bangkok: Thewasathan Botphrahm.

Chirapravati, M.L. Pattaratorn. 2011. *Divination au royaume de Siam: le corps, la guerre, le destin*. Paris: Presses Universitaires France.

Chirasak Dejawongya. 2544 [2001]. *Khwām sapān rawang lānnā lānxāng: Kān seuksā silapakam nai meuang chiang mai lae luang phrabang*. Chiang Mai: Social Research Institute.

Chirasak Dejawongya, Woralan Bunyasurat, and Yuwanat Woramit. 2539 [1996]. *Ho Trai Wat Phra Singh: Prawat laksana silapakam lae naeo thang kan anurak*. Chiang Mai: Social Research Institute.

Chuphon Euachuwong. 2007. "Chitrakam Samkok nai sala Chao Kian An Keng [The romance of the three kingdom paintings in the Chao Kian An Keng Pavilion]." *Muang Boran* 33, 3: 50–8.

Chutima Chunhacha, ed. 2537 [1994]. *Chut chitakam faphanangnai prathet Thai Wat Khongkharam*. Bangkok: Muang Boran.

Coedès, George. 1895. "On some Siamese inscriptions." *Journal of the Asiatic Society of Bengal* 34: 27–38.

________. 1924. *Recueil des inscriptions du Siam*. Bangkok: Bangkok Times Press.

________. 1925. "Documents sur l'histoire politique et religieuse du Laos Occidental." *Bulletin de l'École Française d'Extrême-Orient* 25: 1–200.

________. 1948. *Les Etats Hindouises D'Indochine et D 'Indonesie: Histoire Du Monde* Tome VIII, E. de Boccard, Editeur, Paris.

________. 1964/2507. *Decouverte numismatique au Siam interessant le royaume de Dvaravati.* Paris.

Collins, Steven. 1998. *Nirvana and other Buddhist Felicities*. Cambridge: Cambridge University Press.

________. 2011. *Civilisation et femmes célibataires dans le bouddhisme en Asie du Sud et du Sud-Est: une étude de genre*, Les Editions de Cerf, Paris.

Collins, Steven and McDaniel, Justin. 2010. "Buddhist 'nuns' (mae chi) and the teaching of Pali in contemporary Thailand." *Modern Asian Studies* 44: 1373–1408.

Cowell, E.W., ed. 1907. *The Jātaka or Stories of the Buddha's Former Births*, vol. 6. Cambridge: Cambridge University Press.

Crawfurd, John and Willaim Storm. 1915. *The Crawfurd Papers: A Collection of Official Records Relating to the Mission of Dr. John Crawfurd Sent to Siam by the Government of India*. London: Gregg Books.

Crosby, J. 1910. "Translation of the book of the Birds." *Journal of the Siam Society* 7, 2: 1–90.

Crosby, Kate, Khammai Dhammasami, Jotika Khur-Yearn, and Andrew Skilton, eds. 2009. "Shan Buddhism." *Contemporary Buddhism* 10, 1.

Csordas, Thomas, ed. 2009. *Transnational Transcendence: Essays on Religion and Globalization*. Berkeley: University of California Press.

Damrong Rachanubhap (Somdet Krom Phraya). 1929. "Palace Library Manuscripts." *Occasional Papers of the Santi Pracha Dhamma Institute* 10. [Reprint with English translation in 1969.]

________. 2509 [1966]. *San Somdet*. Bangkok: Khurusapha.

________. 2509 [1966]. *Nithan Borankhadi*. Bangkok: Khurusapha.

________. 2514 [1971]. *Thai rop phamā (chabap ruam lem)*, 5th ed. Bangkok: Rung Wattana.

________. 2543 [2000]. *Tamnan Nangseu Samkok*. Bangkok: Dokya (reprint).

Derrida, Jacques. 1967. *Writing and Difference*. Trans. by Alan Bass. Chicago: University of Chicago Press.

Derris, Karen. 1997. "The Questions We Ask of History." Paper delivered at the Graduate Student Conference in Buddhist Studies, Harvard University.

Desai, S.N. 2005. *Hinduism in Thai Life*. Varanasi: Popular Prakashan Ltd.

Devi, Gauri. 1998. *Hindu Deities in Thai Art*. Varanasi: Aditya Prakashan.

Deuangxai Luangpasi. 1999. *Somdet Phra Chao Xayaxett hāthirāt*. Vientiane: Sangon Likhasit.

________. 2003. *Chao Mahā Uparāt Bungong*. Vientiane: Sangon Likhasit.

Diskul Subhadris. 1995. *Hindu Gods at Sukhodaya*. Bangkok: White Lotus.

Doniger, Wendy. 1999. *The Implied Spider: Politics and Theology in Myth*. The 1996–97 ACLS/AAR Lectures. New York: Columbia University Press.

Douglas, Mary. 1966. "The Abominations of Leviticus." In *Purity and Danger*. New York: Praeger.

Duangchan Khruchayan. n.d. *Prawat khong wat selāratanapabbatārāma lai hin luang kaeo khāng yeun.* Lampang: Wat Lia hin.

Duara, Prasenjit. 1995. *Rescuing History from the Nation: Questioning Narratives of Modern China*. Chicago: University of Chicago Press.

Duroiselle, Charles. 1913. "Talaing Nissaya". *Journal of the Burma Research Society* 3.

Durrenberger, E. Paul. 1980. "Annual Non-Buddhist Religious Observances of Mae Hong Son Shan." *Journal of the Siam Society* 68: 48–56.

________. 1982. "Shan Kho: The Essence of Misfortune." *Anthropos* 77: 16–26.

________. 1983. "Shan Rocket Festival and Non-Buddhist Aspects of Shan Religion." *Journal of the Siam Society* 71: 63–74.

Dykstra, Yoshiko Kurata (trans.). 1983. *Miraculous Tales of the Lotus Sutra from Ancient Japan: The Dainihonkoku hokekyokenki of Priest Chingen*. Kyoto: Kyoto University Press.

Eberhardt, Nancy. 2006. *Imagining the Course of Life*. Honolulu: University of Hawai'i Press.

Evans, Grant. 1999. "What is Lao culture and society?" In *Laos: Culture and society*, ed. Grant Evans. Chiang Mai: Silkworm Books.

________. 2000. "Tai-ization: Ethnic change in northern Indo-China." In *Civility and savagery: Social identity in Tai states*, ed. Andrew Turton. Richmond, Surrey: Curzon.

________. 2002. "Immobile memories: Statues in Thailand and Laos." In *Cultural crisis and social memory*, ed. Charles Keyes and Shigeharu Tanabe. London: Routledge Curzon.

Farid Ud-Din Attar. 1954. *The Conference of the Birds*. Trans. by S.C. Nott. London: Cirwen Press.

________. 1984. *The Conference of the Birds*. Trans. by Afkham Darbandi and Dick Davis. New York: Penguin.

Fernandez, James, ed. 1991. *Beyond Metaphor*. Palo Alto, CA: Stanford University Press.

Fickle, Dorothy H. 1979. *The Life of the Buddha in the Buddhaisawan Chapel*. Bangkok: Krom Sinlapākōn.

Finot, Louis. 1917. "Recherches sur la littérature laotienne." *Bulletin de l'École Française d'Extrême-Orient* 17, 5: 5–224.

Fontein, Jan. 1967. *The Pilgrimage of Sudhana: A Study of Gaṇḍavyuha Illustrations in China, Japan and Java*. The Hague: Mouton.

Foucault, Michel. 1977. *Discipline and Punish: The Birth of the Prison*. New York: Vinatge.

________. 1980. *Power/Knowledge: Selected Interviews and Other Writings 1972–1977*, ed. Colin Gordon. New York: Pantheon Books.

Frankfurter, O. 1909. "Events in Ayudhya from Chulasakaraj 686–966." *JSS* 6, no. 3: 38–62.

Fraser, Sarah E. 2004. *Performing the Visual: The Practice of Buddhist Wall Painting in China and Central Asia*. Chicago: Stanford University Press, pp. 618–960.

Frauwallner, E. 1956. *The Earliest Vinaya and the Beginnings of Buddhist Literature*. Translated from the German by L. Petech. Rome: L'Istituto italiano per il Medio ed Estremo Oriente.

________. 1995. *Studies in Abhidharma Literature and the Origins of Buddhist Philosophical Systems*. Translated from the German by S.F. Kidd under the supervision of Ernst Steinkellner. Albany: State University of New York Press.

Frederic, Louis. 1965. *The Temples and Sculptures of Southeast Asia*. London: Thames and Hudson.

Gaonkar, Dilip. 2001. "Alternative Modernities." *Public Culture*, available online at http://www.socialresearch.newschool.edu/publicculture/backissues/pc27/01-Gaonkar.html.

Gear, Donald and Joan Gear. 2002. *An Ancient Bird-Shaped Weight System from Lan Na and Burma*. Chiang Mai: Silkworm Books.

Gellner, Ernst. 1983. *Nations and Nationalism*. Ithaca: Cornell University Press.

Gethin, R. 1992. "The Mātikās: Memorization, Mindfulness, and the List." In *The Mirror of Memory: Reflections on Mindfulness and Remembrance in Indian and Tibetan Buddhism*, ed. J. Gyatso. Albany: State University of New York Press, pp. 149–72.

Giddens, Anthony. 1995. *The Consequences of Modernity*. Cambridge: Polity Press.

Ginsberg, Henry. 1967. "The Literary Tales Derived from the Sanskrit Tantropākhyāna." Master's Thesis, University of Hawai'i.

________. 1971. "The Sudhana-Manohara Tale in Thai: A Comparative Study Based on Two Texts from the National Library, Bangkok, and Wat Machimawat, Songkhla." PhD thesis, School of Oriental and African Studies, University of London.

________. 1972. "The Manora dance-drama: an introduction." *Journal of the Siam Society* 60, 2: 169–81.

________. 1975. "The Thai Tales of Nang Tantrai and the Pisaca Tales." *Journal of the Siam Society* 63, 2: 279–314.

Girard-Geslan, Maud et al., eds. 1997. *Art of Southeast Asia*. Paris: Harry Abrams Inc.

Gombrich, E.H. 1994. *The Sense of Order: A Study in the Psychology of Decorative Art*. The Wrightsman Lectures, vol. 9. London: Phaidon.

Goubman, Boris. 1998. "Postmodernity as the Climax of Modernity: Horizons of the Cultural Future." Paper presented at the Twentieth World Congress of Philosophy, August 10–15, 1998, Boston, Massachusetts.

Grabar, Oleg. 1995. *The Mediation of Ornament.* Princeton: Princeton University Press.

Grabowsky, Volker. 1994. "Forced resettlement campaigns in Northern Thailand during the early Bangkok period." *Orient Extremus* 37, 1: 45–107 [reprinted in *Journal of the Siam Society* 87, 1 (1999): 45–86].

________. 1997. "Origins of Lao and Khmer national identity: The legacy of the early nineteenth century." In *Nationalism and cultural revival in Southeast Asia: Perspectives from the Centre and the Region*, ed. Sri Kuhnt-Saptodewo, Volker Grabowsky, and M. Großheim. Wiesbaden: Harrassowitz Verlag, pp. 145–67.

________. 2005. "Population and state in Lan Na prior to the mid-sixteenth century." *Journal of the Siam Society* 93: 1–68.

Grabowsky, Volker and Andrew Turton, eds. 2003. *The gold and silver road of trade and friendship: The McLeod and Richardson diplomatic missions to Tai states in 1837.* Chiang Mai: Silkworm Books.

Grappard, Allan. 1982. "Flying Mountains and Walkers of Emptiness: Toward a definition of sacred space in Japanese religions." *History of Religions* 21, 3: 195–221.

Griswold, A.B. 1960 "Notes on Siamese Art." *Artibus Asiae* XXIII: 5–14.

Griswold, A.B. and Prasert na Nagara. 1974. "Epigraphic and Historical Studies, No. 12, Inscription 9." *JSS*, vol. 62, part 1.

________. 1976. "A Siamese Historical Poem." In *Southeast Asian History and Historiography: Essays Presented to D.G.E. Hall*, ed. C.D. Cowen and O.W. Wolters. Ithaca: Cornell University Press.

________. 1992. *Epigraphic and historical studies* [Collected articles from the *Journal of the Siam Society*]. Bangkok: Siam Society.

Guelden, Marlene. 2005. "Ancestral Spirit Mediumship in Southern Thailand: The Nora Performance as a Symbol of the South on the Periphery of a Buddhist Nation-State." PhD dissertation, University of Hawai'i at Manoa.

Gunawardana, R. 1987. "The Kinsmen of the Buddha: Myth as Political Charter in the Ancient and Early Medieval Kingdoms of Ceylon." In *Religion and Legitimation of Power in Sri Lanka*, ed. Bardwell Smith. Chambersburg, PA: Anima Books.

Habermas, Jurgen. 1989. *Der philosophische Diskurs der Moderne*. Frankfurt am Main, Suhrkamp Verlag.

Hall, Rebecca. 2015. "Materiality and Death: Visual Arts and Northern Thai Funerals." *Journal of Southeast Asian Studies* 46, 3: 46–367.

Hansen, Anne. 2007. *How to Behave: Cambodian Buddhism 1860–1930*. Honolulu: University of Hawai'i Press.

Hansen, Miriam. 1991. *Babel and Babylon: Spectatorship in American Silent Film*. Cambridge, MA: Harvard University Press.

Hayashi, Yukio. *Practical Buddhism among the Thai-Lao*. Kyoto: Kyoto University Press, 2003.

Henricks, Thomas. 2006. *Play Reconsidered*. Urbana: University of Illinois Press.

Herail, Francine. 1995. *La Cour du Japon à l'époque de Heian*. Paris: Hachette Livre.

Hinüber, Oskar von. 1983. "Pali manuscripts on canonical texts from Northern Thailand." *Journal of the Siam Society* 71: 75–88.

________. 1993. "Pali und Lanna in den Kolophonen alter Palmblatt handschrift en aus Nord-Thailand." In *Indogermanica et Italica*, ed. G. Meiser. Innsbruck: Universitat Innsbruck.

________. 1996. "Chips from Buddhist workshops: Scribes and manuscripts from Northern Thailand." *Journal of the Pali Text Society* 22: 35–57.

Hinüber, Oskar von and K.R. Norman, eds. and trans. 1994. *The Dhammapada*. London: Pali Text Society.

________. 1996. *A Handbook of Pali Literature*. Berlin: Walter de Gruyter.

Hinüber, Oskar von and K.R. Norman. 1988. "Die Sprachgeschichte des Pāli im Spiegel der südosrasiastischen Handschriftenüberlieferung." *Untersuchungen zur Sprachgeschichte und Handschriftenkunde des Pāli I*. Stuttgart, Germany.

Hirschkind, Charles. 2009. *The Ethical Soundscape: Cassette Sermons and Islamic Counterpublics*. New York: Columbia University Press.

Hobsbawm, Eric. 1987. *Nations and Nationalism since 1870*. Cambridge: Cambridge University Press.

Holt, John. 2004. *The Buddhist Vishnu*. New York: Columbia University Press.

Hooykaas, Christian. 1929. "Tantri de Mittel-javaansche Pancatantra—beworking." PhD dissertation, Leiden University.

Hori, Ichiro. 1958. "On the concept of the hijiri (holy man)." *Numen* V, 2–3: 128–60, 199–231.

________. 1968. *Folk Religion in Japan: Continuity and Change*. Chicago: University of Chicago Press.

Horton, Charles. 2000. "'It Was All a Great Adventure': Alfred Chester Beatty and the Formation of his Library." *History Ireland* 8, 2: 37–42.

Huang, Jo-Fan. n.d. "A Technical Examination of 7 Thai Manuscripts in the 18th, 19th, and 20th Centuries." https://www.ischool.utexas.edu/~anagpic/2006pdf/2006ANAGPIC_Huang.pdf [accessed 25 July 2015].

Hubbard, Jamie and Bastian, ed., prod. [1988]2009. *The Yamaguchi Story: Buddhism and the Family in Contemporary Japan*. London: BBC-Educational Communications, coproduction. DVD.

Huizinga, Johan. 1955. *Homo Ludens: A Study of the Play-element in Culture*. Boston, MA: Beacon Press.

Hundius, Harald. 1990. "Colophons from thirty Pāli manuscripts from Northern Thailand." *Journal of the Pali Text Society* 14: 1–109.

________. 1990. *Phonologie und Schrift des Nordthai*. Stuttgart: Fr. Steiner Verlag-Abhandlungen für die Kunde des Morgenlandes 48.3.

________. 2005. "Lao manuscripts and traditional literature: The struggle for their survival." In *Moladok vannakhadi lao* [The literary heritage of Laos], ed. David Wharton. Vientiane: The National Library of Laos, pp. 1–11.

Inagaki, H. 1972. "Kūkai's Sokushin-Jobutsu-Gi." *Asia Major* XVII, 2: 190–213.

Inoue, Kiyoshi. 1996. *Geschichte Japans: Aus dem Japanischen und mit einem Vorwort von Manfred Hubricht*. Frankfurt: Campus Verlag.

Ishii, Yoneo. 1986. *Sangha, State, and Society: Thai Buddhism in History*. Trans. by Peter Hawkes. Honolulu: University of Hawai'i Press.

Jaini, Padmanabh S. 1966. "The Story of Sudhana and Manoharā: An Analysis of the Texts and the Borobudur Reliefs." *Bulletin of the School of Oriental and African Studies* 29, 3: 533–58.

________. 1989. "The apocryphal Jātakas of Southeast Asian Buddhism." *Indian Journal of Buddhist Studies* 1: 22–37.

________, ed. 1981. *Paṇṇāsajātaka or Zimme Paṇṇāsa (in the Burmese recension)*. Vols. 1 and 2. London: Pali Text Society.

James, Liz. 2007. "Introduction." In *Art and Text in Byzantine Culture*, ed. Liz James. Cambridge: Cambridge University Press.

Jayaywickrama, N.A. 1968. *The sheaf of garlands of the epochs of the conqueror*. London: Pali Text Society.

Jordt, Ingrid. 2007. *Burma's Mass Lay Meditation Movement: Buddhism and the Cultural Construction of Power*. Athens: Ohio University Press.

Jory, P. 2002. "Thai and Western Scholarship in the Age of Colonialism: King Chulalongkorn Redefines the Jatakas." *Journal of Asian Studies* 61, 3: 99–124.

Kaisit Phisanakha. 2545 [2002]. *Chiwa-prawat Borom Khru Phaet: Chiwok Komanphat* [The Biography of the Traditional Doctor: Jīvaka Komārabhacca]. Bangkok: Saradi.

Kamala Tiyavanich. 1997. *Forest recollections*. Honolulu: University of Hawai'i Press.

Kasetsiri, Charnvit. 1976. *The Rise of Ayudhya*. Oxford: Oxford University Press.

Katoshuichi. 1979. *A History of Japanese Literature: The First Thousand Years*. Trans. by David Chibbett. London: Macmillan Press.

Kaung. 1963. "Survey of the history of education in Burma." *Journal of the Burma Research Society* 46, 2.

Keyes, Charles. 1987. *Thailand: Buddhist Kingdom as Modern Nation-State*. Boulder and London: Westview Press.

________. 2002. "National heroine or local spirit? The strug- gle over memory in the case of Thao Suranari in Nakhon Ratchasima." In *Cultural crisis and social memory*, ed. Shigeharu Tanabe and Charles Keyes. Honolulu: University of Hawai'i Press, pp. 113–36.

________. 2006. "The Destruction of a Shrine to Brahma in Bangkok and the Fall of Thaksin Shinawatra: The Occult and the Thai Coup in Thailand of September 2006." Working Paper 80, Asia Research Institute, National University of Singapore.

Keyes, C. and (Phrakhru) Anusaranasasanakiarti. 1980. "Funerary Rites and the Buddhist Meaning of Death: An Interpretative Text from Northern Thailand." *Journal of the Siam Society* 68, 1: 1–28.

Keith-Falconer, Ion G.N. 1970. "Introduction." In *Kalilah and Dimnah or the Fables of Bidpai*, Ion G.N. Keith-Falconer. Amsterdam: Philo Press.

Kham Champakaeomani et al. 2537 [1995]. *Phra Thāt Chedī: Wat samkhan lae phra khrū yot kaeo pon samek*. Chiang Mai: Social Research Institute.

(Phra) Khammai Dhammasami. 2005. "Between idealism and pragmatism: A study of monastic education in Burma and Thailand from the seventeenth century to the present." PhD dissertation, Oriental Studies, Oxford University.

Kieffer-Pulz, P. 1992. *Die Sīm: Vorschriften zur Regelung der Buddhistischen Gemeindegrenze in älteren Buddhistischen Texten*. Berlin: D. Reimer.

Kitagawa, Joseph. 1966. *Religion in Japanese History*. New York: Columbia University Press.

Konthep Thepyothin, ed. n.d. *Tamnan phra reusi* [History of the Rishi]. Bangkok: Sayam panya kanphim.

Ko-Udomvit, Thavorn. 2009. *Young Female Artists of the Year*. Bangkok: Amarin Printing.

Kriangkon Sambhacchalit, ed. 2553 [2010]. *Bhrachum bhakaranam bhak thi 1-6*. Bangkok: Saengdao.

Krom Silapakon [Department of Fine Arts Editorial Team]. 2545 [2002]. *Chareuk tamra ya: Wat Ratcha-orosaram Ratchawihan* [Inscriptions of Medical Manuals: Ratcha-orosaram Royal Monastery]. Bangkok: Krom Silapakon.

Kultida Samabuddhi. 2008. "Sorcerer Sondhi wards off evil: followers don white, clean, pray for victory." *Bangkok Post*, 10 November.

Kumari, Asha. 1990. *Hinduism and Buddhism*. Varanasi: Vishwavidyalaya Prakashan.

Laddawan Saesiang. 2545 [2002]. *200 Pi Bama nai Lanna*. Bangkok: Tenmay.

LaFleur, William. 1983. "In and Out of Rokudo: Kyōkai and the Formation of Medieval Japan." In *The Karma of Words: Buddhism and the Literary Arts in Medieval Japan*, ed. William LaFleur. Berkeley: University of California Press.

LaGirarde, F. 2001. "Gavampati-Kaccayana: Le culte et la legende du disciple ventripotent dans le bouddhisme des Thais." Vols. 1–2. PhD dissertation. Sorbonne, Paris.

Lagirarde, François. 2006. "Three northern Thai histories." Paper presented at Thai Language and Literature conference sponsored by Chulalongkorn University, November 11, Bangkok, Thailand.

Lamun Canhom. 1995. *Wannakam Thong Thin Lanna*. Chiang Mai, Thailand: Suriwong Book Center.

Laumann, Martya, ed. 1991. *Chinese Decorative Design*, vols. 1–4, Taipei: SMC Pub.

Law, V. 1982. *The Insular Latin Grammarians*. Totowa, NJ: Distributed by Biblio Distribution Services.

Lavery, Brian. 2002. "Arts Abroad; An Irish Castle for Religious Manuscripts." *The New York Times*, July 17, 2002. http://www.nytimes.com/2002/07/17/ books/arts-abroad-an-irish-castle-for-religious-manuscripts.html [accessed 13 July 2015].

Lefèvre-Pontalis, Pierre. 1900. "Les Laotiens du royaume de Lan Chang." *T'ouang Pao*: 149–67.

Lieberman, Victor. 1984. *Burmese administrative cycles: Anarchy and conquest, 1580–1760*. Princeton, NJ: Princeton University Press.

________. 1993. "Was the seventeenth century a watershed in Burmese history?" In *Southeast Asia in the early modern era: Trade, power, and belief*, ed. Anthony Reid. Ithaca, NY: Cornell University Press, pp. 214–49.

Lihe and Michael Knight, eds. 2008. *Power and Glory: Court Arts of China's Ming Dynasty*. San Francisco: Asian Art Museum.

Likhit Likhitanonta. 1969. "Pali literature in Northern Thailand." PhD dissertation, Magadh University.

Loos, Tamara. 2006. *Subject Siam: Family, Law, and Colonial Modernity in Thailand*. Ithaca: Cornell University Press.

Lorrillard, Michel. 2004. "Les inscriptions du That Luang de Vientiane: Données nouvelles sur l'histoire d'un stūpa lao." *Bulletin de l'École Française d'Extrême-Orient* 90–91: 289–348.

Ly, Boreth. 2012. "Of Trans(national), Subjects and Translation: The Art and the Body Language of Sopheap Pich." In *Modern and Contemporary Southeast Asian Art: An Anthology*, ed. Boreth Ly and Nora Taylor. Ithaca: Cornell University Press, pp. 117–30.

Maguire, Henry. 2007. "Eufrasius and Friends. On Names and their Absence in Byzantine Art." In *Art and Text in Byzantine Culture*, ed. Liz James. Cambridge: Cambridge University Press, pp. 139–60.

Mahamakut Education Council. 1989. *Acts on the Administration of the Buddhist Order of Saṅgha of Thailand: B.E. 2445, B.E. 2484, B.E. 2505*. Bangkok: Mahamakut Monastic University Press.

(Phra) Mahāniyom Thānathatt. n.d. *Tamnān Phra Borom Thāt Lampang Luang*. n.p.

Mair, Heather, Susan Arai, and Donald Reid, eds. 2010. *Decentering Work*. Calgary: University of Calgary Press.

Malalasekara, G.P. 1986. *The Pali Literature of Ceylon compiled by U Ko Lay*. Rangoon: Burma Pitaka Association.

Mani Phrayomyong. 2546 [2003]. *Sārāphochanānukhrom Lānnā*. Chiang Mai: Dao Computgraphik.

(Phra Mahā) Mani Rattanapathimakone and (Phra) Rattanaphimpheuang. 1999. *Thamnān Phra Kaeo Morakot*. Vientiane: Sangon Likhasit.

Mannell, Roger and Douglas Kleiber. 1997. *A Social Psychology of Leisure*. State College, PA: Venture.

Marcus, Russell. 2013. *Thawan Duchanee: Modern Buddhist Artist*. Chiang Mai: Silkworm Books.

Marra, Michele. 1991. *The Aesthetics of Discontent: Politics and Reclusion in Medieval Japanese Literature*. Honolulu: University of Hawai'i Press.

Marston, John. 2004. "Clay into Stone: A Modern-Day Tāpa." In *History, Buddhism, and New Religious Movements in Cambodia*, ed. John Marston and Elizabeth Guthrie. Honolulu: University of Hawai'i Press, pp. 170–96.

Matics, Kathleen I. 1992. *Introduction to Thai Murals*. Chonburi: White Lotus.

Mattani Mojdara Rutnin. 1996. *Dance, Drama, and Theatre in Thailand*. Chiang Mai: Silkworm Books.

Mayer, Fanny Hagin. 1963. "Religious Elements in Japanese Folk Tales." In *Studies in Japanese Culture*, ed. Joseph Roggendorf. Tokyo: Sophia University Press.

McCargo, Duncan and Krisadawan Hongladarom. 2004. "Contesting Isan-ness: Discourse and Politics in the Northeast of Thailand." *Asian Ethnicity* 5, 2: 219–34.

McDaniel, Justin. 2000. "Creative Engagement: The Sujavanna Wua Luang and Its Contribution to Buddhist Literature." *Journal of the Siam Society* 88: 156–77.

________. 2002. "Transformative history: The Nihon Ryoiki and the Jinakalamalipakaranam." *Journal of the International Association of Buddhist Studies* 25 (1): 151–207.

________. 2002. "The Curricular Canon in Northern Thailand and Laos." *Manusya: Journal of Thai Language and Literature Special Issue*: 20–59.

________. 2003. "Invoking the Source: Nissaya Manuscripts, Pedagogy and Sermon-making in Northern Thailand and Laos." PhD dissertation, Cambridge (USA), Harvard University.

________. 2004. "Paritta and Raksa texts." In *Encyclopedia of Buddhism*, ed. Robert Buswell. New York: Macmillan, pp. 634–5.

________. 2005. "Notes on the Lao influence on Northern Thai literature." In *The literary heritage of Laos: Kongdeuang Nett avong*, Harald Hundius, ed. David Wharton, Dara Kanlaya, and Khanthamali Yangnuvong. Vientiane: National University of Laos, pp. 373–96.

________. 2006. "A Lao Homily: the *Kammavācā Nissaya Sadda*." Paris: École Française d'Extrême-Orient and Vientiane: Études thématiques Laos.

________. 2008. *Gathering Leaves and Lifting Words: Histories of Buddhist Monastic Education in Laos and Thailand*. Seattle: University of Washington Press.

________. 2009. "Philosophical Embryology: Buddhist texts and the Ritual Construction of a Fetus." In *Imagining the Fetus: The Unborn in Myth, Religion, and Culture*, ed. Vanessa R. Sasson and Jane Marie Law. Oxford: Oxford University Press, pp. 91–106.

________. 2009. "Two Buddhist Librarians: The Proximate Mechanisms of Northern Thai Buddhist History." In *Buddhist Manuscript Cultures: Knowledge, Ritual, and Art*, ed. Stephen C. Berkwitz, Juliane Schober, and Claudia Brown. London: Routledge, pp. 124–39.

________. 2011. *The Lovelorn Ghost and the Magical Monk: Practicing Buddhism in Modern Thailand*. New York: Columbia University Press.

________. 2011. "The Agency between Images: The Relationships among Ghosts, Corpses, Monks, and Deities at a Buddhist Monastery in Thailand." *Material Religion* 7, 2: 242–67.

________. 2012. "Encountering corpses: notes on zombies and the living dead in Buddhist Southeast Asia." *Kyoto Review of Southeast Asia, Special Issue on Death and Dying* (translated into Japanese, Bahasa Indonesia and French).

________. 2013. "This Hindu Holy Man is a Thai Buddhist." *Southeast Asia Research* 21, 2: 191–209.

________. 2013. "Encountering Corpses: Notes on Zombies and the Living Dead in Buddhist Southeast Asia." *Kyoto Review of Southeast Asia*, 12, "The Living and the Dead," special issue on death and funerary cultures in Southeast Asia.

________. 2017. *Architects of Buddhist Leisure: Socially Disengaged Buddhism in Asia's Museums, Monuments, and Amusement Parks*. Honolulu: University of Hawai'i Press.

McDaniel, Justin and Lynn Ransom, eds. 2015. *From Mulberry Leaves to Silk Scrolls: New Approaches to the Study of Asian Manuscript Traditions*. The Lawrence J. Schoenberg Studies in Manuscript Culture 1. Philadelphia: University of Pennsylvania Press.

McGill, Forrest, ed. 2005. *The Kingdom of Siam: The Art of Central Thailand, 1350–1800*. San Francisco: Asian Art Museum.

________, ed. 2009. *Emerald Cities: Arts of Siam and Burma, 1775–1950*. San Francisco: Asian Art Museum.

McGovern, Nathan. 2006. "Brahma worship in Thailand: the Erawan Shrine in its social and historical context." MA thesis, University of California, Santa Barbara.

Mingsan Khaosāt. 2525 [1982]. *Wihān Thong Chumchōng Sakun Chāng Lampang*. Chiang Mai: Mahāwithyālai Chiang Mai.

Ministry of Information and Culture (Historical Committee). 2000. *Pavasāt Lao*. Vientiane: Ministry of Information and Culture.

Mishima, Yukio. 1973. *The Temple of the Dawn*. Trans. by E. Dale Saunders and Cecilia Segawa Seigle, New York: Knopf.

Moore, Jerry, ed. 2009. *Visions of Culture*. New York: Rowman and Littlefield.

Mulholland, Jean. 1979. "Thai traditional medicine: ancient thought and practice in a Thai context." *Journal of the Siam Society* 67, 2: 80–115.

________. 1987. *Medicine, Magic, and Evil Spirits: A Study of a Text on Thai Traditional Paediatrics*. Asian Studies Monograph Series, Australian National University, Canberra.

________. 1989. *Herbal Medicine in Paediatrics: Translation of a Thai Book of Genesis*. Asian Studies Monograph Series, Australian National University, Canberra.

Mus, Paul. 1935. *Barabudur: Esquisse d'une histoire du Bouddhisme fondée sur la critique archéologique des textes*, 2 vols. Hanoi: Imprimerie d'Extrême- Orient.

(M.R.) Naengnoi Saksit. 2537 [1994]. *Moradok sathabatyakam krung ratanakosin*. Bangkok: Roongphim krungthep.

Nakamura, Kyoto Motomochi. 1973. *Miraculous Stories from the Japanese Buddhist Tradition: the Nihon Ryōiki of the Monk Kyōkai*. Cambridge: Harvard University Press.

(Mo) Nakhon Bangyikan. 2546 [2003]. *Phra Borom Khru Phaet Chiwok Komarabhat* [The Traditional Doctor Jīvaka Komārabhacca]. Bangkok: Sri Krung wattana.

Newell, C. 2008. "Monks, Meditation and Missing Links." PhD dissertation, School of Oriental and African Studies.

Ni Ni Myint. 1983. *Burma's struggle against British imperialism 1185–1895*. Rangoon: The Universities Press.

________. 2543 [2000]. *Pama kap kan to tan chakrawandinniyom angkrit 1885–1895*. Trans. by Chalong Soontravanich. Bangkok: Munithi krong kan tamra sangkhomsat lae Manusyasat.

Nidda Hongwiwat. 2549 [2006]. *Wessandon Chadok: Thotsachadok kap chitrakam fa-phanang* [The Vessanatara Jataka: The Ten Jatakas Accompanied by their Mural Paintings]. Bangkok: Saeng daet pheuandek.

Nit Ratanasanya et al. 2517 [1974]. "Wat Khongkaram." *ASA: Journal of the Association of Siamese Architects* 3, 1.

Niwa, Motoji. 2001. *Snow, Wave, Pine: Traditional Patterns in Japanese Design*. Trans. by Jay Thomas. Tokyo: Kodansha.

Niyada Laosunthon, ed. 2538 [1995]. *Mural Paintings of Thailand Series: Wat Khongkaram*. Bangkok: Muang Boran.

________, ed. 2538 [1995]. *Sayam sinlapa chitrakam lae sathup-chedi* [Siamese Art, Painting, and Stupas/Cetiyas]. Bangkok: Muang Boran.

________, ed. 2539 [1996]. *Sila-chamlak reuang Ramakian: Wat Phra Chetuphon Wimalamongkhonaram* [Stone Reliefs of the Ramayana: Phra Chetuphon Monastery]. Bangkok: Chon niyom.

________, ed. 2540 [1997]. *Khamphi Narai 20 pang kap khon Thai* [The Twenty Postures found in the Narai Text]. Bangkok: Samnakphim Maekhamphang.

________, ed. 2544 [2001]. *Prachum chareuk Wat Phra Chetuphon* [Collection of the Inscriptions of Phra Chetuphon Monastery]. Bangkok: Amarin Press.

No author. 2510 [1967]. *Rambam chut borankhadi*. Bangkok: Phiphithaphan sathan haeng chat.

No author. 2541 [1998]. *Wat Ratchaorosara Ratchawirawihan*. Bangkok: n.p.

No Na Paknam. 2537 [1994]. *Sinlapa boran nai sayam* [Ancient Art in Siam]. Bangkok: Muang Boran.

________. 2537 [1994]. *Wat Khongkaram: Moradok paen din bon lum nam mae khlong*. Bangkok: Muang Boran.

Norman, K.R. 1983. "Pali Literature." *A History of Indian Literature*, vol. 7.2, ed. J. Gonda. Wiesbaden, Germany: Otto Harrassowitz.

Notton, Camille. 1930. *Annales du Siam*, vol. 2. Paris: Limoges.

Obeyesekere, Gananath. 1999. "Buddhism, Nationhood and Cultural Identity: The Pre-colonial Formations." Draft of unpublished paper.

O'Connor, Stanley. 1982. "Hindu gods of Peninsular Siam." *Artibus Asiae supplementum* 28: 1–73.

Okell, John. 1965. "Nissaya Burmese: A case of systematic adaptation to a foreign grammar and syntax." *Lingua* 15.

________. 1967. "'Translation' and 'Embellishment' in an Early Burmese 'Jātaka' Poem." *The Journal of the Royal Asiatic Society of Great Britain and Ireland* 99, 2: 133–48.

Oldenburg, Ray. 1989. *The Great Good Place: Cafes, Coffee Shops, Community Centers, Beauty Parlors, General Stores, Bars, Hangouts, and How They Get You Through the Day*. New York: Paragon House.

Orzech, Charles. 2002. "Metaphor, Translation, and the Construction of Kingship in the Scripture for Humane Kings and the Mahāmāyūrī Vidyārājñī Sūtra." *Cahiers d'Extrême-Asie* 13: 55–83.

Osipov, Yuri M. 2000. "Buddhist Agiography in Forming the Canon in the Classical Literatures of Indochina." In *The Canon in Southeast Asian Literatures*, ed. David Smyth. London, Curzon, pp. 1–7.

Paitun Dokbuakaeo. 2547 [2004]. *Horasat Lanna*. Chiang Mai: Sathapan Wichai Sangkhom.

Pamaree Surakiat. 2006. "The changing nature of conflict between Burma and Siam seen in the growth and development of Burmese states between the sixteenth and nineteenth centuries." *Asia Research Institute Working Paper* 64:2–47.

________. 2006. "Post-Prince Damrong historical scholarship concerning pre-modern Thai-Burmese warfare: A reappraisal." Unpublished manuscript.

Pampen Rawin. 2538 [1995]. *Mūlasāsanā Samnuan Lānnā*. Chiang Mai: Social Research Institute.

________. 2538 [1995]. *Tamnān Wat Pā Daeng*. Chiang Mai: Social Research Institute.

Pannasami. 1952. *The History of the Buddha's Religion*. Trans. by B.C. Law. London: PTS.

Phanphen Kreuathai. 2543 [2000]. *Mahaphon tamra ya* [The Wonderfully Beneficial Guide to Traditional Medicine]. Chiang Mai: Sathan wichai sangkhom mahawitthayalai.

Parinya Uthichalanon. n.d. *Khu-meu prakop kan chai ya* [Handbook for the Use of Traditional Medicine]. Self-published by Parinya Uthichalanon, Bangkok.

Park, J.P. 2012. *Art by the Book*. Seattle: University of Washington Press.

Parmentier, Henri. 1988. *L'Art du Laos: Iconographie, planche 6*. Paris: École Française d'Extrême-Orient.

Pattaratorn Chirapravati. 1999. *Votive Tablets in Thailand*. Oxford.

________. 2009. "Living the Siamese life: culture, religion, and art." In *Emerald Cities: Arts of Siam and Burma, 1775–1950*, ed. Forest McGill. San Francisco: Asian Art Museum.

Patthana Kitiarsa. 1999. "Postmodernity, remaking tradition and the hybridization of Thai Buddhism." *Anthropological Forum* 9, 2: 163–87.

________. 2008. *Religious Commodifications in Asia*. London: Routledge.

Pelley, Patricia. 1995. "The History of Resistance and the Resistance to History in Post-Colonial Constructions of the Past." In *Essays into Vietnamese Pasts*, ed. Keith Taylor and John Whitmore. Ithaca: Cornell University Press.

Penth, Hans. 1989. "On the history of Chiang Rai." *Journal of the Siam Society* 77.

________. 1993. *A brief history of Lanna*. Chiang Mai: Silkworm Books.

________. 1997. "Buddhist literature of Lān Nā on the history of Lān Nā's Buddhism." *Journal of the Pali Text Society* 23: 43–81.

Penth, Hans, Panpen Kreuathai, and Srilao Kesaprohm. 2541 [1998]. *Chāreuk Phra Chao Kawila: 2334–2357*. Chiang Mai: Corpus of Lān Nā Inscriptions of the Social Research Institute.

________. 2539 [1997]. *Chāruek nai Phiphithaphan Chiang Saen*. Chiang Mai: Corpus of Lān Nā Inscriptions of the Social Research Institute.

Phennapha Sapchaloen et al. 2481 [1938]. *Prawat Mo Chiwok Gomanabhat* [The History of Jīvaka Komārabhacca]. Bangkok: Wat Thepsarin.

Phitya Busararat. 2553 [2010]. *Nathakam haeng lum tale sap Songkhla*. Bangkok: Amarin Printing.

Phoensri Duk, Phaitun Sinlarat, Piyanat Punnat, and Waraphon Chuachaisak. 2536 [1993]. *Watthanatham pheun ban khati khwam cheua* [Traditional Culture and Beliefs]. Bangkok: Chulalongkorn University Press.

Phuchong Chanthawit. 2525 [1982]. "Phra-khreuang samkhan bang rung chak borankhadi [A selection of important amulets from the ancient past]." *Sinlapa watthanatham Thai* 4. Bangkok: Krom silapakon, Bangkok, pp. 21–63.

Pike, Sarah. 2009. "Why Prince Charles Instead of 'Princess Mononoke'? The Absence of Children and Popular Culture in 'The Encyclopedia of Religion and Nature'." *Journal of the American Academy of Religion* 77, 1: 66–72.

Pinitbhand Paribatra. 2006. "Understanding of Myanmar-Thailand relations: Structural development from 19th to late 20th centuries." Unpublished manuscript.

(Phra) Platavisut Guttajayo. 2001. *Guu Meu Kanseuksa Phra Abhidhamma Chan Chulabhidhammikatri*. Bangkok: Mahachulalongkorn Rajavidyalaya.

Pollock, Sheldon. 1989. "Mīmāṃsā and the Problem of History in Traditional India." *JAOS* 109, 3: 603–11.

Pomarin Charuworn. 2006. "Dynamism of Phra Malai Chanting: A Comparative Study of Performance at Kanchanaburi and Chonburi." Talk delivered at the Thai Language and Literature Conference, Bangkok, November 11, 2006.

Pornthip Wongnisanakuson, ed. n.d. *Satsana Phram-Hindu* [Brahmanism]. Bangkok: S.V. Soluchan.

Poshyananda, Apinan. 1992. *Modern Art in Thailand*. Oxford: Oxford University Press.

Poshyananda, Apinan (author) and Melissa Chiu (contributor). 2003. *Montien Boonma: Temple of the Mind*. New York: The Asia Society.

Pottier, Richard. 2007. *Yu Dt Mi Heng: Essai sur les pratiques therapeutiques Lao*. Paris: École Française d'Extrême-Orient.

Prakai Nontawasee, ed. 1988. *Changes in Northern Thailand and the Shan States, 1886–1940*. Singapore: Institute of Southeast Asian Studies.

Prasert na Nagara. 2537 [1994]. *Tamnān Munlasātsanā Wat Suan Dok*. Bangkok: Ekasānwichakān Samakhom Prawatisāt.

Prathip Phayakkhaphon. 2476 [1933]. *Tamra ya mo Thai* [Manual of Traditional Medicine for Thai Doctors]. Chong Heng, Bangkok: Bukkhonanoe Printing, reprinted in 2008.

Prothero, Stephen. 1996. *The White Buddhist: The Asian Odyssey of Henry Steel Olcott*. Bloomington: Indiana University Press.

Pruess, James, ed. 1985. "The That Phanom Chronicle: A Shrine History and its Interpretation." Cornell University Data Paper, no. 104.

Pruitt, William. 1986. "Un Nissaya Birman de la Bibliotheque Nationale, le Patimokkha. Étude linguistique." Part 1. *Cahiers de l'Asie du Sud-Est* 19: 84–119.

________. 1987. "Un Nissaya Birman de la Bibliotheque Nationale, le Patimokkha. Étude linguistique." Part 2. *Cahiers de l'Asie du Sud-Est* 21: 7–45.

________. 1987. "Un Nissaya Birman de la Bibliotheque Nationale, le Patimokkha. Étude linguistique. Part 3. *Cahiers de l'Asie du Sud-Est* 22: 35–57.

________. 1994. *Étude linguistique de nissaya birmans: traduction commentée de textes bouddhiques*. Paris: École Française d'Extrême-Orient.

Rabinovitz, Lauren. 2012. *Electric Dreamland: Amusement Parks, Movies, and American Modernity*. New York: Columbia University Press.

Raksamani, Kusuma. 1978. "Nandakapakarana attributed to Vasubhaga: A Comparative Study of Sanskrit, Lao, and Thai Texts." PhD dissertation, University of Toronto.

Ram Watcharapradit, ed. 2004/2547. *Phap Phra Chanaloet kan prakuat ngan nithatsakan prakuat kan anurak phrabucha phrakhruang lae rian khanachan khrang yingyai*. Phitsanulok.

Raspall, Thieery. 2004. *Kim Sooja: Conditions of Humanity*. Milan: 5Continents Books.

Ratanaporn Sethakul. 1988. "Relations between Kengtung and Chiang Mai." In *Changes in Northern Thailand and the Shan States*, ed. Prakai Nontawasee. Singapore: Institute of Southeast Asian Studies.

________. n.d. *Pawat Meuang Xieng Kaeng*. Vientiane: Khong kān botbat raksā nangseu bailān Lao.

Reid, Anthony. 1993. *Southeast Asia in the Age of Commerce, 1450–1680*. New Haven, Conn.: Yale University Press.

________, ed. 1993. *Southeast Asia in the Early Modern Era: Trade, Power, and Belief*. Ithaca, NY: Cornell University Press.

________. 1999. *Charting the Shape of Early Modern Southeast Asia*. Chiang Mai, Thailand: Silkworm Books.

Reynolds, Craig, 1973. "The Buddhist Monkhood in Nineteenth Century Thailand." PhD dissertation, Ithaca, Cornell University.

________. 1992. "The Plot of Thai History: Theory and Practice." In *Patterns and Illusions: Thai History and Thought in Memory of Richard B. Davis*, ed. Gehan Wijeyewardene and E.C. Chapman. Melbourne: Australian National University Press.

________. 2006. *Seditious Histories: Contesting Thai and Southeast Asian Pasts.* Seattle: University of Washington Press.

________. 2011. "Rural male leadership, religion and the environment in Thailand's Mid South, 1920s–1960s." *Journal of Southeast Asian Studies* 42, 1: 39–57.

Reynolds, Frank and Mani B. Reynolds (trans.). 1982. *Three Worlds According to King Ruang: A Thai Buddhist Cosmology*. Berkeley: University of California Press.

Reynolds, Suzanne. 1996. *Medieval Reading: Grammar, Rhetoric, and the Classical Text*. New York: Cambridge University Press.

Rhys-Davids, C.A. 1974. *Buddhist Manual of Psychological Ethics: Being a Translation, Now Made for the First Time, from the Original Pali, of the First Book in the Abhidhamma Pitaka Entitled Dhammasangani, Compendium of States or Phenomena*, 3rd ed. London: Pali Text Society; distributed by Routledge & Kegan Paul.

Rhys-Davids, C. and Shwe Zan Aung. 1972. *Compendium of Philosophy: Being a Translation Now Made for the First Time from the Original Pali of the Abhidhammatthasangaha*. London: Published for the Pali Text Society by Luzac.

Riccardi, Theodore. 1968. "A Nepali Version of the Vetālapañcaviṃśati Nepali Text and English Translation." Dissertation, University of Pennsylvania.

________. 1971. *A Nepali Version of the Vetālapañcaviṃśati*. Nepali text and English translation. New Haven: American Oriental Society, vol. 54.

Ringis, Rita. 1990. *Thai Temples and Temple Murals*. Oxford: Oxford University Press.

Rojek, Chris. 1995. *Decentering Leisure*. London: Sage.

________. 2000. *Leisure and Culture*. London: Macmillan Press.

Rojek, Chris, Susan Shaw, and A.J. Veal, eds. 2006. *A Handbook of Leisure Studies*. New York: Palgrave.

Salguero, C. Pierce. 2007. *Traditional Thai Medicine: Buddhism, Animism, Ayurveda*. Bangkok: Hohm Press.

Samiti, Antar Rastriya Brahmottham Seva. 1996. "Proceedings of the International Seminar on Brahmanism and Buddhism in Thailand, August 19–21, 1994." Bangkok: Phragru Vamadevamuni Devasathan.

Samuels, Jeffrey. 2004. "Toward an Action-Oriented Pedagogy: Buddhist Texts and Monastic Education in Contemporary Sri Lanka." *Journal of the American Academy of Religion* 72, 4: 955–71.

Sanasen, Uab. 1984. *Ten Contemporary Thai Artists*. Bangkok: Graphis.

Sangkham Changyot. 2548 [2005]. *Kan fon nak kingkala*. Chiang Mai: Nopbori Kanphim.
Sanguan Chotsukra. 1972. *Prachum Tamnan Lanna Thai*, vols. 1 & 2. Krung Thep: Odiansadon.
Sangwon Chotisukrat. 2508 [1965]. *Tamnān Muang Neua*. Bangkok: Odien Store.
________. 2512 [1969]. *Praphenī Thai Phāk Neua.* Bangkok: Odien Store.
________. 2515 [1972]. *Khon dī Muang Neua*. Bangkok: Odien Store.
________. 2515 [1972]. *Prachum Tamnān Lānnā Thai*. Bangkok: Odien Store.
Sanitsida Ekachai. 2008. "Thailand's Gay Past." *Bangkok Post*, February 23.
Sansom, G.B. 1932. "Early Japanese Law and Administration." *Transactions of the Asiatic Society of Japan* 9: 67–110.
________. 1934. "Early Japanese Law and Administration: Part II." *Transactions of the Asiatic Society of Japan* 11: 117–50.
Saokong, Surasit. 2553 [2010]. *Khwam sangob nai lanna lae rajasthan*. Bangkok: Surapon Gallery.
Saranukhrom Wattanatham Thai Phak Neua [Encyclopedia of Thai Culture Northern Region]. 2542 [1999]. 15 volumes. Bangkok: Thanakhan Thai Panich.
Sarassawadee Ongsakun. 2539 [1996]. Prawatsat Lan Na. Bangkok: Amarin Publishing.
______. 2543 [2000]. *Chumchon bōrān nai laeng Chiang Mai-Lamphun.* Chiang Mai: Toyota Foundation and Amarin Publishing.
______. 2005. *The history of Lanna*. Trans. by Chitaporn Tanratanakul. Chiang Mai: Silkworm Books.
Sarikabut, Thep. 1994. *Tamra Phrawet Phisadan*. Bangkok: Silapabannakhan. [Reprint 2547, 2004 CE.]
(Phra) Sasanasobhon. 1975, 1986. *Suatmon chapap Luang*. Bangkok: Mahamakut University Press.
Sasson, Vanessa. 2012. *Little Buddhas*. New York: Oxford University Press.
Sastri, Sivasamba. 1938. *The Tantropākhayāna*. Trivandrum: Government Press.
Satien Goset. 1957. "Wicha Brawattisat." *Silapakorn* 1, 3: 70–4.
_________. 2505 [1962]. *Prapheni kiao kap chiwit* [Life-Cycle Customs]. Bangkok: Siam Printing.
Schearer, Susan, ed. and trans. 2002. *Petrarch: On Religious Leisure*. New York: Italica Press.
Schweisguth, P. 1951. *Étude sur la litterature Siamoise*. Paris: Imprimerie Nationale.
Seeger, M. 2009. "The Changing Roles of Thai Buddhist Women." *Religion Compass* 3, 5: 806–22.
Sharkar, Jagadish Narayan. 1977. *History of History Writing in Medieval India*. Calcutta: Sreenath Press.
Shwe Zan Aung. 1978 [1910]. "Abhidhamma Literature in Burma." *Journal of the Pali Text Society* 6: 106–23.

Singkhla Wannasai. 2519 [1976]. *Kānseuksā choeng wikhro paññāsajātaka chabap lānnāthai*. Chiang Mai: Toyota Foundation.

Sinha, Purnendu Narayana. 1901. *A Study of the Bhagavata Purana; or, Esoteric Hinduism*. Benares: Freeman & Co., Ltd.

Siriwat Khamwansa. 1981. *Song Thai nai 200 pi*. Bangkok: Mahachulalongkorn.

Sis, Peter. 2011. *The Conference of the Birds*. New York: Penguin Books.

Skilling, Peter. n.d. "Compassion, Power, Success: Random remarks on Siamese Buddhist liturgy." Unpublished paper.

________. 1992. "The Raksa literature of the Sravakayana." *Journal of the Pali Text Society* XVI: 109–82.

________. 1998. "Sources for the Study of the Maṅgala and Mora Suttas." *Journal of the Pali Text Society* 24: 185–93.

_______. 2002. "Ārādhanā Tham: Invitation to Teach the Dhamma." *Manusya: Journal of Humanities* (Special Issue) 4: 84–92.

_______. 2007. "Zombies and Half-Zombies: Mahāsūtras and Other Protective Measures." *Journal of the Pali Text Society* 29: 315fn7.

________. 2007. "Kings, Sangha, Brahmans: ideology, ritual, and power in premodern Siam." In *Buddhism, Power and Political Order*, ed. Ian Harris. London: Routledge, pp. 182–215.

Skilling, Peter and Prapod Assavavirulhakarn. 2002. "Tripiṭaka in Practice in the Fourth and Fifth Reigns." *Manusya: Journal of Humanities* (Special Issue) 4: 60–72.

Silpa Bhirasri. 1959. *The Origin and Evolution of Thai Murals*. Bangkok: Fine Arts Department.

Smith, Jonathan. 1987. *To Take Place: Toward Theory in Ritual*. Chicago: University of Chicago Press.

Smyth, David. 1994. *Suat Mon Mueang Nuea Chabap Sombun*. 2537 Chiang Mai, Thanathong.

________, ed. 2000. *The Canon in Southeast Asian Literatures*. London: Curzon.

Snodin, Michael and Maurice Howard. 1996. *Ornament: A Social History Since 1450*, New Haven: Yale University Press.

Sombhong Akharawong. 2550 [2007]. *Chitakam Thai*. Bangkok: Amarin Printing.

Somsak Sakuntanat, ed. 2007/2550. *Takrut khlang chom khlang wet*. Bangkok.

Sonja, Kim, Tae Hyunsun, and Ra Hee Hong Lee. 2000. *Kim Sooja: A Needle Woman*. Seoul: Rodin Gallery.

Sooja, Kim and Oliva Maria Rubio Sooja. 2006. *Kim Sooja: To Breathe*. Madrid: Museo Nacional Centro de Arte Reina Sofia.

Soraphon Sophitkun. 1994. *Tamnan nangsue phrakhruang chak adit thung pacchuban. Sinlapawatthanatham* 15, 3: 90–2.

________. 1997/2540. *Sudyot rian phrakhruang lem thi 1*. Bangkok: Phra Maha.

Sompong Mudito. 2543 [2000]. *Kai khatasatikammatthan* [The Practice of Awareness Meditation]. Bangkok: Thipwisut.

Sorat Hongladarom. 2548 [2005]. *Phra Phaisachayakhuru Waithuraya Phraphattakhatasut* [The Bhaisajyaguru vaiduryaprabharajaya Sutra]. Bangkok: Munitthi Phandara.

Souneth Photisane. 1996. "The Nidān Khun Borom: Annotated translation and analysis." PhD dissertation, University of Queensland.

Spracklen, Karl. 2009. *The Meaning and Purpose of Leisure*. New York: Palgrave.

__________. 2011. *Constructing Leisure*. New York: Palgrave.

Stuart-Fox, Martin. 1998. *The Lao Kingdom of Lān Xāng: Rise and Decline*. Bangkok: White Lotus Press.

________. 1999. *The Lao Kingdom of Lan Xang: Rise and Decline*. Bangkok: White Lotus.

Subhatra Bhumiprabhas. 2007. "Old ceremonies to be revived as Giant Swing returns. History relived." *The Nation*, 10 September.

Suchip, Bunnanuphap. 1996. *Phra Traipidok Chabap samrap Prachachon*. Bangkok: Mahamakut University Press.

Suksamran, Somboon. 1976. *Political Buddhism in Southeast Asia*. New York: St. Martin's Press.

________. 1982. *Buddhism and Politics in Thailand*. Singapore: Institute of Southeast Asian Studies.

(Phraya) Sunthornphiphit. 1972/2515. *Itthipatihan phrakhruangrang khongkhlang*. Bangkok.

Supaphan na Bangchang. 2529 [1986]. *Wiwathanakan ngan khian phasa pali nai prathet thai: chareuk tamnan phongsawadan san prakat*. Bangkok: Mahamakut Monastic University Press.

Surasak Thong. 2010. *Sayam thewa* [Siamese Deities]. Bangkok: Samnak phim Matichon.

Suthachai Yimprasoet. 2004. "The Portuguese in Arakan in the 16th to 17th Centuries." *Manusya* 7, 2: 66–82.

Swanson, Herbert. n.d. "Using missionary records for the study of northern Thai history: An introduction and appraisal." In *Change in Northern Thailand and the Shan states (1886–1910)*. Seminar Papers, Department of History, Chiang Mai University.

Suchita Wongtet. 1985. "Kamnamsaneur." In *Mahagap Kong Usakanae Tao Hung Kun Cheung Wirburussongfangkong*, ed. Suchita Wongtet. Bangkok: Singhakom.

Swearer. 1974. "Myth, Legend and History in Northern Thai Chronicles." *JSS* 62, part 1.

________. 1987. "The Northern Thai City as a Sacred Center." In *The City as Sacred Center: Essays on Six Asian Contexts*. Leiden: E.J. Brill.

Swearer, D. 1996. "A Summary of the Seven Books of the Abhidhamma." In *Buddhism in Practice*, ed. D. Lopez. Princeton, NJ: Princeton University Press, pp. 336–42.

Swearer, Donald and Sommai Premchit. 1977. "A Translation of Tamnan Mulasāsana Wat Pa Daeng: The Chronicle of the founding of Buddhism of the Wat Pa Daeng Tradition." *JSS* 65, part II.

________. 1978. "The Relationship between the Religious and Political Orders in Northern Thailand (14th to 16th centuries)." In *Religion and Legitimation of Power in Thailand, Laos and Burma*, ed. Bardwell Smith. Chambersburg, PA: Anima Books.

________. 1998. *The Legend of Queen Cama: Bodhiramsi's Camadevivaṃsa Translation and Commentary*. Albany: SUNY Press.

Tak Chalermtiarana. 1979. *Thailand: The Politics of Despotic Paternalism*. Bangkok: Thammasat University Press.

Takeshi, Umehara. 1999. "Heian Period: Saichō." In *Buddhist Spirituality II: Later China, Korea, Japan and the Modern World*, ed. Takeuchi Yoshinori. New York: Crossroad.

Tambiah, Stanley. 1976. *World Conqueror, World Renouncer*. Cambridge: Cambridge University Press.

Tanabe, George. 1999. "The Founding of Mount Koya and Kūkai's eternal Meditation." In *Religions of Japan in Practice*, ed. George Tanabe. Princeton: Princeton University Press.

Tanabe, Shigeharu. 2000. "Autochthony and the Inthakhin cult of Chiang Mai." In *Civility and savagery: Social identity in Tai states*, ed. Andrew Turton. Richmond, Surrey: Curzon.

Tannenbaum, Nicola. 2001. *Who Can Compete Against the World?: Power-Protection and Buddhism in Shan Worldview*. Ann Arbor: Association of Asian Studies.

Tannenbaum, Nikki. 2002. "Monuments and memory." In *Cultural crisis and social memory*, ed. Shigeharu Tanabe and Charles Keyes. Honolulu: University of Hawai'i Press.

Taylor, J.L. 1999. "(Post-)modernity, remaking tradition and the hybridisation of Thai Buddhism." *Anthropological Forum* 9, 2: 163–87.

Taylor, Keith. 1998. "Surface Orientations in Vietnam: Beyond Histories of Nation and Region." *Journal of Southeast Asian History* 57, 4.

Teiser, Stephen F. 2007. *Reinventing the Wheel: Paintings of Rebirth in Medieval Buddhist Temples*. Washington: University of Washington Press.

Terwiel, B.J. 1983. *A History of Modern Thailand, 1767–1942*. Lucia, NY: University of Queensland Press.

________. 1994. *Monks and Magic: An Analysis of Religious Ceremonies in Central Thailand*, 3rd rev. ed. Bangkok: White Lotus.

Tha Prian. n.d. *Mo Chiwok Komanphat: Mo Luang pracham Ratcha-samnak-ratchakhru* [Jīvaka Komārabhacca: The Royal Physician]. Bangkok: Duang Kaeo.

________. 2549 [2006]. *Khreuang rang mahasetthi: bucha laeo ruai* [The Ritual Implements of the Millionaire: Use and then Become Rich!]. Bangkok: Khom Ma.

________. 2549 [2006]. *Katha mahasetthi: suat laeo ruai* [The Incantations of the Millionnaire: Chant and then Become Rich!]. Bangkok: Khom Ma.

(Phra) Thammakittiwong. 2548 [2005]. *Wat Ratchaoroasaram Ratchaworawihan.* Bangkok: n.p.

Than Htut and Thaw Kaung. 2003. "Some Myanmar historical fiction and their historical context." *Manusya* 5: 95–106.

Than, Tun, ed. 1988. *The Royal Orders of Burma, AD 1598–1885.* Kyoto: Centre for South East Asian Studies, Kyoto University.

Thanong Khanthong. 2002. "Are we too far gone in hatred for Burma?" *The Nation*, June 9.

Thaw Kaung and Ni Ni Myint. 1996. "Sithu Gamani Thingyan's Zimme Yazawin: A brief history." In *Proceedings of the Sixth international Conference of Thai Studies.* Chiang Mai: International Conference of Thai Studies, pp. 51–63.

Thienchai Aksorndit. 2546 [2003]. *Phra Thāt Lampang Luang.* Chiang Mai: Silkworm Books.

Thienchai Aksorndit, Koroknok Ratanawarābhan, and Wandī Santiwudiwedhī. 2545 [2002]. *Lanna: Chakrawat Tuaton Amnat.* Bangkok: Mahāmakut Monastic University Press.

Thongchai Winichakul. 1994. *Siam mapped: History of the geo-body of a nation.* Honolulu: University of Hawai'i Press.

Thongchai. 2012. *Logiyadharma.* Bangkok: Amarin Printing.

Tin Lwin. 1961. "A study of Pali-Burmese Nissaya." Master's thesis, University of London.

Tontyaphisalasut, Sutthiphong, n.d. *Pramuan Dhamma nai Phra Traipidok.* Bangkok: Rong Phim Kan Sasana.

Trager, Frank and William Koenig. 1979. *Burmese Sit-Tans 1769–1826: Rural life and administration.* Tuscon, AZ: University of Arizona.

Trankell, Ing-Britt. 1999. "Royal relics: Ritual and social memory in Louang Prabang." In *Laos: Culture and society*, ed. Grant Evans. Chiang Mai: Silkworm Books, pp. 191–213.

Triyampawai [pseud.]. 1954/2492. *Pari-atthathibai haeng phrakhruang lem thi 1: Phra somdet Phutthachan.* Bangkok.

Tun Aung Chain. 1996. "Chiang Mai in Bayinnaung's polity." In *Proceedings of the Sixth International Conference of Thai Studies VI.* Chiang Mai: International Conference of Thai Studies.

______. 2004. "The Chiang Mai campaign of 1787–1788: Beyond the Chronicle account." In *Broken glass: Pieces of Myanmar history,* ed. Tun Aung Chain. Yangon: SEAMEO Regional Center for History and Tradition, pp. 79–87.

Turner, Victor. 1974. *Dramas, Fields, and Metaphors: Symbolic Action in Human Society*. Ithaca: Cornell University Press.

________. 1978. *Image and Pilgrimage in Christian Culture: Anthropological Perspectives*. New York: Columbia University Press.

________. 1979. *Process, Performance, and Pilgrimage: A Study in Comparative Symbology*. New Delhi: Concept.

Tyler Rollins Fine Art. 2014. *Transient Shelter: Jakkai Siributr*. http://trfineart.com/wp-content/uploads/2016/12/Jakkai-2014-Catalog.pdf [accessed March 4, 2017].

Vacissaratthera. 1971. *The Chronicle of the Thupa and the Thupavaṃsa*. Trans. by N.A. Jayawickrama. London: Pali Text Society.

Veblen, Thorstein. [1899] 2001. *The Theory of the Leisure Class*. New York: Modern Library.

Veidlinger, Daniel. 2002. "Spreading the Dhamma: The written word and the transmission of Pāli texts in pre-modern Northern Thailand." PhD dissertation, South Asian Studies, University of Chicago.

______. 2002. "Merit-making media: Pali manuscripts from Northern Thailand." Paper presented at American Academy of Religion, November 23–26, Toronto, Ontario, Canada.

______. 2006. *Spreading the Dhamma*. Honolulu: University of Hawai'i Press.

Venkatasubbiah, A. 1965. "A Tamil Version of the Pañcatantra." *The Adyar Library Bulletin* 29: 74–142.

________. 1966. "A Javanese Version of the Pañcatantra." *Annals of the Bhandarkar Oriental Research Institute* 46: 59–100.

________. 1969. "The Pañcatantra Version of Laos." *The Adyar Library Bulletin* 33, 1–4: 195–283.

Vickery, Michael. 1972. "Review of Prachum Chotmaihet Samai Ayuthaya Phak I." *JSS*, 60, part 2.

Vijinthanasarn, Panya, Thongchai Srisukprasert, and Anupong Chantorn. 2012. *Buddha, Dharma, Ecclesiastic*. Bangkok: Amarin Printing.

Vipha Udomchan, ed. 2547 [2004]. *Lai khon yon phamā*. Bangkok: Chulalongkorn University Press.

Wang, Eugene. 2005. *Shaping the Lotus Sutra: Buddhist Visual Culture in Medieval China*. Washington: University of Washington Press.

Warder, A.K., ed. 1961. *Mohavicchedani*. London: Pali Text Society.

Warner, Michael. 2002. *Publics and Counterpublics*. New York: Zone Books.

Weinstein, Stanley. 1999. "Aristocratic Buddhism." In *Cambridge History of Japan*, vol. 2, ed. John Whitney Hall. Cambridge: Cambridge University Press.

Wells, K.E. 1974. *Thai Buddhism: Its Rites and Activities*, 3rd ed. Bangkok: Suriyabun.

Wheatley, Paul. 1983. "Nagara and Commandery: Origins of the Southeast Asian Urban Traditions." University of Chicago, Department of Geography Research Paper.

Wheeler, Matthew. 1999. "Challenges to Narrative History: Bifurcated History and Surface Orientations." Unpublished paper.

Wichienkeeo, Arronrut and David Wyatt. 1998. *The Chiang Mai Chronicle*. Chiang Mai: Silkworm Books.

Williams, C.A.S. 2006. *Chinese Symbolism and Art Motifs*, 4th ed. Tokyo: Tuttle Books.

Wilson, Constance and Lucien Hanks. 1985. *The Burma-Thailand frontier over sixteen decades: Three descriptive documents.* Athens, OH: Ohio University Press.

Wilson, Henry. 2011. *Pattern and Ornament in the Arts of India*. New York: Thames and Hudson.

Wilson, Horace H., trans. 1840. *The Vishnu Purana*. http://www. sacred-texts.com/hin/vp/index.htm [accessed July 13, 2015].

Winnifrith, Tom and Cyril Barrett. 1989. *The Philosophy of Leisure*. New York: St. Martin's Press.

Wong, Deborah. 2001. *Sounding the Center: History and Aesthetics in Thai Buddhist Performance*. Chicago: University of Chicago Press.

(Phra Chao Borom Wongtoe Krom Luang) Wongsathirachasanit lae (Phra Worawongtoe Phra Ong Chao) Saisanitwong. 2534 [1991]). *Tamra saphakhun ya laetamraya Phra Ong Chao Saisanitwong* [The Lost Manual and the Manual of Phra Png Chao Sainsanitwong]. Bangkok: Wacharin Kanphim.

Woodward, Hiram. 2005. *The Art and Architecture of Thailand: From Prehistoric Times Through the Thirteenth Century*. Leiden: Brill.

Wutichai Mulasilpa. 1995. *Kan patirupakanseuksa nai samai phrapansomdej phrachulachom klao chao yu hua*. Bangkok: Thai Wattana Panich.

Wyatt, David. 1969. *The Politics of Reform.* New Haven: Yale University Press.

________. 1975. *Crystal Sands: The Chronicles of Nagara Sri Dharrmaraja*. Cornell University Southeast Asian Studies Program, Ithaca.

________. 1994. *The Nan Chronicle*. Ithaca, NY: Cornell Studies on Southeast Asia.

________. 1994. *Studies in Thai History*. Chiang Mai: Silkworm Books.

Wyatt, David K. 2004. *Reading Thai Murals*. Chiang Mai: Silkworm Books.

Wyatt, David and Aroonrut Wichienkeeo. 1995. *The Chiang Mai Chronicle*. Chiang Mai: Silkworm Books.

Zaleski, Valérie. 1997. "The Art of Thailand and Laos." In *The Art of Southeast Asia*, ed. Bernard Wooding. Paris: Éditions Citadelle et Mazenod.

Zinnoman, Peter. 2001. *Colonial Bastille*. Berkeley: University of California Press.

Index

KYOTO-CSEAS SERIES ON ASIAN STUDIES
Center for Southeast Asian Studies, Kyoto University

List of Published Titles

The Economic Transition in Myanmar after 1988: Market Economy versus State Control, edited by Koichi Fujita, Fumiharu Mieno and Ikuko Okamoto, 2009

Populism in Asia, edited by Kosuke Mizuno and Pasuk Phongpaichit, 2009

Traveling Nation-Makers: Transnational Flows and Movements in the Making of Modern Southeast Asia, edited by Caroline S. Hau and Kasian Tejapira, 2011

China and the Shaping of Indonesia, 1949–1965, by Hong Liu, 2011

Questioning Modernity in Indonesia and Malaysia, edited by Wendy Mee and Joel S. Kahn, 2012

Industrialization with a Weak State: Thailand's Development in Historical Perspective, by Somboon Siriprachai, edited by Kaoru Sugihara, Pasuk Phongpaichit, and Chris Baker, 2012

Popular Culture Co-productions and Collaborations in East and Southeast Asia, edited by Nissim Otmazgin and Eyal Ben-Ari, 2012

Strong Soldiers, Failed Revolution: The State and Military in Burma, 1962–88, by Yoshihiro Nakanishi, 2013

Organising under the Revolution: Unions and the State in Java, 1945–48, by Jafar Suryomenggolo, 2013

Living with Risk: Precarity & Bangkok's Urban Poor, by Tamaki Endo, 2014

Migration Revolution: Philippine Nationhood and Class Relations in a Globalized Age, by Filomeno V. Aguilar Jr., 2014

The Chinese Question: Ethnicity, Nation, and Region in and Beyond the Philippines, by Caroline S. Hau, 2014

Identity and Pleasure: The Politics of Indonesian Screen Culture, by Ariel Heryanto, 2014

Indonesian Women and Local Politics: Islam, Gender and Networks in Post-Suharto Indonesia, by Kurniawati Hastuti Dewi, 2015

Catastrophe and Regeneration in Indonesia's Peatlands: Ecology, Economy and Society, edited by Kosuke Mizuno, Motoko S. Fujita & Shuichi Kawai, 2016

Marriage Migration in Asia: Emerging Minorities at the Frontiers of Nation-States, edited by Sari K. Ishii, 2016

Central Banking as State Building: Policymakers and Their Nationalism in the Philippines, 1933–1964, by Yusuke Takagi, 2016

Moral Politics in the Philippines: Inequality, Democracy and the Urban Poor, by Wataru Kusaka, 2017

Liberalism and the Postcolony: Thinking the State in 20th-century Philippines, by Lisandro E. Claudio, 2017

Networked: Business and Politics in Decentralizing Indonesia, 1998–2004, by Wahyu Prasetyawan, 2018

Writing History in America's Shadow: Japan, the Philippines, and the Question of "Pan-Asianism", by Takamichi Serizawa, 2020

Unraveling Myanmar's Transition: Progress, Retrenchment, and Ambiguity Amidst Liberalization, edited by Pavin Chachavalpongpun, Elliott Prasse-Freeman, and Patrick Strefford, 2020

The Phantom World of Digul: Policing as Politics in Colonial Indonesia, 1926–1941, by Takashi Shiraishi, 2021